Gravetye Ma...
East Grinstead Surrey

GARDENS OPEN TO THE PUBLIC
IN ENGLAND AND WALES

This book will guide the reader to over 1,450 of the most beautiful gardens in England and Wales, 1,250 of which are *private* gardens not normally open to the public.

The National Gardens Scheme is deeply grateful to all the owners for so kindly opening their gardens on the dates shown in this book. There are all sorts and sizes of gardens to visit from the greatest to quite tiny ones packed with treasures and giving ample opportunity to those who are already keen gardeners to pursue their particular interest and for everyone to relax and enjoy peaceful surroundings.

Keep this book with you so that you have it handy for reference, and look out for the yellow National Gardens Scheme posters. The Council of the Gardens Scheme wishes you a very happy year with the Gardens in England and Wales.

Longstock
Hidcote
Bodnant
Kew
Chatsworth

Sissinghurst
Wisley
Wakehurst
Stourhead

INDEX

All other information and further copies of this Guide Book price 75p, including UK postage, may be obtained from the Organising Secretary

THE NATIONAL GARDENS SCHEME
CHARITABLE TRUST
57 LOWER BELGRAVE STREET, LONDON, SW1W 0LR. (01-730 0359)

MARCH 1980

WHEN AND WHY

"The Gardens Scheme", as it was first called, was started at the suggestion of Miss Elsie Wagg, a member of the Council of The Queen's Institute, as part of a national memorial to Queen Alexandra whose deep and sympathetic interest in District Nursing was well known.

During the spring and summer of 1927 over 600 private gardens were open in aid of this memorial fund for the District Nursing service, and large numbers of people were able to enjoy what was then a rare opportunity, to visit some of the best gardens in the country. The idea was so successful that the Gardens Scheme has been organised annually for The Queen's Nursing Institute ever since.

Much of the money raised goes to nurses who still need our help, either in retirement, or in illness, or in difficulties often as a result of the stress and pressure of their work. Special grants are provided to meet unexpected crises as well as regular grants to help those retired on a low pension with the ever-rising cost of living.

In 1949, at the wish of the Gardens Committee, The Queen's Nursing Institute entered into an agreement with The National Trust whereby the Trust, in return for its help and support, would receive a share of The National Gardens Scheme proceeds. This money is used by The National Trust to help maintain certain specified gardens considered to be especially worthy of preservation in the style in which they were designed.

In response to a number of requests from Garden Owners, a policy has been introduced whereby owners may, if they so wish, allocate a proportion of the proceeds from opening a garden for The National Gardens Scheme to another charity. The names of the charities which will benefit from the money raised by the 1980 openings are included in the descriptive entries of the gardens concerned.

For greater simplicity of administration, and with the support and approval of The Queen's Nursing Institute and The National Trust, The National Gardens Scheme has become a charity in its own right, and its official title is now

THE NATIONAL GARDENS SCHEME CHARITABLE TRUST

Who introduced the Ha–Ha? Where do pawpaws grow in London? Where are the dragons' mouths?

And which are the best gardens to visit in Spring, early Summer, late Summer or Autumn?

Which town has 52 parks?

How can you find a company that runs coach tours of gardens?

Why did they call him 'Capability' Brown?

You'll find the answers to these and hundreds of other questions in *Visit an English Garden,* the 75p, 48 page full-colour guide available from most bookshops and Tourist Information Centres or by post (plus 15p p & p) from the English Tourist Board, 4 Grosvenor Gardens, London SW1W 0DU.

VISIT AN ENGLISH GARDEN

Make the most of your own garden

It's always enjoyable to visit and admire the many 'Show Gardens' open to us, but remember, Popular Gardening is the weekly magazine that can help you make the most of your own garden.

Editor Fred Whitsey and his team of experts show week-by-week how to get the very best results for the time and money you spend on your garden.

Whatever its size or shape, 'PG' can help make your garden a happier place to work and relax in.

Popular Gardening

THE GARDENING WEEKLY FOR ALL THE FAMILY

Open to the public six days a week.

The Woolworth garden department. The paradise that's open to every gardener six days a week all year round.

With the very best in equipment, seeds, plants and fertilizers. And, not surprisingly, at typically low Woolworth prices.

It's everything you need to make *your* garden a showplace.

Some items at larger stores only and subject to availability.

EVERYBODY NEEDS WOOLWORTH

Sometime!

And Woolco

Where to see England's rarest roses in full bloom.

In the rose gardens at Castle Howard over two thousand roses will be at their ravishing best this summer. 1,200 Hybrid Tea and Floribunda Roses in ninety varieties, and a similar number of Old Rose plants in four hundred varieties – many of them so rare you might travel England without seeing them anywhere else.

When you've seen the roses, see the rest: a glowing 18th century palace filled with treasures, selections from Britain's largest collection of historic costume, gleaming lakes, a glittering fountain, peacocks . . . bring the children for an unforgettable day out.

Castle Howard is open daily from Easter until the end of October. Grounds and cafeteria from 11am. House and Costume Galleries 11.30 – 5pm. Reduced rate for children 5-13. Enquiries: the Comptroller, Coneysthorpe 333.

Please mention the National Gardens Scheme when replying to the Advertisers

GENERAL INFORMATION

Dogs: Unless otherwise stated in the information about a garden, dogs are usually admitted, *provided they are kept on a lead*. Dogs are not admitted to houses.

● **Gardens Open Frequently.** Certain gardens, which open throughout the season, give a contribution from their takings to The National Gardens Scheme, instead of the whole proceeds from the dates given in this book. These gardens are marked with the sign ●

Charity of the Owner's Choice. Where the owners of 'private' gardens (not normally open to the public) have nominated some other charity to receive a share from an opening for the National Gardens Scheme, the name of the other charity is included in the descriptive entry.

△ **Where this sign** appears alongside dates in the *descriptive* entry for a garden it denotes that the garden will be open in aid of The National Gardens Scheme on the dates shown, but that the garden *is also open* regularly to the public *on other days too*. Details about the regular openings of such gardens can be found in *Historic Houses, Castles and Gardens* obtainable from booksellers; see page x. (In the case of National Trust gardens details can also be found in their *Properties Open in 1980*; See note below).

The National Trust. Certain gardens owned by The National Trust are opened in aid of The National Gardens Scheme on the dates shown in this book. Information about the regular opening of these gardens is given in the booklet *Properties Open in 1980*, published by The National Trust (25p + 15p for postage) and obtainable from 42 Queen Anne's Gate, London, SW1H 9AS, or from any National Trust property.

Open by appointment. Owners who open their gardens by appointment will generally do so for individuals as well as for parties, unless the information given in the details about the garden specifies parties only.

Houses are not open unless this is specifically stated; where the house or part-house is shown an additional charge is usually made.

Tea: When this is available at a garden the information is given in large type, e.g. TEAS or TEA and biscuits etc. (There is, of course, an extra charge for any refreshments available at a garden.) Any other information given about tea, is a guide only to assist visitors in finding somewhere in the area open for tea.

Buses: Continuance of many bus services, and particularly in rural areas, is a matter of considerable uncertainty and especially on SUNDAYS. It is strongly recommended that details should be checked in advance.

Professional photographers: No photographs taken in a garden may be used for sale for reproduction without the prior permission of the garden owner.

The Automobile Association has kindly arranged for information on gardens open for the Scheme to be available from their Service Centres.

The Royal Automobile Club has kindly arranged that their Patrols will direct motorists to gardens when asked.

OTHER BOOKS

Historic Houses, Castles and Gardens in Great Britain and Ireland, 1980 edition. Published by ABC Historic Publications, a division of ABC Travel Guides Ltd. Price 80p at all leading booksellers in Great Britain and Ireland; or £1.40 (including postage and packing) direct from the publishers at Oldhill, London Road, Dunstable, Beds. Published annually in January, gives details of houses, castles and gardens open to the public. Special foreword by the Marquess of Bath.

The National Trust. Certain gardens owned by The National Trust are opened in aid of The National Gardens Scheme on the dates shown in this book. Information about the regular opening of these gardens is given in the booklet *Properties Open in 1980,* published by The National Trust (25p plus 15p for postage) and obtainable from 42 Queen Anne's Gate, London, SW1H 9AS, or from any National Trust property.

Scotland's Gardens Scheme. In 1980 many beautiful gardens in Scotland will be open to the public. An illustrated list with information about the National Trust for Scotland, price 65p including postage and packing, can be obtained from the General Organiser, Scotland's Gardens Scheme, 26 Castle Terrace, Edinburgh EH1 2EL. Information about 2 six-day tours in Scotland (in May and June) and day tours during the Edinburgh Festival may be obtained from the same address.

The National Trust for Scotland. In its care are 80 properties including, as well as gardens and castles, cottages, mountains, islands and historic sites. The National Trust for Scotland, 5 Charlotte Square, Edinburgh, EH2 4DU.

Ulster Gardens Scheme. A list of the private gardens open to the public under the Ulster Gardens Scheme can be obtained from: The Regional Information Officer, The National Trust, Rowallane, Saintfield, Co. Down.

Gardener's Sunday. *Gardens to Visit,* a list of gardens open in aid of The Gardeners' Royal Benevolent Society and The Royal Gardeners' Orphan Fund, is obtainable from Gardener's Sunday, White Witches, Claygate Road, Dorking, Surrey, price 40p, including postage, or from Booksellers, 30p.

The Automobile Association Guide to *Stately Homes, Museums, Castles and Gardens* gives details of around 1,700 places of interest in England, Wales, Scotland and the Channel Islands. Available from AA bookshops, or Mail Order Department, Automobile Association, Fanum House, Basingstoke, Hants RG21 2EA. Price £2.25 plus 25p p. & p. (£2.50 non-members from major booksellers).

Historic Irish Tourist Houses & Gardens Assn. publishes annually an illustrated leaflet with information about nearly 40 properties. Available free from HITHA, c/o Fred's Travel Bureau, 3a Castle Street, Dalkey, Co. Dublin.

Disabled Living Foundation. *The Easy Path to Gardening* price £1.25 inc. postage is obtainable from The Disabled Living Foundation, 346 Kensington High Street, London W14 8NS or The Reader's Digest, 7-10 Old Bailey, London EC99 1AA. The book is based on eight year's work in three hospital research gardens. Any profit will benefit the Disabled Living Foundation.

Please mention the National Gardens Scheme when replying to the Advertisers

FOR EASIER, MORE SUCCESSFUL AND MORE ECONOMICAL GARDENING

SUTTONS SEEDS

Foil-Packed for healthier, more vigorous seedlings.

More than 170 years of care and expert knowledge are behind every flower and vegetable seed variety selected, graded and packed for you by Suttons. That's why you can trust your seeds from Suttons, pioneers of foil packeting.
Most Suttons seeds are sealed in foil for maximum protection. This means they keep harvest fresh until you open the packet ready to sow. From your local shop or garden centre.

Suttons Seeds

Torquay, Devon TQ2 7QJ.

Please mention the National Gardens Scheme when replying to the Advertisers

ROYAL GARDENS

SANDRINGHAM HOUSE AND GROUNDS
(*Norfolk*)

By gracious permission of Her Majesty The Queen, the grounds at Sandringham will be open (except when Her Majesty The Queen or any member of the Royal Family is in residence) on the following days.

April: From April 6 every Tuesday, Wednesday and Thursday.

May, June, July, August and September until Thursday, September 25: Every Sunday, Monday, Tuesday, Wednesday and Thursday. Please note that the HOUSE ONLY will be closed to the Public from July 21 to August 9 inclusive and the Grounds will be closed July 25 to August 2 inclusive. Sandringham House and Grounds will be open on Easter Sunday and Monday, April 6 and 7.

HOURS Sandringham House: 11 (12 noon Sundays) to 4.45; Sandringham Grounds: 10.30 (11.30 on Sundays) to 5. **ADMISSION CHARGES**: House and Grounds: Adults £1, OAP on production of Pension Book 80p, Children 50p; Grounds Only: Adults 70p, OAPs 50p, Children 40p. It is not possible to purchase a ticket to visit the House only. Admission to the Museum is Free.

Advance Party bookings will be accepted during April and May only, except on Bank Holidays and Sundays. There are no reductions in admission fees for parties. Picnicking is not permitted inside the Grounds. Dogs are not permitted inside the Grounds. Free car and coach parking.

Sandringham Church will be open as follows, subject to Weddings, Funerals and Special Services: When Grounds are open as stated above Monday to Thursday inclusive 11–5 (Sundays 2–5 April to Sept.). At other times of the year, the Church will be open from 11–12.30 and 2–5 but the Church is always closed on Fridays and Saturdays throughout the year.

Sandringham Flower Show will be held on Wednesday July 30. Full details may be obtained from the Flower Show Secretary: Mr E. W. Francis, 'Dunphail', Castle Rising, King's Lynn (telephone Castle Rising 315).

Enquiries: Enquiries to Mr R. S. French, Estate Office, Sandringham or by telephone 9–1, 2–4.30 Monday to Friday inclusive at King's Lynn 2675.

FROGMORE GARDENS
(*Berkshire*)

By gracious permission of Her Majesty The Queen, the Frogmore Gardens, Windsor Castle, will be open from 11–7 on the following days:

Wednesday, May 14, and Thursday, May 15

Coaches by appointment only: Apply to The National Gardens Scheme, 57 Lower Belgrave Street, London, SW1W 0LR (Tel. 01-730 0359) stating whether May 14 or 15, and whether morning or afternoon. Admission 30p, children under 14, 10p. Dogs not allowed. Royal Mausoleum also open, free of charge, both days. Entrance to gardens and Mausoleum through Long Walk gate. Visitors are requested kindly to refrain from entering the grounds of the Home Park. Light refreshments will be available at the car park (near the outer gate to the Gardens).

BARNWELL MANOR
(*Northamptonshire*)

By kind permission of Their Royal Highnesses Princess Alice Duchess of Gloucester and the Duke and Duchess of Gloucester, the gardens of Barnwell Manor will be open from 2.30–6 on:

Sunday, April 27, Admission 30p, Children 10p.

By joining the **R.H.S. you can enjoy better gardening . . .**

The
Royal Horticultural Society

 has all kinds of gardeners as members,
amateurs and professionals,
tree men and alpine enthusiasts,
greenhouse owners and cactus collectors,
food producers and flower arrangers,
and many others.

An annual subscription

of £16.00 gives you two tickets;
or £10.00 for one ticket of admission to :
all the flower shows in London, including
Chelsea,
Wisley Garden in Surrey

All members also

Receive the monthly journal *The Garden*
Can obtain advice on gardening problems
Have plants and diseases identified
Use the finest gardening library in the world.

Write now for **illustrated brochure** containing details of these and
other privileges to

The Secretary (NGS)
THE ROYAL HORTICULTURAL SOCIETY
Vincent Square, London, SW1P 2PE

Gardening Books from

RHS Enterprises Ltd.

The Wisley Handbooks, priced from 60p to 95p are practical booklets providing basic information on many gardening subjects. The series is available from most retail booksellers and many garden centres. *Titles in the series include:*

Lawns	Plants for Shade
Roses	Trees for small gardens
Fuchsias	Vegetable Pests, Diseases and Disorders
Houseplants	Pruning Hardy Fruits
Bulbs Indoors	Climbers and Wall Shrubs
Water Gardens	Early Garden Crops
Rhododendrons	Herbaceous Plants
Pelargoniums	Heaths and Heathers
Clematis	Hedges and Screens
Cacti	Pruning Hardy Shrubs
Ferns	Flowers in Greece
Culinary Herbs	Fruit Pests, Diseases and Disorders
Peaches, Apricots, Nectarines, Figs and Grapes	Growing Plants for Flower Arrangement
	Plans for Small Gardens
Ground Cover Plants	Alpines without a Rock Garden
The Small Greenhouse	Grapes: Indoors and Out
Annuals & Biennials	Ivies

New in May:

Gardening in small spaces

Camellias

Details of other books published can be obtained from R.H.S. Enterprises Ltd., 80 Vincent Square, London SW1P 2PE

MODEL VILLAGE
Babbacombe, Torquay

To wander through these beautiful gardens, which are landscaped
to represent a model of the English Countryside is a unique experience and very rewarding to the garden enthusiast. There is a
comprehensive collection of conifers, flowering shrubs and trees
with special emphasis on dwarf conifers. These gardens have been
rightly described as a "Masterpiece of miniature landscaping". The
gardens are open every day except Christmas day Easter to October
9 a.m. to 10 p.m. (illuminations from dusk); November to March
9 a.m. to 5 p.m. Light refreshments, souvenirs and plants are available at the end of your visit. Party rates available.
Tel. Torquay 38669.

LIST OF GARDENS

For Key to Signs and General Information see p ix

BEDFORDSHIRE

Hon County Organiser:
MRS S. WHITBREAD, The Mallowry, Riseley,
Bedford MK44 1EF

DATES OF OPENING

APRIL Sunday 27
HOWARD'S HOUSE, Cardington
MAY Sunday 25
ASPLEY GUISE GARDENS
‡TETWORTH HALL (see Cambridgeshire)
‡WOODBURY HALL, Everton
JUNE Sunday 15
‡ODELL CASTLE, nr Bedford
‡WESTFIELDS, Oakley
JUNE Sunday 22
HOWBURY HALL, Renhold, nr Bedford
JULY Sunday 6
‡BLETSOE CASTLE, Bletsoe
LUTON HOO GARDENS, Luton
‡SOUTHILL PARK, nr Biggleswade
JULY Sunday 13
ODELL CASTLE, nr Bedford

DESCRIPTIONS OF GARDENS

Aspley Guise Gardens, 2 m. W of M1
(Exit 13) via B557, towards Bletchley. *Combined charge for following 3 gardens 40p, or 20p each; Chd. ½ price. Sun. May 25 (2.30–6.30)*

  Aspley House⊕ (Mr & Mrs Stanbury)
  House on E side of village. 5 acres with
  shrubs & lawns. William & Mary house (not
  open). NO DOGS. TEAS

  Manor Close (Sir Kenneth & Lady Allen)
  Small garden. 500 yds from centre of village,
  next to church

  The Rookery (C. R. Randall Esq) 5 acres
  with rhododendrons & woodland. 500 yds
  from village square

Bletsoe Castle †⊕ (Mr & Mrs R. J. Strong)
Bletsoe, 6½ m. N of Bedford. After Falcon Inn,
turn right at Bletsoe sign. House nr church.
Bus: A6 to Falcon Inn, Bletsoe, ¼ m. Small
newly created garden in ancient setting.
TEAS. *Adm. 15p, Chd. 5p. Sun. July 6 (2–7)*

Howard's House⊕ (Humphrey Whitbread
Esq) Cardington, 2 m. SE of Bedford. Station:
Bedford. Walled garden & flower garden;
flowering cherries & clematis. Tea Bedford.
Adm. 20p. Sun. April 27 (2–7)

Howbury Hall⅃⊕ (Mr & Mrs A. N. Polhill)
nr Renhold, 4 m. E of Bedford. Via A428
Bedford–St Neots' coming from Bedford main
drive is about 100 yds after 1st layby. Large
garden with lawns, herbaceous borders, rose
garden, walled kitchen garden & pleasant
woodland. TEAS. *Adm. 20p, Chd. 10p. Sun.
June 22 (2–6.30)*

Luton Hoo Gardens, †⅃⊕ Luton; entrance
at Park St gates. Bus: Green Line 707, 717
London–Luton; London Country 321 Watford–Luton via St Albans. Landscape garden
by Capability Brown. House commenced by
Robert Adams in 1767. NO DOGS. Tea
Wernher Collection Restaurant. *Adm. to
gardens only 50p, Chd. 15p. △Sun. July 6
(2–6)*

Odell Castle⅃ (The Rt. Hon. Lord Luke) NW
of Bedford. From A6 turn W through Sharnbrook; from A428, N through Lavendon &
Harrold. Station: Bedford 10 m. Terrace &
lower garden down to R. Ouse. House built in
1962 on old site, using original stone. TEAS.
Adm. 20p. Sun. June 15 & Sun. July 13 (2–7)

Southill Park⊕ (Mr & Mrs S. C. Whitbread)
5 m. SW of Biggleswade. Large garden. Conservatory. Roses. Plant stall. TEAS. *Adm. 30p.
Sun. July 6 (2–6)*

Westfields (E. F. Davison Esq) Oakley. 5 m.
NW of Bedford; via A6 to turning to W marked
Oakley Station. Medium-sized garden; formal
& informal; rose & water gardens; glades &
shrub walk; herbaceous borders. NO DOGS.
TEAS. *Adm. 25p. Sun. June 15 (2–7)*

Woodbury Hall (Mrs Astell) Everton. 3½ m.
NE of Sandy. Large garden; rhododendrons,
lawns, views. Nearby garden open same day,
Tetworth Hall. See Cambs. *Adm. 15p, Chd.
10p. Sun. May 25 (2–7)*

BERKSHIRE

Hon. County Organiser:

MRS A. M. MANN, Horsemoor House,
Chieveley

DATES OF OPENING

MARCH Sunday 23
ODNEY CLUB, Cookham
MARCH Wednesday 26
THE OLD RECTORY, Burghfield
APRIL Easter Sunday 6 (by appointment only)
OLD RECTORY COTTAGE, Tidmarsh
APRIL Sunday 13
‡FOXGROVE, Enborne, nr Newbury
‡MEADOWAY, Enborne, nr Newbury
APRIL Sunday 20
CULHAM COURT & THE BOTHY,
nr Henley-on-Thames
TYLE MILL, Sulhamstead
WEST WOODHAY HOUSE, Inkpen,
nr Newbury
ENGLEFIELD HOUSE, nr Theale
APRIL Sunday 27
ELCOT PARK HOTEL, nr Newbury
KIRBY HOUSE, Inkpen, nr Newbury
APRIL Wednesday 30
THE OLD RECTORY, Burghfield
MAY Sunday 4
‡BRIMPTON MILL, nr Newbury
OAKFIELD & THE STABLES, Mortimer,
nr Reading
‡STONE HOUSE, Brimpton, nr Newbury
MAY Sunday 11
BUSSOCK MAYNE, Snelsmore Common,
nr Newbury
‡HURST LODGE, Hurst, nr Reading
‡REYNOLDS FARM, Hurst, nr Twyford
PHILLIPS HILL, Snelsmore Common,
nr Newbury
MAY Wednesday 14 & Thursday 15
FROGMORE GARDENS, Windsor Castle
MAY Sunday 18
COLD ASH GARDENS, nr Newbury
MAY Sunday 18 (by appointment only)
OLD RECTORY COTTAGE, Tidmarsh
MAY Sunday 25
ASHRIDGEWOOD COTTAGE, Forest Rd,
Wokingham
FOUNDRY HOUSE, Mortimer, nr Reading
LITTLE BOWDEN, Pangbourne
MAY Wednesday 28
THE OLD RECTORY, Burghfield
JUNE Sunday 1
DONNINGTON CASTLE HOUSE,
nr Newbury
KINGSMOOR, Titlarks Hill, Sunningdale
JUNE Saturday 7
BORLASES, Waltham St Lawrence
JUNE Sunday 8
PURLEY HALL, Pangbourne
WHITE HORSE, Finchampstead,
nr Wokingham

JUNE Sunday 8 (by appointment only)
OLD RECTORY COTTAGE, Tidmarsh
JUNE Sunday 15
‡MORTIMER GARDENS, nr Reading
‡THE PRIORY, Beech Hill, nr Reading
WOODSIDE COTTAGE, Windsor Forest
JUNE Saturday 21
LUXMOORE'S & PROVOST'S &
FELLOWS' GARDENS, Eton
JUNE Sunday 22
ALLANBAY PARK, Binfield
ASHRIDGEWOOD COTTAGE, Forest Rd,
Wokingham
ROOKSNEST, Lambourn Woodlands,
nr Hungerford
JUNE Wednesday 25
THE OLD RECTORY, Burghfield
JUNE Sunday 29
FOLLY FARM, Sulhamstead
FOUNDRY HOUSE, Mortimer, nr Reading
HEADS FARM, Chaddleworth,
nr Newbury
THE OLD RECTORY, Farnborough
JULY Saturday 5
BORLASES, Waltham St Lawrence
JULY Sunday 6
BRADFIELD GARDENS, nr Reading
INKPEN GARDENS, nr Hungerford
NEWINGTON HOUSE, Winkfield, Windsor
WEXHAM SPRINGS, nr Slough
JULY Sunday 13
WASING PLACE, Aldermaston
JULY Sunday 20
BUSSOCK MAYNE, Snelsmore Common,
nr Newbury
JULY Sunday 27 (by appointment only)
OLD RECTORY COTTAGE, Tidmarsh
JULY Wednesday 30
THE OLD RECTORY, Burghfield
AUGUST Saturday 2
BORLASES, Waltham St Lawrence
AUGUST Sunday 3
THE DEANERY, Sonning, nr Reading
AUGUST Sunday 10
ORCHARD COTTAGE, Cookham,
nr Maidenhead
AUGUST Sunday 17
TYLE MILL, Sulhamstead
AUGUST Monday 25 (Summer Bank Hol.)
SHINFIELD GRANGE, Cutbush Lane,
Shinfield, nr Reading
AUGUST Sunday 31
HURST LODGE, Hurst, nr Reading
SEPTEMBER Saturday 6
BORLASES, Waltham St Lawrence
SEPTEMBER Sunday 7
WHITE HORSE, Finchampstead,
nr Wokingham
SEPTEMBER Sunday 14 (by appointment only)
OLD RECTORY COTTAGE, Tidmarsh
SEPTEMBER Wednesday 24
THE OLD RECTORY, Burghfield
OCTOBER Wednesday 29
THE OLD RECTORY, Burghfield

DESCRIPTIONS OF GARDENS

Allanbay Park (Maj. J. L. Wills) Binfield. From Binfield follow B3018, Twyford—Henley Rd. Wrought iron gates opp. pillar box at junction of Shurlock Row & White Waltham Rds. Bus: AV 76, 77 from Maidenhead. Medium-sized garden; lake; park; chiefly roses; foliage border by Lanning Roper. TEAS. *Adm. 20p, Chd. 5p. Sun. June 22 (2–7)*

Ashridgewood Cottage*⊕ (Maj. & Mrs Edwin Crosland) Forest Rd, 2½ m. N of Wokingham. From Wokingham take A321 to Twyford; in 2 m. at Bill Hill X-rds turn right into Forest Rd (B3034); house is on right, ½ m. before Warren Inn P.H. 1-acre garden on alkaline soil started by owners in 1963 & developed on labour-saving principles; island beds of lime-tolerant shrubs, roses & erica carnea; bog garden with willows & other interesting plantings. NO DOGS. Tea Wokingham. *Adm. 40p, Chd. 20p. Sun. May 25 & Sun. June 22 (2–7)*

¶Borlases †⅃ (Jeremy Taylor Esq) Waltham St Lawrence, 3 m. E of Twyford. B3024 Windsor-Twyford; 300 yds after Memorial X at Waltham St Lawrence. Bus: AV76, 77 Maidenhead-Shurlock Row to Wokingham; alight Waltham St Lawrence, Paradise Corner, 300 yds. Large garden; fine trees, various shrubs, roses, azaleas, bulbs, large pond, water lilies; well-landscaped; Gertrude Jekyll features to be seen. Originally a farm dating from Tudor period. Waltham St Lawrence is secluded village of particular beauty & historic interest with fine church. *Adm. 30p. Chd. 10p. Sats. June 7, July 5. Aug. 2, Sept. 6 (2–6)*

Bradfield Gardens, 7 m. W of Reading. From Theale (M4 exit 12) take A340 towards Pangbourne & then turn off W to Bradfield. The following 3 gardens will be open. Cups of TEA at Mariners. *Adm. to each garden 20p. Sun. July 6 (2–6)*
  The Coach House⊕ (Mr & Mrs G. F. Harrison) Horse Leas. ½ m. past Bradfield College X-rds on right of rd to Southend & Bucklebury; house on right. Small informal garden; clay soil on N-facing slope; old roses, mixed shrubs & climbers; pond garden. NO DOGS
  Mariners (Mr & Mrs W. N. Ritchie) Mariners Lane. First right after War Memorial into Mariners Lane. Small, charming garden, owner-maintained; made from heavy clay field since 1973; roses, lilies, herbaceous borders, silver-leaved plants, clematis, flowering shrubs etc
  Potash⊕ (Mr & Mrs J. W. C. Mooney) Mariners Lane. 1-acre garden designed for minimum maintenance with permanent borders, year-round colour & control by plants & chemicals

Brimpton Mill† (The Earl & Countess Lloyd George) Brimpton, SW of Reading. 5 m. E of Newbury, turn S off A4 at Coach & Horses, Midgham, then ½ m. to garden. Medium-sized garden intersected by R. Kennet forming an island with bridges to & from. Queen Anne Mill restored 1976. TEAS. *Adm. 20p, Chd. 10p. Sun. May 4 (2–6.30)*

Bussock Mayne*⊕ (Gerald E. H. Palmer Esq) Snelsmore Common, 3 m. N of Newbury. On B4494 Newbury—Wantage. Medium-sized garden; shrubs, borders, rock garden. 10p extra for bathing in a swimming pool. Tea Newbury (not at garden). *Adm. 20p, Chd. 10p. Sun. May 11 & Sun. July 20 (2–6.30)*

Cold Ash Gardens, NE of Newbury. The following 2 gardens will be open. Ice-cream available at Fencewood House. Tea Thatcham or Newbury. *Combined charge for both gardens, 50p, Chd. 10p. Sun. May 18 (2–6)*
  ¶Copt Heath⊕ (Mr & Mrs Norman Pearson) Coming from Thatcham, towards Coldash, avoid all turnings as far as Down House School, almost opp. Copt. Heath. Mature beautifully grouped azaleas & rhododendrons, skilfully grown on gravel soil; also blossom & interesting shrubs. NO DOGS
  ¶Fencewood House (Miss E. Palmer) Red Shoote Hill. 3–4 acres with rhododendrons, azaleas & spring bulbs. (*Share to Hermitage Village Church*)

Culham Court*⅃ (E. M. Behrens Esq) NE of Henley-on-Thames. Turn N off Remenham Hill, nr Five Horse Shoes Hotel, to Aston. Terraced landscape garden to river. Alpine garden. Tea Henley. *Adm. 30p, Chd. 5p. Sun. April 20 (2–7)*. Also open (within the grounds): **The Bothy*** (Mrs Susan Allison) ½-acre garden; tiny house, a gothic folly with trefoil windows, multiple beams, sitting on edge of R. Thames; garden newly extended with recently planted trees & shrubs occasioned by elm felling; can best be described as a garden in the making. *Adm. 20p, Chd. 5p. Sun. April 20 (2–7)*

The Deanery †⊕ (Mr & Mrs Nigel Broackes) Sonning, 4 m. NE of Reading. ½ m. N of A4. Bus: AV 1A Reading—Maidenhead, alight at garden. 2-acre garden designed by Gertrude Jekyll. House built 1901–2 by Sir Edwin Lutyens for Mr Hudson, founder & editor of *Country Life*. NO DOGS. *Adm. 25p, Chd. 5p. Sun. Aug. 3 (2–5)*

¶Donnington Castle House †⅃ (Dennis Watts Esq) 1½ m. N of Newbury, 1 m. N of Newbury turn off W at signpost to Donnington village off Wantage Rd. Roses herbaceous plants, shrubs. Ruins of Donnington Castle adjoin the grounds. Swimming 10p extra. House (not shown) built 1648. TEAS. *Adm. 25p, Chd. 5p. Sun. June 1 (2–6)*

3

Elcot Park Hotel †&⊕ (H. P. Sterne, Esq) 5 m. W of Newbury .From A4 approx. midway between Newbury & Hungerford, turn off N at signpost to Elcot Park. 16-acre garden overlooking Kennet Valley with extensive views; mainly lawns & woodland; laid out by Sir William Paxton in 1848; magnificent display of daffodils, rhododendrons & other shrubs. Garden in process of being redesigned. TEAS. *Adm. 25p, Chd. 5p. Sun. April 27 (2–6)*

Englefield House*&⊕ (W. Benyon Esq, M.P.) nr Theale, W of Reading. Turn N at roundabout on A4 W of Theale; entrance gates ½ m. on left. Large garden; flowering shrubs; park; deer; commercial garden selling pot plants, etc. (*Share to Englefield Charitable Trust*) NO DOGS. *Adm. 25p, Chd. 10p (under 5, free). Sun. April 20 (2–6)*

Folly Farm*†&⊕ (The Hon. H. W. Astor) Sulhampstead, 7 m. SW of Reading. A4 from Reading, turn left at 'Jack's Booth'. Lutyens & Jekyll design. Medium-sized sunken garden with roses, architectural canal garden; white garden, herbaceous, shrubs, etc. Lutyens house built round old cottage with lawns sloping down to stream. *Adm. 25p, Chd. 10p. Sun. June 29 (2–6)*

¶**Foundry House** (Mr & Mrs J. G. Studholme) Mortimer, 8 m. SW of Reading. 4 m. from M4 Exit 11, via Grazely; at T-junction on edge of Village turn right, 100 yds from garden. 4-acre garden, mainly trees, unusual shrubs, shrub roses. NO DOGS. *Adm. 20p, Chd. 5p. Sun. May 25 & Sun. June 29 (2–6)*

Foxgrove* (Miss Audrey Vockins) Enborne, 2½ m. SW of Newbury. From A343 Newbury–Andover Rd turn right at 'The Gun', 1½ m. from town centre. Bus: AV 126, 127, 128; alight Villiers Way P.O., 1 m. Small family garden; interesting foliage plants, trough gardens, spring bulbs, eucalypts; orchard garden with shrubs, etc; vegetable garden; double primroses, snowdrop species & varieties & other early spring bulbs. Plants for sale. TEAS. *Adm. 15p, Chd. 5p. Sun. April 13 (2–7); also by appt. in Feb.*

Frogmore Gardens*†&⊕ (by gracious permission of Her Majesty The Queen) Windsor Castle; entrance via Park St gate into Long Walk (follow AA signs). Visitors are requested kindly to refrain from entering the grounds of the Home Park. Station & bus stop: Windsor (20 mins walk from gardens); Green Line buses 704, 705, 718 from London. Large garden with lake & lovely trees. The Royal Mausoleum, within the grounds, will also be open free of charge. Refreshment tent in car park on Long Walk (from where there is a 5 min. walk to the gardens). **Coaches by appointment only** (apply to Nat. Gardens Scheme, 57 Lower Belgrave St, London SW1W 0LR. Tel. 01-730 0359 stating whether

May 14 or 15 & morning or afternoon). NO DOGS. *Adm. 30p, Chd. under 14, 10p. Wed. May 14 & Thurs. May 15 (11–7; last adm. 6.30)*

¶**Heads Farm**⊕ (Mr & Mrs T. Egerton) 10 m. NW of Newbury. From A338 Hungerford–Wantage turn uphill for ½ m. 1½-acre garden with shrubs, borders & all types of roses. NO DOGS. *Adm. 20p, Chd. 5p. Sun. June 29 (2–6)*

Hurst Lodge*&⊕ (Lady Ingram) Hurst, 7 m. E of Reading. On A321 opp. village pond. From M4 W use Exit 10 towards Reading on A329(M) exit to Winnersh; left at roundabout towards Wokingham on A329; left at lights X-rds on B3030 for Hurst & Twyford; follow 'Garden open' signs. Station: Twyford, 1½ m. An old garden, approx. 3 acres; spring flowering shrubs & bulbs. Sept: roses & dahlias. TEAS. Free car park. *Adm. 20p, Chd. 5p. Sun. May 11 & Sun. Aug. 31 (2–6)*

Inkpen Gardens, 3 m. S of Hungerford. From A4 in Hungerford High St turn for Hungerford Common & Inkpen. The following 3 gardens will be open. TEA & biscuits. *Combined charge for 3 gardens 60p, Chd. under 10, free. Sun. July 6 (2–7)*

West Court (Mr & Mrs P. C. B. Pockney) 3-acre garden with rose beds & herbaceous borders. C18 house (not open).

Black Latches (Mr & Mrs C. M. Bent) ½-acre garden with herbaceous plants, roses & annuals, vegetables & fruit. Fine view to Inkpen Beacon

¶**Colnbrook Cottage*** (Mr & Mrs R. Skotzen) 2½-acre garden partly on long steep bank & surrounded on 3 sides by woodland; variety of shrubs, rhododendrons & azaleas; roses & herbaceous plants. Work started autumn 1975 clearing & enlarging a neglected cottage garden. Please park cars in rd (except if unable to walk 100 yds). NO DOGS. TEAS

Kingsmoor (Michael Francis Fane Esq) Titlarks Hill, Sunningdale. A30 to Sunningdale; take Chobham & Woking Rd, 1st turning right after railway bridge. 8 acres; special features: rhododendrons, azaleas & conifers. *Adm. 40p. Chd. 10p. Sun. June 1 (2–6)*

Kirby House⊕ (The Hon. John Astor) Inkpen, SW of Newbury. From A4 turn off through Kintbury towards Inkpen & then towards Combe. 4 acres with daffodils, narcissi & blossom. *Adm. 30p. Chd. free. Sun. April 27 (2–6)*

Little Bowden⊕ (Michael Verey Esq). 1½ m. W of Pangbourne on Ashampstead–Yattendon Rd. Azaleas, rhododendrons, bluebells, woodland. 10p extra for bathing in heated swimming pool. *Adm. 30p, Chd. under 15 free. Sun. May 25 (2.30–6.30)*

Luxmoore's Garden: also **Provost's & Fellows' Gardens**⊕ (Provost & Fellows of Eton College) Eton College, Windsor. Stations:

Windsor, Eton S.R. ½ m., W.R. ¾ m. Bus: Green Line 704 & 705 London—Windsor, 1 m. Luxmoore's Garden is an island garden created by a housemaster about 90 years ago; views of college & river. Provost's & Fellows' Gardens adjoin the ancient buildings on N & E sides. Parking in Cannon Yard, New School Yard & Parade Ground. NO DOGS. Tea shops in Eton High St. *Combined charge for all 3 gardens 30p. Sat. June 21 (2–6)*

Meadoway* (Miss Violet Waley) Enborne, 3½ m. SW of Newbury. From Newbury take Enborne Rd & turn left by Craven Arms, 1st right Vanners Lane. Charming cottage garden; exhibition daffodils; unusual plants & shrubs. Plants for sale. NO DOGS. Tea Foxgrove. *Adm. 20p. Sun. April 13 (2–6.30)*

Mortimer Gardens 6 m. SW of Reading. From Reading take Burghfield rd; at Rising Sun turn left; at next X-rds turn left & then right at fork. The following 3 gardens will be open. TEAS at Simms Farm House. *Combined charge 60p. Sun. June 15 (2–6)*

¶**Starvehill House**⊕ (Lady Mowbray) In Lockham Lane. ¾-acre garden, fairly new, with unusual shrubs. Pretty view. NO DOGS

¶**Ashley*** (Mrs Booth) In Lockram Lane. Beautiful small garden of great botanical interest with well-established plants & shrubs. NO DOGS

¶**Simms Farm House** (His Honour Judge Lea & Mrs Lea) Mortimer, turn down Drury Lane to T-junction, then right & house 100 yds along. 1-acre garden with mixed shrub borders; small rockery; some unusual plants. Lovely view

¶**Newington House**⊕ (Mrs H. C. A. Robertson) Winkfield; within 4–5 m. of Windsor, Bracknell & Ascot. From A330 turn off at Maidens Green, Winkfield, towards Winkfield Plain & along ¼ m. 2-acre garden; lawns, rose garden, shrubs, herbaceous, vegetable; pond. Old wood & tiled farm buildings. Two grade II listed houses (Newington House & Abbey Farm House); part shown. (*Share to Winkfield Parish Church*) Home-made TEAS. *Adm., inc. part-house, 30p, Chd. 5p. Sun. July 6 (2–6)*

Oakfield⊕ (Sir Michael & Lady Milne-Watson) Mortimer, SW of Reading. From Reading take Basingstoke Rd, turn right for Grazeley Green & Wokefield. Tea Reading. Large garden; lake, lawns, wild woodland & formal gardens. *Adm. 25p, Chd. 10p. Sun. May 4 (2–6)*

Oakfield, The Stables (Sir Ronald Milne-Watson, Bt) Oakfield, Mortimer, SW of Reading. From Reading take A33 Basingstoke Rd, turn right for Grazeley Green & Wokefield. Small garden recently created from wasteland next to converted stables. *Adm. 20p. Sun. May 4 (2–6)*

Odney Club*&⊕ (John Lewis Partnership) Cookham. Bus: AV 20 & 20A from Maiden-head or High Wycombe, alight The Tarry Stone. Car park in grounds. 120 acres; daffodils; lawns, garden & meadows on R. Thames. Picnics permitted in the meadows. NO DOGS. Tea Cookham village. *Adm. 20p, Chd. 5p. Sun. March 23 (2–6)*

The Old Rectory* (Mr & Mrs R. R. Merton) Burghfield, 5½ m. SW of Reading. Turn S off A4 W of Reading to Burghfield village; turn right after Hatch Gate Inn; entrance gate on right. Medium-sized garden; herbaceous & shrub borders; roses, hellebores, lilies, many rare & unusual plants collected by owners from Japan; old-fashioned cottage plants; autumn colour. Georgian house (not shown). Plants & produce for sale. Tea Reading. *Adm. 30p, Chd. 5p. Weds. March 26, April 30, May 28, June 25, July 30, Sept 24, Oct. 29 (11–6), also by appt.*

The Old Rectory*⊕ (Mrs Michael Todhunter) Farnborough, 4 m. SE of Wantage. From B4494 Wantage—New bury Rd, about 4 m. from Wantage turn E at signpost for Farnborough. Unusual plants; fine view; old-fashioned roses; herbaceous borders. House (not shown) built c. 1749. NO DOGS. Tea Bear Hotel, Wantage. *Adm. 30p. Chd. 5p. Sun. June 29 (2–6)*

Old Rectory Cottage* (A. W. A. Baker Esq) Tidmarsh, ½ m. S of Pangbourne, mid-way between Pangbourne & Tidmarsh turn E down narrow lane & at T-junction turn left. Medium-sized garden; wild garden, small lake, early spring bulbs, shrubs, lilies, roses, autumn colour & berries; sorbus avenue, rose hedge. Plants for sale. *Adm. 30p, Chd. 10p. Garden open by appt. only on following dates, Suns. April 6, May 18, June 8, July 27, Sept. 14 (Tel. Pangbourne 3241)*

Orchard Cottage*⊕ (Mrs Reginald Samuel) Sutton Rd, Cookham, 3 m. N of Maidenhead. Sutton Rd is part of the A4094 at Cookham. 1-acre garden; 500 roses, excluding climbers & shrubs; 500 dahlias; large well-stocked greenhouse; soft fruit garden; water garden; herbaceous & shrub borders. Wide range of horticultural subjects (the late Mr Samuel was Chairman of Windsor Rose Society & Vice-President of National Dahlia Society). NO DOGS. Tea Cookham. Cups of TEA available at garden. *Adm. 30p, Chd. (admitted only with an adult) free. Sun. Aug. 10 (2–7)*

Phillip's Hill†& (Mr & Mrs W. A. Palmer) Snelsmore Common, 3 m. N of Newbury. On B4494 Newbury—Wantage rd. Bluebells. Early Briton Camp. (*Share to British Red Cross Society, Berkshire Branch*) *Adm. 20p, Chd. 10p. Sun. May 11 (2–6)*

The Priory† (O. W. Roskill Esq) Beech Hill, S of Reading. Turn off at Spencers Wood P.O. Bus: AV 6, 12 from Reading. C14 Benedictine priory largely rebuilt 1648. Branch of Lodden flows through garden. Probably laid out in

C17. Lawns, herbaceous borders, shrubberies; kitchen garden. *Adm. 30p, Chd. 15p. Sun. June 15 (2–7)*

Purley Hall †&⊕ (Maj. & Mrs H. W. O. Bradley) ¾ m. E of Pangbourne. Leave M4 at Exit 12 for Pangbourne; in Pangbourne take A329 towards Reading; entrance ¾ m. along on right (flintstone gatehouse). Approx. 8 acres; garden was originally laid out by Bridgeman in 1720 (for which he received the sum of £200); Van Nost statue in lily pool; Seahorse statue possibly by Carpenter or earlier; C18 folly said to commemorate Battle of Culloden; forget-me-nots, paeonies, iris, lilacs, etc. House shown (if fine), 10p extra. *Adm. 30p. Sun. June 8 (2–7)*

Reynolds Farm (Christopher Wells Esq) Hurst, 3 m. S of Twyford. From Hurst Lodge turn left; after 1200 yds take first left, entrance 200 yds on left. Small wild garden of weekend cottage; planted by owner since 1962; designed for minimal maintenance & maximum effect; collection includes some interesting specimens of eucalyptus. NO DOGS. Tea Hurst Lodge. *Adm. 20p. Sun. May 11 (2–7)*

Rooksnest★†&⊕ (Miss M. V. Tufnell) Lambourn Woodlands 6 m. N of Hungerford. 3 m. from M4, junction 14. In parish of Woodland St Mary, signposted off Ermine St. Fascinating medium-sized garden with emphasis on shrubs & ornamental trees, herbaceous plants and roses; pleached limes, etc. Plants for sale. House (not open) dating from 1567. (*Share to Arthritis & Rheumatism Council*) NO DOGS. TEAS. *Adm. 30p, 10p. Sun. June 22 (2–6)*

Shinfield Grange★⊕ (University of Reading, Department of Agriculture & Horticulture) Cutbush Lane, Shinfield, 3 m. SE of Reading. From A327 Reading–Shinfield Rd going S, Cutbush Lane is 1st turning left, after M4 Motorway & Black Boy public House. Bus: Alder Valley 4 & 140 Reading–Wokingham; alight Black Boy public house, ½ m. 15 acres. Developed as a teaching garden with representative plant collections grouped in formal & informal situations; summer borders; annual borders, herbaceous border, rose garden, glade, etc. NO DOGS. TEAS (3.30–5 only). *Adm. 25p; under 16 10p. Mon. Aug. 25 (2–6)*

Stone House★&⊕ (Mr & Mrs Nigel Bingham) Brimpton, 5 m. SE of Newbury. From Newbury via A4 towards Reading; at X-rds turn off S for Brimpton. Medium-sized garden in attractive park; naturalised bulbs; rhododendrons, water garden, flowering cherries, walled kitchen garden, etc. Garden maintained by owners. TEAS. *Adm. 20p, Chd. 5p. Sun. May 4 (2–6.30)*

Tyle Mill&⊕ (L. E. van Moppes Esq) Sulhamstead, SW of Reading. Turn S off A4 at Jack's Booth. Bus: AV 2 Reading–Newbury, alight Jack's Booth 500 yds. Beautiful natural setting with walks by river & waterfalls; bulbs & flowering shrubs; dahlias & herbaceous; fine trees. Tea Theale. *Adm. 30p. Sun. April 20 & Sun. Aug. 17 (2–7)*

Wasing Place&⊕ (Sir William Mount, Bt) Aldermaston, SE of Newbury. Turn S off A4 at Woolhampton; or 3 m. to E, take A340 to Aldermaston. Bus: AV 110 from Newbury, alight Shalford Lodge; ½ m. drive. Large garden; rhododendrons, azaleas, lawns, walled & kitchen garden; greenhouses, herbaceous borders, magnificent cedars. C12 church. Orangeade available. *Adm. 30p. Sun. July 13 (2–6)*

West Woodhay House †&⊕ (J. Henderson Esq) Inkpen, SW of Newbury. Turn S off Bath Rd & on 2½ m. through Kintbury; then follow signposts to West Woodhay. Large garden; roses, shrubs, lake, lawns, woodland garden. Inigo Jones house (not shown). Tea Elcot Park Hotel. *Adm. 20p, Chd. 5p. Sun. April 20 (2–6)*

Wexham Springs★&⊕ (Cement & Concrete Assn) Framewood Rd, Wexham, 2 m. N of Slough. From A40 turn S & French Horn; Wexham Springs approx. 1¾ m. along on left. From M4/A4, in centre of Slough turn into Wexham Rd; Wexham Springs 2 m. along on right. Bus: 335 Windsor–Watford; alight at gate. Large informal garden with mixed shrubs; lake, rhododendrons & azaleas. Formal area with paved & planted courtyards designed by well-known landscape architects, inc. Sylvia Crowe, C. A. Jellicoe & Brian Westwood Terraces & garden walks; patios, paving, screen walling, garden furniture & other permanent displays. Ample free parking space. TEAS. *Adm. 40p, Chd. 20p. Sun. July 6 (2.30–6)*

White Horse★†&⊕ (Lady Liddell) Finchampstead, 3½ m. S of Wokingham. Large garden; shrubs, water gardens, heather, fuchsias; fine views. Alongside ancient church. Plants for sale. TEAS 15p. *Adm. 10p, Chd. free. Sun. June 8 & Sun. Sept. 7 (all day)*

¶**Woodside Cottage**⊕ (Mr & Mrs Kenneth Thornton) Woodside Rd, Windsor Forest. 5 m. SW of Windsor via A332 through Windsor Great Park; by "Crispin" P.H. turn off W on to B383; then bear left & house is 2nd on right. 4-acre garden, mostly shrubs & trees; old-fashioned roses. NO DOGS. Teashops in Windsor *.Adm. 25p, Chd. 5p. Sun. June 15 (2–7)*

BUCKINGHAMSHIRE

Hon. County Organiser:
MRS H. J. MASSINGHAM, Reddings,
Long Crendon, Aylesbury, HP18 5ED

Asst. Hon. County Organiser:
MRS E. N. BARNETT, Lower End,
Long Crendon, Aylesbury

Hon. Treasurer:
G. B. RAVENS, Esq, Buckinghamshire
County Nursing Assn, County Offices,
Aylesbury

DATES OF OPENING

APRIL Sunday 20
HAMBLEDEN MANOR GARDENS,
nr Henley-on-Thames
‡HORSENDEN MANOR, nr Princes
Risborough
‡MANOR FARM, Horsenden
NETHER WINCHENDON HOUSE,
nr Aylesbury
APRIL Sunday 27
ASCOTT, Wing, nr Aylesbury
MAY by appointment
CHURCH END, Bledlow
THE OLD FARM, Bishopstone,
nr Aylesbury
73 TOTTERIDGE LANE, High Wycombe
MAY Sunday 4
CHICHELEY HALL, nr Newport Pagnall
MAY Sunday 18
CLIVEDEN, nr Taplow
MAY Sunday 25
LITTLE PASTON, Fulmer
JUNE by appointment
CHURCH END, Bledlow
THE OLD FARM, Bishopstone,
nr Aylesbury
73 TOTTERIDGE LANE, High Wycombe
JUNE Sunday 1
DORNEYWOOD GARDEN, nr Burnham
STEART HILL, Whaddon Mursley Rd,
Little Horwood, Milton Keynes
WEST WYCOMBE PARK,
nr High Wycombe
JUNE Sunday 15
ASCOTT, Wing, nr Aylesbury
BOSWELLS, Wendover
HADDENHAM GARDENS, nr Thame
(Hill View & Turn End)
JUNE Sunday 22
HADDENHAM GARDENS, nr Thame
(16 Church End & Swanbourne)
THE MANOR HOUSE, Bledlow
JUNE Sunday 29
BOSWELLS, Wendover
LONG CRENDON GARDENS, nr Thame
THE MANOR HOUSE, Little Marlow
JULY by appointment
CHURCH END, Bledlow
THE OLD FARM, Bishopstone,
nr Aylesbury
73 TOTTERIDGE LANE, High Wycombe
JULY Sunday 6
‡HAMBLEDEN MANOR GARDENS,
nr Henley-on-Thames
‡BARNFIELD, Northend Common,
nr Henley-on-Thames
‡THE LITTLE FORGE, Fawley Green,
nr Henley-on-Thames
JULY Sunday 27
THE OLD FARM, Bishopstone,
nr Aylesbury

AUGUST by appointment
CHURCH END, Bledlow
THE OLD FARM, Bishopstone,
nr Aylesbury
SEPTEMBER by appointment
THE OLD FARM, Bishopstone,
nr Aylesbury
SEPTEMBER Sunday 14
CLIVEDEN, nr Taplow

DESCRIPTIONS OF GARDENS

Ascott*⚕ (E. de Rothschild Esq ; The National
Trust—see p. ix) Wing, SW of Leighton
Buzzard, 8 m. NE of Aylesbury. A418. Bus :
United Counties 141 Aylesbury–St Ives passes
entrance. Beautiful surroundings & layout.
Garden part formal, part natural ; many speci-
men trees & shrubs, sunken garden ; lily pond.
Tea Leighton Buzzard. *Adm. 80p, Chd. 40p.*
△*Sun. April 27 & Sun. June 15 (2–6)*

¶Barnfield⊕ (Mr & Mrs John Annan)
Northend Common, 7 m. N of Henley-on-
Thames. From Henley via A423 ; turn right on
to B480 to Stonor then follow signs to
Northend ; or from M40, leave by junction 6
on to B4009 to Watlington & follow sign to
Northend. Medium-sized garden ; shrub roses ;
wandering paths & views. *Adm. 30p, Chd. 5p.*
Sun. July 6 (2–7)

Boswells*⊕ (Sir Thomas & Lady Barlow)
Wendover, SE of Aylesbury. 1 m. S of
Wendover, on A413. Station : Wendover, 1 m.
Medium-sized garden on chalk, all planted
since 1900. TEAS. *Adm. 25p, Chd. 5p. Sun.
June 15 & Sun. June 29 (2–6.30)*

Chicheley Hall †⊕ (The Hon. Nicholas
Beatty) In Chicheley village ; 2 m. E of Newport Pagnell ; 9 m. W of Bedford on A422 ;
5 m. from M1 (junction 14) ; Bus : United
Counties 132, alight nr entrance. Large garden ;
magnificent display of daffodils ; formal 3-
sided canal designed 1700 by George London
who also worked at Hampton Court. Fine
brickwork house built 1719–1723. NO DOGS.
TEAS. *Adm. house & garden £1, Chd. 50p ;
gardens only 40p, Chd. 20p.* △*Sun. May 4
(2.30–6)*

Church End* (Miss P. Dimsdale) Bledlow,
2½ m. SW of Princes Risborough. From A40
turn N via B4009 through Chinnor & on 2 m.
to turning on right to Bledlow. Nr church of
historic interest in centre of village. Small
garden with unusual plants ; flowering shrubs,
old-fashioned roses, lilies. *Collecting box.
Garden open by appt. only, May–Aug ; write
or tel. Princes Risborough 5404*

Cliveden* †⚕⊕ (The National Trust—see p.
ix) 2 m. N of Taplow. B476. Bus : AV 63
Slough–Maidenhead. Bus stop : Feathers Inn,
Cliveden, ¼ m. One of the most beautiful places
in England. Water garden ; grand view of R.
Thames. NO DOGS. *Adm. house & grounds
£1.20 ; grounds only £1.00 ; Chd. ½-price.*
△*Sun. May 18 & Sun. Sept. 14 (11–6.30)*

7

BUCKINGHAMSHIRE—continued

Dorneywood Garden (The National Trust) nr Burnham. 1½ m. N of Burnham village. Between B476 & B473. Bus: Alder Valley 63 (Slough–Dropmore–Maidenhead). Station: Burnham, 2½ m. Natural garden. NO DOGS. Tea Wingroves Tea Gardens, Burnham Beeches. *Adm. 50p. Sun. June 1 (2–7)*

Haddenham Gardens. On *June 15* the following 2 gardens will be open. 3 m. NE of Thame. From A418 turn off S to Haddenham between Thame (3 m.) & Aylesbury (6 m.). Bus: Ox.280 Oxford–Aylesbury. TEAS (2.30–5.30) at Hill View. *Adm. 25p to each garden, Chd. 10p. Sun. Sun. June 15 (2–7)*

   Hill View⊕ (Dr & Mrs C. Johnstone) 37 Churchway. (Bus stop: Willis Rd.) ½-acre garden attractively designed, made & maintained entirely by owners since 1969; fruit, vegetables, herbaceous plants, bonsais, interesting shrubs, alpines, ferns. TEAS

   ¶**Turn End**⊕ (Peter Aldington Esq) Townside. (Bus stop: The Crown.) Secluded ½-acre walled garden in old orchard with variety of large; shade-loving plants; award-winning modern house & small courtyard garden also open. NO DOGS

Haddenham Gardens. On *June 22* the following 2 gardens will be open. (For directions see previous entry.) Bus stop (both gardens): Church End Green. TEAS (3–5) at 16 Church End. *Adm. 25p to Swanbourne; collecting box at 16 Church End. Sun. June 22 (2–6)*

   16 Church End⊕ (Miss Barbara H. Wood) Medium-sized garden; water garden; fruit, flowers, vegetables. TEAS (3–5)

   Swanbourne (Prof. R. S. Pilcher) 21 Church End. Medium-sized garden; walled garden with wide herbaceous borders; fruit & vegetables. Home-made produce & cakes for sale (Miss Betty Arne). *Adm. 25p*

Hambleden Manor Gardens*⚹⊕ (The Viscount Hambleden) NE of Henley-on-Thames. 1 m. N of A4155. Spring bulbs & daffodils. Loggia, shrubs & roses. TEAS. *Adm. 50p, Chd. 10p. Sun. April 20 & Sun. July 6 (2–7)*

Horsenden Manor*⚹⊕ (Mr & Mrs J. Gourlay) 1½ m. W of Princes Risborough; follow A4010 (Wycombe direction) then take right fork B444 for 300 yds & then follow signs for Horsenden. Garden of over 8 acres; fine trees, extensive lawns & massive display of daffodils; herbaceous borders; lake with classical temple, folly, moats & waterfalls. House (not open) C17 & C18. (*Share to N.S.P.C.C.*) NO DOGS. Tea Pepper Pot, 16 Duke St, Princes Risborough. *Adm. 30p, Chd. 15p. Sun. April 20 (2–6)*

¶**The Little Forge**⊕ (Miss Grace Lane) Fawley Green, 3½ m. N of Henley-on-Thames. Leave Henley via Marlow Rd & 1st left signposted Fawley. ½-acre garden; herbaceous &

roses; beautiful view of Chiltern country. NO DOGS. *Adm. 15p, Chd. 5p. Sun. July 6 (2–5)*

Little Paston⊕ (F. P. W. Maynard Esq) Fulmer Common Rd, Fulmer. Fulmer is in triangle formed by A40, A412, A332, N of Slough (map ref. 160/999849). Bus: 335, alight Fulmer Common Rd, 600 yds. 10 acres; woodland garden with lawns; water garden; kitchen garden; mainly rhododendrons. *Adm. 30p, Chd. 10p. Sun. May 25 (2–6)*

Long Crendon Gardens, 2 m. N of Thame, on B4011 to Bicester. TEAS at Windacre. *Sun. June 29 (2–7)*

   Windacre*⚹⊕ (Mr & Mrs K. Urch) Next door to Bernewood School. Garden of approx. 1-acre; trees, roses, shrubs & orchard; main feature is sunken lawn & trees. NO DOGS. Craft Exhibition. *Adm. 20p, Chd. 10p.* TEAS

   ¶**Game Keep** (Mrs A. C. Getley) At end of High St nr church. 1½-acre garden; roses & shrubs; fine view of Vale. *Adm. 30p, Chd. 5p*

Manor Farm⊕ (Mrs C. S. Goldingham) Horsenden, 1½ m. W of Princes Risborough. From Princes Risborough follow A4010 (Wycombe direction) then take right fork B4444 for 300 yds or so; Horsenden signposted from then on; Manor Farm near church gate. 2-acre garden created in 1930s retaining its original design, with formal garden mixed borders and rose garden around a C17 wooden barn; wide lawns, spring bulbs, shrub roses, large walled kitchen garden. NO DOGS. Tea The Pepper Pot, 16 Duke St, Princes Risborough. *Adm. 20p, Chd. 5p. Sun. April 20 (2–6)*

The Manor House, Bledlow⊕ (The Lord & Lady Carrington) ½ m. off B4009 in middle of Bledlow village. Station: Princes Risborough, 2½ m. Medium-sized garden on chalk. Paved gardens & shrub borders. C17 & C18 house. NO DOGS. TEAS. *Adm. 45p, Chd. 10p. Sun. June 22 (2–6)*

The Manor House, Little Marlow†⊕ (Sir Eric & Lady Weiss) 2 m. NE of Marlow. Off A4155, mid-way between Bourne End & Marlow. Approx. 5 acres; extensive lawns; water features; walled garden; heather & woodland garden. Free-flight nun doves. NO DOGS. TEAS. *Adm. 30p, Chd. 15p. Sun. June 29 (2–6)*

Nether Winchendon House*†⚹⊕ (Mrs Spencer Bernard) Nether Winchendon, 5 m. SW of Aylesbury; 7 m. from Thame. Station: Aylesbury. Picturesque village & beautiful church. 3–4 acres; fine trees, variety of hedges; spring bulbs & flowering trees. Newly planted avenue. Tudor manor house (not shown on this date) home of Sir Francis Bernard, Governor of Massachusetts. NO DOGS. Tea Thame, Aylesbury or Waddesdon. *Adm. 50p, Chd. 25p. △Sun. April 20 (2–6)*

The Old Farm*⊕ (Mrs Delap) Bishopstone, SW of Aylesbury. From A418 Thame–Aylesbury, at Stone Church turn off right for Bishopstone. Medium-sized garden; flowering shrubs, borders, trees, pond. Tea Aylesbury. *Adm. 30p, Chd. 5p. Sun. July 27 (2–7); also open by appt. May–Sept.; write or tel. Aylesbury 748236*

Steart Hill*⊕ (Mrs R. Close-Smith) nr Mursley, 4½ m. W of Bletchley. ½-way between Buckingham & Bletchley, turn off A421 at *only* signpost for Mursley; 400 yds from main road. Station: Bletchley. Large collection of roses old & new; shrubberies. TEAS. *Adm. 60p, Chd. 20p.* △*Sun. June 1 (2–6)*

¶**73 Totteridge Lane** (Mr & Mrs R. W. Collingwood) High Wycombe. From centre of High Wycombe via A404; after 1½ m. turn off E; then approx. ½ m. to garden. Bus: LC 363; alight Dolphin P.H., 50 yds. ½-acre garden designed, made & maintained by owners; rockery, raised beds; new herb garden, herbaceous plants & some shrubs. NO DOGS. Collecting box. Garden open by appt. only May–July *(Tel. High Wycombe 28621)*

West Wycombe Park†&⊕ (Sir Francis Dashwood, Bt. The National Trust—see p ix.) West Wycombe. 3 m. W of High Wycombe on A40. Bus: from High Wycombe. Landscape garden & lake with classical Greek & Roman temples. NO DOGS. Tea Cave's Cafe. *Adm. (grounds only) £1 per car or 50p for adults, Chd. 25p. Sun. June 1 (2.15–6)*

CAMBRIDGESHIRE

Hon. County Organisers:

South: MRS MARTIN NOURSE, North End House, Grantchester, Cambridge, CB3 9NQ & MRS PETER PEMBERTON, Maris House, Trumpington, Cambridge

North (Huntingdon, I of Ely, Peterborough): MRS JAMES CROWDEN, 19 North Brink, Wisbech, PE13 1JR

DATES OF OPENING

APRIL Easter Sunday 6
 LONGSTOWE HALL, Longstowe
APRIL Sunday 13
 FELLOWS' GARDEN, King's College, Cambridge
APRIL Sunday 20
 BARTLOW PARK, Linton
MAY Sunday 25
 THE HOO, 46 Church St, Buckden
 ‡TETWORTH HALL, nr Sandy
 ‡WOODBURY HALL—See Bedfordshire
JUNE Sunday 8
 ‡THE CROSSING HOUSE, Shepreth
 ‡DOCWRA'S MANOR, Shepreth
JUNE Sunday 15
 EGERTON HOUSE, Newmarket
 THE LAURELS, Great Shelford, nr Cambridge
 ‡33 GAUL ROAD, March
 ‡THE OLD VICARAGE, Coldham

JUNE Sunday 29
 DUXFORD MILL, Duxford
JULY Sunday 6
 ABBOTS RIPTON HALL, nr Huntingdon
 CROXTON PARK, St Neots
 HARSTON GARDENS, nr Cambridge
JULY Sunday 13
 ‡THE MERCHANT'S HOUSE, Swavesey
 ‡HAWTHORNS, Swavesey
JULY Sunday 20
 WEST WRATTING PARK, West Wratting
JULY Friday 25
 PECKOVER HOUSE, Wisbech
AUGUST Sunday 10
 W. J. UNWIN LTD, Histon, nr Cambridge
AUGUST Sunday 24
 LONGSTOWE HALL, Longstowe
SEPTEMBER Sunday 14
 ‡MELBOURN BURY, nr Royston
 ‡MELBOURN LODGE, nr Royston
OCTOBER Sunday 26
 ANGLESEY ABBEY, nr Cambridge

DESCRIPTIONS OF GARDENS

Abbots Ripton Hall*& (The Lord De Ramsey) 4 m. N of Huntingdon. On B1090. Medium-sized garden; herbaceous border. Large collection of old-fashioned roses; shrubs; grey border; arboretum; tropical house. (*Share to Abbots Ripton Village Gala Week*) NO DOGS. TEAS. *Adm. 30p, Chd. 5p. Sun. July 6 (2–7)*

Anglesey Abbey*†& (The National Trust—see page ix) 6 m. NE of Cambridge. From A45 turn N on to B1102 through Stow-cum-Qay. 100 acres surrounding an Elizabethan manor created from the remains of an abbey founded in reign of Henry I. Garden created during last 50 years; avenues of beautiful trees with lovely autumn colouring; hedges, enclosing small intimate gardens; groups of statuary. NO DOGS. *Adm. 60p, Chd. (accompanied by an adult) 30p.* △*Sun. Oct. 26 (2–6)*

Bartlow Park (Brig. & Mrs Alan Breitmeyer) 1½ m. SE of Linton. 6 m. NE of Saffron Walden; 12 m. SE of Cambridge; from A604 at Linton turn SE for Bartlow. Bus: Cambridge–Haverhill; alight Bartlow X-rds 300 yds. Medium-sized, new garden around recently built house; spring bulbs, flowering shrubs, lawn, ornamental trees, set in fine natural landscape of mature timber. Share to Bartlow Parish Church. *Adm. 30p, Chd. 15p. Sun. April 20 (2–6)*

The Crossing House⊕ (Mr & Mrs Douglas Fuller) Meldreth Rd, Shepreth, 8 m. SW of Cambridge. ½ m. W of A10 Cambridge–Royston Rd. King's Cross–Cambridge railway line runs alongside garden. Small cottage garden with many old-fashioned plants grown in mixed beds in company with modern varieties; shrubs, bulbs, etc; many alpines grown in rock beds & alpine house. Tea & biscuits at Docwra's Manor, Shepreth. *Collecting box. Sun. June 8 (2–7)*

Croxton Park⊕ (The Hon. Lady Fox) 4½ m. E of St Neots. On A45, 13 m. W of Cambridge. Bus: 128 Cambridge–St Neots–Northampton. Elizabethan walled garden (1573), through wrought-iron gates, contains 6 inner gardens; herbaceous borders, rose pergola & box hedges; walled garden is surrounded by shrubberies & lawns, lake & parks. Interesting C14 church with floral decorations. Dogs *only* if on leads. TEAS. Free car park. *Adm. 30p, Chd. 10p. Sun. July 6 (2–7)*

Docwra's Manor✶†⊕ (Mr & Mrs John Raven) Shepreth, 8 m. SW of Cambridge. ½ m. W of Cambridge–Royston Rd (A10). Cambridge–Royston bus stops at gate in Shepreth. Medium-sized garden; unusual shrubs & plants. NO DOGS. TEA & refreshments. Share to Cambs. & Isle of Ely Naturalists Trust. *Adm. 30p, Chd. 10p. Sun. June 8 (2–7); also by appt. for coach parties (April–July) (Tel. Royston 60235)*

Duxford Mill†⊕ (Mr & Mrs Robert Lea) 9 m. S of Cambridge. Close to Duxford village, on B1379, off A505 Royston–Newmarket Rd & 1½ m. from Junction 10, M11 (Cambridge by-pass). Bus: Eastern Counties 112 Cambridge–Saffron Walden. Lawns & borders of modern roses beside the R. Cam. Gardens are landscaped to include vistas of Mill Pool, a Regency stone temple, & sculpture by Wiles. Old water mill & miller's house mentioned in Domesday survey 1080; much visited during Protectorate by Oliver Cromwell. Charles Kingsley stayed for long periods with the Miller & is reputed to have written parts of *The Water Babies* here. TEAS. *Adm. 25p, Chd. 5p. Sun. June 29 (2–7)*

Egerton House (Maj. Sir Reginald & The Hon. Lady Macdonald-Buchanan) 3 m. SW of Newmarket. Route A45. Garden; some interesting trees planted by Royalty; herbaceous borders. Visits to Stud Farm arranged. TEA & biscuits. Free car park. *Adm. 25p, Chd. 5p. Sun. June 15 (2–6)*

Fellows' Garden, King's College,✶†⅄⊕ Cambridge. Bulbs. NO DOGS. Tree leaflets available. *Adm. 20p. Sun. April 13 (2–6)*

33 Gaul Road⊕ (Mr & Mrs F. J. Grounds) March. ¾ m. from centre of March; using March By-Pass, 1st turning off left from Wisbech end roundabout or last turning off right from Chatteris end. House on left-hand side behind privet hedge. 1½-acre garden mainly shrubs, lawns & roses; swimming pool area & orchard; small riverside garden also open, 5 mins. walk from main garden. NO DOGS. TEAS. *Adm. 25p, Chd. 10p. Sun. June 15 (2–6)*

Harston Gardens. 5 m. SW of Cambridge on A10 to Royston. The following 6 gardens will be open. TEA & biscuits at Park House. *Adm. 20p each garden (but collecting box at Weaver Cottage). Sun. July 6 (2–6)*

¶**Park House**✶⅄⊕ (Col G. T. Hurrell) 87 High St (on A10). 4-acre garden with roses & trees

¶**Byron Lodge**⊕ (Mr & Mrs John Cairns) High St (A10) by War Memorial. ¾-acre garden; shrubs, perennial border, vegetables

¶**Elton Way** (Mr & Mrs R. J. Pate) 1 Pightle Close (last turning off main rd at Royston end of village). ½-acre approx. with lawns, flowerbeds & vegetable garden

¶**Harston Manor**⊕ (Robert C. Arnold Esq) At War Memorial turn into Haslingfield Rd. 8 acres with river & many trees

¶**163 High Street** (Dr T. Gibson) Opp. 'Old English Gentleman' P.H. 1-acre garden with flowers, shrubs, vegetables & fruit

¶**Weaving Cottage**⊕ (Miss M. D. Craster) 42 Royston Rd. At Queen's Head turn off W into Haslingfield Rd & entrance immediately on left, opp. stone fountain on Green. (Please leave cars on Green as no room for parking in drive.) A 'secret' garden of ⅓-acre, approached through archway & protected & sheltered by backs of pantiled cottages. NO DOGS. Collecting box

Hawthorns✶ (Dr & Mrs R. W. K. Holland) 45 Gibralter Lane, Swavesey, 8 m. NW of Cambridge. From A604 turn N to Swavesey; through village follow sign left for village college. Bus: Cambridge–St Ives; alight School Lane or Whitton Close. Plantsman's & family garden of ⅓ acre made since 1975 & still in process of development by owner (a professional horticulturist); exposed position on heavy clay; although site was basically flat, parts have been contoured to improve appearance & drainage; features incorporated into design to make best use of peculiarities of land inc. pond, raised alpine bed & shrub roses; glasshouse with notable collection of cacti & other succulents. Tea Merchants House. *Adm. 20p, Chd. 5p. Sun. July 13 (2–7)*

¶**The Hoo**✶⊕ (Mr & Mrs R. W. Peplow) 46 Church St, Buckden. On A1, S of Peterborough N of Biggleswade. 1½-acre garden, mainly herbs & propagation area with collection of old English apples. TEAS. *Adm. 25p, Chd. 10p. Sun. May 25 (2–6)*

The Laurels⊕ (The Misses Collett) Great Shelford, 4 m. S of Cambridge. A130, fork right at War Memorial if coming from Cambridge. Medium-sized, matured garden; large trees; yew hedge; lawns & herbaceous borders. TEAS. *Adm. 25p, Chd. 5p. Sun. June 15 (2–7)*

Longstowe Hall✶⅄⊕ (M. S. M. Bevan Esq) 10 m. W of Cambridge. Nr junction of A14 & B1046. Bus: Eastern Counties 118 Cambridge–Longstowe; alight Fox Inn. Very large garden with extensive lawns, 2 lakes & attractive woodland walks; many fine specimen trees; daffodils & oxlips; formal rose garden & 2 long herbaceous borders. TEAS available. Free car park. *Adm. 30p, Chd. 10p. Sun. April 6 & Sun. Aug. 24 (2–7)*

¶**Melbourn Bury** (Mr & Mrs Anthony Hopkinson) 2½ m. N of Royston & 8 m. S of Cambridge; off the A10 on edge of village, Royston side. 5 acres; small ornamental lake & river with wildfowl; large herbaceous border; fine mature trees with wide lawns & rose garden. NO DOGS. TEAS. *Adm. 25p. Sun. Sept. 14 (2–6)*

¶**Melbourn Lodge***⊕ (J. R. M. Keatley Esq) Melbourn, 3 m. N of Royston, 8 m. S of Cambridge. House in middle of Melbourn village on A10. 2-acre garden, basically C19, which is being gradually adapted for C20 living with accent on ease of upkeep. *Adm. 25p. Sun. Sept. 14 (2–7)*

The Merchant's House* (Mr & Mrs Gordon Norton) 31 Station Rd, Swavesey, 8 m. NW of Cambridge. A604 Cambridge (6½ m.)–Huntingdon (8 m.) turn N to Swavesey; follow rd for 2 m.; through village, house on left where rd forks. Parking by pond. Bus: Cambridge–St Ives; alight opp. house by Swan pond. ½-acre garden; lies on a medieval selion (cultivation strip) & although less than 10 yrs established, has an interesting collection of specimen trees, shrubs & herbaceous plants. House, also medieval & one of the oldest in the village, was brick-fronted in C18 & was then Swan With Two Nicks P.H. for 1½ centuries. Garden catalogue & notes on history of Swavesey (collecting box). TEA & biscuits. *Adm. 20p, Chd. 5p. Sun. July 13 (11.30–7); also open by appt. (Tel. 0954 30809)*

¶**The Old Vicarage**⊕ (Mr & Mrs M. G. Wakeham) Coldham, 4 m. N of March, 6 m. S of Wisbech. Main rd, March-Fridaybridge; next to Coldham Church. 1¾-acre garden with lawns, trees, rockery & flowering shrubs. NO DOGS. TEAS. *Adm. 25p, Chd. 10p. Sun. June 15 (2–6)*

Peckover House*⅃⊕ (The National Trust— see p. ix) Wisbech. In centre of Wisbech town, on N bank of R. Nene (B1441). Garden only open. 2-acre Victorian garden; rare trees, inc. Maidenhair (Gingko) tree. Orange trees growing under glass. NO DOGS. Tea 19 North Brink (adjoining Peckover House). *Adm. 25p, Chd. 10p (with adult). △Fri. July 25 (2–6)*

Tetworth Hall*⅃ (Mr & Mrs D. P. Crossman) 4 m. NE of Sandy. 6 m. SE of St Neots. Woodland & bog garden; rhododendrons & azaleas, unusual shrubs & plants. Nearby garden open on same day, **Woodbury Hall**— see Bedfordshire. TEA & biscuits. *Adm. 20p, Chd. 5p. Sun. May 25 (2–7)*

West Wratting Park⅃⊕ (Lady Ursula d'Abo) 8 m. S of Newmarket. From A11, between Worsted Lodge & Six Mile Bottom, take turning to E to Balsham, & from there turn N along B1052 to West Wratting; Park is at E end of village. Georgian house (orangery shown), beautifully situated in rolling country, with fine trees; rose & herbaceous gardens & walled kitchen garden. NO DOGS. TEAS. *Adm. 25p, Chd. 5p. Sun. July 20 (2–7)*

W. J. Unwin Ltd* Impington Lane, Histon, 3 m. N of Cambridge. Follow A45 to B1049 exit. From Cambridge via B1049; at traffic lights turn right into Impington Lane; follow RAC signs, 'Garden Seed Trials'. Approx. 3 acres of flower & vegetable seed trials containing items from many countries of the world. *Adm. 25p, Chd. 10p. Sun. Aug. 10 (10–6)*

CHESHIRE & WIRRAL (South Merseyside)

Hon. County Organiser:
MAJ. J. A. READMAN, Monarchy Hall, Utkinton, nr Tarporley

DATES OF OPENING

APRIL Sunday 27
‡BARNETT BROOK, Aston, nr Nantwich
‡SALESBROOK FARM, Aston,
nr Nantwich
MAY Sunday 11
TUSHINGHAM HALL, nr Whitchurch
MAY Sunday 18
HAUGHTON HALL GARDENS, nr Bunbury
THE QUINTA, Swettenham
SPELLS, Prestbury
THORNTON MANOR, Thornton Hough,
Wirral
MAY Monday 19 & daily to Saturday 24
THE QUINTA, Swettenham
MAY Sunday 25
PENN, Alderley Edge
MAY Monday 26 (Bank Holiday)
PENN, Alderley Edge
MAY Saturday 31
CAPESTHORNE, nr Macclesfield
THE QUARRY, Prenton, Wirral
JUNE Sunday 1
MANLEY KNOLL, Manley
TIRESFORD, Tarporley
JUNE Sunday 8
ASHTON HEYS, nr Kelsall
‡SPURSTOW HALL, nr Bunbury
‡THE WHITE HOUSE, Bunbury
JUNE Saturday 21
BELL COTTAGE, Vale Royal Abbey,
Whitegate
JUNE Sunday 22
BELL COTTAGE, Vale Royal Abbey
Whitegate
JUNE Sunday 29
SCULSHAW LODGE, Allostock,
nr Knutsford
JULY by appointment
MONARCHY HALL FARM, Utkinton

JULY Sunday 6
‡MILNEGATE, Prestbury
‡WHIRLEY HALL, Macclesfield

JULY Sunday 20
NEWBOLD, Saighton, nr Chester

JULY Sunday 27
‡COBBLESTONES, Malpas
‡OVERTON HALL, Malpas

DESCRIPTIONS OF GARDENS

Ashton Heys*⚭ (Miss E. B. T. Johnson) Ashton, N of Kelsall, N of A54, nr Ashton. Leave A54 Kelsall ($\frac{1}{2}$ m.) at Holland's Lane, or at junction B5393 (bus stop) via Ashton. Mouldsworth Station, $\frac{1}{2}$ m. Chester, 9 m. Large woodland garden; flowering shrubs, trees, three small lakes, rhododendrons, azaleas, rock garden. (*Share to R.S.P.C.A.*) TEAS. *Adm. 35p, Chd. 10p. Sun. June 8 (2–6)*

Barnett Brook*⊕ (Mr & Mrs E. R. Moore) Aston, nr Nantwich, 6 m. NE of Whitchurch, 5 m. SE of Nantwich. Follow signs NW off A530 at Aston, X-rds or off A525 at Rookery Corner W of Audlem. Small garden of specialised plants inc. alpines in troughs & Tufa Rock, River walk. (*Share to Cancer Relief*) TEAS. *Adm. 20p, Chd. 10p. Sun. April 27 (2–7)*

¶**Bell Cottage**⊕ (J. W. Ellis Esq & G. K. Armitstead Esq) Vale Royal Abbey, Whitegate. Turn off A556 to Whitegate; opp. church follow drive for $\frac{3}{4}$ m. to Vale Royal Abbey for parking. Medium-sized garden of general interest developed since 1972 by owners alone; walled garden, wooded area, shrubs, herbaceous, climbers and shrub roses. (*Share to Michaelmas Trust*) *Adm. 25p, Chd. 10p. Sat. June 21 (2–7) & Sun. June 22 (6–8)*

Capesthorne*†⚭ (Sir Walter Bromley-Davenport) 5 m. W of Macclesfield. On A34 7 m. S of Wilmslow. Bus stop: Monks Heath (1$\frac{1}{2}$ m.). Medium-sized garden; daffodil lawn; azaleas, rhododendrons & flowering shrubs; herbaceous border; lake & pool. Georgian chapel built 1722 on view. Cheshire Conservation Trust Nature Trail (leaflet 2p) combined garden & woodland walk. (Hall, park & gardens also open many other days March–Sept; details from Hall Manager, Chelford 861221.) NO DOGS. TEAS. Free car park, *Adm. to garden 50p; house 50p extra. Chd. $\frac{1}{2}$-price.* △*Sat. May 31 (2–6; house 2–5)*

Cobblestones (Mrs E. M. Hilditch) Church St, Malpas. Turn off A41 (Chester–Whitchurch) on to B5069 to Malpas village; house in Church St, approx. 200 yds from church. Small garden, approx. $\frac{3}{4}$ acre; roses, flowering shrubs, herbaceous plants. Wonderfully uninterrupted view over lovely countryside. House (not open) is 3-sided building converted from stable block; attractive entrance with wall plants, troughs & small bedding plants. NO DOGS. TEAS. *Adm. 25p, Chd. 15p. Sun. July 27 (2–7)*

Haughton Hall Gardens*⚭⊕ (Mr & Mrs Geoffrey C. Dean) nr Bunbury; 5 m. NW of Nantwich. 6 m. SE of Tarporley via Beeston Castle; N of A534 Nantwich–Wrexham rd. Medium-sized garden, species of rhododendrons, azaleas, shrubs, rock garden, lake with temple, waterfall. Bird garden with Cuban & Chilean flamingoes, and the largest number of Stanley Cranes in England, black-necked swans, & some 30 species of water fowl. Dogs on leads only. (*Share to British Waterfowl Assn*) TEAS. Free car park. *Adm. 50p, Chd. 15p. Sun. May 18 (2–6.30); also by appt. for parties (Tel: Bunbury 260251)*

Manley Knoll⚭⊕ (D. G. Fildes Esq) Manley, NE of Chester. Nr Mouldsworth. B5393. Quarry garden; azaleas & rhododendrons. TEAS. *Adm. 20p, OAPs & Chd. 5p. Sun. June 1 (2–6.30)*

Milnegate (Mr & Mrs Roger Wood) Castle Hill, Prestbury, 3 m. from Macclesfield. $\frac{1}{2}$ m. from Prestbury via A538 (signposted to Wilmslow) known as Castle Hill; garden near top of hill on left. $\frac{1}{3}$-acre garden; mixed shrub borders & ground cover plants; collection of old-fashioned & modern shrub roses, inc. unusual climbers. (*Share to David Lewis Centre for Epilepsy Appeal Fund*) *Adm. 20p, OAPs & Chd. 10p. Sun. July 6 (2–7); also by appt. (Tel. Prestbury 829156)*

Monarchy Hall Farm (Maj. & Mrs J. A. Readman) Utkinton, 2 m. N of Tarporely. From Utkinton P.O. turn up hill (Quarry Bank) to school; turn left up Tirley Lane for about $\frac{1}{2}$ m. & house on right. 1$\frac{1}{2}$-acre garden of general interest developed by family since 1970. Fine views. *Adm. 25p, Chd. 10p. Garden open by appt. in July (Tel. Kelsall 51363)*

Newbold⚭ (Maj. J. N. Davies-Colley) Saighton, 5 m. SE of Chester. From A41 Chester–Whitchurch, turn at Hatton Heath. Medium-sized old garden; rare trees; vistas. TEAS. *Adm. 25p, OAPs 10p, Chd. 5p. Sun. July 20 (2–6)*

Overton Hall †⚭ (Mr & Mrs Henry Barnett) 1$\frac{1}{2}$ m. NW of Malpas. About 1 m. from Malpas on rd to Tilston turn left & follow signs to Overton Hall. Small garden with water & woodland; herbaceous borders, roses, alpine area; historical environment. Tea at Cobblestones, Malpas. *Adm. 25p, Chd. 10p. Sun. July 27 (2–7)*

Penn* (Mr & Mrs R. W. Baldwin) Macclesfield Rd, Alderley Edge. Approx. $\frac{3}{4}$ m. E of Alderley Edge village, on B5087, Alderley Edge–Macclesfield Rd. Turn left into Woodbrook Rd for car parking. 2$\frac{1}{2}$ acres; rhododendron species & hybrids, deciduous & Japanese azaleas & meconopsis on a hillside backing on to the Alderley Edge (Nat. Trust property). *Adm. 25p, Chd. 5p. Sun. & Mon. May 25 & 26 (2–6)*

The Quarry (Mr & Mrs Chris Jones) Burrell Rd (off Pine Walks), Prenton, Wirral. Station: Hamilton Square. Bus: Birkenhead Corp. 84, 85 & 86, alight Mount Rd or Mendip Rd, 200 yds. 1½-acre garden of unique design, originally a worked-out quarry of which advantage has been taken to make an alpine & rhododendron garden. Lily & fish pond. Unusual flowering trees & shrubs; Exbury strain azaleas, camellias, magnolias, heaths. *Adm. 25p, Chd. 10p. Sat. May 31 (11–7)*

The Quinta* (Sir Bernard & Lady Lovell) Swettenham, E off Holmes Chapel. Turn E off A535 at Twemlow, 2 m. N of Holmes Chapel. Medium-sized garden with trees & shrubs. TEAS (May 18 only). *Adm. 30p, Chd. 10p. Sun. May 18 (2–7); also Mon. May 19 & daily to Sat. 24 (5–9)*

Salesbrook Farm⊕ (Mr & Mrs G. H. Shore) Aston, nr Nantwich, 6 m. NE of Whitchurch, 5 m. SE of Nantwich. Follow signs NW off A530 at Aston X-rds or off A525 at Rookery Corner W of Audlem. Medium-sized garden, herbaceous border, spring display of daffodils, rockery bulbs, gilly-flowers, large heather borders, shrubbery; pleasant brook flowing at bottom of garden with rustic bridge across; barbecue area & brick pillared pergola; alpines. (*Share to Cancer Relief*) Tea at Barnett Brook. *Adm. 20p, Chd. 10p. Sun. April 27 (2–7)*

Sculshaw Lodge⊕ (Mrs Michael Johnson) Allostock, SW of Knutsford. B5082 between Northwich, Middlewich & Knutsford. From M6 turn off at A54 Holmes Chapel–Middlewich intersection. 2½ m. from A556 Chester–Manchester Rd. Medium-sized garden; herbaceous border; delphinium border & iris border; large pond; rockeries; woodland path; kitchen garden. C18 farmhouse (not open). TEAS. *Adm. 30p, Chd. 10p. Sun. June 29 (2–7)*

¶**Spells** (Mr & Mrs R. D. Moule) Withinlee Rd, Prestbury. ¾ m. from Prestbury off A538. At top of Castle Hill, rd signposted to Alderley Edge, is Withinlee, ¼-m. along on right. 1-acre garden; informal landscape with rhododendrons, azaleas, heathers, conifers, mixed shrubs & trees; wood with pond and ornamental waterfowl. NO DOGS. *Adm. 20p, Chd. 10p. Sun. May 18 (2–7)*

¶**Spurstow Hall**⊕ (Mrs R. W. Whineray) Bunbury. Approx. 4 m. S of Tarporley turn E off A49 at X-rds at Spurstow on to minor rd signed Haughton. Garden on left in about ½ m. 2-acre garden of general interest inc. shrubs, shrub roses; mill pool with wildfowl. TEAS. *Adm. 30p, Chd. 10p. Sun. June 8 (2–6.30)*

Thornton Manor (The Viscount Leverhulme) Thornton Hough, Wirral. From Chester A540 to Fiveway Garage; turn right on to B5136 to Thornton Hough village. From Birkenhead B5151 then on to B5136. From Motorway M53, exit 4 to Heswall; turn left after 1 m. Bus: Woodside–Parkgate; alight Thornton Hough village. Large spring garden. Plants & flowers for sale. Dogs on leads only. TEAS available at garden. Free car park. *Adm. 35p, OAPs & Chd. 15p. Sun. May 18 (2–7)*

Tiresford (Mr & Mrs R. J. Posnett) Tarporley. A51 (½ m. S of Tarporley). Bus: Nantwich–Chester, alight 100 yds from garden. Medium-sized garden; water garden & rockery, roses, shrubs & azaleas, well-planted herbaceous border. Home-made TEAS. Free car park. *Adm. 35p, Chd. 10p. Sun. June 1 (2–7)*

Tushingham Hall⊕⊕ (Mr & Mrs F. Moore Dutton) 3 m. N of Whitchurch. A41 Chester–Whitchurch Rd; 17 m. from Chester, turn left after Blue Bell Inn. Medium-sized garden in beautiful surroundings; bluebell wood alongside pool; ancient oak, girth 25 ft.(*Share to St. Chad's Church, Tushingham*) TEAS. *Adm. 25p, Chd. 10p. Sun. May 11 (2–6.30)*

Whirley Hall⊕ (Sir William & Lady Mather) 2½ m. W of Macclesfield. From A537 turn N at signpost to Whirley, between Broken Cross & Monks Heath traffic lights. Bus: Macclesfield–Sandy Lane, Whirley Barn terminus, ¼ m. Medium-sized garden; lawns & shrub borders; shrub roses & flagged terrace in country setting; terrace suitable for wheelchairs. (*Share to St Catherine's Church, Birtles*) TEAS. At 6.30 open-air evensong service (weather permitting); preacher, Gordon Lacey, Vicar of St. Catherine's, Birtles, & Director of Studies, Northern Ordination Course. *Adm. 25p, Chd. 10p. Sun. July 6 (2–7.30)*

¶**The White House**⊕ (Col G. V. Churton) Bunbury (in middle of village). 3 m. S of Tarporley turn E off A49. 2-acre spring garden with lake; speciality: many recently planted specimen & unusual trees & shrubs (rhododendrons & azaleas). (*Share to Bunbury Church Restoration Fund*) NO DOGS. *Adm. 30p, Chd. 10p. Sun. June 8 (2–6.30)*

CLWYD

Hon. County Organiser:
MRS IAN ALEXANDER, Nant Gwilym, Tremeirchion, St Asaph, LL17 0UG

Asst. Hon. County Organiser:
MRS RICHARD HEATON, Plas Heaton, Trefnant, nr Denbigh

DATES OF OPENING

MAY to OCTOBER by appointment only
CEFN BYCHAN COED, Pantymwyn, nr Mold

MAY Sunday 18
HAWARDEN CASTLE, Deeside

MAY Saturday 24
RHAGATT HALL, Corwen

MAY Sunday 25
HAFOD-Y-COED, Tremeirchion
JUNE Sunday 8
RIVER HOUSE, Erbistock, nr Wrexham
JULY Saturday 12
PLAS KINMEL, Abergele
JULY Sunday 20
GWYSANEY HALL, nr Mold
SEPTEMBER Saturday 27
GYRN CASTLE, nr Prestatyn
OCTOBER Thursday 16
EYARTH HOUSE, nr Ruthin

DESCRIPTIONS OF GARDENS

Cefn Bychan Coed* (Mr & Mrs K. W. Gearey) Pantymwyn, 3 m. W of Mold. Mold to Pantymwyn bus terminus, left along Cefn Bychan Rd; right (downhill) at X-rds signed cul-de-sac. (Map ref. 108/192636). ½-acre garden in wooded countryside; rock gardens on steep hillside, rare alpine plants & shrubs, woodland plants & ground cover, mixed flowering shrub & herbaceous plant border; alpine house. Plants for sale. NO DOGS. *Adm. 25p, Chd. (accompanied) free—please telephone first. TEA & biscuits. Garden open May 1 to Oct. 31 (Tel. Mold 740461)*

Eyarth House*⅃ (Mr & Mrs J. T. Fleming) 2 m. S of Ruthin off A525. Bus: Ruthin–Corwen, Ruthin–Wrexham. Medium-sized garden; rock garden; shrubs & ornamental trees. *(Share to St Mary's Church, Llanfair)* TEAS. *Adm. 30p, Chd. 10p. Thurs. Oct. 16 (2.30–6)*

¶Gyrn Castle†⅃ (Sir Geoffrey & Lady Bates) Llanasa, 5 m. SE of Prestatyn. A5151 Holywell–Rhuddlan rd; in Trelawnyd turn right (N) for Newmarket signed Gwaenysgor; 1st right & at Llanasa continue past church & drive gates on left. Large grounds beautifully landscaped; lake, fine trees inc. old Wellingtonia. **Flower Festival** in house (C18) by Rhyl Floral Society. TEA & biscuits. *Adm. inc. house, 40p, OAPs & Chd. 10p. Sat. Sept. 27 (2–6)*

Gwysaney Hall*†⅃⊕ (Capt. & Mrs Davies-Cooke) 1½ m. NW of Mold. Via A541 Mold–Denbigh Rd; 100 yds after end of 30 m.p.h. limit, entrance on right (coming from Mold). 11 acres of pleasure grounds, inc. 1 acre of flowers, 2 acres of lawn, 2 acres of vegetables & forest nursery; 2 acres of arboretum of specimen trees. TEAS. *Adm. 40p, OAPs & Chd. 10p. Sun. July 20 (2–6)*

¶Hafod-y-Coed⊕ (Capt. W. B. Higgin) Tremeirchion, 3 m. E of St Asaph. 2-acre garden with shrubs, rock garden, roses & ornamental duckpond. NO DOGS. Tea The Thatched Cottage, Trefnant. *Adm. 40p, Chd. 10p. Sun. May 25 (2–6)*

Hawarden Castle†⅃⊕ (Sir William & Lady Gladstone) Deeside. On A55 trunk rd, 6 m. W of Chester, just E of Hawarden village. Use Garden Centre entrance. Crosville buses. Large garden & picturesque ruined castle. Picnic area. Free car park. NO DOGS. *Adm. 30p, Chd. (accompanied) 10p. Sun. May 18 (2–6)*

Plas Kinmel†⅃⊕ (Mrs D. H. Fetherston Haugh) 3 m. E of Abergele. 3 m. W of St Asaph via A55, turn off N at signpost to Towyn, then 1st right. 1½-acre garden; roses & herbaceous, shrubs & water garden. House (not open) built 1860 by Nessfield, a fine example of his work. NO DOGS. TEA & biscuits. *Adm. 30p, OAPs & Chd. 15p. Sat. July 12 (2–6)*

¶Rhagatt Hall*⅃⊕ (The Hon. Mrs J. S. Cadman) Carrog, 1 m. NE of Corwen. A5 from Llangollen; 3 m. short of Corwen turn right (N) for Carrog at Esso Garage; cross R. Dee & turn left; 1st opening on right after Carrog. 5-acre garden with azaleas, rhododendrons, trees, rare magnolia; extensive views. Georgian house. TEAS. *Adm. 40p, OAPs & Chd. 10p. Sat. May 24 (2–6)*

River House (Brig. & Mrs Gwydyr-Jones) Erbistock, 5 m. S of Wrexham. On A528 Wrexham–Shrewsbury Rd, ¼ m. before Overton Bridge (opp. turning A539 to Ruabon). Very small garden with interesting plants. NO DOGS. *Adm. 30p. Sun. June 8 (2–6)*

CORNWALL

Hon. County Organiser:
MAJ. E. W. M. MAGOR, Lamellen, St Tudy Bodmin

DATES OF OPENING

MARCH Sunday 23
TRENGWAINTON, nr Penzance
APRIL weekdays by appointment only
CHYVERTON, Zelah, nr Truro
APRIL daily
LONG CROSS HOTEL & GARDEN, Trelights, nr St Endellion
APRIL Easter Sunday 6
TRELISSICK, Feock, nr Truro
TREMEER GARDENS, St Tudy, nr Bodmin
APRIL Sunday 13
PENWARNE, Mawnan Smith, nr Falmouth
APRIL Sunday 27
PENWARNE, Mawnan Smith, nr Falmouth
TREVARNO, Sithney, nr Helston
MAY weekdays by appointment only
CHYVERTON, Zelah, nr Truro
MAY daily
LONG CROSS HOTEL & GARDEN, Trelights, nr St Endellion
MAY Sunday 4
CARCLEW GARDENS, Perran-ar-Worthal, nr Truro
NEWTON FERRERS, nr Callington

MAY Sunday 11
BOCONNOC, nr Lostwithiel
TREMEER GARDENS, St Tudy, Bodmin
MAY Thursday 15
ST MICHAEL'S MOUNT, Marazion
MAY Sunday 18
LANHYDROCK, nr Bodmin
MAY Sunday 25
COTEHELE HOUSE, St Dominick, Calstock
KEN CARO, Bicton, Pensilva
TREWITHEN, Probus
JUNE daily
LONG CROSS HOTEL & GARDEN
Trelights, nr St Endellion
JUNE Sunday 15
TREBARTHA, North Hill, nr Launceston
JULY & AUGUST daily
LONG CROSS HOTEL & GARDEN
Trelights, nr St Endellion
JULY Sunday 20
PENHEALE MANOR, Egloskerry,
nr Launceston
AUGUST Sunday 17
TRERICE, Newlyn East, nr Newquay
AUGUST Sunday 24
TRELISSICK, Feock, nr Truro
AUGUST Sunday 31
LANHYDROCK, nr Bodmin
SEPTEMBER Sunday 7
TREBARTHA, North Hill, nr Launceston
SEPTEMBER & OCTOBER daily
LONG CROSS HOTEL & GARDEN
Trelights, nr St Endellion

DESCRIPTIONS OF GARDENS

Boconnoc†& (Capt. J. D. G. Fortescue) 4 m. NE of Lostwithiel; turning E off A390 Lostwithiel–Liskeard Rd; signs between Lostwithiel & Taphouse. Large garden; flowering shrubs, trees, views. TEAS. *Adm. 50p, Chd. 25p. Sun. May 11 (2–6)*

Carclew Gardens*& (His Honour Judge Chope & Mrs Chope) Perran-ar-Worthal, nr Truro. From A39, mid-way between Truro & Falmouth, turn E at Perran-ar-Worthal. Bus: WN 590 Truro–Falmouth; alight Perran-ar-Worthal, 1 m. Large garden; rhododendron species; terraces & ornamental water. NO DOGS. *Adm. 50p. Sun. May 4 (2–6)*

Chyverton*& (Mr & Mrs N. T. Holman) Zelah, N of Truro. Entrance ¾ m. SW of Zelah on A30. Georgian landscaped garden with lake & bridge (1770); large shrub garden developed since 1925 with extensive collection of trees & shrubs, some of them rare in cultivation; outstanding specimens of Asiatic tree magnolias, rhododendrons & camellias. *Adm. 40p, Chd. 20p. Garden open by appt. only, weekdays April & May (Tel. Zelah 324)*

Cotehele House† (The National Trust—see p. ix) 2 m. W of Calstock. 8 m. SW of Tavistock; 14 m. from Plymouth via Tamar Bridge. Terrace garden falling to sheltered valley with ponds, stream & unusual shrubs. Fine medieval house (one of the least altered in the country); armour, tapestries, furniture. Lunches & TEAS. *Adm. house, garden & mill £1.50, Chd. 75p; garden, grounds & mill 90p, Chd. 45p.* △*Sun. May 25 (11–6; last adm. to house 5.30)*

Ken Caro* (Mr & Mrs K. R. Willcock) Bicton, Pensilva, 5 m. NE of Liskeard. From A390, Liskeard–Callington, turn off N at Butchers Arms, St Ive, & take Pensilva Rd; at next X-rds take rd signposted Bicton. Medium-sized garden, mostly planted in 1970, with rhododendrons, flowering shrubs, conifers & other trees; herbaceous borders, lawns with small fish pond; a flower arranger's garden. Panoramic views. NO DOGS. *Adm. 40p, Chd. 20p. Sun. May 25 (2–6)*

Lanhydrock& (The National Trust—see p. ix) Bodmin. 2½ m. S of Bodmin on B3268. Station: Bodmin Rd, 1¾ m. Bus: WN Bodmin–Lostwithiel; alight Treffry Gate, ¼ m. Large-sized garden; formal garden laid out 1857; shrub garden with good specimens of rhododendrons & magnolias & fine views. NO DOGS. Lunches & TEAS. *Adm. house & garden £1.50, Chd. 75p; garden only 90p, Chd. 45p.* △*Sun. May 18 & Sun. Aug. 31 (11–6; last adm. to house 5.30)*

¶**Long Cross Hotel & Gardens** (Mr & Mrs R. Y. Warrilow) Trelights, nr St Endellion. On Port Quin rd, 1 m. N of B3314. Medium-sized garden being restored; panoramic sea views. *Collecting box. April–Oct. daily (11–2; in summer also 5–8)*

Newton Ferrers& (Sir Valentine Abdy) 3 m. S of Callington. From A390, Tavistock–Liskeard Rd, approx. 2 m. W of Callington, take turning S for Newton Ferrers. Bus stop: Callington. Large garden; flower garden; terraces; water garden. Regret NO DOGS. TEAS. *Adm. 50p, Chd. 25p. Sun. May 4 (2.30–6)*

Penheale Manor*⊕ (Mrs Norman Colville) 5 m. W of Launceston; from Launceston take B3254; turn left at St Stephens Church (1 m.) for Egloskerry; lodge ⅓ m. beyond village on right. Large garden with herbaceous borders, formal rose garden, lawns, shrubs, yew hedges; woodland garden with rhododendrons, azaleas, camellias, etc. Plants for sale. TEA & biscuits. *Adm. 40p, Chd. 20p. Sun. July 20 (2.30–5.30)*

Penwarne* (J. M. Williams Esq) 3¼ m. SW of Falmouth. 1½ m. N of Mawnan Smith. Bus: WN 563 Falmouth–Penjerrick; bus stop 1 m. Flowering shrubs, rhododendrons, magnolias, ornamental ducks. NO DOGS. Jointly with St John Ambulance. *Adm. 40p, Chd. 20p. Sun. April 13 & Sun. April 27 (2–6)*

St Michael's Mount*† (The Rt Hon. Lord St Levan) Marazion. Station: Marazion, ½ m. Bus: Penzance–Helston, alight Marazion, ¼m; ½ m. from shore at Marazion; by causeway (open 10.15–2.30); otherwise by ferry, 20p,

15

Chd. 5p. Flowering shrubs; rock plants; castle walls; fine sea views. Light luncheons & teas at Island Restaurant & Tea Gardens. *Adm. castle & garden £1, Chd. 50p. △Thurs. May 15 (10.30–4.30)*

Trebartha (The Latham family) North Hill, SW of Launceston. Nr junction of B3254 & B3257. Proceed to North Hill village then ask; ½ m. from village. Bus: WN Launceston–Upton Cross; alight in village, ½ m. Wooded area with swan pool surrounded by walks of flowering shrubs; woodland trail through fine woods with cascades & waterfalls; American glade with fine trees. *Adm. 40p, Chd. 20p. Sun. June 15 & Sun. Sept. 7 (2–6)*

Trelissick★ ⊕ (R. Spencer Copeland Esq; The National Trust—see p. ix) Feock, 4 m. S of Truro. Nr King Harry Ferry. On B3289. Large garden; superb view over Falmouth harbour. Georgian house (not shown). NO DOGS. TEAS. *Adm. £1, Chd. 50p. △Sun. April 6 & Sun. Aug. 24 (11–6)*

Tremeer Gardens,★ St Tudy, 8 m. N of Bodmin; W of B3266. 6-acre garden, with water, that has been closely planted in the last 25 years with large variety of rhododendrons & other shrubs. *Adm. 40p, Chd. 20p. Sun. April 6 & Sun. May 11(2–6)*

Trengwainton★ ⊕ (Maj. S. E. Bolitho: The National Trust—see p. ix) 2 m. NW of Penzance. 1½ m. W of Heamoor, on B3312 Penzance–Morvah Rd; ½ m. off St Just Rd A3071 (see Nat. Trust signposts). Large shrub garden with stream & view over Mount's Bay; walled garden with many tender plants which cannot be grown elsewhere in England in the open. Garden only. *Adm. 50p, Chd. 25p. Sun. March 23 (2–6)*

Trerice ⊕ (The National Trust—see p. ix) Newlyn East, 3 m. SE of Newquay. From Newquay via A392 & A3058; turn right at Kestle Mill (Nat. Trust signposts). Bus: 621 Newquay–Truro–Falmouth, or 602 Newquay–St Austell; alight Kestle Mill, 1 m. Small manor house, rebuilt in 1571, containing fine plaster ceilings & fireplaces; oak & walnut furniture & tapestries. TEAS. *Adm. house & garden £1, Chd. 50p. △Sun. Aug. 17 (11–6; last adm. to house 5.30)*

Trevarno★ (Mr & Mrs Peter Bickford-Smith) Sithney, Helston. Helston 3 m., Camborne 7 m. Well signed off B3303 & B3302. Woodland garden with ornamental lake, fine trees & bluebell woods. Free leaflet on history of garden & house. *Adm. 40p, Chd. 20p. Sun. April 27 (1–5)*

Trewithen★ ⊕ (Mr & Mrs A. M. J. Galsworthy) Grampound Rd, nr Truro. 1 m. E of Probus on A390, Probus–Grampound Rd. One of the outstanding gardens of Britain with a collection of rare Asiatic magnolias & rhododendrons & many other plants of distinction; superbly landscaped through a woodland setting & commanding extensive views over traditional C18 parkland. Stunning colours March to mid-June, but variety of trees & shrubs, views & peaceful atmosphere make Trewithen Gardens worth a visit at any time of year. Tea Westway Coffee Shop, Probus. *Adm. 60p, OAPs 40p, Chd. 30p. △Sun. May 25 (2–5)*

CUMBRIA

Hon. County Organiser:
MISS B. CHEW, Box Trees, Crook,
 nr Kendal

DATE OF OPENING

For opening date see local Press
 YEWS, Windermere

APRIL every weekday (not Sundays)
 LINGHOLM, Keswick
APRIL Easter Sunday 6
 ASH LANDING GARDEN, Far Sawrey,
 nr Ambleside
APRIL from Sunday 6, daily except Saturdays
 HOLKER HALL, Grange-over-Sands
APRIL Sunday 13
 ASH LANDING GARDEN, Far Sawrey,
 nr Ambleside
MAY daily except Saturdays
 HOLKER HALL, Grange-over-Sands
MAY every weekday (not Sundays)
 LINGHOLM, Keswick
MAY Sunday 11
 ASH LANDING GARDEN, Far Sawrey,
 nr Ambleside
 BIRKET HOUSES, Winster,
 nr Windermere
MAY Thursday 15
 HUYTON HILL, Pullwoods,
 nr Ambleside
MAY Sunday 18
 ASH LANDING GARDEN, Far Sawrey,
 nr Ambleside
 STAGSHAW, Ambleside
MAY Thursday 22
 HUYTON HILL, Pullwoods, nr Ambleside
MAY Sunday 25
 ASH LANDING GARDEN, Far Sawrey,
 nr Ambleside
 BIRKET HOUSES, Winster, nr Windermere
 STAGSHAW, Ambleside
MAY Thursday 29
 HUYTON HILL, Pullwoods, nr Ambleside
JUNE daily except Saturdays
 HOLKER HALL, Grange-over-Sands
JUNE every weekday (not Sundays)
 LINGHOLM, Keswick
JUNE Sunday 1
 ASH LANDING GARDEN, Far Sawrey,
 nr Ambleside
JUNE Saturday 28
 HALECAT, Witherslack
JULY daily except Saturdays
 HOLKER HALL, Grange-over-Sands

JULY every weekday (not Sundays)
LINGHOLM, Keswick
JULY Sunday 6
ASH LANDING GARDEN, Far Sawrey,
nr Ambleside
JULY Saturday 19
RIGMADEN, Kirkby Lonsdale
JULY Sunday 20
ACORN BANK, nr Penrith
DALLAM TOWER, Milnthorpe, nr Kendal
HIGH LEASGHYLL, Heversham,
nr Kendal
JULY Sunday 27
ACORN BANK, nr Penrith
AUGUST daily except Saturdays
HOLKER HALL, Grange-over-Sands
AUGUST every weekday (not Sundays)
LINGHOLM, Keswick
AUGUST Sunday 3 & Sunday 31
ASH LANDING GARDEN, Far Sawrey,
nr Ambleside
SEPTEMBER daily except Saturdays
HOLKER HALL, Grange-over-Sands
SEPTEMBER every weekday (not Sundays)
LINGHOLM, Keswick
SEPTEMBER Sunday 7
ASH LANDING GARDEN, Far Sawrey,
nr Ambleside
OCTOBER every weekday (not Sundays)
LINGHOLM, Keswick
OCTOBER Sunday 5
ASH LANDING GARDEN, Far Sawrey,
nr Ambleside

DESCRIPTIONS OF GARDENS

Acorn Bank*⅃⊕ (Sue Ryder Foundation; The National Trust—see p. ix) Temple Sowerby. 6 m. E of Penrith on A66; ½ m. N of Temple Sowerby. Bus: Penrith–Appleby or Carlisle–Darlington; alight Culgaith Rd end. Medium-sized garden; good herb garden; parkland. NO DOGS. *Adm. 20p. △Sun. July 20 & Sun. July 27 (10.30–5.30)*

Ash Landing Garden* (Mr & Mrs G. Yates) Far Sawrey, S of Ambleside. Garden 400 yds from the ferry at Ferry House on B5285. Bus: Bowness ferry–Far Sawrey; alight Ferry Nab (440 yds). Medium-sized newly laid-out garden adjoining lake with fine views; natural woodland garden with stream and pools; large collection of hardy heathers, dwarf rhododendrons, primulas & shrubs. Tea Far Sawrey, Near Sawrey or Bowness. Plants for sale (percentage to NGS). NO DOGS. *Collecting box. Suns. April 6, 13, May 11, 18, 25, June 1, July 6, Aug. 3, 31, Sept. 7, Oct. 5 (2–5)*

Birket Houses (B. W. Cave-Browne-Cave Esq) Winster, S of Windermere. From Bowness take A5074 towards Lancaster; at Brown Horse Inn turn right; past Winster church & Bryon Houses Farm; then 1st right down private drive. Medium-sized garden; house & garden designed as a unit by Dan Gibson,

well-known Westmorland architect; formal terraced garden with dry stone walling; daffodils, camellias, azaleas & rhododendrons; topiary work. NO DOGS. TEAS. *Adm. 25p, Chd. 10p. Sun. May 11 & Sun. May 25 (10.30–5.30)*

Dallam Tower*⅃⊕ (Brig. Tryon-Wilson) Milnthorpe, 7 m. S of Kendal. 7 m. N of Carnforth, nr junction of A6 & B5282. Station: Arnside, 4 m.; Lancaster, 15 m. Bus: Ribble 553, 554 Milnthorpe–Lancaster via Arnside, alight lodge gates. Medium-sized garden; natural rock garden, waterfalls, fine display of rambler & polyanthus roses; wood walks, lawns, shrubs. Tea High Leasghyll, Heversham. *Adm. 20p, Chd. 5p. Sun. July 20 (2–7)*

¶High Leasghyll (Miss H. Drew) Heversham, Open same afternoon as **Dallam Tower** (short distance away) to provide TEAS in aid of National Gardens Scheme. (Directions for getting here will be available at Dallam Tower). *Sun. July 20 (2.30–6)*

Halecat⊕ (Mr & Mrs M. C. Stanley) Witherslack, 10 m. SW of Kendal. From A590 turn into Witherslack at Derby Arms; left in township & left again, signpost 'Cartmel Fell'; Lodge gates on left (map ref. 434834). Medium-sized garden; mixed shrub & herbaceous borders, terrace, sunken garden & gazebo; beautiful view over Kent Estuary to Arnside. NO DOGS. Tea Levens Hall or Grange-over-Sands. *Adm. 15p, Chd. 5p. Sat. June 28 (2–7)*

● Holker Hall*⅃⊕ (Mr & Mrs Hugh Cavendish) Cark-in-Cartmel, 4 m. W of Grange-over-Sands. 12 m. W of M6 (exit 36); through Grange-over-Sands & along B5277 (towards Hatherwaite) for a further 4 m. 22-acre garden associated with Joseph Paxton; exotic flowering trees; daffodils; exceptional magnolias, rhododendrons & azaleas; rose garden, cherry & woodland walks. House dates from C16 with C19 additions. Gift shop, children's farm & adventure playground. Picnic area. *Adm. Charges not decided at time of going to press. April 6 to Sept. 30 daily except Sats. (11–6, last adm. 5.15)*

Huyton Hill⅃⊕ (I. G. Butler Esq) Pullwoods. 2 m. S of Ambleside on Hawkshead Rd. Entrance gate on left. Can also be approached from Waterhead or Bowness Bay by boat. Station: Windermere, 6 m. Bus: Ambleside–Hawkshead (infrequent), alight at lodge. Very fine views of Windermere lake & surrounding hills. Variety of trees & flowering shrubs. House C19 but modelled on Bramall Hall (Tudor mansion in Cheshire). *Adm. 10p. Thurs. May 15, 22, 29 (12–5.30)*

● Lingholm⅃⊕ (The Viscount Rochdale) Keswick. On W shore of Derwentwater; Portinscale 1 m.; Keswick 3 m. Turn off A66 at Portinscale on to Grange Rd, C511 & along 1 m. to drive entrance on left. Ferry from Keswick to Nicol End, 10 mins walk. Bus:

Keswick Bus Station to Portinscale, ¾ m.; 'mountain goat' minibus service from town centre passes drive end. Formal garden & woodland walk (1½ m.); rhododendrons, azaleas, etc. Exceptional view of Borrowdale. Plants for sale. NO DOGS. Tea Derwentwater Hotel, Portinscale. Free car park. *Adm. 60p inc. VAT, Chd. if accompanied free. April 1 to Oct. 31 daily except Suns. (10–5)*

Rigmaden*⅃ (G. E. Wilson Esq) 4 m. N of Kirkby Lonsdale on Underley Hall Rd; signposted 2 m. out of Kirkby Lonsdale. Medium-sized garden with shrub roses & herbaceous. NO DOGS. *Adm. 25p, Chd. 5p. Sat. July 19 (2–5.)*

Stagshaw* (The National Trust—see p. ix) 1 m. S of Ambleside. Turn E off A591, Ambleside–Windermere rd, 1 m. S of Ambleside. Bus: Ribble 555, Kendal–Keswick, alight Waterhead, Ambleside, ½ m. Woodland garden inc. modern rhododendrons & azaleas. Views over Windermere. NO DOGS. Tea hotels & cafés at Waterhead. *Adm. 15p, Chd. 5p Suns. May 18 & 25 (all day) & at all other reasonable times throughout the year*

Yews⅃⊕ (Sir Oliver and Lady Scott) Windermere. Bus: Ulverston–Bowness, alight Blackwell School, 50 yds. Medium-sized formal Edwardian garden; fine trees and ha-ha. Garden being renovated. *For opening date see local press*

DERBYSHIRE

Hon. County Organiser:
MISS M. FITZHERBERT, Trusley Manor West, Sutton-on-the-Hill, Derby, DE6 5JG
Asst Hon. County Organiser:
MRS ROWLAND, Flat 1, Trusley Manor, Sutton-on-the-Hill, Derby, DE6 5JG

DATES OF OPENING

JANUARY to DECEMBER daily
 HIGH PEAK GARDEN CENTRE, Bamford, nr Sheffield
APRIL daily during daffodil season
 SHIRLEY HOUSE, nr Ashbourne
APRIL daily from Easter
 LEA RHODODENDRON GARDENS, Lea, nr Matlock
APRIL Sunday 20
 RADBURNE HALL, nr Derby
MAY daily
 LEA RHODODENDRON GARDENS, Lea, nr Matlock
MAY Thursday 1 daily to Sunday 18
 SHIRLEY HOUSE, nr Ashbourne
MAY Sunday 4
 THE LIMES, Apperknowle, nr Chesterfield
MAY Sunday 11
 HAZELBROW, Duffield
MAY Sunday 18
 THE LIMES, Apperknowle, nr Chesterfield

MAY Saturday 24
 DARLEY HOUSE, nr Matlock
MAY Sunday 25
 CATCHFRENCH, nr Belper
 DARLEY HOUSE, nr Matlock
MAY Monday 26 (Spring Bank Hol.)
 CATCHFRENCH, nr Belper
 SHIRLEY HOUSE, nr Ashbourne
JUNE daily to mid-June
 LEA RHODODENDRON GARDENS, Lea, nr Matlock
JUNE Sunday 1
 DERBYSHIRE COLLEGE OF AGRICULTURE, Broomfield, Morley, nr Derby
 THE LIMES, Apperknowle, nr Chesterfield
JUNE Sunday 15
 THE LIMES, Apperknowle, nr Chesterfield
 SHIRLEY HOUSE, nr Ashbourne
JUNE Sunday 22
 SHIRLEY HOUSE, nr Ashbourne
JUNE Sunday 29
 210 NOTTINGHAM RD, Woodlinken, nr Langley Mill
 SHIRLEY HOUSE, nr Ashbourne
JULY every Sunday
 SHIRLEY HOUSE, nr Ashbourne
JULY Saturday 5
 TISSINGTON HALL, nr Ashbourne
JULY Sunday 6
 THE LIMES, Apperknowle, nr Chesterfield
 LOCKO PARK, nr Derby
 MELBOURNE HALL, nr Derby
JULY Sunday 20
 HARDWICK HALL, Doe Lea
 THE LIMES, Apperknowle, nr Chesterfield
AUGUST every Sunday
 SHIRLEY HOUSE, nr Ashbourne
AUGUST Sunday 3
 THE LIMES, Apperknowle, nr Chesterfield
AUGUST Saturday 16
 11 BLANDFORD DRIVE, Pevensey Estate, Newbold
AUGUST Sunday 17
 11 BLANDFORD DRIVE, Pevensey Estate, Newbold
 THE LIMES, Apperknowle, nr Chesterfield
AUGUST Saturday 23
 11 BANDFORD DRIVE, Pevensey Estate, Newbold
AUGUST Sunday 24
 11 BLANDFORD DRIVE, Pevensey Estate, Newbold
AUGUST Monday 25 (Bank Hol.)
 SHIRLEY HOUSE, nr. Ashbourne
AUGUST Sunday 31
 THE LIMES, Apperknowle, nr Chesterfield
SEPTEMBER Sunday 7 & Sunday 14
 SHIRLEY HOUSE, nr Ashbourne

DESCRIPTIONS OF GARDENS

11 Blandford Drive⊕ (J. T. Markham Esq) Pevensey Estate, Newbold. 2 m. N of Chesterfield. Down St John's Rd, from Newbold Church; 1st turn right, then 1st right again, then 1st left. Small garden; prize-winning council house garden on a number of occasions, fuchsias, geraniums, begonias, subtropical plants & usual bedding plants, plants in unusual containers. Tea Chesterfield. *Adm. 20p, Chd. 5p. Sat. & Sun. Aug. 16, & 17 Sat. & Sun. Aug. 23 & 24 (11–7)*

Catchfrench*⊕ (Lt-Col & Mrs R. C. Glanville) Bridge Hill, Belper. Junction of Belper–Ashbourne Rd A517 & Shireoaks Lane at top of Bridge Hill, outskirts of Belper. Bus stop: Belper Triangle, ½ m. Cars: park in Shireoaks Lane; enter through doorway in wall. Medium-sized garden; terraced rose-beds, lawns, pleasant view; roses & interesting shrubs, inc. rhododendrons, azaleas, camellias & heaths. TEAS. *Adm. 30p, Chd. 5p. Sun. & Mon. May 25 & 26 (2–7)*

Darley House*†⊕ (Mr & Mrs G. H. Briscoe) Darley Dale, nr Matlock. Situated 2 m. N of Matlock. On A6 to Bakewell. 1¼ acres; garden originally set out by Sir Joseph Paxton who bought house in 1845, & being restored by present owners; many rare plants & trees; balustrade & steps separating upper & lower garden, a replica of Haddon Hall. Site of original conservatory designed by Paxton who used ridge and furrow principle on the Crystal Palace. NO DOGS. TEA & biscuits. *Adm. 30p, Chd. 15p. Sat. & Sun. May 24 & 25 (2–6)*

Derbyshire College of Agriculture*♿⊕, Broomfield, Morley, 4 m. NE of Derby; entrance on A608. Station: Derby Midland. Bus: Trent 122 or 123 Derby–Heanor, or Derby–Ilkeston, alight at gate. Large garden; rhododendrons, azaleas, rockery, shrubs; small area of glass; demonstration kitchen garden; plots of fruit varieties. NO DOGS. *Adm. 50p, Chd. 5p. Sun. June 1 (2–5)*

Hardwick Hall*†⊕ (The National Trust— see p. ix) Doe Lea, 8 m. SE of Chesterfield. S of A617. Bus: 63 Chesterfield–Mansfield– Nottingham, stops at Glapwell, The Young Vanish Inn, 2 m. Grass walks between horn-beam hedges. Cedar trees. Finest example of Elizabethan house in the country. Very fine collection of Elizabethan needlework & tapestry. *Adm. to house & garden £1.20, Chd. 60p. Gardens only 60p. Chd. 30p. △Sun. July 20 (12–5.30)*

Hazelbrow*♿ (Sir Max Bemrose) Hazel-wood Rd, Duffield, 5 m. N of Derby. ¾ m. NW of Duffield centre; from A6 in Duffield turn off W up King St, which leads into Hazelbrow Rd. Large garden; 3 acres of rhododendrons & beech woods with spring bulbs; interesting quarry rock garden; magnolias, azaleas, camellias & rare specimen trees. Beautiful views. TEA & biscuits. *Adm. 30p, Chd. 10p. Sun. May 11 (2–7)*

● **High Peak Garden Centre***⊕ (The Clifford Proctor Nurseries Ltd) Bamford, 12 m. W of Sheffield. Bamford on A625, 2 m. W of Hathersage, 4 m. E of Castleton; centred amidst rugged grandeur of Peak National Park 7½ acres; complete horticultural service within atmosphere of a garden; exhibition garden with over 8,000 roses; tree & shrub borders; display hedges; rock & heather gardens; rose shows every weekend in summer. NO DOGS. Snack bar available. *All year daily (10 to½hr before dusk)*

● **Lea Rhododendron Gardens***♿ (Mrs Tye & Miss Colyer) Lea, 5 m. SE of Matlock. Large garden of hybrid & specie rhodo-dendrons & azaleas in woodland setting; rock garden. Plants for sale. Tea ¼ m. away *Adm. 30p, Chd. over 5 10p. Easter to mid-June daily (10–8)*

The Limes*♿⊕ (Mr & Mrs W. Belton) Crow Lane, Apperknowle, 6 m. N of Chesterfield from A61 at Unstone turn E for 1 m. to Apperknowle; 1st house past Unstone Grange. Bus: Chesterfield–Apperknowle; Sheffield–Apperknowle. Garden of 2½ acres with daffodils & spring bedding, herbaceous borders, lily ponds with ornamental bridges, roses & flowering shrubs, geraniums & summer bedding plants; greenhouses with pelargonium displays. Putting green. Nature trail over 5 acres. Large natural pond with ornamental waterfowl & birds. Aviaries with pheasants & budgerigars, etc. Donkeys & Jacob sheep. Craft demonstrations of spin-ning, weaving & lace-making on selected Suns. (see press for details). Home-made TEAS. Private parties by arrangement (Tel. Dronfield 412338). Dogs on leads. *Adm. 30p, Chd. 10p. Suns. May 4, 18, June 1, 15, July 6, 20, Aug. 3, 17, 31 (2–6)*

Locko Park*†♿⊕ (Capt. P. J. B. Drury-Lowe) Spondon, 6 m. NE of Derby. From A52 Borrowash Bypass, 2 m. N via B6001, turn to Spondon. Large garden; pleasure gardens; rose gardens. House by Smith of Warwick with Victorian additions. Chapel, Charles II, with original ceiling. TEAS. *Adm. 35p, Chd. 10p. Sun. July 6 (2–6)*

Melbourne Hall*†♿⊕ (The Marquess of Lothian) Melbourne. 8 m. S of Derby on Derby–Ashby-de-la- :ouch Rd. A514. Station: Derby. Bus: Trent 19 from Derby or Barton 3 Nottingham–Melbourne; alight 2 mins from garden. Large garden, early C18, designed by Wise. Fountains. Yew tunnel. TEAS. *Adm. 50p, Chd. 25p. △Sun. July 6 (2–6)*

210 Nottingham Rd⊕ (Mr & Mrs R. Brown) Woodlinkin, Langley Mill. 12 m. NW of Nottingham, nr Codnor; A610 Bypass between Langley Mill & Codnor. ½-acre garden with collections of old & modern shrub & climbing roses; geraniums (cranesbills) euphorbias & hellebores; wide variety of shrubs & small trees & alpines. TEA & biscuits. *Adm. 25p, Chd. 10p. Sun. June 29 (2–6)*

DERBYSHIRE—continued

Radburne Hall* †⅋⊕ (Maj. & Mrs Chandos-Pole) 5 m. W of Derby. W of A52 Derby–Ashbourne Rd; turn off Radburne Lane. Large landscape garden; large display of daffodils; shrubs & formal rose terraces; fine trees & view. Hall (not open) is 7-bay Palladian mansion built *c.* 1734 by Smith of Warwick. Ice-house in garden. NO DOGS. Tea Meynell Arms, Kirk Langley. *Adm. 25p, Chd. 10p. Sun. April 20 (2.30–6.30)*

Shirley House⊕ (Mr & Mrs F. D. Ley) Shirley, 5 m. SE of Ashbourne. A52 Derby–Ashbourne, turn W for Shirley at Ruck O'Stones, or Shirley Lane End. April & May openings: daffodils; June, July, Aug. & Sept. openings: roses, herbaceous, shrubs. *Adm. April & May 20p; June, July, Aug., Sept. 30p; Chd. 10p. April daily during daffodil season; May 1 to 18 daily; May Mon. 26; Suns. June 15, 22, 29; July & Aug. every Sun.; Mon. Aug. 25; Suns. Sept. 7, 14 (11–7)*

Tissington Hall †⅋⊕ (Sir John FitzHerbert, Bt) N of Ashbourne. E of A515. Large garden; roses, herbaceous borders, greenhouses. Tea in village. *Adm. 30p, Chd. 5p. Sat. July 5 (2–6.30)*

DEVON

Hon. County Organisers:
Mr & Mrs H. SAGAR, Windrose, Ilsington, Newton Abbot, TQ13 9RH

Hon. Garden Consultant:
E. M. HARRISON ESQ, Barton House, Otterton, Budleigh Salterton

DATES OF OPENING

By appointment
ANDREW'S CORNER, Belstone, Okehampton (April–Oct)
BIDLAKE MILL, Combebow Bridge, nr Okehampton (all year)
BLACKPOOL HOUSE, Stoke Fleming, nr Dartmouth (all year)
CLAPPER COTTAGE, Bondleigh, North Tawton (April–Oct)
COMBE HEAD, Bampton (all year)
FARRANTS, Kilmington, nr Axminster
THE GARDEN HOUSE, Buckland Monachorum (April 9 to Sept. 17)
LEIGH COTTAGE, Kennerleigh, nr Crediton (May–Aug.)
MIDDLE HILL, Washfield, Tiverton (March–Sept. 7)
PENHAYES, Kenton, nr Exeter (April 8–May 24)
PUTSBOROUGH MANOR, Georgeham (summer months)
RESTHARROW, West Hill, Ottery St Mary (May–Sept.)
SANDERS, Stoke Fleming, nr Dartmouth
STORMSDOWN, Bickington, Ashburton (all year)

THE WARREN, Woodbury, nr Exeter (parties only; May & June)
WOODSIDE, Barnstaple (May to Aug.)
JANUARY & FEBRUARY daily
MARWOOD HILL, nr Barnstaple
MARCH daily
MARWOOD HILL, nr Barnstaple
THE ROCK, Chudleigh
APRIL daily
FERNWOOD, Ottery St Mary
MARWOOD HILL, nr Barnstaple
THE ROCK, Chudleigh
ROSEMOOR, Great Torrington
APRIL every Wednesday
BIDLAKE MILL, Combebow Bridge, nr Okehampton
APRIL Good Friday 4
THE DOWNES, Monkleigh, Bideford
APRIL from Good Friday 4, daily except Mondays (but open Monday 7)
TAPELEY PARK, Instow
APRIL Easter Sunday 6
BICKHAM HOUSE, Roborough
THE DOWNES, Monkleigh, Bideford
PENHAYES, Kenton, nr Exeter
APRIL Easter Monday 7
THE DOWNES, Monkleigh, Bideford
LEE FORD, Budleigh Salterton
PENHAYES, Kenton, nr Exeter
APRIL Wednesday 9
CROSSINGFIELDS COTTAGE, Exmouth
APRIL from April 9 every Wednesday
THE GARDEN HOUSE, Buckland Monachorum
APRIL Sunday 13
BICKHAM HOUSE, Roborough
THE DOWNES, Monkleigh, Bideford
APRIL Monday 14
THE DOWNES, Monkleigh, Bideford
APRIL from April 16 every Wednesday
WEETWOOD, Offwell, Honiton
APRIL Saturday 19
MIDDLE HILL, Washfield, Tiverton
APRIL from April 20 daily
BURROW FARM GARDEN, Dalwood, Axminster
APRIL Sunday 20
ANDREW'S CORNER, Belstone, nr Okehampton
BICKHAM HOUSE, Roborouh
THE DOWNES, Monkleigh, Bideford
MIDDLE HILL, Washfield, Tiverton
APRIL Monday 21
THE DOWNES, Monkleigh, Bideford
APRIL Thursday 24
GREENWAY GARDENS, Churston Ferrers, nr Brixham
APRIL Sunday 27
KILLERTON GARDEN, nr Exeter
APRIL Wednesday 30
COMRIE, Smallridge, nr Axminster
MAY daily
BURROW FARM GARDEN, Dalwood, Axminster
FERNWOOD, Ottery St Mary
MARWOOD HILL, nr Barnstaple

THE ROCK, Chudleigh
ROSEMOOR, Great Torrington
MAY daily except Mondays (but open May 5 & 26)
TAPELEY PARK, Instow
MAY every Sunday
LEIGH COTTAGE, Kennerleigh, nr Crediton
MAY every Wednesday
BIDLAKE MILL, Combebow Bridge, nr Okehampton
COMRIE, Smallridge, nr Axminster
THE GARDEN HOUSE, Buckland Monachorum
WEETWOOD, Offwell, Honiton
MAY Thursdays 1, 8, 15, 22
STORMSDOWN, nr Bickington, Ashburton
MAY Thursday 1
GREENWAY GARDENS, Churston Ferrers, nr Brixham
MAY Saturday 3
MIDDLE HILL, Washfield, Tiverton
MOTHECOMBE HOUSE, Holbeton, nr Plymouth
MAY Sunday 4
BICKHAM HOUSE, Roborough
KNIGHTSHAYES COURT, nr Tiverton
MOTHECOMBE HOUSE, Holbeton, nr Plymouth
PENHAYES, Kenton, nr Exeter
SALTRAM HOUSE, nr Plymouth
WOODSIDE, Barnstaple
MAY Monday 5 (Bank Holiday)
CLAPPER COTTAGE, Bondleigh, North Tawton
LEE FORD, Budleigh Salterton
LEIGH COTTAGE, Kennerleigh, nr Credition
PENHAYES, Kenton, nr Exeter
MAY Sunday 11
ANDREW'S CORNER, Belstone, nr Okehampton
BICKHAM HOUSE, Roborough
CASTLE DROGO, Drewsteignton
MIDDLE HILL, Washfield, Tiverton
MAY Wednesday 14
CROSSINGFIELDS COTTAGE, Exmouth
MAY Saturday 17
DARTINGTON HALL GARDENS, nr Totnes
MAY Sunday 18
DARTINGTON HALL GARDENS, nr Totnes
ENDSLEIGH NURSERIES, Milton Abbot, nr Tavistock
HIGHER KNOWLE, Lustleigh, Bovey Tracey
KILLERTON GARDEN, nr Exeter
MIDDLE HILL, Washfield, Tiverton
RESTHARROW, West Hill, Ottery St Mary
MAY Saturday 24
CLAPPER COTTAGE, Bondleigh, North Tawton
MIDDLE HILL, Washfield, Tiverton

MAY Sunday 25
BICKHAM HOUSE, Roborough
HIGHER KNOWLE, Lustleigh, Bovey Tracey
MIDDLE HILL, Washfield, Tiverton
PENHAYES, Kenton, nr Exeter
THE WARREN, Woodbury, nr Exeter
MAY Monday 26 (Bank Holiday)
HIGHER KNOWLE, Lustleigh, Bovey Tracey
LEE FORD, Budleigh Salterton
LEIGH COTTAGE, Kennerleigh, nr Crediton
MIDDLE HILL, Washfield, Tiverton
PENHAYES, Kenton, nr Exeter
MAY Wednesday 28
THE WARREN, Woodbury, nr Exeter
JUNE daily
BURROW FARM GARDEN, Dalwood, Axminster
FERNWOOD, Ottery St Mary
MARWOOD HILL, nr Barnstaple
THE ROCK, Chudleigh
ROSEMOOR, Great Torrington
JUNE daily except Mondays
TAPELEY PARK, Instow
JUNE every Sunday
LEIGH COTTAGE, Kennerleigh, nr Crediton
JUNE every Wednesday
BIDLAKE MILL, Combebow Bridge, nr Okehampton
THE GARDEN HOUSE, Buckland Monachorum
WEETWOOD, Offwell, Honiton
JUNE every Sunday & Wednesday
THE WARREN, Woodbury, nr Exeter
JUNE Sunday 1
HIGHER KNOWLE, Lustleigh, Bovey Tracey
RESTHARROW, West Hill, Ottery St Mary
JUNE Wednesday 4
COMRIE, Smallridge, nr Axminster
JUNE Sunday 8
BICKHAM HOUSE, Roborough
FARRANTS, Kilmington, nr Axminster
WOODSIDE, Barnstaple
JUNE Wednesday 11
CROSSINGFIELDS COTTAGE, Exmouth
JUNE Sunday 15
ANDREW'S CORNER, Belstone, nr Okehampton
CASTLE DROGO, Drewsteignton
CLIFFE HOUSE, Lynmouth
FARRANTS, Kilmington, nr Axminster
PUTSBOROUGH MANOR, Georgeham
RESTHARROW, West Hill, Ottery St Mary
SHARPITOR, Salcombe
JUNE Monday 16
FARRANTS, Kilmington, nr Axminster
JUNE Saturday 21
CLAPPER COTTAGE, Bondleigh, North Tawton
JUNE Sunday 22
BICKHAM HOUSE, Roborough
FARRANTS, Kilmington, nr Axminster
JUNE Wednesday 25
COMRIE, Smallridge, nr Axminster

DEVON—continued

JUNE Sunday 29
MIDDLE HILL, Washfield, Tiverton
RESTHARROW, West Hill, Ottery St Mary

JULY daily
FERNWOOD, Ottery St Mary
MARWOOD HILL, nr Barnstaple
THE ROCK, Chudleigh
ROSEMOOR, Great Torrington

JULY daily to Sunday 20
BURROW FARM GARDEN, Dalwood,
Axminster

JULY daily except Mondays
TAPELEY PARK, Instow

JULY every Sunday
LEIGH COTTAGE, Kennerleigh, nr Crediton

JULY every Wednesday
BIDLAKE MILL, Combebow Bridge,
nr Okehampton
COMRIE, Smallridge, nr Axminster
THE GARDEN HOUSE, Buckland
Monachorum
WEETWOOD, Offwell, Honiton

JULY Wednesday 2
THE WARREN, Woodbury, nr Exeter

JULY Sunday 6
BICKHAM HOUSE, Roborough
MIDDLE HILL, Washfield, Tiverton
SALTRAM HOUSE, nr Plymouth
THE WARREN, Woodbury, nr Exeter

JULY Sunday 13
BICKHAM HOUSE, Roborough
MIDDLE HILL, Washfield, Tiverton
RESTHARROW, West Hill, Ottery St Mary
SHARPITOR, Salcombe
WOODSIDE, Barnstaple

JULY Sunday 20
KNIGHTSHAYES COURT, nr Tiverton

JULY Sunday 27
MIDDLE HILL, Washfield, Tiverton
RESTHARROW, West Hill, Ottery St Mary

AUGUST daily
FERNWOOD, Ottery St Mary
MARWOOD HILL, nr Barnstaple
THE ROCK, Chudleigh
ROSEMOOR, Great Torrington

**AUGUST daily except Mondays (but
open August 25)**
TAPELEY PARK, Instow

AUGUST every Wednesday
BIDLAKE MILL, Combebow Bridge,
nr Okehampton
COMRIE, Smallridge, nr Axminster
THE GARDEN HOUSE, Buckland
Monachorum
WEETWOOD, Offwell, Honiton

AUGUST Sunday 3
LEIGH COTTAGE, Kennerleigh, nr Crediton

AUGUST Sunday 10
RESTHARROW, West Hill, Ottery St Mary
WOODSIDE, Barnstaple

**AUGUST Wednesdays 13 & 20 &
Thursdays 14 & 21**
THE DOWNES, Monkleigh, Bideford

AUGUST Sunday 24
THE DOWNES, Monkleigh, Bideford
MIDDLE HILL, Washfield, Tiverton
RESTHARROW, West Hill, Ottery St Mary

AUGUST Monday 25 (Bank Holiday)
THE DOWNES, Monkleigh, Bideford

SEPTEMBER daily
FERNWOOD, Ottery St Mary
MARWOOD HILL, nr Barnstaple
THE ROCK, Chudleigh
ROSEMOOR, Great Torrington

SEPTEMBER daily except Mondays
TAPELEY PARK, Instow

SEPTEMBER every Wednesday
BIDLAKE MILL, Combebow Bridge,
nr Okehampton
COMRIE, Smallridge, nr Axminster
WEETWOOD, Offwell, Honiton

**SEPTEMBER Wednesday 3 &
Thursday 4**
THE DOWNES, Monkleigh, Bideford

SEPTEMBER Wednesdays 3, 10, 17
THE GARDEN HOUSE, Buckland
Monachorum

SEPTEMBER Sunday 7
RESTHARROW, West Hill, Ottery St Mary

SEPTEMBER Wednesday 10
CROSSINGFIELDS COTTAGE, Exmouth

SEPTEMBER Sunday 21
RESTHARROW, West Hill, Ottery St Mary

OCTOBER daily
MARWOOD HILL, nr Barnstaple
ROSEMOOR, Great Torrington

OCTOBER daily except Mondays
TAPELEY PARK, Instow

OCTOBER Wednesday 1
COMRIE, Smallridge, nr Axminster

NOVEMBER & DECEMBER daily
MARWOOD HILL, nr Barnstaple

NOVEMBER 1980 to Easter 1981 daily
TAPELEY PARK, Instow

DESCRIPTIONS OF GARDENS

Andrew's Corner⊕ (H. J. Hill Esq) Belstone,
3½ m. E of Okehampton. Parking restricted but
cars may be left on nearby common. A30, E of
Okehampton, signpost to Belstone. Small
garden 1,000 ft up on Dartmoor, overlooking
Cawsand Beacon & Taw Valley; wide interest
throughout year; rock garden, azaleas,
heathers, conifers, etc. NO DOGS. Adm. 20p,
Chd. 10p. Suns. April 20, May 11, June 15
(2.30–6); also by appt. (Tel. Sticklepath 332)

Bickham House*⅍ (The Lord Roborough)
Roborough, 8 m. N of Plymouth. Take
Maristow turning on Roborough Down, ½-way
between Plymouth & Tavistock, then follow
poster directions. Bus stop: nr AA box on
Roborough Down; posters at Maristow
turning 1 m. from house. Shrub garden,
camellias, rhododendrons, azaleas, cherries,
bulbs, trees. Lovely views. NO DOGS. Home-
made TEAS available. Adm. 25p. Suns. April 6,
13, 20, May 4, 11, 25, June 8, 22, July 6, 13
(2–6); parties catered for by appt. with lunch
or tea if required

Bidlake Mill * †⚘ (Mrs Wollocombe) Combebow Bridge, on N side of A30, E of Bridge ½-way between Bridestowe & Lewdown. Parking at Bridge. Terraced rock & water garden in wooded valley, flowering shrubs & trees in variety; created by owners since 1956. Scheduled medieval corn mill & water wheel owned by family since 1268. NO DOGS. *Adm. 25p. April to Sept. 30 every Wed. (11–5); also by appt. all year (Tel. Bridestowe 323)*

Blackpool House * (Lady A. Newman) Stoke Fleming, 4½ m. SW of Dartmouth. Opp. car park at Blackpool Sands. Shrub garden, on steep hillside, containing many rare, mature & tender shrubs. Beautiful sea views. Tea Venus Tea House on sands. *Adm. 15p, Chd. 5p. Garden open by appt. only (Tel. Stoke Fleming 261)*

● **Burrow Farm Garden** *⚘⊕ (Mr & Mrs John Benger) Dalwood, 4 m. W of Axminster. A35 Axminster–Honiton Rd; 3½ m. from Axminster turn N near Shute Garage on to Stockland Rd; ½ m. on right. 4-acre woodland garden created by owners since 1966; rhododendrons, azaleas etc. in natural setting; pond with waterside planting inc. primulas. Plants for sale. Cream TEAS (Suns. only). *Adm. 30p, Chd. 10p. April 20 to July 20 daily (2–7)*

Castle Drogo * (The National Trust—see p. ix) Drewsteignton. W of Exeter, S of A30. Medium-sized garden; shrubs, woodland walk overlooking Fingle Gorge. Grounds only. NO DOGS. *Adm. 90p, Chd. 45p. △Sun. May 11 & Sun. June 15 (11–6)*

Clapper Cottage (Mrs K. Lethbridge) Bondleigh, North Tawton. B3220, 3 m. E of Winkleigh, turn right to Bondleigh & left in ¼ m.; garden 1½ m. by river. Small garden with rockery; 3-acre wild garden with woodland & river walks. Picnics allowed. Plants for sale. *Adm. 15p, Chd. free. Mon. May 5, Sat. May 24, Sat. June 21 (11–7); also by appt. April to Oct. (Tel. North Tawton 209)*

¶**Cliffe House** (Mr & Mrs A. G. Braunton) Lynmouth. Leaving Lynmouth (E) by A39 towards Minehead, after 600 yds turn right. Very limited parking at garden (visitors who leave cars at Lynmouth may walk to garden via zig-zag path through grounds of the Tors Hotel). 3-acre garden; natural rock gardens, & woodland walks. Tea Tors Hotel. *Adm. 30p, Chd. 15p. Sun. June 15 (2–7)*

Combe Head *⚘⊕ (Mr & Mrs A. D. Baxter) Bampton. 1 m. W of Bampton on Dulverton Rd, B3222. Arboretum; collection of many unusual trees, shrubs, climbers, conifers & rose species begun in 1963 in 25 acres of fine old trees. *Adm. 20p. Garden open by appt. all year (Tel. Bampton 287)*

Comrie * (Mrs J. D. Lefeaux) Smallridge, 3 m. N of Axminster; take A358 towards Chard for approx. 2 m. to Weycroft Mill; turn left to Smallridge then 1st right; second house below Post Office. Parking at Village Hall, 3 mins walk from garden. ½ acre, part woodland, garden includes stream, rock garden, shrubs, roses & herbaceous plants; gentians a speciality. Plants for sale. NO DOGS. *Adm. 15p. April 30–June 4 every Wed.; June 25–Oct. 1 every Wed. (2–6)*

Crossingfields Cottage (Mr & Mrs F. N. H. Chalk) 239 Exeter Rd (A376), Exmouth. Good selection of unusual plants & shrubs, in ⅓ acre of S-facing town garden, inc. many species suitable for floral decoration. NO DOGS. *Adm. 15p. Weds. April 9, May 14, June 11, Sept. 10 (10–12 & 5–7)*

Dartington Hall Gardens * †⚘ (Dartington Hall Trust) 2 m. NW of Totnes. Turn off A384 at church. Station: Totnes (1½ m.), then bus. Large landscaped garden with ornamental trees & shrubs laid out around C14 Hall (rest of house not shown) & Tiltyard. Garden centre. *Adm. (donation) 50p recommended. △Sat. & Sun. May 17 & 18 (all day)*

¶**The Downes** *⚘ (Mr & Mrs R. C. Stanley-Baker) Monkleigh, 4½ m. S of Bideford; 3 m. NW of Torrington. On A386 to Bideford turn left (W) up drive, ¼ m. beyond layby. 4-acre garden with landscaped lawns & fine views overlooking Home Farm & woodlands in Torridge Valley; interesting ornamental trees & shrubs; small arboretum; woodland walks. Plants for sale when available. NO DOGS. Teashops in Torrington & Bideford. *Adm. 20p Chd. 10p. Fri. April 4; Suns. & Mons. April 6 & 7, 13 & 14, 20 & 21; Weds. & Thurs. Aug. 13 & 14, 20 & 21; Sun. & Mon. Aug. 24 & 25; Wed. & Thurs. Sept. 3 & 4 (2–6)*

Endsleigh Nurseries *⚘⊕ (M. A. Taylor Esq) Milton Abbot, 7 m. NW of Tavistock. A384 Tavistock–Launceston, turn left ½ m. before Milton Abbot, at school. Garden 1 m. on right. 9-acre nursery garden with good selection trees, shrubs & herbaceous plants. *Adm. 30p, Chd. 10p. Sun. May 18 (2–6)*

Farrants⊕ (Mr & Mrs M. Richards) Kilmington, 2 m. W of Axminster. A35, turn S at Kilmington Cross into Whitford Rd; garden about ¼ m. along on left. 1-acre garden planted since 1963; mostly shrubs & ground cover planted for colour contrast around C16 cottage. Plants for sale if available. *(Share to World Wildlife Assn.)* NO DOGS. *Adm. 20p, Chd. 5p. Suns. June 8, 15, 22; also Mon. June 16 (2–6); also by appt. (Tel. Axminster 32396)*

Fernwood * (Mr & Mrs H. Hollinrake) Toadspit Lane, 1½ m. W of Ottery St Mary. From Exeter take A30 for Honiton. Take B3174 for Ottery St Mary & in 1 m. turn right down Toadspit Lane. House ¼ m. on left. 2-acre woodland garden; wide selection of flowering

DEVON—continued

shrubs, conifers & bulbs, selected to give colour over long period; species & hybrid rhododendrons & azaleas special feature in spring. NO DOGS. *Adm. 20p. April 1 to Sept. 30 daily (all day)*

The Garden House* (Mr & Mrs L. S. Fortescue) Buckland Monachorum, Yelverton. W of A386, 10 m. N of Plymouth. Trees, lawns, terraces in attractive Devon landscape; up-to-date collection of flowering shrubs, ornamental cherries, etc. with good herbaceous plants. Interesting to horticulturists & others throughout spring & summer. Garden shown on other days by previous arrangement. No coaches except by previous appt. NO DOGS. *Adm. 35p, Chd. 5p. April 9 to Sept. 17 every Wed. (3–7); also by appt. (Tel. Yelverton 2493)*

Greenway Gardens*⅄⊕ (Mr & Mrs A. A. Hicks) Churston Ferrers, 4 m. W of Brixham. From B3203, Paignton–Brixham, take rd to Galmpton, thence towards Greenway Ferry. 30 acres. Old established garden with mature trees & shrubs. Rhododendrons, magnolias & camellias. Recent plantings; commercial shrub nursery. Woodland walks by R. Dart. TEAS. *Adm. 30p, Chd. 10p. Thurs. April 24 & Thurs. May 1 (2–6)*

Higher Knowle*⅄ (Mr & Mrs D. R. A Quicke) Lustleigh, 3 m. NW of Bovey Tracey. A382, Bovey Tracey towards Moretonhampstead; in 2¼ m. turn left at Kelly Cross for Lustleigh; in ¼ m. straight on at Brookfield for Manaton; in ½ m. steep drive on left. 3-acre steep woodland garden; rhododendrons, azaleas, magnolias in natural setting; good Dartmoor views. Dogs allowed on leads. *Adm. 35p, Chd. 25p. Suns. May 18, 25, Mon. May 26, Sun. June 1 (2–6)*

Killerton Garden*⅄⊕ (The National Trust— see p. ix) 8 m. N of Exeter. Leave Exeter N on A38 Taunton Rd & fork left in 7 m. on B3185. Garden 1 m., follow N.T. signs. 15 acres of spectacular hillside gardens sweeping down to large open lawns. Delightful walks through fine collection of rare trees & shrubs inc. magnolias, azaleas, cork oak & conifers. NO DOGS. *Adm. 90p, Chd. 45p. △Sun. April 27 & Sun. May 18 (all day)*

Knightshayes Court*⅄ (Lady Amory; The National Trust—see p. ix) 2 m. N of Tiverton. Via A396 Tiverton–Bampton; in Bolham, 1½ m. turn right; drive ½ m. on left. Large woodland garden; rhododendrons, azaleas, alpine plants, unusual shrubs. Formal garden. NO DOGS. TEAS. *Adm. 90p, Chd. 45p. △Sun. May 4 & Sun. July 20 (11–6)*

Lee Ford*†⅄⊕ (Mr & Mrs N. Lindsay-Fynn) Budleigh Salterton. Bus: DG, frequent service between Exmouth railway station, 3½ m., & Budleigh Salterton, alight (Lansdown) at end of drive. Georgian house in 40 acres of parkland, inc. spring bulb planting, woodland walks, herbaceous borders & flowering shrubs. Adam pavilion. *(Share to Gardeners' Sunday)* Car park free. *Adm. 40p. Mons. April 7, May 5 & 26 (2–6); other dates by prior appt. for parties only (minimum 20)*

Leigh Cottage (Mrs N. A. Granger) Kennerleigh, 5 m. N of Crediton. Leave Crediton via Tiverton Rd at Reeds Garage; in 300 yds turn left up Jockey Hill & follow signs to Sandford & Kennerleigh. From Tiverton via A373 & Chulmleigh B3042 take Witheridge Rd; follow signs to Black Dog. Small partly walled garden; great variety of plants, rock garden, scree, pool, herbaceous & roses. Plants for sale if available. NO DOGS. *Collecting box. May 4 to Aug. 3 every Sun.; also Mon. May 5 & Mon. May 26 (2–5.30); also by appt. (Tel. Cheriton Fitzpaine 359)*

Marwood Hill* (Dr J. A. Smart) Marwood, 4 m. N of Barnstaple. In Marwood village, opp. church. Extensive collection of camellias under glass & in open; daffodils, rhododendrons, rare flowering shrubs, new rock & alpine garden in quarry, rose garden; small lake with waterside planting; bog garden; large greenhouse containing exclusively Australian native plants. Plants for sale. *Adm. 20p, Chd. 5p. All year daily (dawn–dusk)*

¶Middle Hill (Mr & Mrs E. Boundy) Washfield, 4½ m. NW of Tiverton. Via B3221 from Tiverton & turn right (N) signed Washfield; straight through village & on for 1 m. Small, enthusiast's garden; raised beds with alpines; bulbs, hellebores & mixed borders in sun & shade. *(Share to Marie Curie Memorial Foundation)* No parties. NO DOGS. Tea Knightshayes Court. *Collecting box. Sat. & Sun. April 19 & 20; Sat. May 3; Suns. May 11, 18; Sat., Sun., Mon. May 24, 25, 26; Suns. June 29, July 6, 13, 27, Aug. 24 (3–7); also by appt. March–Sept. 7 (Tel. Oakford 380)*

Mothecombe House*†⅄⊕ (Anthony Mildmay-White Esq) Holbeton, SE of Plymouth. From A379, between Yealmpton & Modbury, turn S for Holbeton. Woodland walk to sea. Queen Anne house shown. English & Dutch pictures. English & French furniture, porcelain. Flower arrangements by Plymouth & District Flower Club. NO DOGS. TEAS. *Adm. to garden 25p; house 25p extra. Sat. May 3 (11–1 & 2–6), Sun. May 4 (2–6.30)*

Penhayes⊕ (Mr & Mrs John Martin) Kenton, 5 m. S of Exeter. On A379 Exeter–Dawlish coast Rd. Bus: 2, 2A, alight Powderham Castle stop (nearby for both directions). Attractive medium-sized natural garden with good collection of trees, shrubs & herbaceous plants. Pond well stocked with ornamental ducks. Aviary. NO DOGS. TEA & biscuits & soft drinks. *Adm. 30p. Suns. & Mons. April 6 & 7, May 4 & 5, 25 & 26 (2–6); also by appt. (April 8–May 24) (Tel. Starcross 354)*

Putsborough Manor*⊕ (Mr & Mrs T. W. Bigge) Georgeham, NW of Barnstaple. A361 Barnstaple–Braunton; B3231 to Croyde; ¾ m. N of village. Old thatched house (c. 1500) in a valley within 600 yds of the sea; lawn, herbaceous border & stream with waterside plantings, inc. good selection of primulas, May & June; separate walled garden, originally all kitchen garden but now in part laid out in grass with walk flanked by shrub borders. (*Share to Exeter Cathedral Preservation Trust*) *Adm. 20p, Chd. 5p. Sun. June 15 (10–6); also by appt. (summer months) (Tel. Croyde 890484)*

Restharrow (Mrs E. Simpson) Bendarroch Rd, West Hill, 1½ m. SW of Ottery St. Mary; take B3177 to West Hill, after 1½ m. fork right into Bendarroch Rd; garden on left past school. ¾-acre garden started in 1975, designed for year-round effect; mixed borders, heathers, rock plants; collection of silver & gold foliage. NO DOGS. *Adm. 25p, Chd. free. Suns. May 18, June 1, 15, 29, July 13, 27, Aug. 10, 24, Sept. 7, 21 (2–5.30); also by appt. (Tel. Ottery St Mary 2015)*

The Rock*†⊕ (K. F. Boulton Esq) Chudleigh, Newton Abbot. On B3344 Exeter–Plymouth at W end of Chudleigh. Small nursery garden in unusual setting of dells & rockery outcrops with 80-ft cliff. In an area scheduled as of geological & botanical interest. Adjacent to Chudleigh caves & waterfall. *Collecting box. March 1 to Sept. 30 daily (11–1 & 2–6)*

● **Rosemoor Garden Charitable Trust***⊕ (Col J. E. & Lady Anne Palmer) Great Torrington. 1 m. SE of Great Torrington on B3220 to Exeter. Medium-sized garden started in 1959; rhododendrons (species & hybrid), ornamental trees & shrubs, inc. varieties of eucalyptus; primulas; species & old-fashioned roses; scree & raised beds with alpine plants; young arboretum. Plants for sale. TEAS for groups by arrangement (minimum 20 persons). *Adm. 40p, Chd. ½-price; reduction for parties 35p each. April 1 to Oct. 31 daily (dawn–dusk)*

Saltram House †⊕ (The National Trust—see p. ix) Plympton, 3 m. E of Plymouth, S of A38, 2 m. W of Plympton. 8 acres with fine specimen trees; spring garden; rhododendrons & azaleas. C18 orangery & octagonal garden house. George II mansion with magnificent plasterwork & decorations, inc. 2 rooms designed by Robert Adam. NO DOGS. TEAS in house. *Adm. gardens only 90p, Chd. 45p. △Sun. May 4 & Sun. July 6 (11–6)*

Sanders*⊕ (Lady Gascoigne) Stoke Fleming, Dartmouth. 300 yds S of Stoke Fleming church on Kingsbridge Rd. Medium-sized garden with outstanding sea views. Flowering shrubs; fuchsia collection. Woodland garden. NO DOGS. *Adm. 20p, Chd. 10p. Garden open by appt. only. (Tel. Stoke Fleming 341)*

Sharpitor (The National Trust—see p. ix) 1½ m. SW of Salcombe. From Salcombe or Marlborough follow N.T. signs. 6-acre garden with rare plants & shrubs; spectacular views over Salcombe Estuary. NO DOGS. *Adm. to garden only 50p, Chd. 25p. △Sun. June 15 & Sun. July 13 (all day)*

Stormsdown*⊕ (Mrs M. M. Domar) nr Bickington, Ashburton. 1 m. N of A38 on Newton Abbot–Widecombe Rd. 1½-acre garden with choice rhododendrons, azaleas, flowering trees & rare shrubs. Plants for sale. NO DOGS. *Adm. 20p, Chd. 5p. Thurs. May 1, 8, 15, 22 (2–5); also by appt. (all year) (Tel. Bickington 362)*

● **Tapeley Park***⅋⊕ (Miss Rosamond Christie) Instow, 7½ m. SW of Barnstaple. Entrance on A39 Barnstaple–Bideford, 1 m. W of Instow. Beautiful Italian garden, of horticultural interest in all seasons; walled kitchen garden; woodland walk to lily pond. Pets, putting green, picnic area. Conducted tours of house according to demand; fine porcelain, furniture, C18 plasterwork ceilings. Plants & produce for sale. Dogs welcome if on leads. Light lunches, cream TEAS & other refreshments in Queen Anne Dairy. *Adm. charges to be decided. Garden & house: Easter to late Oct. daily except Mons., but open Bank Hols (10–6); Garden only: Nov. 1980 to Easter 1981 daily (daylight hours)*

The Warren*⅋⊕ (in part) (Mrs Anita S. A. Jones) Woodbury, 8 m. E of Exeter. A3052 Exeter–Sidmouth Rd; turn into B3180 towards Exmouth & on 1½ m.; house on right before Woodbury Common. Extensive woodland in sheltered combe of Woodbury Common overlooking R. Exe, with walks through specimen rhododendrons, azaleas & flowering shrubs in natural setting; coniferous & hardwood trees; rare ferns; primulas & other bog plants; Californian redwoods provide a featured landmark. NO DOGS. Tea Woodbury Common. *Adm. 20p, Chd. 10p. May 25 to July 6 every Sun. & Wed. (2–7); also by appt. for parties (Tel. Woodbury 32224)*

Weetwood*⊕ (Mr & Mrs H. Bawden) Offwell. 2 m. E of Honiton on A35, turn off right for Offwell; 50 yds beyond school. Parking at playing field. 1-acre garden; excellent collection of unusual plants, dwarf conifers, rock garden plants, shrubs, autumn gentians, etc. NO DOGS. *Adm. 25p, Chd. 5p. April 16 to Sept. 24 every Wed. (2–6)*

Woodside* (Mr & Mrs Mervyn Feesey) Higher Raleigh Rd, Barnstaple. On outskirts of Barnstaple, A39 to Lynton, turn right 300 yds above fire station. 2-acre garden with outstanding collection of ornamental grasses & sedges & other monocots; extensive range of dwarf, variegated & unusual small shrubs; rock plants & alpines; rhododendrons, foliage plants & conifers. Garden faces S with raised

DEVON—continued

& scree beds & includes ericaceous & large New Zealand collection. *Adm. 30p, Chd. 15p. Suns. May 4, June 8, July 13, Aug. 10 (2–7); also by appt. May–Aug. (Tel. Barnstaple 3095)*

DORSET

(for Bournemouth & Christchurch Districts see Hants.)

Hon. County Organisers:
MRS CHARLES BUDDEN, Wolfeton, Dorchester, &
LADY COOKE, Athelhampton, Dorchester

DATES OF OPENING

FEBRUARY Sundays 17 & 24
HYDE CROOK, nr Dorchester
MARCH from Monday 10, every Monday to Friday
MAPPERTON, Beaminster
MARCH from mid-March daily
ABBOTSBURY GARDENS, nr Weymouth
MARCH Sunday 30
HYDE CROOK, nr Dorchester
APRIL daily
ABBOTSBURY GARDENS, nr Weymouth
COMPTON ACRES GARDENS, Poole
APRIL every Monday to Friday
MAPPERTON, Beaminster
APRIL every Wednesday to Saturday from April 9
FLOREAT GARDEN, Poole
APRIL every Wednesday, Sunday & Bank Holiday
PARNHAM HOUSE, nr Beaminster
APRIL every Sunday & Bank Holiday
HYDE CROOK, nr Dorchester
MINTERNE, Cerne Abbas
APRIL every Wednesday, Thursday, Sunday & Bank Holiday
ATHELHAMPTON, nr Puddletown
APRIL Easter Saturday 5
HYDE CROOK, nr Dorchester
APRIL Easter Sunday 6
DEANS COURT, Wimborne
FORDE ABBEY, nr Chard
SADBOROW MYLL, Thorncombe, nr Chard
APRIL Easter Monday 7
DEANS COURT, Wimborne
FORDE ABBEY, nr Chard
APRIL Sunday 13
BELFIELD HOUSE, Wyke Regis, Weymouth
APRIL Monday 14
BELFIELD HOUSE, Wyke Regis, Weymouth
APRIL Sunday 20
EDMONDSHAM HOUSE, Edmondsham
APRIL Sunday 27
HIGHBURY, West Moors
EDMONDSHAM HOUSE, Edmondsham

MAY daily
ABBOTSBURY GARDENS, nr Weymouth
COMPTON ACRES GARDENS, Poole
MAY every Monday to Friday
MAPPERTON, Beaminster
MAY every Wednesday to Saturday
FLOREAT GARDEN, Poole
MAY every Wednesday, Thursday, Sunday & Bank Hol.
ATHELHAMPTON, nr Puddletown
MAY every Wednesday, Sunday & Bank Hol.
FORDE ABBEY, nr Chard
PARNHAM HOUSE, Beaminster
MAY every Sunday & Bank Hol.
HIGHBURY, West Moors
MINTERNE, Cerne Abbas
MAY Saturday 3
SADBOROW MYLL, Thorncombe, nr Chard
MAY Sunday 4
HYDE CROOK, nr Dorchester
LONG BREDY GARDENS, nr Dorchester
MAY Monday 5 (Bank Hol.)
HYDE CROOK, nr Dorchester
MAY Sunday 11
CULEAZE, nr Wareham
MAY Saturday 17
BUSHEY HOUSE, nr Corfe Castle
MAY Sunday 18
BUSHEY HOUSE, nr Corfe Castle
CULEAZE, nr Wareham
‡MINQUIERS, St Ives, nr Ringwood
‡MOULIN HUET, West Moors
SADBOROW MYLL, Thorncombe, nr Chard
MAY Sunday 25
HIGHWOOD GARDEN, Charborough Park, nr Wareham
MOIGNE COMBE, nr Dorchester
‡MINQUIERS, St Ives, nr Ringwood
‡MOULIN HUET, West Moors
SLAPE MANOR, Netherby
MAY Monday 26 (Bank Hol.)
DEANS COURT, Wimborne
‡MINQUIERS, St Ives, nr Ringwood
‡MOULIN HUET, West Moors
SLAPE MANOR, Netherby
MAY Thursday 29
DEANS COURT, Wimborne
JUNE daily
ABBOTSBURY GARDENS, nr Weymouth
COMPTON ACRES GARDENS, Poole
JUNE every Monday to Friday
MAPPERTON, Beaminster
JUNE every Wednesday to Saturday
FLOREAT GARDEN, Poole
JUNE every Wednesday, Thursday & Sunday
ATHELHAMPTON, nr Puddletown
JUNE every Wednesday & Sunday
FORDE ABBEY, nr Chard
PARNHAM HOUSE, Beaminster
JUNE every Thursday & Sunday
DEANS COURT, Wimborne

JUNE every Sunday
  HIGHBURY, West Moors
  MINTERNE, Cerne Abbas
JUNE Saturday 7
  HIGHWOOD GARDEN. Charborough
  Park, nr Wareham
JUNE Sunday 8
  MOIGNE COMBE, nr Dorchester
JUNE Sunday 15
  SADBOROW MYLL, Thorncombe,
  nr Chard
JUNE Thursday 26
  KINGSTON MAURWARD, nr Dorchester
JUNE Saturday 28
  KINGSTON RUSSELL HOUSE, Long
  Bredy, Dorchester
  SADBOROW MYLL, Thorncombe,
  nr Chard
JUNE Sunday 29
  KINGSTON MAURWARD, nr Dorchester
  KINGSTON RUSSELL HOUSE, Long
  Bredy, Dorchester
  MANOR HOUSE, Hinton St Mary
  RUSSETS, Child Okeford, nr Blandford
JULY daily
  ABBOTSBURY GARDENS, nr Weymouth
  COMPTON ACRES GARDENS, Poole
JULY every Monday to Friday
  MAPPERTON, Beaminster
JULY every Wednesday to Saturday
  FLOREAT GARDEN, Poole
**JULY every Wednesday, Thursday &
Sunday**
  ATHELHAMPTON, nr Puddletown
JULY every Wednesday & Sunday
  FORDE ABBEY, nr Chard
  PARNHAM HOUSE, Beaminster
JULY every Thursday & Sunday
  DEANS COURT, Wimborne
JULY every Sunday
  HIGHBURY, West Moors
JULY Saturday 5
  KINGSTON RUSSELL HOUSE, Long
  Bredy, Dorchester
JULY Sunday 6
  SADBOROW MYLL, Thorncombe,
  nr Chard
  KINGSTON RUSSELL HOUSE, Long
  Bredy, Dorchester
JULY Thursday 17
  ENCOMBE, Kingston
JULY Sunday 20
  SADBOROW MYLL, Thorncombe,
  nr Chard
JULY Wednesday 23
  ENCOMBE, Kingston
JULY Thursday 24
  MELBURY HOUSE, nr Yeovil
AUGUST daily
  ABBOTSBURY GARDENS, nr Weymouth
  COMPTON ACRES GARDENS, Poole
**AUGUST daily except Mondays &
Saturdays (but open Monday 25)**
  ATHELHAMPTON, nr Puddletown
AUGUST every Monday to Friday
  MAPPERTON, Beaminster

**AUGUST Wednesday to Saturday to
August 16**
  FLOREAT GARDEN, Poole
**AUGUST every Wednesday, Sunday &
Bank Hol.**
  FORDE ABBEY, nr Chard
  PARNHAM HOUSE, Beaminster
**AUGUST every Thursday, Sunday &
Bank Hol.**
  DEANS COURT, Wimborne
AUGUST Sunday 3
  HIGHBURY, West Moors
AUGUST Thursday 7
  MELBURY HOUSE, nr Yeovil
AUGUST Sunday 10
  SMEDMORE, Kimmeridge, Wareham
AUGUST Thursday 21
  MELBURY HOUSE, nr Yeovil
SEPTEMBER daily
  ABBOTSBURY GARDENS, nr Weymouth
  COMPTON ACRES GARDENS, Poole
SEPTEMBER every Monday to Friday
  MAPPERTON, Beaminster
**SEPTEMBER every Wednesday,
Thursday & Sunday**
  ATHELHAMPTON, nr Puddletown
**SEPTEMBER every Wednesday &
Sunday**
  FORDE ABBEY, nr Chard
  PARNHAM HOUSE, Beaminster
SEPTEMBER every Thursday & Sunday
  DEANS COURT, Wimborne
SEPTEMBER Thursday 4
  MELBURY HOUSE, nr Yeovil
OCTOBER daily
  COMPTON ACRES GARDENS, Poole
OCTOBER daily to mid-October
  ABBOTSBURY GARDENS, nr Weymouth
**OCTOBER every Monday to Friday to
October 10**
  MAPPERTON, Beaminster
OCTOBER every Wednesday & Sunday
  PARNHAM HOUSE, Beaminster
**OCTOBER Wednesday, 1 Thursday 2,
Sunday 5, Wednesday 8, Thursday 9 &
Sunday 12**
  ATHELHAMPTON, nr Puddletown

DESCRIPTIONS OF GARDENS

● **Abbotsbury Gardens** *&⊕ (Strangways
Estate) 9 m. NW of Weymouth. 9 m. SW of
Dorchester. From B3157 Weymouth–Bridport,
turn off 200 yds W of Abbotsbury village, at
foot of hill. 16 acres; originally garden of
Abbotsbury Castle (which no longer exists),
it was started in early C18 and considerably
extended in the late C19; much replanting
has been done during past few years; very
fine collection of rhododendrons, camellias,
azaleas & wide variety of unusual & tender
trees & shrubs. Peacocks & other birds. Plants
& shrubs for sale. Tea The Flower Bowl,
Abbotsbury. *Adm. charges not yet known.
Mid-March to mid-Oct. daily (10–5.30)*

● **Athelhampton** †*&⊕ (Sir Robert Cooke)
nr Puddletown, NE of Dorchester. Few

27

hundred yds E of Puddletown on main rd to Bere Regis. Station: Dorchester. Bus: 11 & 411 Dorchester—Poole—Bournemouth passes house; alight at Back Lodge. Garden architecture; formal walled gardens, fountains & pools, dovecote, wild gardens & river. Medieval house. NO DOGS. TEAS at house. *Adm. house & garden £1; gardens only 50p, Chd. free in gardens. April 2 to Oct. 12 every Wed., Thurs. & Sun. & Bank Hol.; also every Tues. & Fri. in Aug. (2–6)*

Belfield House† (Capt. & Mrs John Wright) Belfield Park Ave, Wyke Regis. From Weymouth follow signs to Portland; Belfield Park Ave is turning off Buxton Rd (to right). Medium-sized garden, mainly informal with variety of shrubs inc. camellias, azaleas & rhododendrons; many daffodils & primrose, semi-wild. Small Palladian house built *c.* 1777 with columned portico by John Crunden (who designed Boodles Club) for Isaac Buxton; visited several times by George III. NO DOGS. Tea Weymouth (under 1 m.). *Adm., inc. ground floor of house, 30p, Chd. 20p. Sun. & Mon. April 13 & 14 (2–6)*

Bushey House⊕ (D. C. D. Ryder Esq) 2½ m. NE of Corfe Castle. Via A351 Wareham—Corfe Castle; turn off E on to B3351 towards Studland. Medium-sized, new garden & new house (not open); wild rhododendrons; trees; rockery. Panoramic view over heath & harbour. Tea Corfe Castle. *Adm. 20p., Chd. 10p. Sat. & Sun. May 17 & 18 (2–7)*

● **Compton Acres Gardens***⅃⊕ (Mr & Mrs J. R. Brady) Canford Cliffs Rd, Poole. From Poole—Bournemouth Rd turn off on to Canford Cliffs Rd, few yds from Canford Cliffs village, nr Sandbanks. Bus: Hants & Dorset 149, 150, 151 from Bournemouth & Poole; stop at entrance. 15 acres; reputed to be finest gardens in Europe, overlooking Poole Harbour, inc. Japanese, Italian, rock & water gardens; heather; woodland & sub-tropical glen; bronze & marble statuary. Large selection of plants for sale. NO DOGS. TEAS. *Adm. 60p, Chd. 40p. Free car & coach park. April 1 to Oct. 31 daily (10.30–6.30; but to dusk on Thurs. in June, July & Aug.)*

Culeaze*⅃⊕ (Col & Mrs Barne) 7m. NW of Wareham. From Bere Regis take rd S towards Wool; take 2nd turning left, signposted Culeaze; then turn right at Tower. Medium-sized garden; walled garden, rhododendrons, Paulownia in flower, rare trees, flowers & shrubs; greenhouse & conservatory with mimosa. Tea Woodbury Cottage, Bere Regis (1½m.) *Adm. 25p, Chd. 10p. Suns. May 11 & 18 (2–6)*

● **Deans Court** *†⅃⊕ (Sir Michael & Lady Hanham) Wimborne. Just off A31 in centre of Wimborne. 13 acres; partly wild garden; water, specimen trees, free roaming peacocks

& other birds; kitchen garden, with serpentine wall, selling organically produced plants & vegetables as available. House (not open) was originally the Deanery to the Minster. NO DOGS. Tea Yew Tree, opp. Minster (2 mins walk). *Adm. 30p, Chd. 20p. Sun. & Mon. April 6 & 7; May 26 to Sept. 28 every Thurs. Sun. & Bank Hol. (Suns. & Thurs. 2–6; April 7, May 26 & Aug. 25 10–6)*

Edmondsham House⅃⊕ (Mrs Anthony Medlycott) nr Cranborne. B3081, turn at Sixpenny Handley X-rds to Ringwood & Cranborne; thereafter follow signs to Edmondsham. Large garden; spring bulbs, trees & shrubs; walled garden; walled vegetable garden; grass cockpit. Early church nearby. Teas available in Village Hall. *Adm. 30p, Chd. 10p. Suns. April 20 & 27 (2–6); also by appt.*

Encombe†⊕ (Lt-Col H. E. Scott) Kingston, 2½ m. SW of Corfe Castle. Bus: WN 419; alight Kingston, 1 m. Beautiful grounds, lake, lawns & shrubs. Lovely woodland valley walk to sea, ½ m. NO DOGS. Tea Corfe Castle. *Adm. 30p, Chd. 10p. Thurs. July 17 & Wed. July 23 (2.30–6.30)*

Floreat Garden* (Mr. & Mrs. D. C. Morss) 148 Albert Rd, Parkstone, Poole. From Bournemouth or Poole take A35; at Pottery Junction, Branksome, turn on to B3061, Ashley Rd; proceed for ½ m.; turn right by Lloyds Bank down Albert Rd for ½ m. & house on right. Small (¼-acre) S-facing garden of botanical & horticultural interest; alpines, hebes, hellebores, hostas, leptospermums, phormiums, etc, enclosing Hardy Plant Nursery specialising in alpines, unusual foliage & flowering plants & shrubs. *(Share to Gideons International in British Isles)*. NO DOGS. Tea Spinning Wheel, Penhill. *Collecting box. April 9 to Aug. 16 every Wed., Thurs., Fri. & Sat.; (10–5)*

● **Forde Abbey***†⅃⊕ (G. D. Roper Esq) 4 m. SE of Chard. 7 m. W of Crewkerne; well signposted off A30. Large garden (30 acres) containing many fine shrubs & some magnificent specimen trees; herbaceous border, rock garden, water garden, kitchen garden; arboretum established post-war. C12 Cistercian monastery. TEAS. *Adm. charges not yet available. Sun. & Mon. April 6 & 7; May to Sept. every Wed., Sun. & Bank Hol. (2–6)*

Highbury* (Mr & Mrs Stanley Cherry) West Moors, 8 m. N of Bournemouth. In Woodside Rd, off B3072 Bournemouth—Verwood Rd; last rd at N end of West Moors village. Garden of ½-acre in mature setting; many rare & unusual plants & shrubs; conifers, trees, herb garden, ferns, grasses, spring bulbs, sempervivums, silver & variegated collections; propagating & experimental section; botanical & horticultural interest with everything labelled. *(Share to Gardeners' Sunday.)*

28

NO DOGS. Tea Garden Centre in Three Legged Cross, 2 m. *Adm. 20p, Chd. 5p. April 27 to Aug. 3 every Sun.; also Mons. May 5 & 26 (2–6)*

Highwood Garden (H. W. Drax Esq) Charborough Park, Wareham, 6 m. E of Bere Regis. Enter Park by any lodge on A31 & follow signpost to Estate Office, then Highwood Garden. Large garden with rhododendrons & azaleas in woodland setting. NO DOGS. Parish Fete on June 7. *Adm. 30p, Chd. 10p. Sun. May 25 & Sat. June 7 (2.30–6)*

Hyde Crook*& (Maj. P. R. A. Birley) 5 m. NW of Dorchester on A37, Dorchester–Yeovil. 14 acres of woodland garden laid out 1936 by William Bean of Kew & Dr William Fox of Wentworth. Snowdrops (early openings). Flowering trees & shrubs. Japanese cherries, magnolias, camellias, azaleas. Abundance of daffodils & narcissi; orchid house. Visitors welcome to picnic in garden. *Adm. 20p, Chd. 10p. Suns. Feb. 17, 24, March 30, April 6, 13, 20, 27, May 4; also Sat. & Mon. April 5 & 7; Mon. May 5 (2–7); also by appt. for parties* (Tel. Maiden Newton 204)

Kingston Maurward*†&⊕ (Dorset County Council) Dorset College of Agriculture, E of Dorchester. From Dorchester–Puddletown Rd, turn right, 1 m. from Dorchester. Station: Dorchester, 1½ m. Bus: WD 34 & A434, Dorchester–Salisbury, alight Stinsford, ¼ m. Formal & teaching gardens; herbaceous border; shrubberies; rose gardens; Japanese garden; lake & waterfall walk; plant houses, fruit & vegetable plots, & educational plots. NO DOGS. Tea available in nearby village. *Adm. 25p. Thurs. June 26 & Sun. June 29 (2–6)*

Kingston Russell House†⊕ (Charles Worthington Esq) Long Bredy, 8 m. W of Dorchester. ½-way between Dorchester & Bridport; turn S off A35 towards the sea. Garden of 5 acres with yew hedges; Doric Orangery with lemon, orange, grapefruit & banana trees. In July large collection of shrub roses; ¼ m. rose walk. NO DOGS. *Adm. 30p, Chd. 10p. Sats. & Suns. June 28 & 29, July 5 & 6 (2–6)*

Long Bredy Gardens,* ½-way between Bridport & Dorchester, 8 m. from each; S off A35, well signposted. NO DOGS. TEAS at Langebride House. *Combined charge for following gardens 40p, Chd. 10p. Sun May 4 (2–6)*

    Dower Cottage (Mr & Mrs G. W. J. Collyer) Spring flowers in a small garden; pleasant views of hills & stream

    Martins Dower (Dr & Mrs Connor) Picturesque small garden adjacent to Dower Cottage

    Langebride House (Maj. & Mrs. John Greener) Old rectory garden modernised since 1966 for easier management; 200-yr-old beech trees; young flowering trees,

shrub border, yew hedges & fine mixed beech hedge

Friday Cottage (Mrs P. K. Hooper) Small garden with unusual shrubs & flowers.

The Manor House*†⊕ (Mr & Mrs Anthony Pitt-Rivers) Hinton St Mary, 1 m. Sturminster Newton. B3092 from Sturminster Newton; gates on top of hill on right. 5 acres; lawns & shrubs; ponds & yew hedges; collection of shrub roses. Fine view over Blackmore Vale. C15 tithe barn & mainly C19 church. NO DOGS please. *Adm. 30p, Chd. 10p. Sun. June 29 (2–6)*

● **Mapperton**†& (Mr Victor Montagu) 2 m. SE of Beaminster off A356 & B3163. 5 m. NNE of Bridport off A3066. Terraced & hillside gardens with daffodils, formal borders & specimen shrubs & trees. Orangery; C18 stone fish ponds & summerhouse. Soft drinks & ices in cottage garden. Free parking. *Adm. 50p; under 18, 20p; under 5 free. March 10 to Oct. 10 every Mon., Tues., Wed., Thurs. & Fri. (2–6)*

Melbury House*†&⊕ (The Lady Teresa Agnew) 6 m. S of Yeovil. Signposted on Dorchester–Yeovil Rd. 13 m. N of Dorchester. Large garden; very fine arboretum; shrubs & lakeside walk; beautiful deer park. *Adm. 40p, Chd. 20p. Thurs. July 24. Aug. 7, 21, Sept. 4 (2–6)*

¶**Minquiers***⊕ (Mr & Mrs John Newman) 18 Pine Drive, St Ives, 2m. W of Ringwood. Leave A31 at local roundabout W of Ringwood, turning into Woolsbridge Rd, then 1st right into Pine Drive. 1½-acre woodland garden in mature setting, created and maintained by owners; rhododendrons & azaleas (many species & varieties); conifers, camellias, magnolias & peat-loving plants. (Share to Gardeners' Sunday) NO DOGS. Tea Little Chef at roundabout. *Adm. 25p, Chd. 5p. Sun. May 18; Sun. & Mon. May 25 & 26 (2–6)*

● **Minterne***& (The Lord Digby) Cerne Abbas, 10 m. N of Dorchester. Large shrub garden set in beautiful valley; many varieties of Himalayan & Chinese rhododendrons, magnolias, azaleas & rare trees. Japanese cherry trees flowering late April or early May. *Adm. 40p, Chd. 15p. April 6 to June 29 every Sun.; also Mons. April 7, May 5 & 26 (2–7); also by appt. for parties on weekdays*

Moigne Combe& (Maj.-Gen. H. M. G. Bond) 6 m. E of Dorchester. 1½ m. N of Owermoigne turning off A352 Dorchester–Wareham Rd. Medium-sized garden; wild garden & shrubbery; heathers, azaleas, rhododendrons, etc.; woodland paths & lake walk. Tea Trees Stores, Crossways. *Adm. 25p, Chd. 10p. Sun. May 25 & Sun. June 8 (2–6)*

¶**Moulin Huet***⊕ (Mr & Mrs Harold Judd) 15 Heatherdown Rd, West Moors. 7 m. N of

Bournemouth. Leave A31 at West Moors Garage into Pinehurst Rd, then take 1st right into Uplands Rd, then 3rd left into Heatherdown Rd. Small garden ($\frac{1}{3}$ acre) of considerable botanical interest; large collection of dwarf conifers (90); many plants & shrubs rare in cultivation; alpines, sink gardens, bonsai, rockeries, wood sculpture. (*Share to Gardeners' Sunday*) NO DOGS please. Tea Azalia Restaurant (on A31). *Adm. 20p, Chd. 5p. Sun. May 18; Sun. & Mon. May 25 & 26 (2-7)*

● **Parnham House**＊†&⊕ (John Makepeace Esq) nr Beaminster. On A3066, $\frac{3}{4}$ m. S of Beaminster; 5 m. N of Bridport. Garden 14 acres, exensively reconstructed early this cent.; variety of form & interest; riverside walk & picnic area; Yew Terrace comprising topiary of 50 clipped yews; spring-fed water channels which cascade beside steps to Great Lawn; balustraded Ladies Terrace leads to formal East Court; Italian Garden, Glade & Wilderness which wrap around the walled kitchen garden (not open). House (Grade 1 listed building dating from 1540 with additions by John Nash) also open, inc. John Makepeace Furniture Workshops. TEAS. *Adm. to whole site 90p, Chd. 50p. April 1 to Oct. 31 every Sun. Wed. & Bank Hol. (10-5); also by prior arrangement on Tues. & Thurs. for parties (Tel. Beaminster 862204)*

¶**Russets**＊⊕ (Mr & Mrs G. D. Hartham) Rectory Lane, Child Okeford. 6 m. NW Blandford. From Blandford via A357 & turn off N at Shillingstone; or from A350 turn off W at signpost for Child Okeford. Parking space in Rectory Lane (ask nr centre of village). Garden of $\frac{1}{2}$ acre specialising in shrubs & perennials. (*Share to Oxfam*) *Adm. 20p, Chd. 10p. Sun. June 29 (2-6)*

Sadborow Myll (Cmdr W. J. Eyre, R.N. (Retd)) Thorncombe, SE of Chard. From Lyme—Crewkerne Rd B3165 turn W at Rose & Crown, Birdsmoor gate & on 1$\frac{1}{2}$ m. Bear left at Sadborow Pound; 1 m. down narrow lane & on right. $\frac{1}{2}$-acre, new garden with modern bungalow attached to C19 water mill with mill pond. Bog garden 800 yds up lane. *Adm. 25p. Suns. April 6, May 18, June 15, July 6, 20; also Sats. May 3 & June 28 (2-6.30)*

Slape Manor&⊕ (Mr & Mrs Tom Nicole) Netherbury. 2 m. S of Beaminster; 4 m. N of Bridport; W of A3066. Medium-sized garden; flowering shrubs, lawns & hedges. Tea Wooden Spoon, Beaminster. *Adm. 30p, Chd. 10p. Sun. & Mon. May 25 & 26 (2-6)*

Smedmore＊⊕ (Maj. J. C. Mansel) Kimmeridge, 7 m. S of Wareham. A351 from Wareham or Swanage to Corfe Castle; turn W at signpost to Church Knowle & Kimmeridge; follow signs to Kimmeridge. 2 acres; colourful herbaceous borders; walled flower gardens & vegetable garden; display of hydrangeas.

Plants for sale. Gardens are adjacent to C17 & C18 grey stone manor house with many fine Queen Anne & Georgian features. Tea Kimmeridge Post Office (1 m.), Corfe Castle (5 m.) or Wareham. *Adm. 40p, Chd. 20p.* △*Sun. Aug. 10 (2.30-5.30)*

CO. DURHAM

Hon. County Organiser:
MRS IAN BONAS, Bedburn Hall, Hamsterley
  Bishop Auckland

DATES OF OPENING

ALL YEAR daily
  ST AIDAN'S COLLEGE, Durham
APRIL from April 5 & MAY every Wednesday, Sunday & Bank Holiday weekend (Sat.–Tues.)
  RABY CASTLE, Staindrop
MAY Sunday 18
  THE COLLEGE OF ST HILD & ST BEDE, Durham
JUNE every Wednesday & Sunday
  RABY CASTLE, Staindrop
JUNE Sunday 1
  WESTHOLME, Winston, nr Darlington
JUNE Sunday 15
  BEDBURN HALL, Hamsterley
JUNE SUNDAY 29
  ELDON HOUSE, Heighington,
    nr Darlington
  WILDWOODS, Rowlands Gill,
    nr Newcastle-on-Tyne
JULY daily except Saturdays
  RABY CASTLE, Staindrop
JULY Sunday 6
  AUCKLAND CASTLE, Bishop Auckland
  LOW WALWORTH HALL, nr Darlington
JULY Sunday 13
  GAINFORD GARDENS, nr Barnard Castle
JULY Sunday 20
  FAWNLEES HALL, Wolsingham
  SPRING LODGE, Barnard Castle
JULY Sunday 27
  BRANCEPETH GARDENS, nr Durham
AUGUST & SEPTEMBER daily except Saturdays (but open Aug. 23) to September 30
  RABY CASTLE, Staindrop

DESCRIPTIONS OF GARDENS

Auckland Castle †&⊕ (The Right Reverend The Lord Bishop of Durham & Mrs Habgood) Bishop Auckland. Bus stop: Market Place, 100 yds (clock over main gate). 8$\frac{1}{2}$-acre garden inc. kitchen gardens & greenhouses. Guided tours of State Rooms. Castle dates back to Norman times & has been favourite residence of Bishops of Durham for over 800 yrs & therefore of historical interest. Postcards & brochures on sale. NO DOGS. TEAS. *Adm. grounds & castle (State Rooms) 40p, Chd. 20p. Sun. July 6 (2-6)*

Bedburn Hall&⊕ (Ian Bonas Esq) Hamsterley, 9 m. NW of Bishop Auckland. From A68 at Witton-le-Wear, turn off W to Hamsterley; turn N out of Hamsterley—Bedburn & down 1 m. to valley. From Wolsingham on B6293 turn off SE for 3 m. Medium-sized garden; terraced garden on S facing hillside with streams; lake; woodland & lawns; rhododendrons; herbaceous borders; roses. TEAS. *Adm. 30p, Chd. 15p. Sun. June 15 (2–6)*

Brancepeth Gardens, 6 m. SW of Durham on A690 between villages of Brandon & Willington. An attractive sandstone village consisting of a few Georgian & later houses at the gates of the Castle & Church which originate from late C12. A number of gardens will be open, inc. the following. (*Share to Brancepeth Church*) TEAS available. *Combined charge for all following gardens 50p, Chd. 15p (tickets from 1 Foxes Row & Quarry Hill). Sun. July 27 (2–6)*

　Quarry Hill⊕ (P. D. Nicholson Esq) Medium-sized garden of fine proportions; herbaceous borders, shrubs & topiary; vegetable garden; greenhouse

　1 Foxes Row (D. Quayle Esq)

　Also other gardens

The College of St Hild & St Bede, Durham. From A1(M) via A690; entrance just below roundabout on edge of town. Large garden noted for its lawns, rose beds, rockeries & island beds. Extensive views over Castle & Cathedral. TEAS. *Adm. 30p, Chd. 10p. Sun. May 18 (2–5)*

¶**Eldon House**⊕ (Mr & Mrs G. C. Bartram) Heighington, 6 m. NW of Darlington. From A1(M) turn off N along A68 (towards Bishop Auckland) & then A6072 to Heighington. From NW via A68 take turning left (opp. Dog Inn) signposted Heighington. Garden on edge of Heighington village green. 1½ acres; walled garden, well laid out; mature shrubs. TEAS. *Adm. 30p, Chd. 15p. Sun. June 29 (2–6)*

Fawnlees Hall&⊕ (Sir James Steel) 1m. from Wolsingham via Leazes Lane, by old Grammar School, Wolsingham, 1 m. Bus: From Stanhope, Crook or Bishop Auckland; alight Grammar School. Medium-sized garden; rock garden; herbaceous borders; roses; walled vegetable garden. TEA & biscuits *Adm. 30p, Chd. 15p. Sun. July 20 (2–6)*

Gainford Gardens. On A67, 8 m. W of Darlington, 8 m. E of Barnard's Castle. One of the loveliest villages in the county; it lies round a large & tranquil green between A67 & the Tees; Georgian flavour predominates. TEAS available at Headlam Hall. *Combined charge for all gardens 50p, Chd. 20p. Sun. July 13 (2–6)*

　Headlam Hall (J. H. Robinson Esq) 2 m. N of Gainford. 3 acres; formal garden with beech & yew hedges; small walled rose garden; troutwater; vegetables; extensive lawns

The White House (The Dowager Lady Barnard)

25 Low Green (Mrs N. M. Spalding)

5 Spa Road (Mrs W. B. Tucker)

◖**Wispering Waters** (Mr & Mrs R. G. Davison) Winston Rd

Low Walworth Hall★⊕ (Mr & Mrs Peter Edwards) 3½ m. NW of Darlington. Bus: 12, Darlington—West Auckland; alight at gate (½ m. drive). Old walled garden; herbaceous borders, shrubs, roses; trout rearing pond. Home-made TEAS. *Adm. 40p, Chd. 15p. Sun. July 6 (2–6)*

● **Raby Castle**★†&⊕ (The Rt Hon. The Lord Barnard) Staindrop, NW of Darlington. 1 m. N of Staindrop on A688 Barnard Castle—Bishop Auckland. Buses: 75 & 77 Darlington—Barnard Castle; 8 Bishop Auckland—Barnard Castle; alight Staindrop, North Lodge, ¼ m. 10-acre gardens; Castle also dates principally C14 with alterations made 1765 & mid-C19; fine pictures & furniture. Collection of horse-drawn carriages & fire engines. TEAS at the Stables. Special terms for parties on application. *Adm. Charges not available at time of going to press. April 5 to June 30, Weds. & Suns.; July 1 to Sept. 30 daily except Sats.; also Easter & Bank Hol. Weekends. Sat.-Tues.; (Castle 2–5; garden & park 1–5.30 last adm. 4.30); also by appt. for parties (Tel. Staindrop 60202)*

St Aidan's College★ (By kind permission of the Principal, Miss Irene Hindmarsh) Durham. 1 m. from City centre. A1050 N towards Durham City; turn W at South End House, where St Aidan's College signposted. St Aidan's College was designed by Sir Basil Spence & the grounds laid out according to a plan by Prof. Brian Hackett about 1966. The maturing garden (3 acres) includes shrub planting, rose beds, a laburnum walk & raised beds; several specimen trees of interest, inc. gingko, liquidamber & cedrus libani, have been planted. From the garden there are unequalled views of Durham Cathedral, Durham City & Durham University Observatory, designed by Anthony Salvin. In porter's lodge are available booklet 15p & postcards 5p; also collecting box for entry fee. *Adm. 20p, Chd. 10p. All year daily (all day)*

Spring Lodge★&⊕ (Col W. I. Watson) Barnard Castle. A66 Scotch Corner–Carlisle, turn off 1st right after Greta Bridge coming from E; or left in Bowes from W. Bus: UAS Darlington—Barnard Castle, alight terminus, ½ m., opp. the Bowes Museum. Medium-sized garden. Roses, good variety herbaceous plants. TEA & biscuits. *Adm. 20p, Chd. 10p. Sun. July 20 (2–7)*

Westholme★†⊕ (Mr & Mrs McBain) Winston, W of Darlington. From A67 Darlington—Barnard Castle, nr Winston turn N on to B6274; Lodge 100 yds beyond old railway crossing. Bus: UAS 75, Darlington—Barnard

CO. DURHAM—continued

Castle; alight Lodge Gates, 100 yds. Medium-sized garden; rhododendrons; flowering shrubs; mixed borders; old fashioned rose garden; lawns. (*Share to Church of England Children's Soc.*) TEA & biscuits. *Adm. 30p, Chd. 10p. Sun. June 1 (2-7)*

Wildwoods* (Mrs Raymond Dobson) Orchard Rd, Rowlands Gill, 10 m. SW of Newcastle-upon-Tyne. From Newcastle take A694; through Rowlands Gill ¼ m. from shopping area take 1st right into Orchard Rd. From Durham take A692 to Ebchester & turn right into A694 approaching Rowlands Gill from W. Medium-sized garden; scree, shrub borders & woodland garden. TEAS. *Adm. 30p, Chd. 10p. Sun. June 29 (2-6)*

DYFED

Hon. County Organisers:
North (Ceredigion District) MRS P. A. LATHAM, Garreg Farm, Glandyfi, Machynlleth SY20 8SS
South (Carmarthenshire, Dinefwr, Pembrokeshire & Preseli Districts) THE LADY JEAN PHILIPPS, Slebech Hall, Haverfordwest

DATES OF OPENING

ALL YEAR by appointment
    PENRALLT FFYNNON,
    nr Newcastle Emlyn
MARCH to OCTOBER
    YNYSHIR HALL HOTEL, nr Machynlleth
APRIL, MAY, AUGUST & SEPTEMBER by appointment
    PANT-YR-HOLIAD, Rhydlewis
APRIL Easter Sunday 6
    BLACKALDERN, Narberth
APRIL Saturday 19
    ‡COSHESTON HALL, Pembroke Dock
    ‡MAYESTON HOUSE, Cosheston
MAY Saturday 3, Sunday 4 & Monday 5
    SLEBECH HALL, nr Haverfordwest
JUNE Sunday 1
    WINNARD'S PERCH, Burton Ferry,
    nr Milford Haven
JUNE Sunday 8
    LLANCEFN MILL, Clynderwen
JUNE Sunday 15
    ‡BRIAR COTTAGE, Ferryside
    ‡GLAN-YR-AFON, Ferryside
JUNE Sunday 22
    CARMAENAU FAWR, Clynderwen
JUNE Saturday 28
    COLBY LODGE, Stepaside, nr Amroth
JUNE Sunday 29
    CARROG, Llanddeiniol, nr Llanrhystyd
    COLBY LODGE, Stepaside, nr Amroth
AUGUST Sunday 3
    BOTANY GARDEN, Penglais Rd,
    Aberystwyth

DESCRIPTIONS OF GARDENS

Blackaldern*⅃ (Mrs A. M. De Quincey) 1 m. from Narberth. From A40 at roundabout (6 m. W of Whitland) turn right & follow signs saying "Crematorium" for 2 m.; drive gate on right. 5½ acres of woodland garden with magnolias, camellias, rhododendrons & other shrubs & flowering trees. (*Share to Crinow Church*) Tea cafés in Narberth. *Adm. 25p, Chd. 10p. Sun. April 6 (2-6)*

Botany Garden* (University College of Wales) Penglais Rd, Aberystwyth. From A44 turn on to A487. Car parking on main College campus on opp. side of A487. 1 m. from Aberystwyth. Local buses stop at gate. Medium- to large-sized garden; botanical collections of herbaceous plants, shrubs & trees; also nursery & general greenhouse collection. NO DOGS. TEA & biscuits. *Adm. 25p. Sun. Aug. 3 (2-6)*

Briar Cottage (Maj. W. K. Buckley) Ferryside 10 m. S of Carmarthen. ½ m. from Ferryside village. 1½ acre garden with shrubs & herbaceous borders; conservatory also shown. Tea at Glan-yr-Afon. *Adm. 25p. Sun. June 15 (2-6.30)*

Carmaenau Fawr⊕ (Mr & Mrs Richard Lewis) Clynderwen, 2 m. N of Narberth. A40 at Penblewin Roundabout turn N towards Clynderwen; go slowly & in 500 yds drive is on right. Charming small garden. TEA & Welshcakes. *Adm. 25p. Sun. June 22 (2-6.30)*

Carrog*⅃⊕ (Mr & Mrs Geoffrey Williams) Llanddeiniol, NE of Llanrhystyd. From A487 Aberystwyth–Aberaeron Rd, 6 m. S of Aberystwyth & approx. 1 m. beyond Blaenplwyf TV mast. Bus stop: 1 m. from house (Aberystwyth–Aberaeron). 5 acres; garden, in setting of mature trees, reclaimed, replanted & maintained entirely by owners; mainly in early years of planting; walled garden; lawns; shrubs; young ornamental trees; pond with bog & water plants; shrub roses. NO DOGS. TEA & biscuits. *Adm. 30p, Chd. 20p. Sun. June 29 (2-6)*

Colby Lodge⅃⊕ (Mr & Mrs I. O. Chance) Stepaside, 6 m. S of Narberth. From A477, on opp. side of rd from signpost to Ludchurch, turn off S into lane downhill. 3 m. NE of Saundersfoot. Walkers can come from Amroth by footpath. Woodland garden with stream; rhododendrons & azaleas; large walled garden. (*Share to Gardeners' Sunday*) TEA & biscuits. *Adm. 30p, Chd. 10p. Sat. & Sun. June 28 & 29 (2-6)*

Cosheston Hall⊕ (Maj. & Mrs R. Ivor Ramsden) 3 m. N of Pembroke. From A477 3 m. E of Pembroke Dock, turn off N for Cosheston. Medium-sized spring garden; daffodils; mature trees and shrubs. *Adm. 25p. Sat. April 19 (2-6)*

Glan-yr-Afon⊕ (Dr Graham Jenkins) In Ferryside village, 10 m. S of Carmarthen. 4-acre garden; terraced gardens & woodland paths overlooking Towy estuary; conservatory. TEAS. *Adm. 25p. Sun. June 15* (2–6.30)

Llancefn Mill* (Mr & Mrs Donald Macdonald) Clynderwen, 6 m. N of Narberth, 12 m. ENE from Haverfordwest. Turn N off A40 at Redstone Cross on to B4313; at Llancefn Cross turn right & follow yellow signs. 10-acres; riverside garden planted since 1967; rhododendrons, azaleas, & many interesting shrubs. TEAS. *Adm. 25p, Chd. 10p. Sun. June 8 (2–6.30)*

' Mayeston House*⊕ (Mr & Mrs George Wheeler) Cosheston, 3 m. N of Pembroke. From A477, 3 m. E of Pembroke Dock, turn off N for Cosheston. 9 acres; avenue of trees; rosebeds, shrubs, specimen trees. Croquet on the lawn. NO DOGS. TEAS. *Adm. 30p. Chd. 15p. Sat. April 19 (2–6)*

Pant-yr-Holiad* (Mr & Mrs G. H. Taylor) Rhydlewis, NW of Llandysul; 12 m. NE of Cardigan. From coast rd take B4334 S towards Rhydlewis; after 1 m. turn left; driveway 2nd on left. Medium-sized garden; garden embraces a well-stocked herb garden of distinctive design, dwarf rhododendrons, rare trees & shrubs in a woodland setting terrain. NO DOGS. *Collecting box. By appt. only during April, May, August & September (Tel. Rhydlewis 493)*

¶Penrallt Ffynnon (Mr R. D. Lord) Cwmcou, 3 m. NW of Newcastle Emlyn. Follow Cwm-cou to Cardigan rd (B4570) up long hill for 1¼ m.; turn right for 150 yds; ignore sharp left-hand bend & bear slightly right along narrow lane for 400 yds. 4½-acre garden of trees & shrubs with good views, made by owner since 1971; camellia hedge, daffodils & other bulbs; Japanese & other cherries; eucalypts; sorbus, acer, malus & willow species; shrub roses, rhododendrons; conifers; many other trees, shrubs, herbaceous plants, some uncommon. NO DOGS. *Collecting box. Garden open, by appt. only, all year. (Tel. Newcastle Emlyn 710654)*

Slebech Hall†⊕ (The Lady Jean Philipps) 6 m. E of Haverfordwest. From Carmarthen via A40, take 1st turn left after Canaston Bridge, signposted The Rhos; drive on left, about ½ m., with 1 white lodge. Bus: Haverfordwest–Tenby or Haverfordwest–Carmarthen; bus stop 3 m. Large garden; picturesque ruins of the Church of St John of Jerusalem in garden. *Adm. 30p, Chd. 10p. Sat., Sun. & Mon. May 3, 4 & 5 (10–6.30)*

Winnard's Perch* (Mr & Mrs A. J. Davies) Burton Ferry, 7 m. E of Milford Haven. At 'Jolly Sailor', Burton Ferry, drive through 'Jolly Sailor' car park & along private rd; cattle grid to garden. 1 acre; small well-filled garden of flowers and foliage of interest to flower arrangers. *Adm. 25p. Sun. June 1 (2–7)*

Ynyshir Hall Hotel*⚲⊕ (Mr & Mrs John Hughes) Eglwysfach, 6 m. SW of Machynlleth. Aberystwyth 13 m. 700 yds from A487; turn off next to Eglwysfach Church. Large garden; shrubs, fine trees, rhododendrons, azaleas & hydrangeas. *Collecting box. March to Oct.* (2–5)

ESSEX

Hon. County Organiser:
MRS N. CLARKE, Birch Hall, Theydon Bois

DATES OF OPENING

ALL YEAR daily except Sundays & Bank Hols
WHITE BARN HOUSE, Elmstead Market
APRIL Sunday 13
BIRCH HALL, Theydon Bois, nr Epping
HYDE HALL, Rettendon, nr Chelmsford
APRIL Sunday 20
TERLING PLACE, Terling, nr Chelmsford
THEYDON PRIORY, Theydon Bois,
nr Epping
APRIL Sunday 27
EAST HALL, Mersea Island, nr Colchester
MAY daily except Sundays & Bank Hols
WHITE BARN HOUSE, Elmstead Market
MAY Sunday 11
LE PAVILLON, Newport
MAY every Wednesday, Thursday & Friday from May 14
SALING HALL, Great Saling
MAY Sunday 25
HYDE HALL, Rettendon, nr Chelmsford
TILTY HILL FARM, Dutton Hill, nr Dunmow
JUNE daily except Sundays
WHITE BARN HOUSE, Elmstead Market
JUNE every Wednesday, Thursday & Friday
SALING HALL, Great Saling
JUNE Sunday 1
GLAZENWOOD, Bradwell, nr Braintree
JUNE Sunday 8
LE PAVILLON, Newport
JUNE Sunday 15
WALTONS, nr Saffron Walden
JUNE Sunday 22
BRIZES PARK, Kelvedon, nr Brentwood
JUNE Sunday 29
HYDE HALL, Rettendon, nr Chelmsford
JULY daily except Sundays
WHITE BARN HOUSE, Elmstead Market
JULY every Wednesday, Thursday & Friday
SALING HALL, Great Saling
JULY Sunday 6
LOFTS HALL, Elmdon, nr Royston
JULY Sunday 13
KILN HOUSE, Great Horkesley,
nr Colchester
LITTLE CHESTERFORD MANOR,
nr Saffron Walden
AUGUST daily except Sundays & Bank Hols
WHITE BARN HOUSE, Elmstead Market

SUSSEX—continued

AUGUST Friday 1
SALING HALL, Great Saling
AUGUST Sunday 3
TERLING PLACE, Terling, nr Chelmsford
AUGUST Sunday 10
MOUNT HALL, Great Horkesley,
nr Colchester
AUGUST Sunday 17
HYDE HALL, Rettendon, nr Chelmsford
SEPTEMBER daily except Sundays
WHITE BARN HOUSE, Elmstead Market
SEPTEMBER every Wednesday, Thursday & Friday
SALING HALL, Great Saling
SEPTEMBER Sunday 21
LITTLE CHESTERFORD MANOR,
nr Saffron Walden
OCTOBER every Wednesday, Thursday & Friday to October 17
SALING HALL, Great Saling
OCTOBER 1980 to MARCH 1981 daily except Sundays & Bank Hols
WHITE BARN HOUSE, Elmstead Market

DESCRIPTIONS OF GARDENS

Birch Hall (Mrs N. Clarke) Theydon Bois, S of Epping, B1393; N of Woodford A104; W of Abridge A113. Informal garden with flowering shrubs; woodland through which visitors may walk (adjoining Epping Forest Deer Sanctuary). It is hoped to also have an exhibition from private collection of veteran & vintage motor cars. (*Share to Epping Forest Centenary Trust*) TEAS. *Adm. 30p, Chd. 10p Sun. April 13 (2–6)*

Brizes Park⚭⊕ (The Hon. Simon Rodney) Kelvedon Hatch, NW of Brentwood. A128 from Brentwood, 4½ m. Bus: EN 339 Brentwood–Harlow; EN 260 Brentwood–Blackmore; alight at Lodge bottom of drive, ¼ m. Medium-sized garden; walled kitchen garden; long walks through woods. Park. C18 house, built 1722 (not shown). TEAS. *Adm. 20p, OAPs & Chd. 5p Sun. June 22 (2–7)*

East Hall⊕ (Mr & Mrs J. H. G. Sunnucks) Mersea Island, 10 m. S of Colchester. From Colchester via B1025; after crossing Strood causeway fork left & after approx. 2¼ m. turn right. House mainly Tudor & adjacent to C13 parish church, associated with the hymn writer the Rev. Sabine Baring Gould, both set within a moated area of approx. 5 acres; lawn, shrubs & young specimen trees. (*Share to The Samaritans, Colchester Branch*) TEAS. *Adm. 30p, OAPs & Chd. 10p. Sun. April 27 (2–5)*

Glazenwood⊕ (Mr & Mrs D. A. H. Baer) Bradwell, 4 m. E of Braintree, ½ m. S of A120 (follow signs). Informal garden recently replanted with roses, shrubs, foliage plants & ground cover; woodland setting; semi-circular avenue of limes; original planting *c.* 1805 by Samuel Curtis of the *Botanical Magazine.* (*Share to Nat. Trust Mid-East Anglia Centre*) Plants for sale. Picnic area. TEA & biscuits. *Adm. 30p, OAPs & Chd 15p. Sun. June 1 (2–6)*

Hyde Hall★⊕ (Mr & Mrs R. H. M. Robinson) Rettendon, 7 m. SE of Chelmsford; 6 m. NE of Wickford. From A130 Chelmsford–Southend, in Rettendon, turn off NE towards East Hanningfield & then into Buckhatch Lane. Varied collection of trees & shrubs, spring bulbs, roses & ornamental greenhouse plants. (*Share to other charities*) TEAS. *Adm. 35p, Chd. 10p. Suns. April 13, May 25, June 29, Aug. 17 (2–7); also by appt. at other times*

Kiln House⊕ (Mr & Mrs G. P. Pattinson) Gt Horkesley, 3 m. N of Colchester. A134 Colchester–Sudbury; turn off at Half Butt Inn, Gt Horkesley. 5-acre garden; lawns, shrubs, herbaceous beds, roses, alpines, water garden. All plants etc clearly labelled. TEAS. *Adm. 30p, OAPs & Chd. 15p. Sun. July 13 (2–6)*

Le Pavillon (H. A. J. Butler Esq) Newport. From A11 turn right at sign N of Newport; from Saffron Walden via B1052 follow signs. Station: Audley End 1½ m. Bus: EN 301 Bishop's Stortford–Saffron Walden; alight Coach & Horses, Newport, 1 m. Medium-sized garden; herbaceous & shrub borders; roses. Tea Paragon Café, Newport. *Adm. 25p. OAPs & Chd. 10p. Sun. May 11 & Sun. June 8 (2–7)*

Little Chesterford Manor★†⊕ (Mr & Mrs W. H. Mason) 3 m. N of Saffron Walden. Via A11, 1 m. N of Littlebury, turn off E at signpost to Little Chesterford. House next to church. Via A130, 3 m. N of Saffron Walden, turn off W at signpost to Little Chesterford. 3½-acre garden; flowering trees & shrubs; herbaceous borders; small pond. C12 manor (not open) is oldest inhabited house in East Anglia. C15 dovecote. Plant stall. NO DOGS. TEAS. *Adm. 35p, Chd. 10p. Sun. July 13 & Sun. Sept. 21 (2–6)*

Lofts Hall⊕ (Maj. & Mrs C. R. Philipson) Elmdon, 8 m. E of Royston, 5 m. W of Saffron Walden off B1039. Large garden; roses, herbaceous & shrub border, kitchen garden, greenhouses. Lake & C16 carp pond; early C17 dovecote (reputedly 2nd largest in England). Stud farm & herd of pedigree Charolais cattle on view. (*Share to Gardeners' Sunday*) TEAS. *Adm. 30p, Chd. 10p. Sun. July 6 (2–7)*

¶Mount Hall (Mr & Mrs Edward Carbutt) Great Horkesley, 4½ m. N of Colchester. A134 to Sudbury, through village & turn off left at London Rd; left at turning to West Bergholt; 2nd drive on left. 3-acre garden; herbaceous & shrub borders; attractive walled garden & pool. Plants for sale. NO DOGS. TEAS. *Adm. 30p, Chd. 15p. Sun. Aug. 10 (2–7)*

Saling Hall★†⚭⊕ (Mr & Mrs Hugh Johnson) Great Saling, 6 m. NW of Braintree. A120, mid-way between Braintree & Dunmow turn off N at the Saling Oak. Large garden; walled garden dated 1698; small park with fine trees; extensive new collection of unusual plants with emphasis on trees; water gardens. (*Share to St James' Church, Gt. Saling*) NO DOGS please. *Adm. 30p, Chd. 15p. May 14—Aug. 1 & Sept. 3—Oct. 17 every Wed., Thurs. & Fri. (2—5); parties other days by arrangement*

Terling Place*†⅋ (The Lord Rayleigh) Terling, NE of Chelmsford. Between A12 & A131. Spring flowering bulbs & shrubs. Formal garden of clipped yew, roses, many coniferous trees. House built 1772; wings added 1818. Architect: John Johnson. (*Share to Cancer Research Fund.*) *Adm. 25p. Chd. 10p. Sun. April 20 & Sun. Aug. 3 (2—7)*

Theydon Priory*⅋ (Sir William Keswick) Theydon Bois, S of Epping. N of A113. Station: Theydon Bois (Tube). Bus: LT 250 Hornchurch—Romford—Epping; alight Coopersale Lane. Bulbs, flowering trees, shrubs, walled garden. Dogs on leads. *Adm. 25p, OAPs & Chd. 15p. Sun. April 20 (2—6)*

Tilty Hill Farm*⊕ (Mr & Mrs F. E. Collinson) Duton Hill, 4 m. N of Dunmow. A130, midway between Dunmow & Thaxted, turn off at Duton Hill through village, turn right, follow signs. Medium-sized garden; many conifers & plants grown from seeds; roses, shrubs; C17 beeboles. Extensive views of surrounding countryside. Semi-tropical greenhouse. (*Share to Riding for the Disabled Assn.*) NO DOGS. TEA & biscuits. *Adm. 25p, OAPs & Chd. 15p. Sun. May 25 (2—7)*

Waltons*⊕ (E. H. Vestey Esq) Ashdon, 4 m. NE of Saffron Walden. ½ m. E of Saffron Walden—Bartlow Rd. Herbaceous borders; roses, flowering shrubs; walled kitchen garden. Tea Saffron Walden. *Adm. 30p, OAPs & Chd. 15p. Sun. June 15 (2—6)*

White Barn House*⊕ (Mrs Beth Chatto) Elmstead Market, 4 m. E of Colchester. Leave Colchester on A133 for Clacton through Elmstead Market; in ¼ m. signs on right. 3 acres of attractively landscaped garden with many unusual plants, shown in wide range of conditions from hot & dry to water garden. Adjacent nursery open. NO DOGS. Parties by arrangement. *Adm. 30p, Chd. free. All year daily, except Suns. & Bank Hols. (9—5)*

GLAMORGANS

Hon. County Organisers:

(Mid & South) LT-COL & MRS ROY E. HORLEY, Llys-y-Coed, Church Rd, Pentyrch, Mid Glamorgan, CF4 8QF

(West) MRS R. C. HASTIE, Upper Hareslade, Bishopston, Swansea, West Glamorgan

DATES OF OPENING

APRIL Sunday 27
  COEDARGRAIG, Newton Porthcawl

MAY Sunday 4
  EWENNY PRIORY, Ewenny, Bridgend
MAY Monday 5 (Bank Hol)
  MERTHYR MAWR HOUSE, nr Bridgend
MAY Sunday 11
  RHOOSE FARM HOUSE, Rhoose, nr Barry
JUNE Saturday 7
  4 & 5 THE GROVE, Mumbles, nr Swansea
JUNE Sunday 8
  COEDARHYDYGLYN, nr Cardiff
JUNE Sunday 15
  LLANDAFF GARDENS, Cardiff
JULY Sunday 6
  AILSA CRAIG, Caswell Bay, nr Swansea, West Glam.
  THE GRANGE, St Brides-super-Ely, nr Cardiff
JULY Sunday 20 & AUGUST Sunday 3
  DUMGOYNE, 90 Heol Isaf, Radyr
AUGUST Sunday 10
  RHOOSE FARM HOUSE, Rhoose, nr Barry

DESCRIPTIONS OF GARDENS

Ailsa Craig (Mr & Mrs K. C. Austin Bailey) Caswell Bay, approx. 7 m. SW of Swansea; on district rd between Bishopston & Caswell Bay. 2 acres; formal garden with croquet lawn, swimming pool, & vegetable garden. Fine view of Caswell Bay & Channel. NO DOGS. Plant & produce stall. *Adm. 25p, Chd. 10p. Sun. July 6 (2—6)*

Coedargraig (Sir Leslie Joseph) Newton, Porthcawl. Car park off main rd. Bus: Bridgend—Porthcawl, alight gates. Ornamental plants with indigenous trees & shrubs; herbaceous borders; rose, rock, water, vegetable & fruit gardens. (*Share to Kenfig Hill & District Spastics Society*) TEAS available. *Adm. 30p, Chd. 15p, Cars 20p. Sun. April 27 (2—7)*

Coedarhydyglyn⅋ (Sir Cennydd & Lady Traherne) 5 m. W of Cardiff. Bus: Western Welsh, Cardiff—Cowbridge, alight gates. Natural terrain, pleasant situation. Lawns, flowering shrubs, view, Japanese garden, fine trees. (*Share to The Samaritans, Cardiff Branch*) TEA available. *Adm. 25p. Sun. June 8 (2.30—6.30)*

Dumgoyne (Mr & Mrs Hubert Jackson) 90 Heol Isaf, Radyr. A4119 Cardiff—Llantrisant Rd; 2 m. W of Llandaff turn right on to B4262 for Radyr. Station: Radyr (trains from Queen St, Cardiff). Rhondda buses: alight at Radyr turning. Small, immaculate, Chelsea-inspired suburban garden; largely bedded out; glasshouse with interesting plants. (*Share to Y.M.C.A.*) Plants for sale (from May). Collecting box. *Sun. July 20 & Sun. Aug. 3 (2—5.30)*

Ewenny Priory †⊕ (R. C. Q. Picton Turbervill Esq) Ewenny, 2 m. S of Bridgend. Bus: Bridgend—Ogmore, alight Ewenny Bridge, ½ m. Medium-sized garden. Old walled priory dating from 1137 (house not shown). (*Share to The National Trust*) Picnic area available. *Adm. 25p. Sun. May 4 (2-7)*

The Grange (Mr & Mrs John Cory) St Brides-super-Ely, W of Cardiff. Between A48 & A4119. Medium-sized garden; roses, trees, flowering shrubs. TEAS available. *Adm. 20p. Sun. July 6 (2-7)*

'4 & 5 The Grove (Mrs M. P. Burgess-James) Mumbles, 5 m. SW of Swansea. In Mumbles, to the rear of Queen's Rd & its junction with Langland Rd. Example of how a small hillside garden can be terraced in an ornamental manner, inc. a small water garden. Excellent view of Swansea Bay. NO DOGS. TEAS. *Adm. 30p, Chd. 10p. Sat. June 7 (12-7)*

Llandaff Gardens. 2 m. from centre of Cardiff via A4119 towards Llantrisant. Bus: Cardiff Corpn from Cardiff; Rhondda & Western Welsh trom Valleys; alight Malsters Arms. The following 4 gardens will be open. TEA at Llys Esgob. *Combined charge 30p. Sun. June 15 (2-6)*

> **The Clock House** (Prof. & Mrs Bryan Hibbard) Cathedral Close. Small walled garden with fine old trees; wide variety of shrubs & plants & an important collection of roses (old, shrub & species). (*Share to Friends of Llandaff Cathedral*)
>
> **Llys Esgob** (The Rt Revd The Bishop of Llandaff) The Cathedral Green. (*Share to Church in Wales Partners in Mission Appeal*) TEAS available
>
> **Penpentre** (Dr & Mrs Michael Richards) Bridge St. Medium-sized walled garden; interesting trees, shrubs & roses; kitchen garden. (*Share to Friends of Llandaff Cathedral*)
>
> **Saint Michael's Theological College** (The Revd John Hughes, Warden, & the Council of St Michael's College) Cardiff Rd. The garden & fine College Chapel, designed by the late George Pace, will be open. (*Share to Vietnam Refugee Fund*)

Merthyr Mawr House† (Mr & Mrs Murray McLaggan) 2 m. SW of Bridgend. Station: Bridgend. Bus: Bridgend-Island Farm Camp ½ m. Flowering shrubs, bulbs, wood garden. Chapel ruin c. 1400 on site of Iron Age fort. (*Share to British Red Cross (Mid-Glamorgan Branch)*). Refreshments available. *Adm. 25p, Mon. May 5 (2-6)*

' Rhoose Farm House (Prof. A. L. Cochrane) Rhoose, Barry. Nr Y.M.C.A. Coleg-y-Fro, Rhoose. Buses from Cardiff, Barry & Llantwrt Major to Rhoose. B4265 Barry-Bridgend rd. Large informal garden with shrubs, roses, herbaceous plants & an important scree garden. Sculpture by Barbara Hepworth & Peter Nicholas (sculpture gallery of Peter Nicholas adjoining may also be seen). House partly C17

& C18; 2 Victorian rooms shown. (*Share to Rhoose & Penmark Civic Trust*) TEAS. *Adm. 30p, Sun. May 11 & Sun. Aug. 10 (2.30-6)*

GLOUCESTERSHIRE & NORTH AVON

Hon. County Organiser:
MRS R. E. WAINWRIGHT, 42 Cecily Hill, Cirencester GL7 2EF
Assistant Hon. County Organisers:
T. E BRYANT, Esq, 49 Oxbutts Park, Woodmancote, Cheltenham, GL52 4HW; MRS T. F. HEWER, Vine House, Henbury, Bristol, BS10 7AD; MRS JAMES LEES-MILNE, Essex House, Badminton GL9 1DD; MRS J. F. MOORE, Grange Cottage, Blockley, Moreton-in-Marsh

Hon. County Auditor:
H. J. SHAVE, Esq, ACCA (Brading & Co.), 31 Castle St, Cirencester

DATES OF OPENING

MARCH by appointment
> BROOK COTTAGE (ALPINE), nr Cheltenham
> THE LEVEL, nr Lydney
> ST FRANCIS, Minchinhampton
> VINE HOUSE, Henbury, Bristol
> WESTEND HOUSE, Wickwar
> YEW TREE COTTAGE, Ampney St Mary

MARCH every Wednesday
> BARNSLEY HOUSE, nr Cirencester

MARCH every Monday
> THE OLD MANOR, Twyning

MARCH Sunday 23
> YEW TREE COTTAGE, Ampney St Mary

APRIL by appointment
> BROOK COTTAGE (ALPINE), nr Cheltenham
> HILL HOUSE, Wickwar
> DEAN LODGE, Iron Acton
> LASBOROUGH MANOR, nr Tetbury
> THE LEVEL, nr Lydney
> ST FRANCIS, Minchinhampton
> VINE HOUSE, Henbury, Bristol
> WESTEND HOUSE, Wickwar
> YEW TREE COTTAGE, Ampney St Mary

APRIL every Wednesday
> BARNSLEY HOUSE, nr Cirencester

APRIL every Sunday, Wednesday & Thursday & Easter Monday
> KIFTSGATE COURT, nr Chipping Campden

APRIL every Monday
> THE OLD MANOR, Twyning

APRIL Easter Sunday 6
> FOSSEBRIDGE MANOR, nr Northleach
> YEW TREE COTTAGE, Ampney St Mary

APRIL Easter Monday 7
> MISARDEN PARK, nr Stroud
> YEW TREE COTTAGE, Ampney St Mary

APRIL Easter Monday 7 & Fridays April 11, 18 & 25
> SEZINCOTE, nr Bourton-on-the-Hill

APRIL Saturday 12
> THE OLD MANOR, Twyning

APRIL Saturday 19
EASTINGTON GARDENS, nr Northleach
APRIL Sunday 20
ABBOTSWOOD, nr Stow-on-the-Wold
EASTINGTON GARDENS, nr Northleach
CHURCH HOUSE, Lechlade
WESTONBIRT SCHOOL, nr Tetbury
APRIL Sunday 27
WILLERSEY HOUSE, nr Broadway
‡SOUTHROP GARDENS, nr Lechlade
‡QUENINGTON GARDENS, nr Fairford
KEMBLE GARDENS, nr Cirencester
‡‡HODGES BARN, Shipton Moyne
‡‡EASTON GREY HOUSE (Wiltshire),
nr Malmsebury
APRIL Monday 28
WILLERSEY HOUSE, nr Broadway
MAY by appointment
BROOK COTTAGE (ALPINE),
nr Cheltenham
DEAN LODGE, Iron Acton
HILL HOUSE, Wickwar
LASBOROUGH MANOR, nr Tetbury
THE LEVEL, nr Lydney
ST FRANCIS, Minchinhampton
VINE HOUSE, Henbury, Bristol
WESTEND HOUSE, Wickwar
YEW TREE COTTAGE, Ampney St Mary
MAY every Wednesday
BARNSLEY HOUSE, nr Cirencester
MAY every Friday and Bank Holiday
Mons. May 5 & 26
SEZINCOTE, nr Bourton-on-the-Hill
MAY every Sunday, Wednesday,
Thursday & Bank Holiday Mondays
May 5 & 26
KIFTSGATE COURT, nr Chipping Campden
MAY every Monday
THE OLD MANOR, Twyning
MAY Sunday 4
BLOCKLEY GARDENS
STANWAY HOUSE, nr Winchcombe
BARNSLEY HOUSE, nr Cirencester
YEW TREE COTTAGE, Ampney St Mary
MAY Wednesday 7 & Thursday 8
BAGPATH COURT, nr Tetbury
MAY Saturday 10
BATSFORD PARK, nr Moreton-in-Marsh
THE OLD MANOR, Twyning
MAY Sunday 11
HIDCOTE MANOR, nr Chipping Campden
BATSFORD PARK, nr Moreton-in-Marsh
MAY Saturday 17
SEVERN VIEW (ALPINE), nr Thornbury
(by appt. only)
MAY Sunday 18
LITTLE BARROW, between Moreton &
Stow
GLOUCESTERSHIRE COLLEGE OF
AGRICULTURE, Hartpury
SEVERN VIEW (ALPINE), nr Thornbury
(by appt. only)
MAY Saturday 24
KIFTSGATE COURT, nr Chipping Campden
EASTINGTON GARDENS, nr Northleach

MAY Sunday 25
EASTINGTON GARDENS,
nr Northleach
ALGARS MANOR, Iron Acton
VINE HOUSE, Henbury, Bristol
MAY Monday 26 (Bank Hol.)
MISARDEN PARK, nr Stroud
ALGARS MANOR, Iron Acton
VINE HOUSE, Henbury, Bristol
JUNE by appointment
BROOK COTTAGE (ALPINE),
nr Cheltenham
HILL HOUSE, Wickwar
DEAN LODGE, Iron Acton
LASBOROUGH MANOR, nr Tetbury
THE LEVEL, nr Lydney
ST FRANCIS, Minchinhampton
VINE HOUSE, Henbury, Bristol
WESTEND HOUSE, Wickwar
YEW TREE COTTAGE, Ampney St Mary
JUNE every Wednesday
BARNSLEY HOUSE, nr Cirencester
JUNE every Friday
SEZINCOTE, nr Bourton-on-the-Hill
JUNE every Monday
THE OLD MANOR, Twyning
JUNE every Sunday, Wednesday &
Thursday
KIFTSGATE COURT, nr Chipping Campden
JUNE Sunday 1
SOUTHAM GARDENS, nr Cheltenham
BARNSLEY HOUSE, nr Cirencester
SOUTHROP GARDENS, nr Lechlade
JUNE Monday 2
SOUTHAM GARDENS, nr Cheltenham
JUNE Sunday 8
9 SANKEY GROVE (ALPINE),
Moreton-in-Marsh
STANWAY HOUSE, nr Winchcombe
YEW TREE COTTAGE, Ampney St Mary
JUNE Saturday 14
THE OLD MANOR, Twyning
JUNE Sunday 15
STOWELL PARK, nr Northleach
THE CHESTNUTS, nr Minchinhampton
JUNE Saturday 21
STANDISH PARK & MARTINS,
nr Stonehouse
JUNE Sunday 22
HIDCOTE VALE, nr Chipping Campden
RODMARTON MANOR, between
Cirencester & Tetbury
STANDISH PARK & MARTINS,
nr Stonehouse
STANCOMBE PARK, nr Dursley
LYEGROVE, nr Badminton
JUNE Monday 23
STANCOMBE PARK, nr Dursley
JUNE Saturday 28
KIFTSGATE COURT, nr Chipping Campden
‡BRADLEY COURT, nr Wotton-under-Edge
‡ALDERLEY GRANGE,
nr Wotton-under-Edge
‡TALBOT END HOUSE,
nr Wotton-under-Edge
‡HILL HOUSE, Wickwar

GLOUCESTERSHIRE & NORTH AVON—continued

JUNE Sunday 29
STANTON, nr Broadway
THE GLEBE HOUSE, Coln Rogers
THE CROFT HOUSE, Fairford
KEMBLE GARDENS, nr Cirencester
‡BRADLEY COURT, nr Wotton-under-Edge
‡TALBOT END HOUSE,
    nr Wotton-under-Edge
BADMINTON GARDENS

JUNE Monday 30
THE CROFT HOUSE, Fairford
KEMBLE GARDENS, nr Cirencester
BADMINTON GARDENS (Dower House
    & Essex House only)

JULY by appointment
ADSETT COURT, Wesbury-on-Severn
BROOK COTTAGE (ALPINE),
    nr Cheltenham
DEAN LODGE, Iron Acton
HILL HOUSE, Wickwar
LASBOROUGH MANOR, nr Tetbury
THE LEVEL, nr Lydney
ST FRANCIS, Minchinhampton
VINE HOUSE, Henbury, Bristol
WESTEND HOUSE, Wickwar
YEW TREE COTTAGE, Ampney St Mary

JULY every Wednesday
BARNSLEY HOUSE, nr Cirencester

JULY every Friday
SEZINCOTE, nr Bourton-on-the-Hill

JULY every Monday
THE OLD MANOR, Twyning

JULY every Sunday, Wednesday & Thursday
KIFTSGATE COURT, nr Chipping Campden

JULY Saturday 5
THE LEVEL, nr Lydney

JULY Sunday 6
LITTLE BARROW, between Moreton &
    Stow
‡SUDELEY LODGE, nr Winchcombe
‡RUSHBURY HOUSE, nr Winchcombe
LOWER DEAN GARDENS, nr Northleach
WITHINGTON GARDENS,
    nr Andoversford
THE LEVEL, nr Lydney
‡‡BARNSLEY HOUSE, nr Cirencester
‡‡CERNEY HOUSE, nr Cirencester
‡‡‡BEVERSTON CASTLE, nr Tetbury
‡‡‡HODGES BARN, Shipton Moyne
‡‡‡‡KINGSMEAD, Didmarton
‡‡‡‡ALDERLEY GRANGE, nr Wotton-
    under-Edge
HUNTS COURT, nr Dursley

JULY Monday 7
LITTLE BARROW, between Moreton &
    Stow
‡BEVERSTON CASTLE, nr Tetbury
‡HODGES BARN, Shipton Moyne

JULY Saturday 12
KIFTSGATE COURT, nr Chipping Campden
THE OLD MANOR, Twyning

JULY Sunday 13
HIDCOTE VALE, nr Chipping Campden
WILLERSEY HOUSE, nr Broadway
FOSSEBRIDGE MANOR, Coln St Denys
‡WESTBURY COURT, Westbury-on-Severn
‡ADSETT COURT, nr Westbury-on-Severn
YEW TREE COTTAGE, Ampney St Mary
‡‡COTSWOLD FARM, nr Cirencester
‡‡DUNTISBOURNE VALLEY GARDENS,
    nr Cirencester
‡‡‡BISLEY GARDENS
‡‡‡SYDENHAMS, nr Bisley
DEAN LODGE, Iron Acton

JULY Monday 14
WILLERSEY HOUSE, nr Broadway
SYDENHAMS, nr Bisley
DEAN LODGE, Iron Acton

JULY Sunday 20
‡BOURTON-ON-THE-HILL GARDENS,
    nr Moreton-in-Marsh
‡SEZINCOTE, nr Bourton-on-the-Hill
WITCOMBE PARK, nr Gloucester
ILSOM, nr Tetbury
SPRINGFIELD BARN, Upton Cheyney

JULY Sunday 27 & Monday 28
ST FRANCIS, Minchinhampton

AUGUST by appointment
ADSETT COURT, nr Westbury-on-Severn
BROOK COTTAGE (ALPINE), nr
    nr Cheltenham
DEAN LODGE, Iron Acton
HILL HOUSE, Wickwar
LASBOROUGH MANOR, nr Tetbury
THE LEVEL, nr Lydney
ST FRANCIS, Minchinhampton
VINE HOUSE, Henbury, Bristol
WESTEND HOUSE, Wickwar
YEW TREE COTTAGE, Ampney St Mary

AUGUST every Wednesday
BARNSLEY HOUSE, nr Cirencester

AUGUST every Friday & Bank Holiday Monday
SEZINCOTE, nr Bourton-on-the-Hill

AUGUST every Monday
THE OLD MANOR, Twyning

AUGUST every Sunday, Wednesday & Thursday & Bank Holiday Monday
KIFTSGATE COURT, nr Chipping Campden

AUGUST Sunday 3
WESTONBIRT SCHOOL, nr Tetbury

AUGUST Saturday 9
THE OLD MANOR, Twyning

AUGUST Sunday 10 & Sunday 17
42 CECILY HILL, Cirencester

AUGUST Sunday 24
THE GLEBE HOUSE, Coln Rogers
YEW TREE COTTAGE, Ampney St Mary

AUGUST Monday 25 (Bank Hol.)
CAMPDEN HOUSE, nr Chipping Campden

AUGUST Saturday 30
EASTINGTON GARDENS, nr Northleach

AUGUST Sunday 31
EASTINGTON GARDENS, nr Northleach
BARTON MILL HOUSE, Cirencester

SEPTEMBER by appointment
BROOK COTTAGE (ALPINE), nr Cheltenham
DEAN LODGE, Iron Acton
HILL HOUSE, Wickwar
LASBOROUGH MANOR, nr Tetbury
THE LEVEL, nr Lydney
ST FRANCIS, Minchinhampton
VINE HOUSE, Henbury, Bristol
WESTEND HOUSE, Wickwar
YEW TREE COTTAGE, Ampney St Mary

SEPTEMBER every Wednesday
BARNSLEY HOUSE, nr Cirencester

SEPTEMBER every Friday
SEZINCOTE, nr Bourton-on-the-Hill

SEPTEMBER every Monday
THE OLD MANOR, Twyning

SEPTEMBER every Sunday, Wednesday & Thursday
KIFTSGATE COURT, nr Chipping Campden

SEPTEMBER Saturday 6
KIFTSGATE COURT, nr Chipping Campden

SEPTEMBER Sunday 7
HYAM & THE LAMMAS, Minchinhampton
WESTONBIRT SCHOOL, nr Tetbury

SEPTEMBER Sunday 14
HIDCOTE VALE, nr Chipping Campden

SEPTEMBER Sunday 21
SNOWSHILL MANOR, nr Broadway

OCTOBER by appointment
BROOK COTTAGE (ALPINE), nr Cheltenham
THE LEVEL, nr Lydney
ST FRANCIS, Minchinhampton
VINE HOUSE, Henbury, Bristol
WESTEND HOUSE, Wickwar
YEW TREE COTTAGE, Ampney St Mary

OCTOBER every Wednesday
BARNSLEY HOUSE, nr Cirencester

OCTOBER every Monday
THE OLD MANOR, Twyning

NOVEMBER 1980 to MARCH 1981 by appointment
THE LEVEL, nr Lydney
ST FRANCIS, Minchinhampton
VINE HOUSE, Henbury, Bristol
WESTEND HOUSE, Wickwar
YEW TREE COTTAGE, Ampney St Mary

NOVEMBER 1980 to MARCH 1981 every Wednesday
BARNSLEY HOUSE, nr Cirencester

DESCRIPTIONS OF GARDENS

Abbotswood*♿⊕ (Dikler Farming Co.) 1 m. W of Stow-on-the-Wold. Bus: Pulhams from Cheltenham, alight Lower Swell, ¼ m. Beautiful & extensive heather, stream & alpine gardens; massed plantings of spring bulbs & flowers; rhododendrons, flowering shrubs, specimen trees; extensive herbaceous borders, roses & formal gardens; fine example of garden landscape. Buses not allowed inside grounds. TEA & biscuits. Car park free. *Adm. 50p, Chd. 20p. Sun. April 20* (2–6)

Adsett Court♿⊕ (Adsett Court Assn) Westbury on Severn, 8 m. SW of Gloucester. 1 m. off A38 Gloucester–Chepstow route turn towards Northwood Green. 3½-acre garden; formal herbaceous borders enclosed by series of hedges; large lawns & mature trees. TEAS. *Adm. 25p, Chd. 10p. Sun. July 13* (2–6)*; also July & August by appt.*

Alderley Grange*†♿ (Mr Guy & The Hon. Mrs Acloque) Alderley, 2 m. S of Wotton-under-Edge. Turn NW off A46, Bath–Stroud Rd, at Dunkirk. (2 m. equidistant from Hawkesbury Upton & Wotton-under-Edge.) Walled garden with fine old trees & shrub roses; herb garden. Jacobean house (not open) with classical facade. NO DOGS. Tea Hill House (June 28) & Kingsmead (July 6). (*Share to Glos. Trust for Nature Conservation*). *Adm. 25p, Chd. 10p Sat. June 28 & Sun. July 6* (2–6)

Algars Manor†♿ (John M. Naish Esq) Iron Acton, N of Bristol. 3 m. Yate, Sodbury. Turn S off Iron Acton bypass B4059, past village green, 200 yds, then over level crossing (Station Rd). 3 acres; woodland garden beside R. Frome; millstream; native plants mixed with azaleas, rhododendrons, camellias, magnolias, eucalyptus. Picnic area (with tree climbing for children) just beyond garden. Early Jacobean house (not open) & old barn. Plants for sale. DOGS on leads. TEA in barn. (*Share to British Digestive Foundation* (*Bristol Branch*)). *Adm. 30p, Chd. 10p. Sun. & Mon. May 25 & 26* (12–6)

Alpine Gardens. Most alpine gardens are small & able to accommodate only a limited number of visitors at one time. As they are of especial interest to the growing number of alpine garden enthusiasts they are listed together here:

Brook Cottage (Miss G. Wright) Sevenhampton, 7 m. E of Cheltenham. From A40 turn N on to Stow Rd (A436) at Andoversford traffic lights; follow Sevenhampton signs (2 m.). Very small garden with fast-flowing brook, largely alpines, bulbs & waterside plants. Old Cotswold cottage (scheduled) in beautiful surroundings. Nearby Church garden, well known particularly for rose & alpine beds described in *Country Life, The Countryman* & many guide books. Plants for sale if available. (*Share to Glos. Trust for Nature Conservation*). *Adm. 25p. Garden open by appt. only March to Oct.* (*Tel. Andoversford 493*)

9 Sankey Grove* (Mr & Mrs R. Haywood) Moreton-in-Marsh. ¼ m. from town centre; from Fosseway (A429) turn into Fosseway Ave; then 2nd left into Sankey Grove. Small specialist's garden of alpines, dwarf conifers & unusual plants; also alpine house. NO CHILDREN or DOGS. Tea Moreton-in-Marsh (Cotswold Café), (*Share to Glos. Trust for Nature Conservation*). *Adm. 25p. Sun. June 8* (2–6)

Severn View* (Mr & Mrs Eric Hilton) Grovesend, 1½ m. SE of Thornbury. On A38 on Bristol side of Severn Vale Nurseries. 1-acre garden of special interest to the rock garden enthusiast, a considerable section being devoted to growing alpine plants, many of them rare in cultivation. Plants for sale. Fine views of the Severn Valley. NO DOGS please. *(Share to Glos. Trust for Nature Conservation). Adm. 30p. Garden open by appt. only on Sat. & Sun. May 17 & 18 (Tel. Thornbury 413343) (2–7)*

Yew Tree Cottage (see p. 46)

Badminton Gardens. 5 m. E of Chipping Sodbury. The following 4 gardens will be open. Home-made TEAS Badminton House Orangery. *(Share to Glos. Trust for Nature Conservation). Combined charge for 4 gardens 80p, Chd. 10p. Sun. June 29 (2–6)*

Badminton House †⅃⊕ (The Duke & Duchess of Beaufort) Ornamental grounds in classical setting; orangery. NO DOGS.

The Dower House* (The Lady Caroline Somerset) Large, formal garden with informal planting; ornamental kitchen garden; herb garden. Dogs on leads only. *Also open Mon. June 30 (2–6) Collecting box (No tea)*

Essex House (Mr & Mrs J. Lees-Milne) Small garden redesigned & planted since 1975 by present owners. NO DOGS. *Also open Mon. June 30 (2–6) Collecting box (No tea)*

The Old Vicarage (Col & Mrs Guinness) Pretty walled garden in picturesque setting. NO DOGS

Bagpath Court⊕ (Mr & Mrs S. L. Lloyd) Kingscote, 6 m. W of Tetbury. From A4135 Tetbury–Dursley turn S at Hunters Hall Inn, Kingscote & on 1 m. Small to medium-sized garden largely replanted & laid out since 1962; planned for easy upkeep; lily pool & rock garden; shrubs; lovely situation in valley. *(Share to Glos. Trust for Nature Conservation). Adm. 25p, Chd. free. Wed. & Thurs. May 7 & 8 (2–30.–6.30)*

● **Barnsley House***†⅃⊕ (Mr & Mrs David Verey) 4 m. NE of Cirencester on Burford Rd A433. Old garden, altered since 1962; interesting collection of shrubs & trees; ground cover; herbaceous borders; pond garden; laburnum walk; knot garden & herb garden; kitchen garden laid out in formal style; C18 summer-houses. Plants for sale. C17 house (not open). Tea Greyhound Farm House, Barnsley (parties by appt. Tel. Bibury 406). *Adm. 40p, OAPs 30p, Chd. free. All year every Wed. (10–6); also Suns. May 4, June 1, July 6 (2–7)*

Barton Mill House (Mrs Mullings) Barton Lane, Gloucester St, Cirencester. Turn left up Barton Lane at N end of Gloucester St. Bus:

B 561, 562 from Cheltenham. Medium-sized garden with river & streams; water garden & wildfowl; herbaceous, dahlias & roses, Old Cotswold mill-house. Gifts for sale. TEAS (home-made cakes) 50p. *Adm. garden & part house 30p, Chd. 10p. Sun. Aug. 31 (2.30–6.30)*

Batsford Park †⅃ (Batsford Estates Company) 2 m. NW of Moreton-in-March, A44/A429 intersection. Nearest bus & train Moreton-in-Marsh. Arboretum; over 900 named varieties of trees (some rare) & shrubs; flowering cherries & bulbs; beautiful views from Cotswold escarpment. NO DOGS. Tea Moreton-in-Marsh (Cotswold Café). *(Share to Guide Dogs for the Blind). Adm. 65p, School Chd. 20p. △Sat. & Sun. May 10 & 11 (2–6)*

Beverston Castle †⊕ (Maj. & Mrs L. Rook) 1½ m. W of Tetbury on A4135. Herbaceous & shrub borders. C17 house attached to C12–15 castle ruin. Plants for sale. TEAS (July 6 only). *(Share to Riding for the Disabled). Adm. 25p. Sun. & Mon. July 6 & 7 (2–6)*

Bisley Gardens. 4 m. NE of Stroud. Following 3 gardens open. TEAS. *Combined charge 50p, Chd. free. Sun. July 13 (2–6.30)*

Buckhorn House (Mr & Mrs G. T. St J. Sanders) Small garden made in 1963 by present owners. Unusual plants

Jaynes Court (Mr & Mrs Gordon W. Clarry) Large garden with lawns, herbaceous borders, shrubs & kitchen garden. C18 dovecote & cockpit

The Wells Cottage (Mr & Mrs Richard Flint) Close to historic wells. 1-acre "family" garden. Herbaceous borders, shrubs & vegetables

Blockley Gardens,⊕ 4 m. NW of Moreton-in-Marsh. A44 Moreton-Broadway; turning E to Blockley clearly signed. The following 5 gardens will be open. TEAS by Blockley WI. *(Share to Blockley Church Roof Restoration Fund). Combined charge 80p, Chd. 20p. Sun. May 4 (2–6)*

The Old Silk Mill (Sir Robert & Lady Lusty)
Sleepy Hollow (Mrs O. Dicks) originally 1 large garden now divided into 2. Bulbs, trees & shrubs; trout streams & mill race
The Old Mill (Dr & Mrs Shackleton Bailey) Mill pond & water garden
Malvern Mill (Mr & Mrs Robert Cook) Medium-sized garden beside stream with bulbs & spring flowers.
¶**The Old Quarry** (A. T. Hesmondhalgh Esq) On edge of village on Broadway Rd. 1-acre landscaped garden in old quarry with grass walks & lovely views

Bourton-on-the-Hill Gardens, 1½ m. W of Moreton-in-Marsh on A44 Moreton–Broadway. Turn into car park at 30 mph limit sign at bottom of hill. The following 2 gardens will be open. *(Share to Glos. Trust for Nature Conser-*

vation). NO DOGS. Tea Sezincote. *Combined charge 40p, Chd. free. Sun. July 20 (2–6)*

¶**Bourton House** † (Mr & Mrs E. M. Watson-Smyth) 12-acre garden includes white rose garden & Victorian basket from the Great Exhibition. Grade II Queen Anne mansion with C16 cottages & brew house; tithe barn dated 1549 is an ancient monument. Visitors should leave garden via long Church Walk taking turn to the Manor House

¶**Manor House**⊕ (Mr & Mrs John Christie-Miller) 1½-acre hillside garden; wild garden with specie roses & shrubs. Magnificent views

Bradley Court † (Mr & Mrs A. Garnett) Bradley Green, Wotton-under-Edge. Take Dursley Rd out of Wotton; fork left ½ m. from war memorial for Bradley Green; house is on right-hand side. 3-acre garden re-made by present owners since 1970; herbaceous plants & shrubs; very original planting; secret garden. Elizabethan house (not open). Queen Anne gazebo; contemporary grotto. NO DOGS. Tea Wotton; café by war memorial or Hill House (June 28) or Badminton House (June 29). *(Share to N.S.P.C.C.). Adm. 25p, Chd. 10p. Sat. & Sun. June 28 & 29 (2–6)*

Broughton Poggs & Filkins Gardens
See Oxfordshire

¶**Campden House** (Mr & Mrs Philip Smith) 2 m. SW of Chipping Campden. Drive entrance on Chipping Campden–Weston Sub-Edge rd, about ¼ m. SW of Campden. 2-acre walled garden with mixed borders; rose walk; fine parkland. Manor house with fine C17 tithe barn. Tea Bantam Tea Rooms (parties, please book: Tel. 0386 840386). *Adm. 30p, Chd. under 10 free. Mon. Aug. 25 (2–6)*

42 Cecily Hill⊕ (Mr & Mrs Robin Wainwright) Cirencester. On W side of Cirencester at gates into Park. Medium-sized town garden with good walls; clematis a speciality; roses & herbaceous border, shrubs, pond & rock garden. NO DOGS. Tea The Mad Hatter, 30 Castle St. *Adm. 25p, Chd. free. Suns. Aug. 10 & 17 (2–6)*

Cerney House (Mr & Mrs C. P. Francis) North Cerney. 4 m. N of Cirencester on A435 Cheltenham rd; turn W at church & ½ m. up hill. Large garden with lawns, great variety of shrubs, walled garden with herbaceous, roses & vegetables. Georgian house (not open) in beautiful country. TEAS (by Glos. Trust). *(Share to Glos. Trust for Nature Conservation). Adm. 30p, Chd. 10p. Sun. July 6 (2–6)*

The Chestnuts* (Mr & Mrs E. H. Gwynn) Minchinhampton, 1 m. E of Nailsworth. From Nailsworth by Avening Rd A434, turn left at Weighbridge Inn & ¼ m. up hill. From Minchinhampton 1 m. on Nailsworth Rd via New Rd or Well Hill. ⅔-acre enclosed garden; walls, terraces; shrubs & bulbs; climbing, shrub & other roses; rock garden; pool garden.

Adjoining field also ⅔ acre, planted since 1972 with trees & shrubs inc. species & shrub roses. Cotswold Stone Georgian house (not open). NO DOGS. *(Share to Glos. Trust for Nature Conservation). Adm. 30p, Chd. free. Sun. June 15 (2–6)*

Church House (Mr & Mrs M. Boustead) Lechlade. 2 mins walk from Market Place through churchyard. Bus: B 447 from Cirencester or Swindon; alight Market Place. Medium-sized garden; early C18 gazebo & summerhouse of architectural interest; spring bulbs. Tea Marlborough House, Lechlade. *Adm. 25p, Chd. 10p. Sun. April 20 (2–6)*

Cotswold Farm*⅃ (Maj. & Mrs. P. D. Birchall) 5 m. N of Cirencester on A417; signpost ¼ m. from Five Mile House Inn. Cotswold garden in lovely position with terraces, shrubs, mixed borders, rock borders & shrub roses. NO DOGS. Tea at Duntisbourne Abbots. *(Share to Glos. Trust for Nature Conservation). Adm. 25p, Chd. 10p. Sun. July 13 (2–6)*

The Croft House*⊕ (Miss P. M. Dugdale & Miss B. A. Scott) Fairford, 8 m. E of Cirencester. Entrance through archway on E side of Market Place. Old walled garden with unusual plants & shrubs, herb garden & gazebo; formal vegetable garden. Close to beautiful church, famous for C15 stained glass windows. Plants for sale. TEAS (June 29 only). *(Share to Glos. Trust for Nature Conservation). Adm. 25p. Sun. & Mon. June 29 & 30 (2.30–6.30)*

Dean Lodge (Mr & Mrs Godfrey Cook) Iron Acton, 3 m. W of Chipping Sodbury. A432 from Chipping Sodbury, turn NW on to B4059; turn off Iron Acton bypass into village High St. Almost 2 acres; lawns, small spinney, rose garden, trees old & new, shrubs, herbaceous plants; streamlet running through; spring bulbs. C17 house (not open). Plants for sale. NO DOGS. TEAS (July 13 only). *(Share to Glos. Trust for Nature Conservation). Adm. 25p, Chd. 5p. Sun. & Mon. July 13 & 14 (1–6); also by appt. April to Sept. (Tel. Rangeworthy 202)*

Duntisbourne Valley Gardens, † 12 m. S of Gloucester on A417 turn W for 1 m.; or from Cirencester fork left via Daglingworth through fine scenery. Lovely cluster of Cotswold villages of historic interest. In Duntisbourne Rous, Saxon church with crypt, much loved by John Betjeman. Following gardens open. TEAS (3.30–5.30) by Duntisbourne Abbots Youth Hostel Assn in Youth Hostel. *(Share to C.P.R.E.). Adm. to each garden 10p. Sun. July 13 (2–6)*

Duntisbourne Abbots:
   Church Farm (Mr & Mrs J. A. Paterson-Morgan)
   Youth Hostel Association (Mr & Mrs Lane)

Holt's Hill (Mr & Mrs John Spencer)
The Old Cottage (Mrs S. E. Crawford)
Duntisbourne Leer:
Longford (Mr & Mrs Nigel Harris)
Trustrams House (Mrs E. Smail)
Duntisbourne Rous:
The Old Rectory (Mrs Charles Renshaw)

Eastington Gardens, 1 m. SE of Northleach (A40). Charming Cotswold village with lovely views. Bus stop: Northleach. Following 3 gardens open. TEAS only on Suns. *40p ticket admits to all gardens. Sats. & Suns. April 19 & 20; May 24 & 25; Aug. 30 & 31 (2–6)*

Eastington (Mr & Mrs Owen Slatter) Middle End. Medium-sized Cotswold garden of general interest
Yew Tree Cottage (Mr & Mrs M. Bottone) Lower End. Rockery, plants & shrubs
Bank Cottage (Mr & Mrs E. S. Holland) Lower End. Cottage garden; alpines. Plants for sale.

Fossebridge Manor⊕ (Maj. & the Hon. Mrs John Shedden), Coln St Denys. 3 m. SW of Northleach & ½ m. E of Fossebridge on A429 (Fosseway). Old Cotswold farmhouse with Norfolk thatch. Bulbs, herbaceous, roses, river & lake. Donkeys. Band (July 13 only). NO DOGS. TEAS. *(Share to Chedworth Branch, Royal British Legion). Adm. 25p, Chd. 10p. Sun. April 6 & Sun. July 13 (2–6)*

The Glebe House&⊕ (Mr & Mrs David N. Foster) Coln Rogers. 7 m. NE of Cirencester; via Fosseway & turn right at Coln Rogers. From Northleach via Fosseway & turn left at Coln St Denys. Large garden between R. Coln (with trout) & old Cotswold house (not open); pond with carp. NO DOGS. TEAS. *(Share to Sue Ryder Homes, Leckhampton). Adm. 20p, Chd. 10p. Sun. June 29 & Sun. Aug. 24 (2–6)*

Gloucestershire College of Agriculture*&⊕ (Gloucestershire County Council) Hartpury House, 5 m. N of Gloucester. Take A417 Gloucester–Ledbury; clearly signposted. 4 acres; large lawns; trees, shrubs & terraces; glasshouses; kitchen garden; demonstration gardens, ornamental gardens. Miniature golf course. Tea Gloucester. NO DOGS. *Adm. 40p, Chd. 15p. Sun. May 18 (2–6)*

Hidcote Manor Gardens*&⊕ (The National Trust—see Nat. Trust, p. ix) 3 m. NE of Chipping Campden. Bus: B 524 from Evesham or Stratford-on-Avon, alight X-rds ½ m. S of Mickleton. Series of formal gardens, many enclosed within superb hedges, inc. hornbeam on stems. Many rare trees, shrubs, plants. (In addition to the dates shown below in aid of the NGS, the garden is open, 11–8 (no entry after 7 or an hour before dusk if earlier) daily except Tues. & Fri., April 1 to Oct. 31.) NO DOGS. TEAS. *Adm. £1.10, Chd. 55p.* △*Sun. May 11 (11–8; no adm. after 7)*

Hidcote Vale*⊕ (Miss B. C. Muir) Hidcote Boyce. 3 m. NE of Chipping Campden. 1 m. from Hidcote N.T. Garden via Chipping Campden rd from there. Small garden with good collection of interesting & unusual shrubs & plants with particular attention to colour schemes. NO DOGS. Tea Campden & Mickleton, Three Ways Hotel. *Adm. 25p, OAPs 15p, Chd. 25p. Suns. June 22, July 13, Sept. 14 (2–6)*

Hill House*&⊕ (Sally, Duchess of Westminster) Wickwar, 4 m. N of Chipping Sodbury. On B4060, mid-way between Chipping Sodbury & Wotton-under-Edge. From Chipping Sodbury through Wickwar; left by wall signed to Motorway 5 & entrance 200 yds on left. Medium-sized garden; tree & shrub paddocks & mixed herbaceous & rose borders. 2 aviaries of foreign birds & flock of Welsh mountain sheep. NO DOGS. TEAS (by Glos. Trust). *(Share to Glos. Trust for Nature Conservation). Adm. 25p, Chd. 10p Sat. June 28 (2–6); also by appt. April–Sept. for parties only (Tel. Wickwar 304)*

Hodges Barn*†&⊕ (Mr & Mrs C. N. Hornby) Shipton Moyne; 3 m. S of Tetbury, on Malmesbury side of Shipton Moyne. 8 acres; woodland garden with many spring bulbs; water garden, herbaceous borders & fine roses & shrubs; mature tapestry hedge. TEAS (April 27 & July 6 only). *(Share to Glos. Trust for Nature Conservation). Adm. 30p, Chd. 15p. Sun. April 27; Sun. & Mon. July 6 & 7 (2–6)*

¶**Hunts Court**⊕ (Mr & Mrs T. K. Marshall) North Nibley, Dursley. 2 m. NW of Wotton-under-Edge. From Wotton on B4060 Dursley rd turn right in Nibley at Black Horse; fork left after ¼ m. 1-acre garden with shrubs, lawns & about 200 old roses; herbaceous & heather beds. Plants & strawberries for sale if available. NO DOGS. TEAS. *Adm. 25p, Chd. 10p Sun. July 6 (2–6)*

Hyam†&⊕ (Douglas Anderson Esq) Minchinhampton, 3 m. SE of Stroud. From Market Square turn right at Cross; bear left at West End to iron gates 50 yds from bus stop. Medium-sized, home-made, garden with lawns & glorious views; fine wrought-iron work & some ancient stones; herbaceous borders, lavender hedges, sweet peas, dahlias. Plants & cut flowers for sale. Band. TEAS. *Adm. inc. The Lammas 50p. Sun. Sept. 7 (12–6.30)*

Ilsom⊕ (Sir Kenneth Preston) 1 m. NE of Tetbury; A433. Bus B432 Cirencester–Bristol; alight at entrance to drive. Herbaceous borders; large walled kitchen garden. TEAS. *Adm. 25p, Chd. 10p. Sun. July 20 (2–6)*

Kemble Gardens, 4 m. SW of Cirencester on A429 to Malmesbury. The following 3 gardens will be open. DOGS on leads. TEAS by W.I. at Kemble House (April 27 & June 29 only). (*Share to All Saints' Church, Kemble*). *Combined charge for 3 gardens 60p. Sun. April 27; Sun. & Mon. June 29 & 30 (2–6)*

Glebe Barn⊕ (Mr & Mrs Gordon Gregory) Small garden started in 1972 on site of former vicarage; old walls; roses; clematis; shrubs

Kemble House⊕ (Mrs Donald Peachey) Large, mature & old-fashioned garden pertaining to a C17 manor house & overlooking its own parkland; adjoining church. Informal planting of shrubs, herbaceous plants; old-fashioned & floribunda roses. Plants for sale if available.

The Pigeon House⊕ (Dr & Mrs John Grove-White) Medium-sized garden started 1972 in yard of converted C18 barn with scheduled pigeon loft. Roses; water garden; lily pond with exotic fish; rockery; tapestry hedge; fruit & flowering trees

● **Kiftsgate Court***⅍ (Mrs D. H. Binny) 3 m. NE of Chipping Campden, adjacent to Hidcote Nat. Trust Garden. 1 m. E of A46 & B4081. Bus: Stratford-on-Avon–Broadway, alight Mickleton, 1 m. Magnificent situation & views; many unusual plants & shrubs; tree paeonies, hydrangeas, abutilons, etc; collection of specie & old-fashioned roses, inc. largest rose in England, R. Filipes Kiftsgate. Plants from garden for sale on open days. NO DOGS. TEAS. *Adm. 80p, Chd. 20p. April 1 to Sept. 30 every Sun., Wed., Thurs. & Bank Hol.; also Sats. May 24, June 28, July 12, Sept. 6 (2–6)*

¶**Kingsmead**⊕ (The Earl & Countess of Westmorland) Didmarton, Badminton. 6 m. SW of Tetbury on A433 Cirencester–Bath rd. 4-acre garden; many varieties of roses; old kitchen garden has been completely redesigned & replanted with roses, shrubs & trees by present owners. Topiary yew house. NO DOGS (but can be walked in fields by drive). TEAS. *Adm. 30p, Chd. 10p. Sun. July 6 (2–6)*

The Lammas*†⅍⊕ (Mr & Mrs G. V. Sherren) Minchinhampton, 3 m. SE of Stroud. Entrance through **Hyam**, which see for directions. 5-acre, mature garden with many fine trees & shrubs; herbaceous borders & rose garden; water garden. Historic house rebuilt Queen Anne (not open); magnificent tithe barn (open); walled kitchen garden; tropical greenhouse. Band. TEAS. *Adm. inc. Hyam 50p. Sun. Sept. 7 (12–6.30)*

Lasborough Manor (Maj. & Mrs C. A. Fisher) 5 m. W of Tetbury. 4½ m. S of Nailsworth, 1½ m. S of Calcot X-rds on main Stroud–Bath Rd A46. House stands just below Lasborough Church. Large herbaceous border; shrubs. Cotswold manor, 1609. Beautiful fireplaces. Old family pictures, china & furniture. NO DOGS. Plants for sale if available.

Adm. house & garden 50p. Open by appt. only. April 1 to Sept. 30 (Tel. Leighterton 222)

The Level* (Mr & Mrs R. H. H. Taylor) Pillowell, 3½ m. N of Lydney. B4234 from Lydney, turn right just before level crossing; car park on right at top of 2nd hill. 2½ acres; new garden (begun 1975) on 2 slag heaps; heather border; rock garden; rare & old roses; fine collection of hebes (over 70 varieties); young trees & shrubs, mixed borders; many rare & unusual plants. Plants for sale. NO DOGS please. (*Share to Glos. Trust for Nature Conservation*). *Adm. 25p, Chd. 10p. Sat. & Sun. July 5 & 6 (2–6); also by appt. all year (Tel. Whitecroft 562867)*

Little Barrow⊕ (Sir Charles & Lady Mander) Moreton-in-Marsh. On E side of A429 halfway between Stow-on-the-Wold & Moreton-in-Marsh. Infrequent bus passes house. Medium-sized garden with sunken garden, spring flowers, lawns, roses, herbaceous borders & yew hedges; vegetable & fruit gardens. Plants for sale if available. *Adm. 25p, Chd. 10p. Sun. May 18; Sun. & Mon. July 6 & 7 (2–6)*

Lower Dean Gardens, 1 m. NW of Northleach, turn off Fosseway on rd to Turkdean; after 1 m. fork left down lane to Lower Dean. NO COACHES. 4 small gardens in charming small hamlet tucked under a beech-wooded hill. NO DOGS. TEA & biscuits at The Grey House. (*Share to All Saints' Church, Turkdean*) *Combined charge 40p, Chd. 20p. Sun. July 6 (2–6)*

The Snicket (Col & Mrs H. W. King)

The Grey House (Mr & Mrs M. W. Whitbread). TEA & biscuits

¶**Willowbrook House** (Mr & Hon. Mrs A. E. O. Welton)

¶**The Old House** (Mr & Mrs D. King)

Lyegrove*⊕ (The Dowager Countess of Westmorland) 2 m. SW of Badminton on B4040. Bus: Lyegrove, alight bottom of drive. Formal garden with lily pool; herbaceous borders; roses & delphiniums; various shrubs. DOGS on leads. Tea Cross Hands Hotel. *Adm. 40p, Chd. 20p. Sun. June 22 (2.30–6.30)*

Misarden Park†⅍ (Mrs Huntly Sinclair) 7½ m. NE of Stroud. Bus: Stroud or Cheltenham, alight Miserden village, 5 mins. walk. Spring flowers, shrubs & herbaceous borders; old Tudor manor house standing high overlooking Golden Valley. *Adm. 30p. Mon. April 7 & Mon. May 26 (2–6)*

¶**The Old Manor***⅍⊕ (Maj. & Mrs Wilder) Twyning. 3 m. N of Tewkesbury. From A38 Tewkesbury–Worcester rd turn off Eat signpost to Twyning. 1-acre garden with variety of shrubs, trees, herbaceous & alpine plants; pool garden, rock beds, terrace plants, troughs. Small nursery open for sale of plants every Mon. March–Oct. inc., 2–7 (when

GLOUCESTERSHIRE & NORTH AVON—continued

garden may be seen to help choose plants). Field walks for picnicking. NO DOGS. TEA & biscuits. (*Share to Gardeners' Sunday*). *Adm. 25p, Chd. 15p. Sats. April 12, May 10, June 14, July 12, Aug. 9 (2–7); also other Sats. March-Oct. by appt.*

Quenington Gardens, 2 m. N of Fairford. The following 5 gardens will be open. NO DOGS. TEAS at Old Mill House. *Combined charge 50p, Chd. 20p. Sun. April 27 (2–6)*
3 gardens on R. Coln with spring bulbs:
>   **The Old Rectory** (Sir Alex & Dame Henriette Abel Smith) Adjoining village church with interesting Normal doorways & Tympana
>   **Old Mill House** (Mr & Mrs W. A. Foster). TEAS
>   ¶**Riverside** (Mrs V. Goddard)
1 garden at top of village:
>   ¶**Mallards** (Mr & Mrs B. R. Roebuck) Spring bulbs & polyanthus
Garden 1 m. from village on Roman Akeman St:
>   **Coneygar Farm** (Mr & Mrs A. W. Morris) Walled garden with unusual foliage & flowering plants

Rodmarton Manor⋆⊕ (Maj. & Mrs Anthony Biddulph) 6 m. SW of Cirencester & 4 m. NE of Tetbury, turn N off A433. Large garden; herbaceous borders; terraced garden; leisure garden; variegated & unusual plants; beech, holly & yew hedges. Cotswold house designed by Ernest Barnsley (not open, except chapel). Plants for sale. NO DOGS. Picnic area. TEAS & lemonade. *Adm. 40p, OAPs 30p, Chd. 20p. Sun. June 22 (2–6)*

Rushbury House† (Lt-Col & Mrs C. J. Sidgwick) 2½ m. from Winchcombe. At top of Cleave Hill on A46 Winchcombe–Cheltenham turn off at sign to Rushbury House. Medium-sized garden with shrubs & flowers. Farmyard animals & horses. Beautiful view. House (not open) presented in 1582 by Elizabeth I to her Keeper of the Privy Seal. DOGS on leads. Tea at Sudeley Lodge. *Adm. 25p, Chd. 10p. Sun. July 6 (2–6)*

St Francis, Lammas Park⋆†⅄⊕ (Mr & Mrs Falconer) Minchinhampton, SE of Stroud. From Minchinhampton Market Square down High St 100 yds; then turn right at X-rds; in 300 yds bear left at West End; gate on left at next junction. Medium-sized garden made in old park round modern Cotswold stone house. Fine beech avenue; terraced garden; trough gardens; bonsai trees; C18 ice-house. Plants for sale. Picknickers welcome. Home-made TEAS. *Adm. 25p, Chd. 10p. Sun. & Mon. July 27 & 28 (2–6); also by appt. all year*

● **Sezincote**⋆†⅄ (Mr & Mrs David Peake) 1½ m. SW of Moreton-in-Marsh. From More-ton-in-Marsh turn W along A44 towards Broadway & Evesham; after 1 m. (just before Bourton-on-the-Hill) take turn to left (South), near a stone lodge with white gate. Water garden by Repton & Daniell & practically unaltered. Trees of unusual size. House in Indian manner, inspiration for The Pavilion, Brighton; architect Samuel Pepys Cockerell. TEAS by W.I. (July 20 only). *Adm. 60p, Chd. 20p. Sun. July 20 (2–6); also April 7 to Sept. 26 every Fri. & Bank Hol.*

Snowshill Manor⋆† (The National Trust—see Nat. Trust, p. ix) 3 m. S of Broadway. 4 m. W of A424. Small terraced garden with ponds, old roses & old-fashioned flowers. House with architectural features & large & unique collection of musical instruments, clocks, toys, bicycles. (In addition to the date shown below in aid of NGS the house & garden are open, April & Oct. Sats. & Suns.; May to Sept. daily except Mons. & Tues. (but open on Bank Hols.). 11–1 & 2–6 (or sunset if earlier). NO DOGS. *Adm. house & garden £1.10. Chd. 55p.* △*Sun. Sept. 21 (11–1, 2–6)*

Southam Gardens,⊕ 3 m. N of Cheltenham. Just off A46 Cheltenham–Broadway rd, or 1½ m. E of A435 Cheltenham–Evesham rd. The following 4 gardens in centre of village at foot of Cleeve Hill will be open. Fine views over Cheltenham to Leckhampton Hill. NO DOGS please. TEAS (3.30–5.30) by W.I. at Village Hall. Also car park. *(Share to Glos. Trust for Nature Conservation). Combined charge 80p, Chd. 20p. Sun. & Mon. June 1 & 2 (2–6)*
>   **Byways** (Mr & Mrs G. Robinson) Small cottage garden
>   **Old Gable House** (Mr & Mrs M. L. Shinn) Old sloping garden of 1 acre; wisteria-covered pergola; topiary
>   **Old School House** (Mrs I. G. Robinson) ¾-acre garden on 3 levels; roses & rose species in mixed borders, iris, rhododendrons, conifers
>   **Orchard Lea** (Mr & Mrs A. L. Jones) Medium-sized garden of general interest; flowers, shrubs, fruit & vegetables. Beehive

Southrop Gardens, 1½ m. N of Lechlade, turn off A361 at signposts to Southrop. Riverside daffodils at neighbouring village of Eastleach may be in flower at time of April opening. TEAS at Southrop Lodge. *Combined charge 50p, OAPs & Chd. 25p. Sun. April 27 & Sun. June 1 (2–6)*
>   **Southrop Manor**† (Mr & Mrs Kenneth Combe) Large garden with R. Leach running through; stew pond where monks kept carp & trout; river & water garden. House originally Norman. C16 tithe barn. Adjacent to Saxon church. (*Sun. April 27 only*)
>   **Southrop Lodge**†⅄ (Lady Steel) 1-acre garden with show of bulbs of all kinds, wallflowers & polyanthus; very fine cedar

of Lebanon & ginkgo tree; old box hedges. Late Georgian house which was the Vicarage where John Keble was curate to his father. In middle of village opp. Swan Inn

Fyfield Manor (Sir Guy & Lady Millard) 1-acre garden with spring bulbs; flowering trees & shrubs

Springfield Barn★ (Mr & Mrs H. Joseph Woods) Upton Cheyney, Bitton. 5 m. NW of Bath; 8 m. SE of Bristol. Take A431 Bath–Hanham–Bristol & turn off for Upton Cheyney; turn right in front of cottages. Please observe parking advice. Garden just over an acre, started from scratch in 1960, designed & planted with several hundred species, many from own propagation, by present owners. Plants for sale. TEAS (if fine). *Adm. 30p, Chd. 10p. Sun. July 20 (2–6)*

Stancombe Park★&⊕ (Mr & Mrs B. S. Barlow) Dursley ½-way between Dursley & Wotton-under-Edge on B4060. Bus stop: 30 yds from gates. Folly garden & Temple; herbaceous borders, new tree & shrub planting. Plants for sale if available TEAS on June 22; TEA & biscuits on June 23. *Adm. 40p, Chd. 10p. Sun. & Mon. June 22 & 23 (2–6)*

Standish Park & Martins★†& 2 m. NW of Stonehouse. From B4008 Stonehouse–Gloucester rd take turning for Oxlynch & proceed 1 m. from main rd. The following 2 gardens will be open. NO DOGS. TEAS (home-made cakes). *Share to Glos. Trust for Nature Conservation. Combined charge 50p, OAPs 25p, Chd. 10p. Sat. & Sun. June 21 & 22 (2–6)*

¶**Standish Park** (John Oldacre Esq) Interesting garden on differing levels, with rose walks & good kitchen garden surrounding Old Farm House, restored. Picnicking permitted on farm in area of outstanding natural beauty

¶**Martins** (Mr & Mrs F. L. Cross) Terraced garden with wide variety of shrubs & plants collected over 25 years surrounding delightful thatched cottage. Special interest for flower arrangers

Stanton,⊕ nr Broadway. A number of village gardens may be seen for a combined charge of 50p. Alpine & other plants for sale. TEA & biscuits can be purchased in Village Hall from 3–5.30. *Sun. June 29 (2.30–7)*

Stanway House★†&⊕ (Trustees of the Lord Wemyss Trust) 4 m. NE of Winchcombe. A46 Broadway–Winchcombe rd, turn at Toddington roundabout towards Stow-on-the-Wold; about 1 m. from roundabout turn left for Stanway. A438, B4037, Stanway 1 m. from Toddington roundabout on the Stow side. 20 acres of lawns & trees; beautiful setting. Tithe barn (open). Tea The Bakehouse, Stanway (parties of 20 or more please book tea in advance, Tel. Stanton 204). *Adm. 20p, Chd. 10p Sun. May 4 & Sun. June 8 (2–6)*

Stowell Park†& (The Lord & Lady Vestey) 2 m. SW of Northleach. Off Fosseway A429. Large garden; terraced lawns with magnificent views; large kitchen garden; peach & vine houses; greenhouses. House (not open) originally C14 with later additions. Nearby church built 1172 & with original hand paintings of that date on walls. NO DOGS. TEAS. *Share to Chedworth Branch, Royal British Legion. Adm. 30p, Chd. 15p. Sun. June 15 (2–6)*

Sudeley Lodge (Mr & Mrs K. J. Wilson) 1½ m. SE of Winchcombe; take A46 to Bourton-on-Water/Guiting Power; drive on right, about 1 m. up hill, signposted. Sudeley Lodge. Medium-sized garden in lovely setting with lawns, borders & stone walls; greenhouses. Swimming pool available for use. NO DOGS. TEAS. *Share to Glos. Trust for Nature Conservation. Adm. 25p, Chd. 10p. Sun. July 6 (2–6)*

Sydenhams (Mr & Mrs G. G. Cradock-Watson) 1 m. N of Bisley on Stroud rd turn right at Stancombe Corner. Small garden; herbaceous borders, roses, formal beds. Tudor Cotswold house (not open), partly C14 in lovely situation overlooking Slad Valley. Picturesque farm buildings & medieval stone pillars. Tea Bisley Gardens (July 13 only). *(Share to Glos. Trust for Nature Conservation). Adm. 25p, Chd. 10p. Sun. & Mon. July 13 & 14 (2–6)*

Talbot End House (G. E. C. Dougherty Esq) Cromhall, 5½ m. SW of Wotton-under-Edge. From Bristol via B4058, to X-rds in Cromhall & turn right to Talbot End. 2 acres; Edwardian garden adapted by some replanting in recent years. NO DOGS. Tea Hill House (June 28); Badminton House (June 29). *Adm. 25p, Chd. 10p. Sat. & Sun. June 28 & 29 (2–6)*

Vine House★&⊕ (Prof. & Mrs T. F. Hewer) Henbury, N of Bristol. Bus stop: Salutation Inn, Henbury, 50 yds. 2-acre garden; trees, shrubs, water garden, bulbs, naturalised garden landscaped & entirely planted by the present owners since 1946. Subject of article in R.H.S. Journal Nov. 1968. *(Share to Glos. Trust for Nature Conservation). Adm. 25p, OAPs & Chd. 10p. Sun. & Mon. May 25 & 26 (2–7); also by appt. all year (Tel. Bristol 503573)*

Westbury Court★†⊕ (The National Trust—see Nat. Trust, p. ix) Westbury-on-Severn, 9 m. SW of Gloucester. On A48. Medium size; a formal water garden with canals & yew hedges laid out between 1696 & 1705, the earliest of its kind remaining in England. Restored by The National Trust in 1971. (In addition to the dates shown below in aid of the NGS, the garden is open April & Oct. Sats. & Suns.; May to Sept. daily except Mons. & Tues. (but open Bank Hols.). (11–6). NO DOGS. Picnic area. *Adm. 60p, Chd. 30p. △Sun. July 13 (11–6)*

Westend House*⚥ (Keith Steadman Esq) Wickwar, 4 m. N of Chipping Sodbury. In Wickwar at N end of Main St, signposted M5, turn left & very shortly left again signposted Rangeworthy & Cromhall; 2nd house on right, 600 yds. Large & varied collection of trees & shrubs, many of them rare & unusual, form a natural planting of about 3 acres; pond garden with many willows & small informally planted walled garden. Whole garden has been made since 1950 & was designed to be labour-saving when mature. There is a nursery where many plants grown in garden may be obtained. NO DOGS. *Adm. 50p. Garden open by appt. only, all year (Tel. Wickwar 208)*

Westonbirt School,* †⚥⊕ 3 m. S of Tetbury. Bus: B 432 Tetbury–Bristol. Formal Italian garden, terraced pleasure garden, rustic walks & lake. Approx. 25 acres. Many rare & exotic trees & shrubs. Bus stop & Tea Hare & Hounds Hotel, Westonbirt, ½ m. (parties by appt. W'birt 233). *Adm. 25p, Chd. 10p. Suns. April 20 Aug. 3, Sept. 7 (2–6)*

Willersey House*†⊕ (Col & Mrs P. Arkwright) 1½ m. N of Broadway on Chipping Campden Rd out of Willersey village. Bus: Evesham–Broadway. Bus stop: 300 yds. Beautiful old Cotswold house. Extensive views. Bulbs & flowering shrubs; daffodils a feature. July openings: Rose gardens & flowering shrubs; herbaceous borders. TEAS (April 27 only) in aid of CPRE. *(Share to Glos. Trust for Nature Conservation). Adm. 25p. Sun. & Mon. April 27 & 28 (2–6); Sun. & Mon. July 13 & 14 (2–7)*

Witcombe Park*⚥⊕ (Mrs W. W. Hicks Beach) 4 m. E of Gloucester on A436 turn S by 12 Bells; signpost to Gt Witcombe. Medium-sized garden; roses, flowering shrubs & sunk garden set in beautiful Cotswold scenery. NO DOGS. TEAS. *(Share to Glos. Trust for Nature Conservation). Adm. 25p, Chd. 10p. Sun. July 20 (2–6,30)*

Withington Gardens, † 3 m. S of Andoversford. One of the loveliest of Cotswold villages Norman church 1150–1400 on Saxon site with two magnificent Norman doorways. A number of old houses. The following 8 gardens will be open. Car park at Mill Inn (by kind permission). TEAS & refreshments. *Combined charge for all gardens 50p, Chd. under 12, free. Sun. July 6 (2–6)*

> **Manor House** (Mr & Mrs Robert Fender)
> **Halewell Close** (Mrs Carey Wilson)
> **The Old House**⊕ (Mrs H. G. Mason)
> **Withington House**⊕ (Sir Derrick & Lady Carter)
> **The Close** (Mr & Mrs Richard Walker)
> **Lower Farm House** (Miss N. P. Gray)
> **Upcote Farm** (Mr & Mrs John Platt)
> **Garden House** (Mr & Mrs C. F. G. Max-Muller)

Yew Tree Cottage*⊕ (Brig. & Mrs H. Shuker & Miss P. Strange) Ampney St Mary. At E end of Ampney St Peter on A417 fork left at Red Lion Inn, 1st left to Ampney St Mary, then 1st right in village. Medium-sized garden full of interest; shrubs, bulbs, perennials; alpines a speciality. Old Cotswold cottage. Plants for sale. TEAS (by W.I.). *(Share to Ampney St Peter & Mary church repairs). Adm. 25p. Sun. March 23 (2–6); Sun. & Mon. April 6 & 7; Suns. May 4, June 8, July 13, Aug. 24 (2–7); also by appt., all year (Tel. Poulton 333)*

GWENT
(formerly Monmouthshire)

Hon. County Organiser:
LADY CRAWSHAY, Llanfair Court, Abergavenny

Asst. Hon. County Organiser:
MRS G. H. C. CLAY, Lower House Farm, Nantyderry, Abergavenny

DATES OF OPENING

JANUARY to NOVEMBER every Sunday, also by apptment only on weekdays (but not Tuesdays or Fridays)
   THE YEW TREE, Lydart, nr Monmouth
MAY Sunday 4
   MATHERN, Mathern, nr Chepstow
MAY Saturday 24 & Sunday 25
   ‡LLANOVER, nr Abergavenny
   ‡LOWER HOUSE FARM, Nantyderry
JUNE Sunday 1
   THE CHAIN GARDEN, Abergavenny
JUNE Sunday 8
   ‡CLYTHA PARK, nr Abergavenny
   ‡NORTH PARADE HOUSE, Monmouth
JUNE Sunday 15
   THE CRAIG, Pen-y-Clawdd, nr Monmouth
JUNE Sunday 22
   BRYNDERWEN, Bettws Newydd, nr Usk
JUNE Sunday 29
   LLANSOY GARDENS, nr Devauden
JULY Sunday 6
   COURT ST LAWRENCE, Llangovan, nr Usk
JULY Sunday 13
   ROCKFIELD HOUSE, nr Monmouth
JULY Sunday 20
   LLANFAIR COURT, nr Abergavenny

DESCRIPTIONS OF GARDENS

Brynderwen⊕ (Mr & Mrs Arthur Bull) Bettws Newydd, nr Usk. A40, Monmouth–Abergavenny; turn off opp. Clytha Lodge up Bettws Lane, signposted Bettws Newydd; garden is 1¼ m. up lane. Medium-sized garden with pretty rose garden. TEAS. *Adm. 25p, Chd. under 12, 5p. Sun. June 22 (2–7)*

The Chain Garden (Mr & Mrs C. F. R. Price) Chapel Rd, 1 m. N of Abergavenny. Turn off

A40 (on Brecon side of town) into Chapel Rd, garden at top of rd. 2-acre garden with stream running through; lawns; rhododendrons; flowering shrubs & rock gardens. (*Share to Cancer Research Campaign*) TEAS. *Adm. 25p. Sun. June 1 (2-7)*

Clytha Park †&⊕ (R. Hanbury-Tenison Esq; The National Trust) 6 m. SE of Abergavenny. On A40, ½-way between Abergavenny & Raglan. 5 acres; specimen trees, shrubs & lake. TEAS. *Adm. 25p, Chd. 10p. Sun. June 8 (2-7)*

Court St Lawrence (Lt-Col & Mrs G. D. Inkin) Llangovan, SW of Monmouth. 5 m. NE of Usk; from A449 access at Usk take B4235 for Chepstow for 1 m.; on sharp right bend continue straight on for Monmouth; after approx. 3 m. entrance on right. ½-acre of garden & woods with conventional shrubs, roses & wood with rough grass. NO DOGS. TEAS. *Adm. 25p, Chd. over 5, 10p. Sun. July 6 (2-7)*

The Craig*⊕ (Mrs Rainforth) Pen-y-Clawdd, SW of Monmouth. Turn off S from Raglan–Monmouth Rd (*not Motorway*) at sign to Pen-y-Clawdd. Bus: Newport–Monmouth, alight Keen's shop, ½ m. Small mixed cottage garden with heather hedges, heather beds, shrubs & bog garden. TEA. *Adm. 25p. Sun. June 15 (2-7)*

Llanfair Court* †&⊕ (Sir William Crawshay) 5 m. SE of Abergavenny. Route A40. Bus: Abergavenny–Raglan, alight Herbert Arms, 1 m. Medium-sized garden; herbaceous border, flowering shrubs, roses, water garden; modern sculpture. TEA. *Adm. 25p. Sun. July 20 (2-7)*

Llanover*&⊕ (R. A. E. Herbert Esq) S of Abergavenny. Bus: Abergavenny–Pontypool, alight drive gates. Large water garden; rare conifers. (*Share to British Red Cross (May 24)*) TEAS. *Adm. 30p. Sat. & Sun. May 24 & 25 (2-7)*

Llansoy Gardens. Between Devauden & Llansoy. 7 m. NW of Chepstow, 7 m. SW of Monmouth. From B4293 Chepstow–Monmouth rd turn off W at signpost to Raglan & Llansoy & down Star Hill for ½ m. From Usk or Raglan via Crosshands X-rds; 1 m. from Star Inn. Tea Star Inn (if booked in advance). *Combined charge for following 2 gardens 30p, Chd. 15p. Sun. June 29 (2-7)*

¶**Rockshiel*** (Mrs O. Cowburn) ½-acre garden constructed on hillside; terraced & planted for easy maintenance; small vegetable garden also terraced

¶**Torymynydd Farm*** (Rear-Adml & Mrs M. S. Townsend) From Rockshiel turn up steep & narrow council rd & bear left at junction. 1-acre garden on steep hillside, designed, planted & maintained by owners; small water garden & paved garden; natural woodland; panoramic views

Lower House Farm*⊕ (Mr & Mrs Glynne Clay) Nantyderry, 7 m. SE of Abergavenny. From A471 Usk–Abergavenny Rd, turn off at Chain Bridge. Labour-saving, family-maintained garden with mixed borders & some interesting plants. Plant stall. Tea available at Llanover, also open May 24 & 25. *Adm. 25p. Sat. & Sun. May 24 & 25 (2-7)*

Mathern †⊕ (British Steel Corporation) Mathern, S of Chepstow. Station: Chepstow, 3 m. Bus: Newport–Chepstow, alight New Inn, Pwll-Meyric, 1 m. Pleasure garden associated with historical house: dating from 1400. TEA & biscuits. *Adm. 25p. Sun. May 4 (2-7)*

North Parade House †⊕ (Mr & Mrs John P. K. Rennie) Monmouth. At N end of North Parade (A466 Monmouth–Hereford) nr entrance to Monmouth School for Girls. Bus stop & parking outside house. ½-acre garden enclosed by high mellow red brick wall; lawn, herbaceous border, ornamental trees & vegetable garden. House (not open) & woolstaplers warehouse adjoining built late C18. NO DOGS. TEA. *Adm. 25p, Chd. 15p. Sun. June 8 (2-7)*

Rockfield House*&⊕ (Lt-Col J. C. E. Harding-Rolls) 2 m. NW of Monmouth on B4233. Fork left at Rockfield P.O. Free car park in field above garden. Trees, shrubs, borders, roses galore, lily ponds, paved water garden with goldfish, small lake, ducks, swans. NO DOGS. TEA. *Adm. 30p, Chd. under 14, 15p. Sun. July 13 (2-7)*

● **The Yew Tree***& (Lt-Cdr A. F. Collett) Lydart, 2 m. S of Monmouth. 2 m. S of Monmouth via B4293; fork left for Penallt; house 300 yds on left. Private car park, 50 yds. (Weekdays visitors (by appt. only) may drive up to house, enabling elderly or those in wheelchairs to get to the terrace.) Garden of over 3 acres with stupendous views & many vistas; large & unusual range of plants, rare trees & shrubs & a stream garden. Visitors by appt. are requested to phone at short notice to ensure fine weather; otherwise send s.a.e. Coach parties by appt. only. Tea Monmouth or Wye Valley. *Adm. 25p. Jan. 1 to Nov. 30 every Sun. (May–Oct. 11–1 & 2–6; other months 10–1 & 2–4); also by appt. only Mons., Weds., Thurs. & Sats. (except Dec.)* (*Tel. 0600 2293*)

GWYNEDD

Hon. County Organisers:
(North Gwynedd) MERIOL, LADY
 WILLIAMS, Trewyn, Beaumaris
(Mid Gwynedd) MRS JAMES BAILY
 GIBSON, Fronheulog, Llanfrothen,
 Penrhyndeudraeth, LL48 6LX
(South Gwynedd) MRS P. A. LATHAM,
 Garreg Farm, Glandyfi, Machynlleth,
 Powys, SY20 8SS

DATES OF OPENING

ALL YEAR DAILY
 HAFODTY, between Caernarvon &
 Beddgelert
ALL YEAR by appointment
 BRYNHYFRYD, Corris, nr Machynlleth
MARCH 27 daily to NOVEMBER 4
 PORTMEIRION, Minffordd, nr
 Penrhyndeudraeth
**APRIL to OCTOBER first Wednesday in
every month**
 PLAS BRONDANW, Llanfrothen,
 Penrhyndeudraeth
**Mid-APRIL to mid-JUNE by
appointment**
 CEFN BERE, Dolgellau
MAY Friday 16
 PLAS NEWYDD, Anglesey
MAY Sunday 18 & Wednesday 21
 HAFOD GARREGOG, Nantmor,
 nr Beddgelert
MAY Monday 26 (Bank Hol.)
 PLAS BRONDANW, Llanfrothen,
 nr Penrhyndeudraeth
JUNE Friday 20
 PENRHYN CASTLE, nr Bangor
JULY Sunday 13 & Wednesday 16
 TIR UCHA, Criccieth
JULY Wednesday 30
 VAYNOL, nr Portdinorwic
AUGUST Monday 25 (Bank Hol.)
 PLAS BRONDANW, Llanfrothen,
 nr Penrhyndeudraeth

DESCRIPTIONS OF GARDENS

Brynhyfryd* (Mr & Mrs David Paish) Corris,
6 m. N of Machynlleth. 10 m. S of Dolgellau.
At Corris turn off A487 ; garden is ¼ m. up hill
on old rd from Corris. Garden may be visited at
any time of year ; 4-acre garden on rocky
mountainside, constructed & planted by
owners since 1961 ; species & hybrid rhododendrons & other peat-loving plants ; specie &
shrub roses ; flowering shrubs ; alpine, water
& cover plants. Much of interest at medium &
low level, but flat-heeled shoes recommended.
NO DOGS please. *Collecting box. By appt.
only, all year* (*Tel. Corris 278*)

Cefn Bere* (Maldwyn Thomas Esq) Dolgellau. 1st turning right after crossing
Dolgellau bridge on the Barmouth Rd, turn
right behind school & up hill. Small garden ;
extensive collection of alpines & rare plants.
NO DOGS. Tea Dolgellau. *Collecting box. By
appt. only, mid-April to mid-June* (*Tel.
Dolgellau 422768*)

Hafod Garregog† (Mr & Mrs Hugh Mason)
Nantmor, 5 m. N of Penrhyndeudraeth
towards Aberglaslyn. Small garden made since
1971 in woodland setting with fine mountain
views ; trees, shrubs, flowers & vegetables ;
woodland bluebell walk. Home of Rhys Goch
Eryri AD 1430. Situated above R. Hafod. Tea

Beddgelert, 3 m. *Adm. 30p, Chd. 10p. Sun.
May 18 & Wed. May 21 (2–6)*

Hafodty⊕ (Mr & Mrs Pierce) Bettws
Garmon, in Snowdonia National Park. Route
A487, 6 m. SE of Caernarvon on Beddgelert
Rd, A487. Bus : Whiteways from Caernarvon
or Beddgelert, alight at gate. Very small
garden ; part suitable for wheelchairs. Nant
Mill Waterfall (migration of elvers, June–
Aug. ; salmon leaping Sept.–Dec.) Rock &
water garden. *Collecting box. Daily all year
10.30–dusk)*

Penrhyn Castle†⅃⊕ (The National Trust—
see p. ix) E of Bangor. 1 m. E of Bangor at
junction of A5 & A55. Coach trips from
Llandudno. Buses from Llandudno, Caernarvon, Betws-y-Coed. Bus stop : Grand Lodge
Gate. Large gardens ; fine trees, shrubs, river
garden, good views. Castle was rebuilt in 1830
for 1st Lord Penrhyn, incorporating part of
15th-cent. building on 8th-cent. site of home
of Welsh Princes. Exhibition of 1,000 dolls in
period & national costume ; collection of
butterflies ; museum of locomotives & quarry
rolling stock. TEAS & refreshments. No reduction for coach parties. *Adm.* (*inc. castle,
grounds, museum & parking*) *£1.20; coach
parties £1; Chd. up to 16, 60p.* △*Fri. June 20
(11–6; castle 11–5)*

Plas Brondanw†⅃⊕ (Lady Williams-Ellis)
Llanfrothen. Station : Penrhyndeudraeth, 2 m.
Bus : Crosville, Garreg village, alight lodge,
¼ m. Entrance : arched gatehouse, Llanfrothen.
An architectural & topiary, terraced & vista'd
garden below C17 house with superb mountain views. Part only of garden suitable for
wheelchairs. *Adm. 20p, Chd. 10p. Mon. May
26 & Mon. Aug. 25 (10–6); collecting box on
gate for Weds. April 2, May 7, June 4, July 2,
Aug. 6, Sept. 3, Oct. 1 (1.30–4)*

Plas Newydd† (The Marquess of Anglesey ;
The National Trust) Isle of Anglesey. 1 m. SW
of Llanfairpwll & A5 on A4080. Gardens with
massed shrubs, fine trees, & lawns sloping
down to Menai Strait. Magnificent views to
Snowdonia. C18 house by James Wyatt contains Rex Whistler's largest wall painting ; also
Military Museum. NO DOGS. TEAS & light
lunches. *Adm. house & garden £1, Chd. 50p
(booked parties over 20 in number, 80p, Chd.
40p); garden only 50p, Chd. 25p.* △*Fri. May
16 (12.30–5.30)*

● **Portmeirion***†⅃ (Portmeirion Foundation) Minffordd, SW of Penrhyndeudraeth.
Station : Minffordd. Bus : Crosville, Port-
madoc–Blaenau Ffestiniog. Sub-tropical
coastal, cliff & woodland gardens, surrounding
scenic village. Not very suitable for wheelchairs. Meals : Portmeirion Hotel Restaurant ;
snacks : Hercules Hall Self-Service Restaurant. *Adm. 95p, Chd. 25p. March 27–Nov. 4
daily (9.30–6)*

Tir Ucha⊕ (Mr & Mrs Peter Barrett) Lon
Ednyfed, Criccieth. 600 yds from Criccieth ;

48

follow signs for Golf Club; Tir Ucha is on right 200 yds past the cemetery. 2 acres; shrubs, herbaceous borders, roses, heathers, vegetables, orchard. Extensive views over Tremadog Bay to Rhinog Mountains. Toy exhibition. TEA & biscuits. Car park. *Adm. 25p, Chd. 10p. Sun. July 13 & Wed. July 16 (2–6)*

Vaynol⊕ (Sir Michael Duff, Bt) nr Portdinorwic. Bus: Llandudno via Bangor–Caernarvon, alight lodge gate. Free transport from main gate to garden. Herbaceous borders. Herd of ancient breed of white cattle. Victorian Chapel. Garden of Tudor Manor House, by permission of David Gladstone Esq, also open, no extra charge. Home-made TEAS. *Adm. 25p. Chd. 10p. Wed. July 30 (2–6)*

HAMPSHIRE

Hon. County Organiser:
MRS WILLOUGHBY NORMAN, Hurst Mill, Petersfield

Assistant Hon. County Organisers:
HON. MRS C. R. CHETWODE, Hill House, Cheriton, nr Alresford SO24 0NU; MRS G. E. COKE, Jenkyn Place, Bentley; MRS DAVID GIBBS, Braishfield Manor, Romsey; MRS ROLLO HOARE, The Dower House, Dogmersfield; THE LADY O'NEILL, Lisle Court Cottage, Lymington SO4 8SH; MRS PETER WAKE, Fairfield House, Hambledon PO7 6RY

DATES OF OPENING

JANUARY to DECEMBER daily
  FURZEY GARDENS, nr Lyndhurst
  MACPENNYS, Bransgore
JANUARY & FEBRUARY every Saturday & Sunday
  WELLINGTON COUNTRY PARK
FEBRUARY every Saturday & Sunday from February 9
  WYCK PLACE, nr Alton
FEBRUARY Sunday 17
  BRAMDEAN HOUSE, nr Alresford
MARCH daily
  FURZEY GARDENS, nr Lyndhurst
  MACPENNYS, Bransgore
  WELLINGTON COUNTRY PARK
MARCH Saturday 1, Sunday 2, Saturday 8 & Sunday 9
  WYCK PLACE, nr Alton
MARCH Sunday 16
  CASTLETOP, Burley, nr Ringwood
MARCH Sunday 30 & Monday 31
  EXBURY, nr Southampton
  HOLYWELL, Swanmore
  STRATFIELD SAYE HOUSE, nr Basingstoke
APRIL daily
  EXBURY, nr Southampton

FURZEY GARDENS, nr Lyndhurst
MACPENNYS, Bransgore
WELLINGTON COUNTRY PARK
APRIL every Sunday
  HURST MILL, nr Petersfield
APRIL daily except Fridays
  STRATFIELD SAYE HOUSE, nr Basingstoke
APRIL Easter Sunday 6
  HARCOMBE HOUSE, Ropley, nr Alresford
  MICHELMERSH COURT, nr Romsey
  SOBERTON MILL, Wickham
  WOODCOTE MANOR, Bramdean, nr Alresford
APRIL Easter Monday 7
  HURST MILL, nr Petersfield
  SOBERTON MILL, Wickham
  WOODCOTE MANOR, Bramdean, nr Alresford
APRIL Sunday 13
  ASHFORD GARDENS, nr Petersfield
  BRAMDEAN HOUSE, nr Alresford
  CRANBURY PARK, Otterbourne, nr Winchester
  HARCOMBE HOUSE, Ropley, nr Alresford
  LAVERSTOCK HOUSE, nr Whitchurch
  PENNINGTON CHASE, Lymington
  TICHBORNE PARK, nr Alresford
  WOODCOTE MANOR, Bramdean, nr Alresford
APRIL Saturday 19
  KINGSMEAD, Winchester
APRIL Sunday 20
  BINSTED PLACE, nr Alton
  BRAISHFIELD MANOR, nr Romsey
  THE DEANE HOUSE, Sparsholt, nr Winchester
  GREATHAM MILL, Liss, nr Petersfield
  HACKWOOD PARK (THE SPRING WOOD), nr Basingstoke
  LONGPARISH HOUSE, nr Andover
  MARTYR WORTHY MANOR, nr Winchester
  SEGENSWORTH HOUSE, Titchfield, nr Farnham
  SUTTON MANOR, Sutton Scotney, nr Winchester
  WOODCOTE MANOR, Bramdean, nr Alresford
APRIL Sunday 20 and daily except Mondays
  SPINNERS, Boldre, nr Lymington
APRIL Sunday 27
  LITTLEHAY, Burley, nr Ringwood
  THE VYNE, Sherborne St John, nr Basingstoke
MAY daily
  EXBURY GARDEN, nr Southampton
  FURZEY GARDENS, nr Lyndhurst
  MACPENNYS, Bransgore
  WELLINGTON COUNTRY PARK
MAY daily except Mondays
  SPINNERS, Boldre, nr Lymington

HAMPSHIRE—continued

MAY daily except Fridays
STRATFIELD SAYE HOUSE,
nr Basingstoke

MAY every Sunday
HURST MILL, nr Petersfield

MAY Sunday 4
ALVERSTOKE GARDENS, Gosport
JUNE, Walkford, nr Christchurch
UPPER RAKE HANGER, Rake, nr Liss
VERNON HILL HOUSE, Bishops Waltham

MAY Monday 5 (May Day Hol.)
GREATHAM MILL, Liss, nr Petersfield
HURST MILL, nr Petersfield
UPPER RAKE HANGER, Rake, nr Liss

MAY Sunday 11
CASTLETOP, Burley, nr Ringwood
THE DOWER HOUSE, Dogmersfield
HINTON AMPNER HOUSE, nr Alresford
JENKYN PLACE, Bentley
KILN COPSE, Eversley, nr Fleet
PYLEWELL PARK, nr Lymington

MAY Monday 12
THE DOWER HOUSE, Dogmersfield

MAY Sunday 18
CHANTRY, Wickham, nr Fareham
COLD HAYES, Steep Marsh, nr Petersfield
THE DOWER HOUSE, Dogmersfield
HACKWOOD PARK (THE SPRING
WOOD), nr Basingstoke
HARCOMBE HOUSE, Ropley,
nr Alresford
KILN COPSE, Eversley, nr Fleet
LEPE HOUSE, Exbury
PENNINGTON HOUSE, Lymington
ROTHERFIELD PARK, nr Alton
RUMSEY GARDENS, Clanfield
WALHAMPTON, Lymington

MAY Monday 19
THE DOWER HOUSE, Dogmersfield
RUMSEY GARDENS, Clanfield

MAY Saturday 24
NORTHREPPS COTTAGE, East Boldre,
nr Lymington

MAY Sunday 25
BROCKENHURST PARK, Brockenhurst
HERRIARD PARK, Basingstoke
HOLLINGTON HERB NURSERIES,
nr Newbury
HOUSE-IN-THE-WOOD, Beaulieu
JENKYN PLACE, Bentley
PYLEWELL PARK, nr Lymington
SHRONER WOOD, Martyr Worthy
WINTERSHILL HALL, Durley
THE WYLDS, Liss, nr Petersfield

MAY Monday 26 (Spring Bank Hol.)
GREATHAM MILL, Liss, nr Petersfield
HURST MILL, nr Petersfield
NORTHREPPS COTTAGE, East Boldre,
nr Lymington

JUNE daily
FURZEY GARDENS, nr Lyndhurst
MACPENNYS, Bransgore
WELLINGTON COUNTRY PARK

JUNE daily to Sunday 15
EXBURY GARDENS, nr Southampton

JUNE daily except Mondays
SPINNERS, Boldre, nr Lymington

JUNE daily except Fridays
STRATFIELD SAYE HOUSE,
nr Basingstoke

JUNE every Sunday
HURST MILL, nr Petersfield

JUNE Sunday 1
ASHFORD GARDENS, nr Petersfield
STOCKS FARM, Burley Street,
nr Ringwood

JUNE Sunday 8
BENTLEY GARDENS, Bentley
‡BRAISHFIELD MANOR, nr Romsey
CHILWORTH MANOR, nr Southampton
JENKYN PLACE, Bentley
‡MERDON MANOR, nr Winchester

JUNE Sunday 15
LONGSTOCK PARK GARDENS,
Stockbridge
ROTHERFIELD PARK, nr Alton
SUTTON MANOR, Sutton Scotney,
nr Winchester

JUNE Saturday 21
KINGSMEAD, Winchester

JUNE Sunday 22
BROOK HOUSE, nr Fleet
DRAYTON HOUSE, East Meon,
nr Petersfield
HINTON AMPNER HOUSE, nr Alresford
JENKYN PLACE, Bentley
KILN COPSE, Eversley, nr Fleet
SOMERLEY, nr Ringwood
VERNON HILL HOUSE, Bishops Waltham

JUNE Wednesday 25
HIGHCLERE CASTLE, nr Newbury

JUNE Thursday 26
FIELD HOUSE, Monxton, nr Andover

JUNE Sunday 29
‡‡BRAMDEAN HOUSE, nr Alresford
BROADHATCH HOUSE, Bentley
‡CLIDDESDEN DOWN HOUSE,
nr Basingstoke
DROXFORD GARDENS, nr Wickham
FAIRFIELD HOUSE, Hambledon
FIELD HOUSE, Monxton, nr Andover
GREATHAM MILL, Liss, nr Petersfield
HOLLINGTON HERB NURSERIES,
nr Newbury
LITTLE CHILLAND, Martyr Worthy
‡‡MANOR FARM, Bramdean, nr Alresford
THE MANOR HOUSE, Buriton,
nr Petersfield
MOTTISFONT ABBEY, nr Romsey
ODIHAM GARDENS, nr Basingstoke
‡TUNWORTH OLD RECTORY,
nr Basingstoke

**JUNE Monday 30 daily to July
Saturday 5**
BRAMDEAN HOUSE, nr Alresford
FAIRFIELD HOUSE, Hambledon

JULY daily
FURZEY GARDENS, nr Lyndhurst

MACPENNYS, Bransgore
WELLINGTON COUNTRY PARK
JULY daily (except Mondays) to July 11
SPINNERS, Boldre, nr Lymington
JULY daily except Fridays
STRATFIELD SAYE HOUSE, nr
Basingstoke
JULY Sunday 6
BENTWORTH LODGE, nr Alton
BRAMDEAN HOUSE, nr Alresford
BROADHATCH HOUSE, Bentley
CHILLAND, Martyr Worthy,
nr Winchester
CHITHURST MANOR, Rogate,
nr Petersfield
COURT HOUSE, East Meon,
nr Petersfield
FAIRFIELD HOUSE, Hambledon
FROYLE GARDENS, nr Alton
HILL HOUSE, Old Alresford
HURST MILL, Petersfield
JENKYN PLACE, Bentley
THE MANOR HOUSE, Buriton,
nr Petersfield
MOUNDSMERE MANOR,
nr Basingstoke
THE WEIR HOUSE, Alresford
JULY Sunday 13
ALVERSTOKE GARDENS, Gosport
BENTWORTH LODGE, nr Alton
BOHUNT MANOR, Liphook
CULVERLEA HOUSE, Pennington
Common, Lymington
HOCKLEY HOUSE, Twyford,
nr Winchester
HURST MILL, Petersfield
‡THE OLD RECTORY, Rotherwick,
nr Basingstoke
‡OLD TOLL GATE, Mattingley, nr Hartley
Wintney
‡THE RICKS, Rotherwick
RUMSEY GARDENS, Clanfield
JULY Monday 14
RUMSEY GARDENS, Clanfield
JULY Sunday 20
HURST MILL, Petersfield
JENKYN PLACE, Bentley
KILMESTON GARDENS, nr Winchester
VERNON HILL HOUSE, Bishops Waltham
JULY Sunday 27
HOLLINGTON HERB NURSERIES,
nr Newbury
SPARSHOLT MANOR, nr Winchester
TICHBORNE PARK, nr Alresford
AUGUST daily
FURZEY GARDENS, nr Lyndhurst
MACPENNYS, Bransgore
WELLINGTON COUNTRY PARK
AUGUST daily except Fridays
STRATFIELD SAYE HOUSE,
nr Basingstoke
AUGUST Sunday 3
18 GLENAVON RD, Highcliffe-on-Sea,
nr Christchurch
HILL HOUSE, Old Alresford
JENKYN PLACE, Bentley

AUGUST Sunday 10
18 GLENAVON RD, Highcliffe-on-Sea
Christchurch
MERDON MANOR, nr Winchester
OAKLEY MANOR, Church Oakley,
nr Basingstoke
AUGUST Saturday 16
HAMBLEDON VINEYARD, Mill Down,
Hambledon, nr Portsmouth
AUGUST Sunday 17
JENKYN PLACE, Bentley
AUGUST Sunday 24
SUTTON MANOR, Sutton Scotney,
nr Winchester
AUGUST Sunday 31
HOLLINGTON HERB NURSERIES,
nr Newbury
JENKYN PLACE, Bentley
VERONA COTTAGE, Mengham, Hayling
Island
SEPTEMBER daily
FURZEY GARDENS, nr Lyndhurst
MACPENNYS, Bransgore
WELLINGTON COUNTRY PARK
SEPTEMBER daily except Fridays
STRATFIELD SAYE HOUSE,
nr Basingstoke
SEPTEMBER Sunday 14 & Sunday 21
MILL COURT, Alton
SEPTEMBER Sunday 28
HOLLINGTON HERB NURSERIES,
nr Newbury
OCTOBER daily
FURZEY GARDENS, nr Lyndhurst
MACPENNYS, Bransgore
WELLINGTON COUNTRY PARK
OCTOBER Sunday 19
UPPER RAKE HANGER, Rake, nr Liss
THE WYLDS, Liss, nr Petersfield
OCTOBER Monday 20
UPPER RAKE HANGER, Rake, nr Liss
OCTOBER Sunday 26
HACKWOOD PARK (THE SPRING
WOOD), nr Basingstoke
NOVEMBER & DECEMBER daily
FURZEY GARDENS, nr Lyndhurst (except
Dec. 25 & 26)
MACPENNYS, Bransgore
**NOVEMBER 1980 to FEBRUARY 1981
every Saturday & Sunday**
WELLINGTON COUNTRY PARK

DESCRIPTIONS OF GARDENS

Alverstoke Gardens, nr Gosport. Follow
A32 S of Fareham to 2nd lot of traffic lights,
3 m., turn right to Stokes Bay; 2nd left turn
after Roundabout is Western Way & Vectis Rd
is 30 yds along on left. From Gosport Ferry
take buses 72, 73 & 93 to Western Way, 2 m.
TEAS at Green Pastures. *Combined charge for
following 2 gardens 25p, Chd. 10p. Sun.
May 4 & Sun. July 13 (2–6)*

Green Pastures*⊕ (Mrs F. R. Mason) 26
Western Way. Garden backs on to Stanley

Park. Spacious varied garden; spring bulbs & shrubs; small vegetable garden, fruit trees; herbaceous border & flowering shrubs; small fish pond. NO DOGS.

59 Vectis Rd* (Miss M. W. Singleton) Small suburban garden of botanical interest on corner site; bulbs, rare shrubs, small pond & herbaceous border; new bog garden & rock pool

Ashford Gardens*⅃⊕ Steep, nr Petersfield. 2 m. N of Petersfield, off Alresford Rd (no. C18); turn right ½ m. past Cricketers Inn at Steep. About 12 acres of gardens set in valley of the Ash under steep wooded hangers of Stoner & Wheatham, described by poet Edward Thomas (who lived for a time at Berryfield before he was killed in France in 1917). Landscaped pools & waterfalls, beautiful trees & unusual shrubs, banks of azaleas & rhododendrons add colour & variety to this naturally lovely setting. *Combined charge for 3 adjoining gardens 50p, Chd. 25p. Sun. April 13 & Sun. June 1 (2–6)*

   Ashford Chace (Ashford Chace Ltd)
   Berryfield (Mr & Mrs Douglas Harris)
   Old Ashford Manor (J. Abrahams Esq)

Bentley Gardens,⊕ 4 m. SW of Farnham, on A31 between Farnham & Alton. Church car park may be used (by kind permission of the Rector). Bus: AV 452 Guildford–Winchester; alight School Lane, Bentley 400 yds. *Combined charge for following 5 gardens 30p, Chd. 10p. Sun. June 8 (2–6)*

   Bowerlands (L. L. Pike Esq) On A31 facing W, turn right in middle of Bentley & take 2nd turning right & house is 2nd on right. 2-acre garden with roses.
   Inwoods (Mrs J. Secker Walker) Small garden with old-fashioned roses & interesting trees. NO DOGS
   Orchard House (Maj. Iain Scorgie Price) Medium-sized garden; roses, trees, shrubs & rockery
   Pamplins (Maj. C. G. Seymour) Medium-sized garden; borders & roses
   ¶**Field House** (M. T. Coulton Esq) Medium-sized garden; borders & roses

Bentworth Lodge⅃⊕ (Mrs H. K. Andreae) 3½ m. NW of Alton. On A339, 9 m. S of Basingstoke. Medium-sized garden; old & new roses, pergola, yew hedges, shrubs & pond garden. Swimming in heated pool 20p extra. TEAS. Share to A.R.C. *Adm. 30p, Chd. 10p. Suns. July 6 & 13 (2–6)*

Binsted Place⊕ (Mr & Mrs C. J. Wills) 4 m. NE of Alton, 5 m. SW of Farnham; from A325 Farnham–Petersfield Rd turn off W at Binsted signpost by Halfway House P.H. at Bucks Horn Oak. 2½ acres; walled gardens comprising shrubbery, flower garden, rose garden, lily pond, vegetable garden; swimming

pool. Daffodils for sale. TEAS. *Adm. 25p, Chd. 10p. Sun. April 20 (2–6.30)*

Bohunt Manor*⅃⊕ (Lady Holman) Liphook. On A3 in village. Bus: AV 24 Guildford–Petersfield, alight at drive entrance. Medium-sized woodland garden; pleasant lakeside walk; water garden; herbaceous borders, roses, flowering shrubs. Collection of over 100 ornamental ducks, geese, pheasants, West & East African crowned cranes in natural surroundings. NO DOGS. TEA & biscuits. *Adm. 40p, Chd. 5p. Car park free. Sun. July 13 (2–7)*

Braishfield Manor (D. E. Gibbs Esq) 3 m. N of Romsey. Signposted to Braishfield on A31 (between Ampfield & Romsey) or on A3057 at Kings Somborne. 4-acre garden; young shrubs, roses & specimen trees planted since 1967. ½-acre vineyard. TEAS (June 8 only). *Adm. 30p, Chd. 10p. Sun. April 20 (2–5) & Sun. June 8 (2–6)*

Bramdean House* (Mr & Mrs H. Wakefield) 4 m. SE of Alresford. On A272. Bus: HD 69 Winchester–Petersfield, alight Bramdean village. Walled gardens with famous herbaceous borders, large collection of unusual plants & roses; carpets of many different spring bulbs. NO DOGS admitted. *Adm. 40p, Chd. 10p. Sun. Feb. 17 & Sun. April 13; also daily Sun. June 29 to Sun. July 6 inc. (2–6); also by previous appt.*

Broadhatch House*⊕ (Mr & Mrs Patrick Powell) Bentley, 4 m. NE of Alton. On A31 between Farnham & Alton. Bus: AV 452; alight School Lane, Bentley, ½ m. 3½ acres; formal garden with yew hedges; herbaceous borders, unusual flowering shrubs & variety of roses. Share to Br. Red Cross Soc. NO DOGS. *Adm. 25p, Chd. 10p. Suns. June 29 & July 6 (2–7)*

Brockenhurst Park⅃⊕ (The Hon. Denis & Mrs Berry) Brockenhurst. Entrance nr old church. Bus: Hants & Dorset 56, Southampton –Lymington; alight Island Shop, Brockenhurst, 1 m. 7 acres; woodland garden; rhododendrons, azaleas; old trees, ponds, steps, hedges, topiary. Modern house on site of old house. Beautiful undulating parkland. Tea Brockenhurst. *Adm. 30p. Sun. May 25 (2–6)*

Brook House⅃⊕ (Mr & Mrs Carron Greig) 1½ m. N of Fleet. B3013; immediately N of M3 Motorway bridge. Medium-sized garden; walled garden with swimming pool; lawns & herbaceous borders with water; walled kitchen garden; woodland walks. TEAS. *Adm. 25p, Chd. 5p. Sun. June 22 (2–6)*

Castletop* (Mrs Mackworth-Praed) Castle Hill Lane, Burley, E of Ringwood. A31 to Picket Post, turn S to Burley, approx. ¼ m. Bus: HD X17, alight Burley St. Woodland walks; bulbs, rhododendrons. TEAS. *Adm. 20p. Sun. March 16 & Sun. May 11 (2–6)*

Chantry (Adm. Sir Geoffrey & Lady Norman) 100 Acres, 1 m. E of Wickham. 4 m. N of Fareham via A32. From Wickham Church turn E along A333 for 1 m. then left up 100 Acre Rd for 300 yds. Garden entirely made by owners, with a view to easy maintenance; included in *Gardens of Britain*. NO DOGS. Tea Olde Tea Shoppe, Wickham. (*Share to Br. Red Cross Soc.*). *Adm. 30p, Chd. 5p. Sun. May 18 (2–7)*

Chilland*⅛⊕ (L. A. Impey Esq) Martyr Worthy. 4 m. NE of Winchester, ½ m. from Itchen Abbas. Bus: AV 214 Winchester–Aldershot, alight signpost marked 'Chilland' on B3047. Medium-sized garden of modern design for present-day conditions; herbaceous plants, shrub borders, roses, lilies, peonies. View of R. Itchen valley. *Adm. 50p, Chd. 10p. Sun. July 6 (2–7)*

Chilworth Manor,*⅛⊕ (University of Southampton) Chilworth, N of Southampton. Signposted from Clump Inn on A27, 1 m. NW of its junction with A33. Bus: Hants & Dorset 62 Romsey–Southampton, alight Clump Inn, Chilworth, ¼ m. 15 acres, largely informal; well-matured flowering shrubs, mainly rhododendrons & azaleas; conifers; fine specimen trees; walks through woodland beyond garden with indigenous varieties. *Adm. 40p, Chd. 20p. Sun. June 8 (2–7)*

Chithurst Manor,†⊕ (Mrs M. E. de Udy) Rogate, E of Petersfield, 2½ m. W of Midhurst via A272 Petersfield–Midhurst rd; turn off to Chithurst; there is a signpost saying Residential Hotel at Trotton by the Common. Small typical formal Elizabethan paved garden & riverside walk in small coppice. Tiny Norman Church in field. Tea South Downs Hotel, Trotton. *Adm.* (*inc. part-house*) *30p, Chd. 15p. Sun. July 6 (2.30–6.30)*

Cliddesden Down House*⅛⊕ (Michael Peto Esq) 1 m. S of Basingstoke. In centre of Cliddesden village. Medium-sized garden of horticultural interest designed some 20 yrs ago with many interesting specie roses & climbing plants, surrounding charming early Georgian house (not shown). *Adm. 25p, Chd. 5p. Sun. June 29 (2–6)*

Cold Hayes*⅛ (Mr Brian Blacker & Lady Doris Blacker) Steep Marsh. Turn off A325 Petersfield–Farnham Rd to Steep Marsh. Turn off Petersfield–Alresford Rd 3 m. from Petersfield. From Steep village observe direction signs. Medium-sized garden; flowering shrubs, trees, beautiful views. *Adm. 30p, Chd. 10p. Sun. May 18 (2.30–7)*

Court House†⊕ (Arthur D. Gill Esq) (but several flights of steps) East Meon, 5 m. W of Petersfield. Turn off A32 at West Meon; or off A272 at Langrish. Bus: Southampton–Petersfield, or Winchester–Petersfield; alight opp. church at garden gate. Approx. 2 acres;

formal walled garden, herbaceous borders, yew hedges. C14 ecclesiastical hall also shown (no extra charge). NO DOGS. *Adm. 30p, Chd. 10p. Sun. July 6 (2.30–6.30)*

Cranbury Park †⊕ (Mr & Mrs Chamberlayne-Macdonald) Otterbourne, 5 m. S of Winchester. 2 m. N of Eastleigh; main entrance on old A33 between Winchester & Southampton, by bus stop at top of Otterbourne Hill. Extensive pleasure grounds laid out in late C18 & early C19; fountains; rose garden & specimen trees; lakeside walk. Stables & family carriages will be on view. Picnic area provided in grounds. *Adm. 50p, Chd. 25p Sun. April 13 (2–6)*

¶**Culverlea House***⊕ (Brig. & Mrs R. A. Blakeway) Pennington Common, 1 m. W of Lymington. A337 Lymington–Bournemouth; turn N at Pennington Cross, through village, 1st house on left past common. 1-acre garden with wide variety of trees, flowering shrubs & old & new roses. Tea Lymington. *Adm. 20p, Chd. 10p Sun. July 13 (2–6)*

The Deane House (Mr & Mrs Brian Downward) Sparsholt, 3 m. W of Winchester. Via A272 Winchester–Stockbridge rd to Littleton/Sparsholt X-rds. Car park. Garden on S slope with views; varied spring bulbs & shrubs. Pony rides. TEAS. (*Share to Peacehaven Home for Horses*). *Adm. 30p, Chd. 10p. Sun. April 20 (2–5)*

The Dower House*⊕ (Mr & Mrs Rollo Hoare) Dogmersfield. Turn N off A287 for Dogmersfield. Bus: AV 7 Farnham–Odiham; alight Dogmersfield turning, 1½ m. Medium-sized garden; bluebell wood with collection of over 200 different varieties of rhododendron & azalea; magnolias & other flowering trees & shrubs; fine views. TEAS (May 11 & 18 only). *Adm. 30p, Chd. 10p. Sun. & Mon. May 11 & 12, 18 & 19 (2–6)*

Drayton House (Baroness Dacre) East Meon, 6 m. SW of Petersfield. Take East Meon turning on S side of A272. Bus: Petersfield–Winchester; alight bottom of hill, 100 yds. Medium-sized garden; old-fashioned roses; herbaceous; views over the lovely Meon valley. Part-time gardener only. TEAS. *Adm. 30p, Chd. 10p. Sun. June 22 (2–6)*

Droxford Gardens, 4½ m. N of Wickham. On A32 approx. mid-way between Alton & Portsmouth, the following 5 gardens will be open. Combined charge 50p, OAPs & Chd. 25p. Sun. June 29 (2–6)
  Fir Hill (Mrs Derek Schreiber). In Droxford village. 5 acres; roses, shrubs; swimming pool. Country TEAS.
  The Manor⊕ (Mr & Mrs Robin Denham) medium-sized garden; roses; swimming pool. William & Mary house (not open).
  Myrtle Cottage⊕ (Miss Joan Spurgin) small garden

Rosemary Cottage (Tony Vintcent Esq) small garden

The Small House (Maj. & Mrs David Colville) Small garden

● **Exbury Gardens**＊⚹⊕ (Mr & Mrs Edmund de Rothschild) Exbury, 2½ m. SE of Beaulieu; 15 m. SW of Southampton. Via B3054 SE of Beaulieu; after 1 m. turn sharp right for Exbury. 200 acres of woodland garden incorporating the Rothschild Collection of azaleas, rhododendrons, magnolias, maples & camellias. TEAS & light refreshments available. *Adm. 80p (parties 70p); Chd. 40p. March 30 to June 15 daily (2–6.30)*

Fairfield House⚹⊕ (Mr & Mrs Peter Wake) Hambledon, 10 m. SW of Petersfield. In Hambledon village on B2150. Medium-sized garden; daffodils (April opening), flowering shrubs, mixed borders, walled gardens, fine cedar trees. Scheduled Regency house (not open). Refreshments available June 29 & July 5 & 6. *Adm. 40p, Chd. 15p. Sun. June 29 daily to Sun. July 6 (2–6); also by appt. (Tel. Hambledon 431)*

¶**Field House**⊕ (Dr & Mrs Pratt) Monxton, 3 m. W of Andover, between A303 & A343; in Monxton take Abbots Ann Rd; last house on right. 2-acre garden made & maintained by owners; herbaceous borders; orchard; chalk-pit garden with pond & kitchen garden. Thatched cottage (not open). Parking & picnicking in field opp. NO DOGS. *Adm. 25p, Chd. 10p. Thurs. June 26 & Sun. June 29 (2–6)*

Froyle Gardens. Approx. 4 m. NE of Alton. From A31 Alton–Bentley turn off by side of Ham & Chicken Inn. & Filling Station. TEAS at Brocas Farm. *Combined charge for following 3 gardens 30p, Chd. 10p. Sun. July 6 (2–7)*

¶**Park Edge**⊕ (Mrs E. Bootle-Wilbraham) 1–1½ acres with hybrid musk roses & other roses; peonies; herbaceous plants; shrubs

¶**Blundens House**⊕ (Mr & Mrs D. J. Evans) ¾-acre garden with herbaceous, rose & shrub borders, all planted since 1974. Small Tudor house (not open) with later additions in keeping

¶**Brocas Farm** (A. A. Robertson Esq) Lower Froyle (½ m. up from turning on A31 to Lower Froyle). 2-acre garden with shrubs, shrub roses & herbaceous. Early C18 farmhouse (not open) & buildings. NO DOGS

● **Furzey Gardens**＊†⚹⊕ (H. J. Cole Esq & Mrs M. A. Selwood) Minstead, 8 m. SW of Southampton. 1 m. S of A31; 2 m. W of Cadnam & end of M27; 3½ m. NW of Lyndhurst. 8 acres; informal shrub garden; comprehensive collections of azaleas & heathers; water garden; fernery; summer & winter flowering shrubs. Botanical interest at all seasons. Also open Will Selwood Gallery & Ancient Cottage (A.D. 1560); high-class arts & crafts by 150 local craftsmen. NO DOGS. Tea Compton Arms Hotel 1 m. *Adm. 55p (winter 25p), Chd. 25p (winter 15p). Daily all year except Dec. 25 & 26 (10–7; dusk in winter)*

18 Glenavon Road (L. A. Vilches Esq) Highcliffe on Sea, 2 m. E of Christchurch. From A35 turn along Ringwood Rd towards Walkford, then 1st turn on right to Holmhurst Estate. From A337 turn up Hinton Wood Ave & right up Braemar Drive. Small garden on Holmhurst Estate designed & planted by owner in natural surroundings; variety of trees, shrubs & flowers. Share to Nat. Institute for the Blind. *Adm. 10p, Chd. 5p. Suns. Aug. 3 & 10 (2–7)*

Greatham Mill＊ (Mrs E. N. Pumphrey) Liss, 5 m. N of Petersfield. From A325, Petersfield–Farnham, turn off W at Greatham on to B3006 towards Alton; after 600 yds turn left into 'No Through Rd' lane leading to garden. Interesting garden with large variety of plants surrounding mill house, with mill stream. Plants for sale. NO DOGS. *Adm. 25p, Chd. free. Sun. April 20, Mon. May 5, Mon. May 26, Sun. June 29 (2–7)*

Hackwood Park (The Spring Wood)＊†⚹ (The Viscount Camrose) 1 m. S of Basingstoke. Entrance off Tunworth Rd. Signposted from A339 Alton–Basingstoke. The Spring Wood is a large 80-acre delightful C17–C18 semi-formal wood with Pavilions, walks, glades, ornamental pools, amphitheatre, interesting trees & bulbs. No Dogs. HOME-MADE TEAS & produce for sale. *Adm. 40p, Chd. 10p. Suns. April 20, May 18, Oct. 26 (2–6)*

Hambledon Vineyard＊⊕ (Maj.-Gen. Sir Guy Salisbury-Jones) Mill Down, Hambledon. 9 m. SW of Petersfield, 12 m. N of Portsmouth. Turn off A3 London–Portsmouth Rd at signpost to Hambledon or at Waterlooville. Bus: SD 139, Portsmouth–Hambledon. Bus stop: 10 mins walk. Talk given in press house. Small pleasure garden. Vineyard produces a dry white wine of subtle charm & pleasing fragrance. Vineyard lies on slope above village of Hambledon. TEAS & light refreshments. (*Share to Hambledon Village Hall.*) *Adm. Adults (includes wine-tasting) 80p; Senior Citizens (includes wine-tasting) 55p; Persons under 18, 35p. Sat. Aug. 16 (2.30–5.30)*

Harcombe House⊕ (Sir Derek Vestey, Bt) Ropley, E of Alresford. Leave A31 Alton–Winchester Rd at The Anchor, Ropley; follow rd to West Tisted for ½ m; turn up *first* narrow lane on right & on to Harcombe. Bus: AV 14 Aldershot–Winchester. Large garden; bulbs in season; flowering shrubs, small water garden; good views. *Adm. 30p, Chd. 5p. Suns. April 6, 13, May 18 (2–6)*

Herriard Park＊⚹⊕ (J. Loveys Jervoise Esq) S of Basingstoke. A339. Bus: WD 107 Alton–Basingstoke, alight Herriard Church, ¼ m.

Large garden; botanical interest; flowering shrubs, greenhouses, pinetum. Pots & plants for sale. (*Share to Gardeners' Sunday*). TEAS. *Adm. 20p, Chd. 10p. Sun. May 25 (2–6)*

Highclere Castle⚬⊕ (The Earl of Carnarvon) S of Newbury. A34 Newbury–Whitchurch, turn at Cherrycot X-rds; A343 Newbury–Andover, turn at Highclere village. Bus: Newbury–Whitchurch, alight Cherrycot X-rds, ½ m.; Newbury–Andover, alight Highclere village, 2 m. Large garden; extensive lawns with fine cedars, rhododendrons & azaleas. House not open. Tea Yew Tree Cafe, Highclere on A343. *Adm. 25p. Wed. June 25 (2–6)*

Hill House⊕ (Maj. & Mrs W. F. Richardson) Old Alresford. From Alresford, 1 m. along B3046 towards Basingstoke, then turn right by church. 2-acre garden; large herbaceous border & formal beds set round large lawn; kitchen garden. TEA & biscuits. *Adm. 25p, Chd. 10p. Sun. July 6 & Sun. Aug. 3 (2–6)*

Hinton Ampner House*⚬⊕ (Ralph Dutton Esq) S of Alresford. On Petersfield–Winchester Rd A272. 1 m. W of Bramdean village. Bus: HD 67 Petersfield–Winchester, alight at Lodge, 5 mins. Large garden; formal layout; flowering shrubs & trees; roses. Subject of article in *Country Life*. Good views. *Adm. 30p, Chd. 15p. Sun. May 11 & Sun. June 22 (2–6)*

Hockley House⊕ (Mr & Mrs J. R. L. Hill) Church Lane, Twyford, 2½ m. S of Winchester. From A333 Winchester–Portsmouth turn, just N of Twyford village, down Church Lane. Garden runs down to R. Itchen; shrubs, annual beds, lawns. *Adm. 30p, Chd. 10p. Sun. July 13 (2–6)*

Hollington Herb Nurseries*⊕ (Hollington Nurseries Ltd; Judith & Simon Hopkinson) Woolton Hill, 5 m. SW of Newbury. A343 from Andover or Newbury; turn for Woolton Hill; take 2nd left & after ½ m. fork left (next to Hollington House). 1½-acre working herb nursery for wholesale & retail trade situated in old walled kitchen garden; working greenhouse/tunnels plus display & stock beds; approx. 200 different herbs & scented geraniums can be seen. NO DOGS. (*Share to Cancer Research*). *Adm. 20p, Chd. 5p. Suns. May 25, June 29, July 27, Aug. 31, Sept. 28 (11–5)*

Holywell*†⚬⊕ (The Lord Rhyl) Swanmore. The Bungalow Lodge is on A32, mid-way between Wickham & Droxford, well postered. Bus: HD 69 from Fareham, alight Hill Pound (1 m.). Medium-sized garden; daffodils, camellias, flowering cherry trees, woodland walks. Plants for sale. Dogs welcome. TEA & biscuits March 30 only; March 31 picnic area. *Adm. 30p, Chd. 10p. Sun. & Mon. March 30 & 31 (2–6)*

House-in-the-Wood (Countess Michaelowski) 1½ m. from Beaulieu; signposted from Motor Car Museum, Beaulieu (on B3054 Lymington–Hythe). 13 acres of Woodland Garden. TEAS. *Adm. 40p, Chd. free. Sun. May 25 (2.30–6)*

Hurst Mill*⚬ (Mr & Mrs Willoughby Norman) 2 m. SE of Petersfield. On B2146 mid-way between Petersfield & South Harting. Large garden in lovely position overlooking lake; terraces; waterfall, bog gardens, camellias, rhododendrons, magnolias, flowering shrubs, ornamental trees, shrub & climbing roses, large kitchen garden. NO DOGS. Tea Punch & Judy, High St, Petersfield. *Adm. 40p, Chd. 10p. April 6 to July 20 every Sun.; also Mons. April 7, May 5 & 26 (2–6); also by appt. April to end of Aug. for Garden Clubs & parties (Tel. Harting 216)*

Jenkyn Place*⊕ (G. E. Coke Esq) Bentley. 400 yds N of X-rds in Bentley signposted Crondall. Bus: 452 Guildford–Winchester, alight Bentley village, 400 yds. Well-planned large garden of variety & botanical interest. Subject of an article in *Country Life*. Old-fashioned & species roses, herbaceous borders, interesting collection of rare shrubs. NO DOGS. Car park free. *Adm. 40p, Chd. 16 & under (accompanied) 10p. Suns. May 11, 25, June 8, 22, July 6, 20, Aug. 3, 17, 31 (2–7); also by previous appt. all year, for organised parties*

June*⊕ (Mr & Mrs G. A. Carter) Seaview Rd, Walkford. 1 m. from Cat & Fiddle; 200 yds from Walkford Hotel. Bus: HD 123, 124, 125, 126 from Bournemouth or Lymington. ¼-acre, well designed garden for all seasons (situated alongside wooded common), featured on Southern ITV & in Hampshire magazine 1968; many varieties of shrubs & plants, spring bulbs, outdoor grapes. NO DOGS. *Adm. 20p, Chd. 5p. Sun. May 4 (2.30–6)*

Kilmeston Gardens. 7 m. E of Winchester. Kilmeston lies 1 m. S of A272, turning at New Cheriton X-rds. The following 3 gardens will be open. Variety of plants & vegetables for sale. Cream TEAS at Manor Farm Cottage. *Combined charge for 3 gardens 50p, Chd. 10p. Sun. July 20 (2–6.30)*

¶**Manor Farm House** (Adml & Mrs Graham) Medium-sized garden with good views & variety of interesting plants & shrubs. Plants for sale

¶**Manor Farm Cottage** (Mr & Mrs R. A. Mardling) ½-acre typical cottage garden with herbaceous borders, shrubs & rockeries

¶**Dean House** (Mr & Mrs P. Gwyn) Well laid-out gardens surrounding Georgian house (not open)—lawns, fine trees, shrubs, topiary, walled garden, greenhouses

Kiln Copse*⊕ (Mr & Mrs Jervis O'Donohoe) Eversley, 4 m. N of Fleet. From A30 on to B3016 & from A327 on to B3016. 8 acres; daffodils in wood followed by bluebells &

foxgloves; good collection of rhododendrons; new mixed border; roses; bog garden. Produce for sale. NO DOGS. TEAS. *Adm. 30p, Chd. 5p. Suns. May 11 & 18, June 22 (2-7)*

¶**Kingsmead** (Mr & Mrs Hopkinson) Kingsgate Rd, Winchester. A33 to St Cross Rd, Winchester; turn off at Norman Rd; house on corner of Norman Rd & Kingsgate Rd. Garden of ½ acre with collection of roses; rare shrubs & plants; extensive rock garden. (*Share to St Lawrence Church Appeal*). TEAS. *Adm. 30p, Chd. 10p. Sat. April 19 & Sat. June 21 (2-7)*

Laverstoke House*⚘⊕ (Mrs Julian Sheffield) Approx. 2 m. E of Whitchurch; 10 m. W of Basingstoke. Garden with fine trees, shrubs & bulbs, surrounding C18 house (not open). Large collection of shrub roses. *Adm. 30p, Chd. 10p. Sun. April 13 (2-6)*

Lepe House*⊕ (The Dowager Lady Wardington) Exbury, S of Southampton. From N as for Fawley follow signs for Lepe. From W as for Beaulieu follow signs for Lepe. Bus: Southampton–Lepe, alight Lepe Point, 1 m. Large woodland & wild garden with rhododendrons; on the sea at mouth of R. Beaulieu. TEA & biscuits. *Adm. 30p. Car park 10p. Sun. May 18 (2-6)*

Little Chilland⊕ (Mr & Mrs Nelson) Martyr Worthy. 4 m. NE of Winchester; ½ m. from Itchen Abbas. Bus: AV 14 Winchester–Aldershot; alight signpost marked 'Chilland' on B3047; 100 yds down Chilland Lane. Garden of ¾ acre; herbaceous, rock, small greenhouses, conifers, shrubs, pot plants. NO DOGS. TEAS. *Adm. 25p, Chd. 5p. Sun. June 29 (2-7)*

Littlehay* (Mr John & Lady Janet Gore) Burley, E of Ringwood. Just out of Burley, opp. cricket ground. Small pretty garden (originally laid out by Miss Jekyll) in charming forest surroundings. *Adm. 20p, Chd. 5p. Sun. April 27 (2-6)*

Longparish House*† (Lt-Col. & Mrs C. P. Dawnay) Longparish, 5½ m. E of Andover. 3½ m. SW of Whitchurch, on B3048. Approx. 3½ acres; mainly wild garden with daffodils & other spring bulbs naturalised in grass. R. Test runs through garden. Elizabethan granary on straddle stones. Col Peter Hawker (1786–1853), famous sportsman, lived here. *Adm. 30p, Chd. 15p. Sun. April 20 (2-6)*

Longstock Park Gardens* (Leckford Estate Ltd; Part of John Lewis Partnership) 3 m. N of Stockbridge. From A30 turn N on to A3057 & follow signs to Longstock. 7 acres woodland & water garden; extensive collection of aquatic & bog plants. Walk through park from water garden leads to arboretum, grey garden, herb garden & rose garden; herbaceous, summer bulbs & dahlia border. Plants may be purchased from nursery. Free car park. *Adm. 40p, Chd. 20p. Sun. June 15 (2-5)*

Macpennys* (D. B. & Tim Lowndes Esq) Bransgore. Mid-way between Christchurch & Burley. Bus: HD 15 Christchurch–Burley, alight at gate. Large woodland garden. Nurseries, camellias, rhododendrons, azaleas, heathers. Mist propagation. Tea Burley. *Collecting box. All year daily (Mons.–Sats. 9–5, Suns. 2–5)*

¶**Manor Farm**⊕ (Mrs Cecil Feilden) Bramdean, 4 m. SE of Alresford. A272, ½-way between Winchester & Petersfield (both 9 m.); in Bramdean turn up Church Lane; 1st house on left. 1-acre garden, newly made; primarily shrubs planted mainly in 1977. NO DOGS. *Collecting box. Sun. June 29 (2-6)*

The Manor House, Buriton†⚘⊕ (Mr & Mrs C. R. Wood) 4 m. S of Petersfield; turn E off A3 Portsmouth Rd at signpost Buriton (N of Butser Hill); drive up to the church, entrance to the left of church by the village pond. 5 acres of garden; formal rose walk, mixed border, walled garden with old-fashioned roses & summer house; 3 walnuts 400 yrs old; lawns & conservatory. C16 Tithe Barn of great architectural beauty; hexagonal dovecote. Lovely views of Queen Elizabeth Forest (Edward Gibbon described the view in his writings). NO DOGS. TEAS. (*Share to Handicapped Adventure Playground Assn.*). *Adm. 25p, Chd. 10p. Suns. June 29 & July 6 (2-6)*

Martyr Worthy Manor⚘⊕ (Cmdr & Mrs Rivett-Carnac) 3 m. NE of Winchester. From Alresford, or Winchester Bypass, turn on to B3047; white gates in Martyr Worthy, opp. War Memorial & by bus stop. 4-acre garden; massed bulbs, interesting trees & shrubs. Next to fine C11 church. Tea Winchester. *Adm. 25p, Chd. 5p. Sun. April 20 (2-6)*

Merdon Manor (D. A. H. Wilkie Cooper Esq) Hursley, SW of Winchester. From A3090 at Standon turn on to Slackstead Rd & along 2 m. Medium-sized garden; fine views, roses, herbaceous border, small formal walled water garden. *Adm. 30p, Chd. 10p. Sun. June 8 & Sun. Aug. 10 (2-6)*

Michelmersh Court†⚘⊕ (Sir Jocelyn Lucas, Bt & Lt-Cmdr & Mrs R. S. de Chair) 4 m. N of Romsey. From A3057 Romsey–Stockbridge, turn E at Timsbury for Michelmersh. Medium-sized garden; peacocks, herb garden, roses, woodland walks. Some plants for sale. Pony rides. Historic church adjoins. *Refreshments, Adm. 35p, Chd. 20p. Sun. April 6 (2-6)*

Mill Court*⚘ (Leila, Viscountess Hampden) 3 m. NE of Alton, on S side of A31. Turn off at County sign marked Mill Court; immediately after crossing R. Wey, gate & lodge. Medium-sized garden bounded by early stone farm buildings & walls & fine large stone granary with Tudor dwelling attached; herbaceous border & roses, many climbing with clematis; varied collection of shrubs, many with good autumn colours; rare weeping beech at main gate. NO DOGS. (Share to Church of England Children's Society). Adm. 25p, Chd. 10p. Suns. Sept. 14 & 21 (2.30–6)

Mottisfont Abbey*⊕ (The National Trust) Mottisfont, 4½ m. NW of Romsey. From A3057 Romsey–Stockbridge turn off W at sign to Mottisfont. One wheelchair available at garden. 30 acres; originally a C12 Priory; landscaped grounds with spacious lawns bordering R. Test; magnificent trees, inc. a giant plane; river walk; remarkable ancient spring pre-dating the Priory; walled garden contains Nat. Trust's large collection of old-fashioned roses. Tea Mottisfont Post Office. Adm. 60p, Chd. 30p. Sun. June 1 (2–6)

Moundsmere Manor*⅄⊕ (Mr & Mrs M. P. Andreae) Preston Candover, S of Basingstoke, 10-acre garden; herbaceous borders, ornamental yew hedges, roses, greenhouses. Adm. 30p. Sun. July 6 (2–6)

Northrepps Cottage*⊕ (Mrs Richardson) Main Rd, East Boldre, 5 m. NE of Lymington. Small garden made & maintained by owner since 1971, with flowering shrubs & trees, NO DOGS. Tea Montague Arms, Beaulieu. Adm. 25p, Chd. 10p. Sat May 24 (2–6) & Mon. May 26 (10–6)

Oakley Manor⊕ (Mr & Mrs Priestley) Church Oakley, W of Basingstoke. From B3400, Basingstoke–Whitchurch, take turning to Church Oakley. Bus: WD 103 Basingstoke–Church Oakley. Medium-sized garden; lawns; trees; small water garden; borders; greenhouses. NO DOGS. TEAS. Adm. 20p, Chd. 5p. Sun. Aug. 10 (2–7)

Odiham Gardens. Attractive gardens, each with period house (not open). TEAS at The Priory. Combined charge for 4 gardens 50p. Sun. June 29 (2–7)

  The Priory (Mr & Mrs Hugh Lee)
  The Bury House (Cmdr & Mrs Edwin Morrison)
  The White House (Mr & Mrs Christopher Chetwode)
  ¶**The Long House** (Mr & Mrs Ian Gornall)

¶**The Old Rectory, Rotherwick**⅄⊕ (B. L. B. Hutchings Esq) NE of Basingstoke; 2½ m. NW of Hook. Via A32 N for 1 m. then straight on to Rotherwick; left on entering village; past church; house at T-junction at end of village. 2-acre typical Victorian parsonage garden; lawns, rosebeds, orchard, kitchen garden; good trees inc. beech & lime. TEA & biscuits. Adm. 20p, Chd. 5p. Sun. July 13 (2–6)

Old Toll Gate (Lady Scobie) Mattingley, 3½ m. NW of Hartley Wintney. On A32 between Hook & Reading, on Reading side of Hound Green Garage. Small garden made & worked by owner for colour & design. Some plants for sale. NO DOGS. Tea The Old Rectory, Rotherwick. Adm. 20p. Sun. July 13 (2.30–6)

Pennington Chase*⅄⊕ (John Coates Esq) Lower Pennington Lane, Lymington. A337 Lymington–Bournemouth Rd, turn S at Pennington Cross into Lower Pennington Lane. Bus stop: Fox Pond & Pennington Cross, ½ m. 4-acre garden; interesting collection of flowering shrubs & trees, many in fine state of maturity; spring bulbs. NO DOGS. Adm. 30p, Chd. 15p. Sun. April 13 (2–7)

Pennington House*†⊕ (Col Brownlow) 2 m. S of Lymington. From A337 Lymington–Bournemouth turn off S at X-rds. Large garden; interesting collection of trees, shrubs & herbaceous plants; water garden. Adm. 50p, Chd. 25p. Sun. May 18 (2–7)

Pylewell Park*⅄⊕ (W. Whitaker Esq) 2½ m. E of Lymington. Bus: HD 107 Lymington–Hythe, alight S Baddesley, ¼ m. Large garden of botanical interest; good trees, flowering shrubs, rhododendrons, lake woodland garden. Adm. 30p, Chd. 10p. Sun. May 11 & Sun. May 25 (2–7)

The Ricks⊕ (J. J. Morris Esq) The Street, Rotherwick, 2 m. N of Hook. M3/A30 or M4/A33 then A32 & turn at signpost to Rotherwick (next to Falcon pub). Medium-sized garden; herbaceous border, shrub borders, vegetable garden, greenhouse, lawns. Tea The Old Rectory, Rotherwick. Adm. 30p, Chd. 10p. Sun. July 13 (2–6.30)

Rotherfield Park †⅄⊕ (Sir James & Lady Scott) East Tisted, 4 m. S of Alton. On A32. Bus: SD 38 Portsmouth–Alton. Large garden; wall garden; rose garden, herbaceous borders; lovely grounds with beautiful trees; very good greenhouses open. TEA & biscuits. Adm. 30p, Chd. free. Sun. May 18 & Sun. June 15 (2–6)

Rumsey Gardens*⊕ (Mr & Mrs N. R. Giles) 117 Drift Rd, Clanfield, 6 m. S of Petersfield. Turn off A3 N of Horndean, at Hill Top Petrol Station, which is at junction with Drift Rd. 2 acres; alpine, herbaceous & water gardens; heather, rhododendrons & wild gardens planted in raised beds of acid soil. Container-grown plants for sale in adjacent Nursery. NO DOGS. Adm. 20p, Chd. 10p. Suns. & Mons. May 18 & 19, July 13 & 14 (2–7)

¶**Segensworth House**⅄⊕ (Mr & Mrs Gerald A. Day) Mill Lane, Titchfield, 3 m. W of Fareham. From Fareham via A27 towards Southampton, turn right (N) at sign to Titchfield Abbey; house is past Abbey, on right. 4-acre garden running down to R. Meon with natural pond; many varieties of daffodils & spring bulbs; rhododendrons, shrubs & trees. Tudor Barn. TEA & biscuits. Adm. 30p, Chd. 15p. Sun. April 20 (2–6); also by appt.

¶**Shroner Wood**⅄ (Mr John & Lady Mary Gaye Anstruther-Gough-Calthorpe) Martyr Worthy, 5 m. N of Winchester. On A33 ¼ m. from Lunways Inn. 4 acres; arboretum, formerly planted by Hilliers, consisting of shrubs & fine trees; orchard & fine views; rhododendrons, azaleas, bluebells. TEAS. *Adm. 30p, Chd. 10p. Sun. May 25 (2–6.30)*

Soberton Mill †⅃ (Mrs Arthur Sutherland) N of Wickham. On A32 mid-way between Droxford & Wickham, each 2 m. Medium-sized garden intersected by mill stream & bordered by R. Meon. (*Share to Hampshire Federation for the Blind* (Droxford Branch)). *Adm. 30p, Chd. 15p. Sun. & Mon. April 6 & 7 (2–7)*

Somerley †⅃ (The Earl of Normanton) N of Ringwood. Turn W off A338 at Ellingham. Bus: HD/WD 38 Bournemouth–Salisbury, alight Ellingham Cross, 1 m. Medium-sized garden; wonderful views over R. Avon valley; formal lay-out; herbaceous borders; rose garden. NO DOGS. *Adm. 40p. Sun. June 22 (2–6)*

Sparsholt Manor⊕ (Mr & Mrs David Martineau) Sparsholt, 3 m. W of Winchester. Via A272 Winchester–Stockbridge Rd to Littleton/Sparsholt X-rds; turn left for Sparsholt to Plough Inn; entrance opp. Medium-sized garden; lawns, bedding plants; good views. Use of swimming pool 25p extra. NO DOGS. TEAS. *Adm. 25p, Chd. 10p. Sun. July 27 (2–5.30)*

● **Spinners*** (Mr & Mrs P. G. G. Chappell) School Lane, Boldre, 1½ m. N of Lymington. From A337 Brockenhurst–Lymington, turn E for Boldre (*not* rd to Boldre Church); cross Boldre Bridge; just short of Pilley village, turn right into School Lane. Garden entirely made & maintained by owners; azaleas, rhododendrons, camellias, magnolias, etc., interplanted with primulas, blue poppies & other choice woodland & ground cover plants. Rare plants & shrubs for sale. Sale of flower paintings. NO DOGS. *Adm. 20p, April 20 to July 11 daily except Mons. (2–6.30)*

Stock's Farm⊕ (John W. Richardson Esq) Burley St, 2½ m. E of Ringwood. A31 to Picket Post; turn off at signpost to Burley; go through Burley St village, past Flying G. Ranch, up hill & 1st house on right. About 1⅓ acres; mature garden of old farmhouse (not open (; flowering shrubs, azaleas, camellias, magnolias & rhododendrons. Tea Mann Tea Rooms, Burley, ½ m. *Collecting box. Sun. June 1 (2–6)*

● **Stratfield Saye House***†⅃⊕ (Home of the Dukes of Wellington) Off A33, equidistant between Reading & Basingstoke. House built 1630 & presented to the Great Duke in 1817; unique collection of paintings, prints, furniture, china, silver & personal mementoes of the Great Duke. Special Wellington Exhibition & (during 1980). Costume Exhibition from BBC TV Blue Peter Special Assignment on the Duke of Wellington.

Wildfowl sanctuary; American, rose & walled gardens & grounds. *Inc. adm. £1.40, Chd. 70p. Special rates for pre-booked parties (Tel. Basingstoke 682882 or Turgis Green 602). Daily (except Fris.) March 30–Sept. 28 (11.30–5)*

Sutton Manor⅃⊕ (C. A. Davies Esq) Sutton Scotney. 7 m. N of Winchester. In Sutton Scotney village; coming from Winchester on A34, 1st drive on left. 30 acres; herb farm with herb display beds planted in walled garden & shop. Many greenhouses; in park lovely trees & shrub walks. Teashop on Whitchurch Rd (2 m. away). *Adm. 30p, Chd. 10p. Suns. April 20, June 15, Aug. 24 (2–6)*

Tichborne Park †⅃ (Mrs John Loudon) 2 m. S of Alresford. Drive gate between Cheriton & Alresford. Large garden with R. Itchen running through & a waterfall surrounded by fine park. Property famous for annual distribution of Tichborne Dole. Village church with Roman Catholic and Protestant altars. *Adm. 20p, Chd. 10p. Sun. April 13 (2–6) & Sun. July 27 (2–6)*

Tunworth Old Rectory †⊕ (Col the Hon. Julian Berry) 5 m. SE of Basingstoke. 3 m. from Basingstoke, turn S off A30 at sign to Tunworth. Medium-sized garden; shrubs, lawns, yew hedges, rose borders; fine beech trees & ilex. Interesting beech-lined walk to church. House (not shown) scheduled as Ancient Monument, part dating to 1210; in *Domesday Book* with adjacent farmhouse & church. TEAS. *Adm. 25p, Chd. 10p. Sun. June 29 (2–6.30)*

Upper Rake Hanger (Dr Stephen Laing) Liss, 4 m. N of Petersfield. Towards London via A3; garden ¼ m. beyond The Jolly Drover on right, 1 m. S of Rake. Approx. 2 acres; wild garden of heathers, azaleas, conifers & sand-liking shrubs, set in 7 acres of woodland on side of a hill; owner making & maintaining a woodland garden by himself in his spare time. Spectacular views over 3 counties. Plants for sale. TEAS. *Collecting box. Sun. May 4 (2–6), Mon. May 5 (10–1), Sun. Oct. 19 (2–5), Mon. Oct. 20 (10–1); also by appt.*

Vernon Hill House⅃ (The Lord & Lady Newton) 1 m. from Bishop's Waltham. Turning off Beeches Hill. Attractive spring & summer garden of 6 acres; wild garden with tulips growing informally followed by lilies (July); fine trees, roses, unusual shrubs. Plant stall. Picnickers welcome. *Adm. 30p. Suns. May 4, June 22 & July 20 (2–7)*

¶**Verona Cottage**⊕ (David J. Dickinson Esq) Webb Lane, Mengham, Hayling Island. 4 m. S of Havant. From A3023 fork off left to Mengham; shops & free public car park 100 yds. Regular bus service Havant–Mengham. Entrance to garden opp. Rose in June P.H. New garden (one-tenth acre) partly created out of overgrown building site during summer 1979; designed by owner for year-round interest inc. frost-tender shrubs, flowers & lilies & for maximum 3 hrs work per week. Plants for sale. NO DOGS. Cups of TEA available. *Adm. 25p, Chd. 10p. Sun. Aug. 31 (2–6)*

The Vyne★†&⊕ (The National Trust—see Nat. Trust, p. ix) Sherborne St John, 4 m. N of Basingstoke. Between Sherborne St John & Bramley. From A340 turn off E at Nat. Trust signposts. 17 acres of grounds with extensive lawns, lake, fine trees, herbaceous border. TEAS. *Adm. house & garden £1, Chd. 50p; garden only 40p, Chd. 20p. △Sun. April 27 (2–6)*

¶**Walhampton** (Walhampton School Trust) Lymington. 1 m. along rd to Beaulieu. 20 acres with azaleas & rhododendrons; shell grotto. *Adm. 40p, Chd. 10p. Sun. May 18 (2–6)*

¶**The Weir House** (Joseph Addison Esq) Alresford (5 mins walk); go down Broad St, Alresford (B3046) & immediately after end of the Great Weir (pond on right) turn left (signed Abbotstone); in 150 yds take drive on left. 3-acre garden with lawns bordered by R. Arle. Tea in Alresford. *Adm. 40p, Chd. 10p. Sun. July 6 (2–6)*

● **Wellington Country Park,** Stratfield Saye. Off A33, between Reading & Basingstoke (on separate part of Estate, 3 m. from house). Lovely natural woodlands & lake developed for recreational activities inc. Nature Trails, Boating, Fishing, Children's Adventure Playground & Children's Animals; also National Dairy Museum. *Adm. 80p, Chd. 40p; special rates for pre-booked parties (Tel. Heckfield 444). Daily March 1–Oct. 31; also Sats. & Suns. Nov.–Feb. (10–5.30 or 1 hr. before dusk)*

Wintershill Hall&⊕ (Cmdr Colin Balfour, R.N.) Durley, 7 m. NE of Southampton & 8 m. SE of Winchester. NW of Bishop's Waltham; nr junction of A333 & B3037. Medium-sized garden; fine views, rhododendrons & azaleas; kitchen garden. *Adm. 30p. Sun. May 25 (2–7)*

Woodcote Manor& (J. S. Morton Esq) Bramdean, SE of Alresford. On A272 Winchester–Petersfield, ½ m. E of Bramdean. Woodland garden; bulbs, shrubs. C17 manor house (not open). Tea Alresford. *(Share to Br. Red Cross Soc. (Hants). Adm. 20p, Chd. 5p. Sun. & Mon. April 6 & 7; Suns. April 13 & 20 (2–5)*

Wyck Place★&⊕ (Lady Bonham Carter) 3 m. E of Alton, between A31 & B3004. Bus: Altonian (Saturdays) to gate from Alton· Display of aconites & other winter flowers, early flowering shrubs. Picnics welcomed, weather permitting. *Adm. 10p, Chd. under school age free. Feb. 19 to March 9 every Sat. & Sun. (2.30–5)*

The Wylds★&⊕ (Gulf International) Liss. 6 m. N of Petersfield; garden will be signposted from Greatham on A325 & Rake on A3.

40-acre garden; 10-acre lake; 100 acres of woodland; rhododendrons, azaleas, heathers; many other shrubs & trees. *Adm. 30p. Chd. 10p. Sun. May 25 & Sun. Oct. 19 (2–6)*

HEREFORD & WORCESTER

Hon County Organisers:
(Hereford) MRS P. GETHING LEWIS, Dinmore Manor, Leominster
MRS E. CHARLTON, Mansel Court, Mansel Gamage, Hereford (Asst. Hon. County Organiser)
(Worcester) MRS C. G. F. ANTON, Summerway, Torton, nr Kidderminster

DATES OF OPENING

JANUARY to DECEMBER daily
    ABBEY DORE COURT, nr Hereford
APRIL from April 5, every Wednesday, Saturday & Sunday, also Monday 7 & Tuesday 8
    BREDON SPRINGS, Ashton-under-Hill
APRIL Good Friday 4
    SPETCHLEY PARK, nr Worcester
APRIL Easter Sunday 6 & Easter Monday 7
    HERGEST CROFT GARDENS, Kington
APRIL Sunday 13
    ‡CONDERTON MANOR, nr Tewkesbury
    ‡OVERBURY COURT, nr Tewkesbury
APRIL Sunday 20
    THE COURTHOUSE, Birlingham, nr Pershore
    DUNLEY HALL, nr Stourport-on-Severn
    WIND'S POINT, British Camp, nr Malvern
APRIL Monday 21 & daily to Sunday 27
    SUMMERWAY, Torton, nr Kidderminster
APRIL Sunday 27
    THE COURTHOUSE, Birlingham,
MAY daily
    ABBEY DORE COURT, nr Hereford
    HERGEST CROFT GARDENS, Kington (from May 3)
MAY every Wednesday, Saturday & Sunday, also Bank Hols & Tuesdays 6 & 27
    BREDON SPRINGS, Ashton-under-Hill
MAY every Thursday
    STONE HOUSE COTTAGE, nr Kidderminster
MAY Sunday 4
    THE COURTHOUSE, Birlingham, nr Pershore
    DINMORE MANOR, Leominster
MAY Sunday 11
    THE COURTHOUSE, Birlingham, nr Pershore
    DUCKSWICH HOUSE, Upton-on-Severn
    SPETCHLEY PARK, nr Worcester
MAY Saturday 17
    LOEN, Bewdley

MAY Sunday 18
BEAUCASTLE, Bewdley
CLENT HALL, nr Stourbridge
THE COURTHOUSE, Birlingham,
nr Pershore
MAY Monday 19
BEAUCASTLE, Bewdley
CLENT HALL, nr Stourbridge
MAY Sunday 25 & Monday 26 (Bank Hol.)
CLENT HALL, nr Stourbridge
JUNE daily
ABBEY DORE COURT, nr Hereford
HERGEST CROFT GARDENS, Kington
JUNE every Wednesday, Saturday & Sunday
BREDON SPRINGS, Ashton-under-Hill
JUNE every Thursday
THE PRIORY, Kemerton
STONE HOUSE COTTAGE,
nr Kidderminster
JUNE Sunday 1
ARLEY HOUSE, Upper Arley
CLENT HALL, nr Stourbridge
HAFFIELD, nr Ledbury
JUNE Monday 2
CLENT HALL, nr Stourbridge
JUNE Sunday 8 & Monday 9
CLENT HALL, nr Stourbridge
JUNE Sunday 15
CLENT HALL, nr Stourbridge
STONE HOUSE COTTAGE,
nr Kidderminster
JUNE Monday 16
CLENT HALL, nr Stourbridge
JUNE Sunday 22
BELL'S CASTLE, Kemerton
THE BROOK HOUSE, Colwall,
nr Malvern
HARTLEBURY CASTLE,
nr Kidderminster
WITLEY PARK HOUSE, Great Witley,
nr Worcester
JUNE Monday 23 & daily to Sunday 29
SUMMERWAY, Torton, nr
Kidderminster
JUNE Saturday 28
GATLEY PARK, nr Leominster
JUNE Sunday 29
STONE HOUSE COTTAGE,
nr Kidderminster
JULY daily
ABBEY DORE COURT, nr Hereford
HERGEST CROFT GARDENS, Kington
JULY every Wednesday, Saturday & Sunday
BREDON SPRINGS, Ashton-under-Hill
JULY every Thursday
THE PRIORY, Kemerton
STONE HOUSE COTTAGE, nr
Kidderminster

JULY Saturday 5
BALLARDS FARM, Hinton-on-the-Green,
nr Evesham
JULY Sunday 6
BALLARDS FARM, Hinton-on-the-Green,
nr Evesham
BERRINGTON HALL, Leominster
BRAMPTON BRYAN HALL, Bucknell,
nr Knighton
BROADFIELD COURT, Bodenham,
nr Leominster
CROFT CASTLE, Leominster
HAFFIELD, nr Ledbury
WHITFIELD, Wormbridge
JULY Sunday 13
CLENT HALL, nr Stourbridge
‡CONDERTON MANOR, nr Tewkesbury
‡OVERBURY COURT, nr Tewkesbury
‡THE PRIORY, Kemerton
JULY Sunday 20
STONE HOUSE COTTAGE,
nr Kidderminster
AUGUST daily
ABBEY DORE COURT, nr Hereford
HERGEST CROFT GARDENS, Kington
AUGUST every Wednesday, Saturday, Sunday, Bank Hol. & Tuesday 26
BREDON SPRINGS, Ashton-under-Hill
AUGUST every Thursday
THE PRIORY, Kemerton
STONE HOUSE COTTAGE,
nr Kidderminster
AUGUST Sunday 10
STONE HOUSE COTTAGE,
nr Kidderminster
AUGUST Saturday 16 & Sunday 17
PONTRILAS COURT, nr Hereford
AUGUST Sunday 24
CLENT HALL, nr Stourbridge
MONNINGTON COURT,
Monnington-on-Wye
THE PRIORY, Kemerton
STONE HOUSE COTTAGE,
nr Kidderminster
AUGUST Monday 25
CLENT HALL, nr Stourbridge
AUGUST Sunday 31
WORMINGTON GRANGE, nr Broadway
SEPTEMBER daily
ABBEY DORE COURT, nr Hereford
HERGEST CROFT GARDENS, Kington
SEPTEMBER every Wednesday, Saturday & Sunday
BREDON SPRINGS, Ashton-under-Hill
SEPTEMBER every Thursday
THE PRIORY, Kemerton
STONE HOUSE COTTAGE,
nr Kidderminster
SEPTEMBER Sunday 7
CLENT HALL, nr Stourbridge
DINMORE MANOR, Leominster
RIPPLE HALL, nr Tewkesbury
SEPTEMBER Sunday 14
THE PRIORY, Kemerton

OCTOBER daily to October 19
 HERGEST CROFT GARDENS, Kington
OCTOBER every Wednesday, Saturday & Sunday to October 26
 BREDON SPRINGS, Ashton-under-Hill
OCTOBER every Thursday
 STONE HOUSE COTTAGE,
 nr Kidderminster
OCTOBER Sunday 19
 GARNONS, nr Hereford
OCTOBER to DECEMBER daily
 ABBEY DORE COURT, nr Hereford

DESCRIPTIONS OF GARDENS

Abbey Dore Court⊕ (Mrs C. L. Ward) 11 m. SW of Hereford; from A465 mid-way between Hereford & Abergavenny turn W, signposted Abbey Dore; then 2½ m. An old garden of approx. 3 acres being reclaimed by owner with family help; shrubs & herbaceous plants; fern border, herb garden, river walk.; walled kitchen garden & young orchard. (*Share to Mother Teresa of Calcutta*) NO DOGS. Plants & fruit for sale. *Collecting box. All year daily (all day)*

Arley House& (R. D. Turner Esq) Upper Arley, 5 m. N of Kidderminster. A442 Kidderminster–Bridgnorth; signpost to Arley at Shatterford. Bus: MR 296 Kidderminster–Bridgnorth. Arboretum containing specimen conifers & hardwoods, rhododendrons, camellias, magnolias, heathers; Italianate garden; greenhouses with orchids, alpines. Aviary with ornamental pheasants, budgerigars, peafowl. NO DOGS. TEAS. *Adm. 30p, Chd. 10p. Sun. June 1 (2–7)*

Ballards Farm⊕ (Mrs M. J. Eaton) Hinton-on-the-Green, 3 m. S of Evesham. A435 from Evesham, approx. 2 m. to Hinton Cross. Turn right to Hinton, left at top of village, farm on left. Almost 1 acre; lawn, choice shrubs, herbaceous plants; greenhouse. (*Share to Imperial Cancer Research*) Plants for sale. Tea Evesham or Broadway. *Adm. 20p, Chd. 5p. Sat. & Sun. July 5 & 6 (2–7)*

Beaucastle*&⊕ (Mr & Mrs G. Clancey) Bewdley. On A456 Bewdley–Cleobury Mortimer. Bus: MR 192 Birmingham–Ludlow, alight at gate. Large garden; rock, water & formal gardens. Home-made TEAS (May 18 only). *Adm. 25p, Chd. 15p. Sun. & Mon. May 18 & 19 (2–7)*

Bell's Castle (Lady Holland-Martin) Kemerton, NE of Tewkesbury. Turn off main Evesham–Cheltenham Rd at Beckford. Bus: B 535 Evesham–Gloucester; 540 Evesham–Cheltenham; alight War Memorial, Kemerton. 3 small terraces with battlements; wild garden outside wall. The small Gothic castellated folly was built by Edmund Bell (Smuggler) *c.* 1820; very fine views. Home-made TEAS (by Overbury W.I.). *Adm. 25p, Chd. 10p. Sun. June 22 (2–6.30)*

Berrington Hall †⊕ (The National Trust—see p. ix) 3 m. N of Leominster. ¼ m. W of A49. Bus: Midland Red 435 Leominster–Stockton Cross, alight Berrington South Lodge. Extensive views. Herbaceous border. TEAS. *Adm. 85p (Chd. 40p) or combined charge with Croft Castle £1.50 (Chd. 75p). △ Sun. July 6 (2–6)*

¶**Brampton Bryan Hall** †&⊕ (Mr & Mrs Christopher Harley) Bucknell, 6 m. E of Knighton, on A4113 Knighton–Ludlow rd. Medium-sized garden; large lawns & old cedars, limes & other trees; fine yew hedges & collection of interesting trees. Medieval castle adjoining C18 house. TEA & biscuits. *Adm. 30p, Chd. 10p. Sun. July 6 (2–7)*

Bredon Springs* (Ronald Sidwell Esq) Paris, Ashton-under-Hill, 6 m. SW of Evesham. Take Ashton turning off A435, Evesham–Cheltenham Rd; turn right in village & take 1st left. Very limited parking. Coach parties must alight at the church (by the old cross) & walk through churchyard (6 mins), following the mown footpath over 2 fields. Tea Evesham (6 m.), Broadway (8 m.) or Tewkesbury (8 m.). 1½ acres; mainly wild garden with large collection of hardy plants; maintained with minimum labour. Plants for sale. *Collecting box. April 5 to Oct. 26 every Sat., Sun., Wed.; also Bank Hol. Mons. & Tues. following (10–dusk)*

Broadfield Court †⊕ (Mr & Mrs Keith James) Bodenham, 7 m. SE of Leominster. A49 from Leominster or Hereford & A417 to Bodenham; turn left to Risbury opp. Texaco Garage. 4 acres of unspoilt old English garden; rose gardens, yew hedges, herbaceous border, flowering trees & shrubs. Picnic area. Developing commercial vineyard, 6 acres; Old Cider Mill & press. Manor house (not open) mentioned in Domesday Book. NO DOGS. TEA & biscuits. *Adm. 30p, Chd. 10p. Sun. July 6 (2–7)*

The Brook House⊕ (J. D. Milne Esq) Colwall, 4 m. W of Malvern. On B4218 ½-way between Malvern & Ledbury via Wyche Cutting; opp. Horse & Jockey Hotel, Colwall. Water garden; flowering trees & shrubs; walled garden. Old Herefordshire farm house with mill stream. Plants for sale. Cups of TEA. *Adm. 25p, Chd. 10p. Sun. June 22 (2.30–6.30)*

Clent Hall †&⊕ (C. Parkes Esq) Clent, 3 m. S of Stourbridge. Parking for 500 cars adjoining lodge entrance. Turn off main Birmingham–Kidderminster Rd to Clent, Clent Hall adjoins church. Georgian mansion (not open) with fascinating history dating before Domesday Book (1086). Gardens planted in latter part of last cent.; extensive rhododendrons, azaleas; holly & yew specimens; fine old trees. Other features 'The Water Garden', 'Sarah's Secret Garden', 'The formal rose garden', 'Pets' Cemetery', extensive parkland

& woodland walks with magnificent views over unspoilt country. Plants for sale if available. NO DOGS. Home-made TEAS (Sun. openings & Mon. 25 only). *Adm. 25p, Chd. 10p. Suns. & Mons. May 18 & 19, 25 & 26, June 1 & 2, 8 & 9, 15 & 16; Sun. July 13, Sun. & Mon. Aug. 24 & 25; Sun. Sept. 7 (2.30–5.30); also by appt. for coach parties*

Conderton Manor*⊕ (Mr & Mrs William Carr) 5½ m. NE of Tewkesbury. Between A435 & B4079. Bus: B540 Cheltenham–Evesham; 535 Gloucester–Evesham; alight Conderton. Cotswold stone manor house (not shown), magnificent views of Cotswolds; young trees; shrubs; bulbs; very fine flowering cherries; roses & herbaceous border. NO DOGS. Tea at Overbury Court. *Adm. 30p, Chd. 10p. Sun. April 13 & Sun. July 13 (2–6)*

The Courthouse*⊕ (Mr & Mrs Ian Macpherson) Birlingham, 2 m. S of Pershore. A44, Worcester–Pershore–Evesham Rd; in Pershore take A4104 towards Upton-on-Severn; 1st left at top of hill to Birlingham village only. Daffodils, flowering trees & shrubs; lawns. View to Bredon Hill. (*Share to St John Ambulance in County of Worcs. & Hereford*) Tea Pershore. *Adm. 25p, Chd. 5p. April 20– May 18 every Sun. (2–6)*

Croft Castle†&⊕ (The National Trust—see p. ix) 5 m. NW of Leominster. On B4362 (off B4361, Leominster–Ludlow). Large garden; borders & walled garden; landscape park & walks in Fishpool Valley; fine old avenues. Tea Berrington Hall. *Adm. 85p (Chd. 40p) or combined charge with Berrington Hall £1.50 (Chd. 75p).* △ *Sun. July 6 (2–6)*

Dinmore Manor*†&⊕ (G. H. Murray Esq) Leominster, 6 m. N of Hereford. Route A49. Bus: Midland Red Hereford–Leominster, alight Manor turning, 1 m. Small garden, C12 & C14 Church of Knights Hospitaller. *Collecting box.* △*Sun. May 4 & Sun. Sept. 7 (2–6)*

Duckswich House⊕ (Mr & Mrs E. C. S. Howard) Upton-on-Severn. From Upton take A4104 & turn left opp. Tunnel Hill P.O. Medium-sized garden with flowering shrubs, pool & spring flowers. House (not open) built & garden begun 1952–3. Tea Upton-on-Severn, 1 m. *Adm. 20p, Chd. 10p. Sun. May 11 (2–7)*

Dunley Hall& (J. S. B. Lea Esq) 1¾ m. SW of Stourport-on-Severn. On A451 Stourport–Gt Witley Rd. Mainly lawns with flowering trees & shrubs, cherries, magnolias, azaleas, rhododendrons, also major collection of exhibition daffodils & narcissus species. In greenhouse, hippeastrum hybrids & orchids. Amongst trees are examples of the 'Cork Tree', Quercus Suber. A clone of the original 'Service

Tree' which came from Wyre Forest & Metasequoia Glyptostrobiodes, the 'Dawn Redwood' from the first consignment of seed sent to this country in 1948. TEAS (by Areley Kings Church). *Adm. 30p, Chd. 10p. Sun. April 20 (2–6)*

¶**Garnons**&⊕ (Sir John & Lady Cottrell) 7 m. W of Hereford on A438 towards Brecon; lodge gates on right. Large garden landscaped by Repton; attractive autumn colour. Part of house shown; only 1 wing (mid C19 addition) remains. TEAS. *Adm. inc. part-house, 30p, Chd. 15p. Sun. Oct. 19 (2–6)*

Gatley Park (Capt. & Mrs Thomas Dunne) Leinthall Earls, 9 m. NW of Leominster; 9 m. SW of Ludlow. Turn E off A4110 between Aymestrey & Wigmore; drive approx. 1 m. long. Medium-sized garden; terraced rose gardens; wall herbaceous borders; double walk of clipped yew hedges; small kitchen garden. Fine views over park & woods. Jacobean house (not open) standing at 700 ft. Flower Festival in Norman Church inside park gates. Tea Aymestrey Church Flower Festival. *Adm. 25p, Chd. 10p. Sat. June 28 (2–7)*

¶**Haffield**⊕ (Mr & Mrs Alan Cadbury) 3 m. S of Ledbury on A417. 4 mins. from M50, Exit 2 towards Ledbury (just past Herefordshire county sign). Quarry garden; outstanding tulip & ginkgo trees; shrubs, herbaceous borders; view. House (not open) 1815 by Robert Smirke. TEA & biscuits. *Adm. 25p, Chd. 10p. Sun. June 1 & Sun. July 6 (2–6)*

Hartlebury Castle†& (The Rt Revd The Lord Bishop of Worcester) S of Kidderminster. A449 Worcester–Kidderminster turn off at Hartlebury village. Bus: MR 315 Worcester–Kidderminster–Stourbridge; alight village. Medieval moated castle reconstructed 1675, restored 1964. Many Tudor & Hanoverian Royal connections. Rose garden in forecourt. NO DOGS. TEA & biscuits. *Adm. gardens & state rooms of castle, 30p, Chd. 10p. Sun. June 22 (2–5.30)*

● **Hergest Croft Gardens***†& (W. L. Banks Esq & R. A. Banks Esq) 20 m. NW of Hereford on outskirts W of Kington off A44; signposted at end of speed limit. Gardens, which are famous with connoisseurs for their immense variety of trees & shrubs; lawns, flower & herbaceous borders, rockery & large kitchen garden; as well as the more formal plantings round the house there are the Azalea Garden with many rare trees underplanted with azaleas & the Park Wood which contains a valley filled with rhododendrons up to 30 ft. tall. Home-made TEAS by arrangement for parties over 20 (Tel. Kington 230218). *Adm. 60p, Chd. 30p. Sun. & Mon. April 6 & 7; May 3–Oct. 19 daily (11–7)*

Loen⊕ (Mr & Mrs S. K. Quayle) Long Bank, 2 m. W of Bewdley via A456; after 1¾ m. turn left, beside a red brick church, into a small lane. 6 acres; rock & water garden; interesting collection of shrubs in woodland setting. Plants for sale. *Adm. 20p, Chd. 10p. Sat. May 17 (2–6)*

Monnington Court*†⊕ (Angela Conner & John Bulmer) Monnington-on-Wye, 9 m. W of Hereford. Garden, lake with island & stepping stones, pond, rockeries, climbing plants. Medieval churchyard. Fine view, Kilvert's famous Monnington Walk; C13 & C17 house; Sculpture by owner; indoor film show; boat rides. Foundation Stud of American Morgan Horse. **Costumed Ride/ Drive Display** 3 p.m. (in indoor school if it rains). TEA, soft drinks & BARBECUED FOOD. *Adm. house & garden 50p. Sun. Aug. 24 (12–7)*

Overbury Court⟐⊕ (E. Holland-Martin Esq) 5 m. NE of Tewkesbury, 2½ m. N of Teddington Hands Roundabout, where A438 (Tewkesbury –Stow-on-the-Wold) crosses A435 (Cheltenham–Evesham). Daffodils. Georgian house 1740 (not shown) & landscape gardening of same date with stream & pools. Plane trees, yew hedges. Large herbaceous border. Norman church adjoins garden. Plants for sale. TEAS. *Adm. 30p, Chd. 10p. Sun. April 13 & Sun. July 13 (2–7)*

Pontrilas Court⟐⊕ (Mr & Mrs D. A. Keown-Boyd) 11 m. S of Hereford. Just off A465, mid-way between Hereford & Abergavenny. Bus stop at gate (Sat. only). Medium-sized garden with riverside walks; trees planted by George Bentham (of Bentham & Hooker). Suitable for wheelchairs if dry. Home-made TEAS. *Adm. 25p, Chd. 10p. Sat. & Sun. Aug. 16 & 17 (2–7)*

● The Priory* (Mr & The Hon. Mrs Peter Healing) Kemerton, NE of Tewkesbury. Turn off main Evesham–Cheltenham Rd at Beckford. Main feature of this 3-acre garden is the long herbaceous borders planned in colour groups; stream, sunk garden. Many interesting & unusual plants & shrubs. Plants for sale. Aug. 24 only TEAS by Kemerton W.I. *Adm. 25p, Chd. 5p. Suns. July 13, Aug. 24, Sept. 14; also June 5 to Sept. 25 every Thurs. (2–7)*

Ripple Hall⊕ (Sir Hugo Huntington-Whiteley, Bt) 4 m. N of Tewkesbury. Off A38 Worcester–Tewkesbury (nr junction with motorway); Ripple village well signposted. 6 acres; lawns & paddocks with donkeys; walled vegetable garden; cork tree & orangery. TEAS. *Adm. 25p, Chd. 10p. Sun. Sept. 7 (2–6)*

Spetchley Park*⟐⊕ (R. J. Berkeley Esq) 3 m. E of Worcester. A422 ½ m. Large garden of general interest; daffodils. Only deer park in Worcestershire; red and fallow deer. Regret NO DOGS. TEAS. *Adm. 70p, Chd. 35p. △Fri. April 4 & Sun. May 11 (2–6)*

Stone House Cottage*⊕ (Maj. & the Hon. Mrs Arbuthnott) Stone, 2 m. E of Kidder-

minster via A448 towards Bromsgrove; in Stone, next to church, turn up drive. Local buses stop by church. 1-acre sheltered wall garden, recently planted; rare wall shrubs & climbers & interesting herbaceous plants. (*Share to Catholic Assn for Food & Development*) Large selection of unusual shrubs & climbers for sale. NO DOGS. *Adm. 25p, Chd. 10p. Suns. June 15, 29, July 20, Aug. 10, 24; also May–Oct. every Thurs. (2–6); also by appt. all year*

Summerway⊕ (Mr & Mrs Graeme Anton) Torton, 3 m. S of Kidderminster. A449, 3 m. S of Kidderminster, turn off up lane signposted Wilden Top. 3-acre garden with interesting collection of young trees, mixed borders, new pool & rock garden. TEAS (June 29 only). *Adm. 25p, Chd. 5p. April 21–27 daily; also June 23–29 daily (2–6)*

Whitfield⟐ (G. M. Clive Esq) Wormbridge 8 m. SW of Hereford on Abergavenny Rd Parkland & extensive gardens. Picnic parties welcome. *Adm. 30p. Sun. July 6 (2–6)*

Wind's Point †⟐⊕ (Cadbury Trustees) British Camp. 3 m. SW of Malvern on Ledbury Rd. Medium-sized garden; unusual setting, lovely views. Last home of great Swedish singer Jenny Lind & where she died 1887. Tea British Camp Hotel (next door). *Adm. 20p, Chd. 10p. Sun. April 20 (10–7)*

Witley Park House⊕ (Mr & Mrs W. A. M. Edwards) Great Witley, 9 m. NW of Worcester. On A443 1 m. W of Little Witley Garage on left coming from Worcester & Droitwich. 18 acres inc. pool; lakeside walk; many varieties young trees, roses. *Adm. 25p, Chd. 5p. Sun. June 22 (2–7)*

Wormington Grange⟐⊕ (The Hon. Mrs Michael Evetts) 4 m. W of Broadway. From A46 Broadway–Cheltenham, turn off at 2nd turning for Wormington (Wormington Grange) driving from Broadway. Large natural garden with rose & other small gardens leading off. Croquet lawn & very good views. TEAS (scones & biscuits). *Adm. 20p, Chd. 10p. Sun. Aug. 31 (2–6)*

HERTFORDSHIRE

Hon. County Organiser:
MRS MARTIN ACLAND, Standon Green
End, nr Ware, SG11 1BN
DATES OF OPENING
APRIL Easter Sunday 6
BENINGTON LORDSHIP, nr Stevenage
MACKERYE END, nr Harpenden
APRIL Saturday 19
ARKLEY MANOR, nr Barnet
APRIL Sunday 20 & Monday 21
COKENACH HOUSE, Barkway
APRIL Sunday 27
FURNEAUX PELHAM HALL,
nr Buntingford

THE MANOR HOUSE, Chipperfield,
  nr Berkhamsted
ST PAUL'S WALDEN BURY, nr Hitchin
MAY every Wednesday & Sunday
  BENINGTON LORDSHIP, nr Stevenage
MAY Saturday 10
  MYDDELTON HOUSE, Enfield
MAY Sunday 11
  ST PAUL'S WALDEN BURY, nr Hitchin
MAY Sunday 25
  HIPKINS, Broxbourne
JUNE every Wednesday & Sunday
  BENINGTON LORDSHIP, nr Stevenage
JUNE Sunday 1
  WOODHALL PARK, Watton-at-Stone,
    nr Hertford
JUNE Sunday 8
  NORTHCHURCH FARM, nr Berkhamsted
  ST PAUL'S WALDEN BURY, nr Hitchin
JUNE Saturday 14
  ARKLEY MANOR, nr Barnet
  MYDDELTON HOUSE, Enfield
JUNE Sunday 15
  MOOR PLACE, Much Hadham
JUNE Sunday 22
  MACKERYE END, nr Harpenden
  THE ROYAL NATIONAL ROSE SOCIETY'S
    GARDEN, Chiswell Green, St Albans
JUNE Saturday 28 & Sunday 29
  BENINGTON LORDSHIP, nr Stevenage
JUNE Sunday 29
  OLD RECTORY, Sarratt, nr Watford
  ST PAUL'S WALDEN BURY, nr Hitchin
JULY every Wednesday & Sunday
  BENINGTON LORDSHIP, nr Stevenage
JULY Sunday 6
  CAPEL MANOR, Waltham Cross,
    nr Enfield
  LEVERSTOCK GREEN & GORHAMBURY
    GARDENS, nr Hemel Hempstead
    (Westwick Cottage, King Charles II
    Cottage, Green End, Hill End Farm &
    Hill End Farm Cottage)
JULY Saturday 12
  ARKLEY MANOR, nr Barnet
JULY Sunday 13
  FURNEAUX PELHAM HALL, nr
    Buntingford
JULY Sunday 27
  KNEBWORTH HOUSE, nr Stevenage
AUGUST Sunday 10
  25 Berry Way, Rickmansworth
  (see London section)

DESCRIPTIONS OF GARDENS

Arkley Manor* (Dr W. E. Shewell-Cooper)
Arkley, W of Barnet. In Rowley Lane, Arkley,
just off A1. Station: New Barnet, 2½ m. High
Barnet Underground, 1½ m. Bus: LT 107,
107A from Enfield; alight War Memorial. Dr.
Shewell-Cooper gives lectures on composting,
etc., during afternoon. Collection of bulbs.
Minimum work gardening; no digging, forking
or hoeing anywhere in garden; compost
methods; no chemical fertilisers or injurious
sprays; model orchards; soft fruit plots &
vegetable gardens; unusual vegetables;
double-glazed & plastic greenhouses & access
& cloche frame area; rose, heather, fern, iris,
hemerocollis & weeping gardens; fern collection; cut-flowers section. Elizabethan garden.
Cactus house. Herbaceous borders. Miniature
plants. Grey & green borders. Pot plants &
collection of Rochford house plants. Guide to
garden 35p. (*Share to Gardeners Sunday &
Good Gardeners' Assn.*) TEAS 15p. *Adm. 30p,
Chd. 20p. Sats. April 19, June 14, July 12
(2.30–6)*

● **Benington Lordship***† (Mr & Mrs
C. H. A. Bott) Benington, 5 m. E of Stevenage.
Mid-way between Walkern (on B1037) &
Watton-at-Stone (on A602). Terraced garden
overlooking lakes, formal rose garden;
Victorian folly, Norman keep & moat; rock &
water garden; spectacular double herbaceous
borders. Plants for sale. NO DOGS. June 28
& 29 *only*: TEAS at garden & Floral Festival in
adjacent church. *Adm. 50p, Chd. 10p. Sun.
April 6; May, June & July every Wed. & Sun.
(2–5); Sat. & Sun. June 28 & 29 (2–6); also
by appt.*

**Capel Manor Institute of Horticulture &
Field Studies***†&⊕ (London Borough of
Enfield) Bullsmoor Lane, Waltham Cross.
2½ m. NE of Enfield & ¼ m. W of A10 at Bullsmoor traffic lights. Bus: Green Line 734, 735;
310 to Bullsmoor Lane. Station: Turkey St,
1¼ m. Comprehensive collection of hardy &
glasshouse plants; many fine trees, inc. what is
possibly the oldest copper beech in Britain;
large collection of old-fashioned & species
roses; shrub & herbaceous borders; annual
borders, large rock & water garden; C17
garden of contemporary plants & herbs;
botanical beds, model vegetable garden,
garden & glasshouse designed for physically
handicapped gardeners; collection of tender
economic plants, banana, sugar cane, etc.
Grounds shared by Horses & Ponies Protection
Society. TEAS. *Adm. 25p, Senior Citizens &
Chd. 15p. Sun. July 6 (2–6)*

¶**Cokenach House**&⊕ (Mr & Mrs J. E. L.
Lebus) Barkway, 5 m. S of Royston. On B1368
Puckeridge–Cambridge Rd on N side of
Barkway; or turn E off A10, 2 m. S of Royston,
signposted Barkway. 13 acres; informal
garden surrounded by water in parkland
setting; spring bulbs; walled garden, vine-
houses, fine trees. Sale of plants if available.
NO DOGS. TEAS. *Adm. 30p, Chd. 10p. Sun. &
Mon. April 20 & 21 (2.30–6.30)*

Furneaux Pelham Hall*†&⊕ (Mr & Mrs
Peter Hughes) nr Buntingford. From A120 N
of Little Hadham, NE of Puckeridge; E of A10.
Lake, ornamental duck; water garden with
fountains playing; walled rose garden; yew
hedges; shrubs. Elizabethan house (not

open). No cameras or photography. (*Share to St. Mary Church, Furneaux Pelham*). NO DOGS. TEAS. *Adm. 40p, Chd. 10p. Sun. April 27 & Sun. July 13 (2–6)*

Hipkins*⅄⊕ (Stuart Douglas Hamilton Esq) Broxbourne. From A10 to Broxbourne turn up Bell or Park Lane into Baas Lane. Station: Broxbourne, 1 m. Bus: LC 310 Enfield–Hertford; GL 715, 715A London–Hertford; alight Station Rd, ½ m. 3 acres; natural garden with flowering shrubs, especially azaleas. DOGS on leads. TEAS. *Adm. 30p, Chd. 10p. Sun. May 25 (2.30–6)*

Knebworth House†⅄⊕ (The Hon. David Lytton Cobbold) Knebworth. 28 m. N of London; direct access from A1(M) motorway at Stevenage. Station & Bus stop: Stevenage, 3 m. Pleached lime avenues, roses, herbaceous borders. Historic house, home of Bulwer Lytton. Restaurant. *Adm. charges available from Knebworth Estate Office (Tel. Stevenage 812661). △Sun. July 27 (11.30–5.30)*

Leverstock Green & Gorhambury Gardens, via A414 mid-way between Hemel Hempstead & St Albans. Car parking at all gardens. Coffee, lunch and TEAS available at Hill End Farm. *Combined charge for following 5 gardens 50p, Chd. (accompanied) free. Sun. July 6 (11–6)*

Westwick Cottage⊕ (Mrs Sheila Macqueen) Westwick Row. Medium-sized garden specialising in plants for flower arranging, & many unusual specimens. Flower arrangements in the house (weather permitting) by Mrs Sheila Macqueen (no extra charge). Plant stall

King Charles II Cottage⊕ (Mr & Mrs F. S. Cadman) Westwick Row. 1-acre garden; roses a special feature; small, well-stocked ornamental pond. Part house also shown (weather permitting) with flower arrangements by Mrs Sheila Macqueen (no extra charge)

Green End⊕ (Mr & Mrs F. W. Buglass) Leverstock Green Rd. Approx. 1 acre; collection of alpines, shrubs, & other plants, a number of them unusual, rare & selected forms; species cyclamen. Garden laid out, planted & maintained by present owners since 1953

Hill End Farm⊕ (Mr & Mrs A. M. Warwick) Beech Tree Lane, Gorhambury. Coffee, Lunch, TEAS & Car park

Hill End Farm Cottage⊕ (Mrs J. Spilman) Gorhambury. Small Tudor cottage set in small old-world garden made from scratch by owner since 1971. Part house also shown if fine. Dogs on leads please

Mackerye End*†⅄⊕ (Mr & Mrs Douglas Cory-Wright) NE of Harpenden. NW of Wheathampstead. N of A6129. Bus: LC 355 from St Albans or Harpenden, alight Batford Mill; 355 from St Albans or Luton. Daffodils. Lent lilies, flowering shrubs, yew hedges,

ancient tulip tree. June opening: herbaceous border, rose garden, peonies & delphiniums. TEAS (June 22 only). *Adm. 25p, Chd. 10p. Sun. April 6 & Sun. June 22 (2–7),*

The Manor House (The Earl of Dartmouth) Chipperfield, 3 m. NW of Watford. From Watford N up A41 (or exit 5 from M1) to Kings Langley; turn left (W) at sign to Chipperfield; left at X-rds & left again at X-rds in Chipperfield; house 200 yds beyond common. 6-acre garden with daffodils, cherry blossom; shrub border. Roses (possibility of late June opening; see local press then) *Adm. 25p, Chd. 10p. Sun. April 27 (2.30–6).*

Moor Place*⅄⊕ (B. M. Norman Esq) Much Hadham. Enter through lodge gates by War Memorial or turning at Hadham Cross on A119. Station: Bishop's Stortford, 6 m. Bus: LC 350 Bishop's Stortford–Ware–Hertford, alight Much Hadham Cross, ¼ m. Medium-sized garden; C17 kitchen garden, part converted into shrubs & lawns; fine trees & shrubs. TEAS available. *Adm. 30p, Chd. 10p. Sun. June 15 (2–7)*

Myddelton House*⅄⊕ (Lea Valley Regional Park Authority) Bull's Cross, Enfield, Middx. From A10 turn off W via Turkey St or Bullsmoor Lane & into Bull's Cross. Bus: LC 310 & GL 715 to Turkey St; 5 mins from bus stop. Rare plants & trees; flowering shrubs. Gardens of the Authority's headquarters. NO DOGS. *Adm. 20p. Sat. May 10 & Sat. June 14 (2–7)*

Northchurch Farm⊕ (Mr & Mrs J. R. Fonnereau) W of Berkhamsted. Adjacent to Ashridge (Northchurch Common) N.T. Parking & picnicking permitted in the vicinity. Off B4506, 1 m. from Northchurch village (on A41). Medium-sized garden; herbaceous plants & shrubs, rockery, woodland garden with rhododendrons. *Adm. 25p, Chd. 10p. Sun. June 8 (2–7)*

Old Rectory⅄⊕ (Sir Alexander & Lady Spearman) Sarratt, 7 m. NW of Watford. In Church Lane, Sarratt; last drive on right. Fairly large gardens with lawns & roses; magnificent view over Chess Valley. Wheelchairs welcome, though garden is hilly. Light refreshments available. *Adm. 25p, Chd. 10p. Sun. June 29 (2–7)*

The Royal National Rose Society's Garden. Chiswell Green Lane, 3 m. S of St Albans. M1 to junction 6 and then A405; or A1 to Hatfield and then A405 signposted Watford. 12-acre display garden; roses of all types inc. species, old-fashioned and modern varieties.; 30,000 plants, over 900 varieties also Trail Ground for new varieties. TEAS. *Adm. 60p, Chd. free. Sun. June 22 (2–6)*

St Paul's Walden Bury*†⅄⊕ (Simon Bowes Lyon Esq & The Hon. Lady Bowes Lyon) Whitwell, on B651 5 m. S of Hitchin; ½ m. N of Whitwell. Formal woodland garden laid out about 1740, covering more than 30 acres with temples, statues, lake & ponds; there are also rhododendron & flower gardens. (*Shared with other charities*) TEAS. *Adm. 30p, Chd. 10p. Suns. April 27, May 11, June 8 & 29 (2–7)*

Woodhall Park⊕ (Mr & Mrs Thomas Abel Smith) N of Hertford. Entrance on A602, 5 m. N of Hertford & 1 m. S of Watton-at-Stone. Medium-sized garden set around C18 stables & courtyard converted into dwellinghouse; well sited in centre of park. Mostly herbaceous plants & shrubs. Picnics allowed in park beside drives (dogs *strictly* on leads). *Adm. 30p, Chd. 5p. Sun. June 1 (1.30–6)*

ISLE OF WIGHT

Hon. County Organisers:
MR & MRS PHILIP GRIMALDI, Cedar Lodge, Puckpool, Ryde

Hon. Treasurer:
J. CURETON Esq, Cornerways, Niton Undercliff, PO38 2NE

DATES OF OPENING

APRIL every Sunday
　THE CASTLE, St Helens
　MORTON MANOR, Brading
APRIL Easter Sunday 6
　GATCOMBE PARK, nr Newport
APRIL Easter Monday 7
　THE CASTLE, St Helens
APRIL Sunday 13
　THE ORCHARD, Gatcombe
　THE SHIELING, Gatcombe
APRIL Sunday 20
　UPPER CHINE SCHOOL, Shanklin
APRIL Sunday 27
　WOOLVERTON HOUSE, St Lawrence, nr Ventnor
MAY every Sunday
　THE CASTLE, St Helens
MAY Sundays 4, 11, 18
　MORTON MANOR, Brading
MAY Monday 5 (Bank Hol.)
　THE CASTLE, St Helens
MAY Sunday 11
　WATERDIP, York Lane, Totland Bay
MAY Sunday 25
　CEDAR LODGE, Puckpool, nr Ryde
MAY Monday 26 (Bank Hol.)
　THE CASTLE, St Helens
JUNE Sunday 1
　WATERDIP, York Lane, Totland Bay
　THE CASTLE, St Helens
JUNE Sunday 8
　DODPITS HOUSE, Newbridge
JUNE Sunday 15
　TYNE HALL, Bembridge
JUNE Sunday 22
　PARK VIEW, Wroxall, nr Ventnor
JUNE Sunday 29
　NUNWELL PARK, nr Brading

JULY Sunday 6
　OWL COTTAGE, Mottistone
JULY Sunday 13
　PARK VIEW, Wroxall, nr Ventnor
JULY Sunday 27
　WESTOVER HOUSE, Calbourne
AUGUST Sunday 17
　HAMSTEAD GRANGE, nr Yarmouth

DESCRIPTIONS OF GARDENS

● **The Castle**&⊕ (Mr & Mrs D. H. Bacon & Mrs A. Drake) St Helens, 5 m. E of Ryde. At crest of Duver Rd about 100 yds from village green. No. 8 bus route. Approx. 4 acres; gardens about 100 ft above sea-level facing S, with spectacular views of Bembridge Harbour; walk through white garden to short chestnut & lime avenue bordered by formal lawns; walled herbaceous border, greenhouses & rose garden; woodland walk featuring massed spring bulbs; wild garden with old & interesting trees. Scheduled house (not open) dates from 1820. Plants for sale. NO DOGS. Parties midweek by arrangement (Tel. Bembridge 2164). *Adm. 20p, Chd. 5p. April 6 to June 1 every Sun.; also Mons. April 7, May 5, 26 (2–6)*

Cedar Lodge*& (Mr & Mrs Philip Grimaldi) Puckpool, Ryde. Bus: Seaview service; stop opp. Puckpool Holiday Camps. Parking in field above garden, almost opp. entrance to Holiday Camps. Garden with flowering trees & shrubs. NO DOGS. *Adm. 20p, Chd. 5p. Sun. May 25 (2.30–5.30)*

Dodpits House* (Mr & Mrs Cyril Lucas) Newbridge; 4 m. SE of Yarmouth. Entrance to car parking in field off B3401 between Wellow & Newbridge. 3-acre garden with shrub plantings inc. many shrub roses. NO DOGS. *Adm. 20p, Chd. 5p. Sun. June 8 (2–6)*

Gatcombe Park †&⊕ (Sir Robert Hobart, Bt) 3 m. SW of Newport. On bus route from Newport. Medium-sized garden; lawns, shrubs, flowers, swimming pool, lake, park. Part house shown. Norman church. TEAS 45p. *Adm. to garden 20p; car park 10p; house 20p extra, Chd. 10p. Sun. April 6 (2.30–6.30)*

Hamstead Grange⊕ (Lt-Col & Mrs Kindersley) nr Shalfleet, 3 m. NE of Yarmouth. Bus: 12 Yarmouth–Newport, alight Ningwood. Rose garden with shrubs. Fine views of Solent & Newtown Creek. Swimming pool. Picnic parties welcome. *Adm. 20p, Chd. 5p. Sun. Aug. 17 (2.30–6)*

● **Morton Manor***†&⊕ (Mr & Mrs J. B. Trzebski) Brading. Terraced walled garden with distant views of Sandown Bay; lovely water garden; formal lily pond, shrub & rhododendron borders; rose gardens; lawns, woodland. Collecting box for NGS. *April 6 to May 18 every Sun. (2–6)*

Nunwell Park †&⊕ (Mrs Oglander) ½ m. from Brading. Medium-sized garden with trees & shrubs; very old wall garden. Wonderful view over Bembridge Harbour. *Adm. 20p, Chd. 5p.* Sun. June 29 (2–5.30)

The Orchard⊕ (Mr & Mrs Corbett) Gatcombe, S of Newport between A3020 & B3323. Medium-sized garden with trees, shrubs, spring flowers & lovely views. TEA & biscuits (20p). *Adm. 20p, Chd. 5p.* Sun. April 13 (2.30–5)

Owl Cottage★ (Mrs A. L. Hutchinson & Miss S. L. Leaning) Hoxall Lane, Mottistone, 9 m. SW of Newport. From B3399 Newport–Freshwater, at Mottistone Green bus stop turn down Hoxall Lane; 200 yds to garden. Interesting cottage garden (⅓ acre). View of the sea. Part house also shown. Plant stall. Home-made TEAS. *Adm. to garden 20p, Chd. 5p; house 10p extra, Chd. 5p.* Sun. July 6 (2–6)

¶Park View⊕ (Mr & Mrs Pearce) Avenue Rd, Wroxall, 3 m. N of Ventnor, via Ventnor–Newport rd & turn left (W) into Appledurcombe Rd; then 1st left into unadopted rd. ½-acre, formal garden; mostly lawns with flowerbeds; herbaceous & annual plants; terraced garden. TEAS. *Adm. 20p, Chd. 5p.* Sun. June 22 & Sun. July 13 (11–5.30)

The Shieling (Mrs Elizabeth Lord) Gatcombe, S of Newport, between A3020 & B3323. Medium-sized garden with trees & shrubs & lovely views. TEA & biscuits (10p). *Adm. 20p, Chd. 5p.* Sun. April 13 (2–6)

Tyne Hall⊕ (Mr & Mrs D. F. Peel) Love Lane' Bembridge. In middle of village, at corner of High St, turn down Love Lane (cul-de-sac); entrance at far end; parking in field off drive. 3–4 acres; trees, lawns, shrubs & roses. Views across Solent to mainland. TEAS. *Adm. 20p, Chd. 5p.* Sun. June 15 (2–5.30)

Upper Chine School★⅋⊕ (Miss Gifford) S of Shanklin. Bus: 16 Shanklin–Ventnor, alight gates. Chine stream through gardens; swimming pool New School Theatre in grounds, *Chd. 5p.* Sun. April 13 (2–6)

Waterdip★†⊕ (Dr & Mrs J. Waring) York Lane, Totland Bay. From Totland Bay turn right up York Lane opp. Christchurch lytch gate; house at top on right, entrance has stone pillar (home-made). Parking in Cliff Rd & Church Hill. Entirely shrubs; camellias, rhododendrons, azaleas, tulip trees, sophora, microphylla, Davidia (handkerchief tree); magnolia campbellii, grandiflora & stellata; hydrangeas, cleodendrons, coronilla, agapanthus in home-made tubs, osmanthus, etc., etc. Home-made weathercock. Part house shown. *Adm. house & garden 20p, Chd. 5p.* Sun. May 11 & Sun. June 1 (2.30–5.30)

Westover House†⅋⊕ (Dr & Mrs Walter S. Killpack) Calbourne, 6 m. W of Newport. B3401 Newport–Calbourne village; entrance at beginning of Winkle St. Large garden with lawns, shrubs, trees; swimming pool; lake, park, walled kitchen garden; icehouse. *Adm. 20p, Chd. 5p.* Sun. July 27 (2–6)

Woolverton House★⅋ (Mrs G. E. Twining) St Lawrence, W of Ventnor. Bus: 16 from Ryde, Sandown, Shanklin. Flowering shrubs; bulbs; fine position. TEAS. *Adm. 15p, Chd. 5p.* Sun. April 27 (2–6)

KENT

Hon. County Organiser:
MRS ALAN HARDY, Hillhurst Farm, Hythe, CT21 4HU

DATES OF OPENING

ALL YEAR by appointment
43 LAYHAMS RD, West Wickham
MARCH Sunday 30
HEVER CASTLE, nr Edenbridge
APRIL daily except Mondays & Tuesdays (but open on Monday 7)
SCOTNEY CASTLE, Lamberhurst
APRIL every Tuesday, Wednesday, Friday, Sunday & Bank Hol. (but closed Friday 4)
HEVER CASTLE, nr Edenbridge
APRIL every Sunday
HOLDEN HOUSE, Southborough, Tunbridge Wells
APRIL Good Friday 4
HOLDEN HOUSE, Southborough, Tunbridge Wells
APRIL Easter Sunday 6
CRITTENDEN HOUSE, Matfield
ELBRIDGE HOUSE, Sturry, nr Canterbury
GODINTON PARK, Ashford
APRIL Monday 7
CRITTENDEN HOUSE, Matfield
HOLDEN HOUSE, Southborough, Tunbridge Wells
APRIL Sunday 13
STREET END PLACE, nr Canterbury
APRIL Wednesday 16
SELLING GARDENS, nr Faversham
APRIL Sunday 20
CRITTENDEN HOUSE, Matfield
‡CROACH'S, Ide Hill
DENTON COURT, Denton, nr Canterbury
DOGHOUSE FARM (on Stone St), nr Canterbury
GOODNESTONE PARK, next Wingham, Canterbury
HOLE PARK, Rolvenden
LADHAM HOUSE, Goudhurst
MERE HOUSE, Mereworth, nr Maidstone
MOUNT EPHRAIM, Hernhill, nr Faversham
‡THE OLD VICARAGE, Ide Hill
STREET END PLACE, nr Canterbury
WOODLANDS MANOR, Adisham
APRIL Monday 21
MOUNT EPHRAIM, Hernhill, nr Faversham

APRIL Thursday 24
  LADDINGFORD HOUSE, Laddingford,
    nr Maidstone
APRIL Sunday 27
  ‡BALI-HAI, 91 Chestnut Ave, Walderslade
  ‡2 GENTIAN CLOSE, Walderslade
  LUTON HOUSE, Selling, nr Faversham
APRIL Wednesday 30
  HOLE PARK, Rolvenden
MAY daily except Mondays &
  Tuesdays (but open May 5 & 26)
  SCOTNEY CASTLE, Lamberhurst
MAY every Tuesday, Wednesday,
  Friday, Sunday & Bank Hol.
  HEVER CASTLE, nr Edenbridge
MAY every Sunday
  ‡BALI-HAI, 91 Chestnut Ave, Walderslade
  ‡36 CAMPION CLOSE, Walderslade
  ‡2 GENTIAN CLOSE, Walderslade
  HOLDEN HOUSE, Southborough,
    Tunbridge Wells
MAY Sunday 4
  CRITTENDEN HOUSE, Matfield
  DOGHOUSE FARM (on Stone St),
    nr Canterbury
  THE GRANGE, Benenden
  HOLE PARK, Rolvenden
  NORTHBOURNE COURT, nr Deal
  SANDLING PARK, nr Hythe
MAY Monday 5 (May Day Holiday)
  CRITTENDEN HOUSE, Matfield
  HOLDEN HOUSE, Southborough,
    Tunbridge Wells
MAY Sunday 11
  BRADBOURNE HOUSE GARDENS,
    East Malling, nr Maidstone
  CROWN POINT NURSERY, Ightham,
    nr Sevenoaks
  THE GRANGE, Benenden
  HALL PLACE GARDENS, Leigh,
    nr Tonbridge
  HEARTS OF OAK BENEFIT SOCIETY
    CONVALESCENT HOME, Broadstairs
  LONG BARN, Weald, nr Sevenoaks
  SANDLING PARK, nr Hythe
MAY Wednesday 14
  SISSINGHURST CASTLE GARDEN,
    Cranbrook
MAY Saturday 17
  ROCK FARM, Nettlestead, Maidstone
  STONEWALL PARK, Chiddingstone
    Hoath, Edenbridge
MAY Sunday 18
  ‡CROACH'S, Ide Hill
  DODDINGTON PLACE, nr Sittingbourne
  HOLE PARK, Rolvenden
  HUSH HEATH MANOR, nr Goudhurst
  ‡THE OLD VICARAGE, Ide Hill
  SANDLING PARK, nr Hythe
  STONEWALL PARK, Chiddingstone
    Hoath, Edenbridge
  TANNERS, Brasted
  WATERGATE HOUSE, Fordwich
  WOOLTON FARM, Bekesbourne

MAY Monday 19
  WATERGATE HOUSE, Fordwich
MAY Thursday 22
  LADDINGFORD HOUSE, Laddingford,
    nr Maidstone
MAY Saturday 24
  ROCK FARM, Nettlestead, Maidstone
MAY Sunday 25
  COLDHAM, Little Chart Forstal, Ashford
  DOGHOUSE FARM (on Stone St),
    nr Canterbury
  ELBRIDGE HOUSE, Sturry,
    nr Canterbury
  FOXWOLD, Brasted Chart, nr Westerham
  GOODNESTONE PARK, next Wingham,
    Canterbury
  HALES PLACE, Tenterden
  LADHAM HOUSE, Goudhurst
  NORTHBOURNE COURT, nr Deal
  OXON HOATH, Hadlow, nr Tonbridge
  THE RED HOUSE, Crockham Hill
  SALTWOOD CASTLE, nr Hythe
  SANDLING PARK, nr Hythe
  ‡UPDOWN FARM, Betteshanger, nr Deal
  ‡UPDOWN HOUSE, Betteshanger, nr Deal
  WARDERS, Tonbridge
  WAYSTRODE MANOR, Cowden
  WOOLTON FARM, Bekesbourne
MAY Monday 26 (Spring Bank Hol.)
  HOLDEN HOUSE, Southborough,
    Tunbridge Wells
  MOUNT EPHRAIM, Hernhill,
    nr Faversham
  ROCK FARM, Nettlestead, Maidstone
  SALTWOOD CASTLE, nr Hythe
MAY Tuesday 27
  MOUNT EPHRAIM, Hernhill,
    nr Faversham
MAY Wednesday 28
  HOLE PARK, Rolvenden
  ROCK FARM, Nettlestead, Maidstone
MAY Thursday 29
  WARDERS, Tonbridge
MAY Saturday 31
  ROCK FARM, Nettlestead, Maidstone
JUNE daily except Mondays & Tuesdays
  SCOTNEY CASTLE, Lamberhurst
JUNE every Tuesday, Wednesday,
  Friday & Sunday
  HEVER CASTLE, nr Edenbridge
JUNE every Sunday
  ‡BALI-HAI, 91 Chestnut Ave, Walderslade
  ‡36 CAMPION CLOSE, Walderslade
  ‡2 GENTIAN CLOSE, Walderslade
  SALTWOOD CASTLE, nr Hythe
JUNE Sunday 1
  CRITTENDEN HOUSE, Matfield
  DODDINGTON PLACE, nr Sittingbourne
  HALL PLACE GARDENS, Leigh,
    nr Tonbridge
  HOLDEN HOUSE, Southborough,
    Tunbridge Wells
  MARLE PLACE, Brenchley
  SANDLING PARK, nr Hythe
  SEA CLOSE, Hythe
  SPRIVERS, Horsmonden, nr Tonbridge

JUNE Wednesday 4
 HOLE PARK, Rolvenden
 KNOLE, Sevenoaks
 ROCK FARM, Nettlestead, nr Maidstone
JUNE Saturday 7
 SISSINGHURST PLACE, Cranbrook
JUNE Sunday 8
 CONGELOW HOUSE, Yalding
 GOODNESTONE PARK, next Wingham,
  Canterbury
 HOLDEN HOUSE, Southborough,
  Tunbridge Wells
 LUTON HOUSE, Selling, nr Faversham
JUNE Wednesday 11
 ROCK FARM, Nettlestead, nr Maidstone
 SISSINGHURST CASTLE GARDEN,
  Cranbrook
 WAYSTRODE MANOR, Cowden
JUNE Saturday 14
 ROCK FARM, Nettlestead, Maidstone
JUNE Sunday 15
 DOGHOUSE FARM (on Stone St)
  nr Canterbury
 GOODNESTONE PARK, next Wingham,
  Canterbury
 KYPP COTTAGE, Biddenden
 ‡MERE HOUSE, Mereworth, nr Maidstone
 ‡MEREWORTH CASTLE, nr Maidstone
 NORTHBOURNE COURT, nr Deal
JUNE Monday 16 & Tuesday 17
 KYPP COTTAGE, Biddenden
JUNE Saturday 21
 ROCK FARM, Nettlestead, Maidstone
JUNE Sunday 22
 BERWICK HOUSE, Lympne, nr Hythe
 BRENCHLEY MANOR, Brenchley
 GOODNESTONE PARK, next Wingham,
  Canterbury
 HUSH HEATH MANOR, nr Goudhurst
 THE OLD PARSONAGE, Sutton Valence,
  nr Maidstone
 OTHAM GARDENS, nr Maidstone
 WEST FARLEIGH HALL, nr Maidstone
JUNE Monday 23
 BERWICK HOUSE, Lympne, nr Hythe
JUNE Wednesday 25
 CHEVENING, Sevenoaks
 ROCK FARM, Nettlestead, Maidstone
JUNE Saturday 28
 ILAM, Hawkhurst
 ROCK FARM, Nettlestead, Maidstone
JUNE Sunday 29
 ELBRIDGE HOUSE, Sturry,
  nr Canterbury
 THE GRANGE, Plaxtol, nr Sevenoaks
 ILAM, Hawkhurst
 LADDINGFORD HOUSE, Laddingford,
  nr Maidstone
 MOUNT EPHRAIM, Hernhill,
  nr Faversham
 THE OLD PARSONAGE, Sutton Valence,
  nr Maidstone
 THE POSTERN, Tonbridge
 ST CLERE, Kemsing, nr Sevenoaks
 WAYSTRODE MANOR, Cowden

 WEEKS FARM, Egerton Forstal, Headcorn
 WOODLANDS MANOR, Adisham
JUNE Monday 30
 LADDINGFORD HOUSE, Laddingford,
  nr Maidstone
 MOUNT EPHRAIM, Hernhill, nr
  Faversham
JULY daily, except Mondays & Tuesdays
 SCOTNEY CASTLE, Lamberhurst
**JULY every Tuesday, Wednesday,
 Friday & Sunday**
 HEVER CASTLE, nr Edenbridge
JULY every Saturday
 ROCK FARM, Nettlestead, Maidstone
JULY every Sunday
 ‡BALI-HAI, 91 Chestnut Ave, Walderslade
 ‡36 CAMPION CLOSE, Walderslade
 SALTWOOD CASTLE, nr Hythe
JULY Wednesday 2
 ROCK FARM, Nettlestead, Maidstone
JULY Sunday 6
 COBHAM COURT, Bekesbourne,
  nr Canterbury
 CRITTENDEN HOUSE, Matfield
 DOGHOUSE FARM (on Stone St),
  nr Canterbury
 FOXHOLE, Sandling, nr Hythe
 GOODNESTONE PARK, next Wingham,
  Canterbury
 THE GRANGE, Plaxtol, nr Sevenoaks
 HORTON PRIORY, Sellindge
 KYPP COTTAGE, Biddenden
 MARLE PLACE, Brenchley
 NORTHBOURNE COURT, nr Deal
 OLDBURY PLACE, Ightham,
  nr Sevenoaks
 THE POSTERN, Tonbridge
 RINGFIELD, Knockholt
 THE SALUTATION, Sandwich
 SEA CLOSE, Hythe
 ‡UPDOWN FARM, Betteshanger, nr Deal
 ‡UPDOWN HOUSE, Betteshanger, nr Deal
 WEEKS FARM, Egerton Forstal, Headcorn
 WITHERSDANE HALL, Wye
JULY Monday 7
 DOGHOUSE FARM (on Stone St),
  nr Canterbury
 KYPP COTTAGE, Biddenden
JULY Tuesday 8
 KYPP COTTAGE, Biddenden
JULY Wednesday 9
 BOG FARM, Brabourne Lees, nr Ashford
 COBHAM COURT, Bekesbourne,
  nr Canterbury
 SISSINGHURST CASTLE GARDEN,
  Cranbrook
JULY Sunday 13
 COLDHAM, Little Chart Forstal, Ashford
 FOXHOLE, Sandling, nr Hythe
 LONG BARN, Weald, nr Sevenoaks
 MERE HOUSE, Mereworth, nr Maidstone
 WEEKS FARM, Egerton Forstal, Headcorn
JULY Wednesday 16
 ROCK FARM, Nettlestead, Maidstone

KENT—continued

JULY Sunday 20
  BELMONT PARK, Throwley,
    nr Faversham
  ‡COURT LODGE, Groombridge
  ‡GROOMBRIDGE PLACE, Groombridge
  LADHAM HOUSE, Goudhurst
  WATERGATE HOUSE, Fordwich

JULY Monday 21
  WATERGATE HOUSE, Fordwich

JULY Wednesday 23
  WEST FARLEIGH HALL, nr Maidstone

JULY Sunday 27
  DOGHOUSE FARM (on Stone St),
    nr Canterbury
  NORTHBOURNE COURT, nr Deal

JULY Wednesday 30
  ROCK FARM, Nettlestead, Maidstone

**AUGUST daily except Mondays &
  Saturdays (but open August 25)**
  SALTWOOD CASTLE, nr Hythe

**AUGUST daily except Mondays &
  Tuesdays (but open on August 25)**
  SCOTNEY CASTLE, Lamberhurst

**AUGUST every Tuesday, Wednesday,
  Friday, Sunday & Bank Hol.)**
  HEVER CASTLE, nr Edenbridge

AUGUST Sunday 3
  ‡BALI-HAI, 91 Chestnut Ave, Walderslade
  ‡36 CAMPION CLOSE, Walderslade
  SEA CLOSE, Hythe
  YEOMANS, Great Chart, Ashford

AUGUST Wednesday 6
  KNOLE, Sevenoaks

AUGUST Saturday 9
  GREAT COMP, Borough Green

AUGUST Sunday 10
  36 CAMPION CLOSE, Walderslade
  GREAT COMP, Borough Green
  HEARTS OF OAK BENEFIT SOCIETY
    CONVALESCENT HOME, Broadstairs

AUGUST Wednesday 13
  BOG FARM, Brabourne Lees, nr Ashford

AUGUST Sunday 17
  BILTING HOUSE, nr Ashford
  36 CAMPION CLOSE, Walderslade
  WEST STUDDAL FARM, West Studdal,
    nr Dover

AUGUST Sunday 24
  36 CAMPION CLOSE, Walderslade
  HOLDEN HOUSE, Southborough,
    Tunbridge Wells
  NORTHBOURNE COURT, nr Deal

AUGUST Monday 25 (Bank Hol.)
  HOLDEN HOUSE, Southborough,
    Tunbridge Wells

AUGUST Sunday 31
  ELBRIDGE HOUSE, Sturry,
    nr Canterbury
  HOLDEN HOUSE, Southborough,
    Tunbridge Wells

**SEPTEMBER daily except Mondays &
  Tuesdays**
  SCOTNEY CASTLE, Lamberhurst

**SEPTEMBER every Tuesday,
  Wednesday, Friday & Sunday**
  HEVER CASTLE, nr Edenbridge

SEPTEMBER Sunday 7
  HOLDEN HOUSE, Southborough,
    Tunbridge Wells
  HOLWOOD, Keston
  HORTON PRIORY, Sellindge
  WITHERSDANE HALL, Wye

SEPTEMBER Sunday 14
  HOLDEN HOUSE, Southborough,
    Tunbridge Wells

SEPTEMBER Thursday 25
  LADDINGFORD HOUSE, Laddingford,
    nr Maidstone

**OCTOBER daily except Mondays &
  Tuesdays**
  SCOTNEY CASTLE, Lamberhurst

OCTOBER Sunday 5
  LADHAM HOUSE, Goudhurst

OCTOBER Sundays 12 & 19
  HOLE PARK, Rolvenden

OCTOBER Sunday 26
  TANNERS, Brasted

DESCRIPTIONS OF GARDENS

Bali-Hai⋆⊕ (Mr & Mrs L. O. Miles) 91
Chestnut Ave, Walderslade, 3 m. S of Chatham.
From M2 leave by Exit 3 on to A229 Maidstone—Chatham; follow Walderslade signs;
turn left into Tunberry Ave, then right into
York Ave & right again into Chestnut Ave.
Bus: 184 from Chatham Pentagon to doorstep.
Interesting small garden (½ acre) with alpine
& rare plants incorporated in rockeries, bog
gardens, peat beds, ponds & borders. (*Share
to Gardeners' Sunday*) NO DOGS. TEA &
cold drinks. *Adm. 25p, Chd. 10p. April 27–
Aug. 3 every Sun. (2–6); also by appt. at
other times (Tel. Medway 63329).*

Belmont Park⅃⊕ (The Lord Harris) Throwley, 5 m. SW of Faversham. Walled garden,
lawns & orangery; small pinetum & kitchen
garden. Long walk & folly; Victorian grotto.
House by Samuel Wyatt, *c.* 1792. Tea Eastling,
3 m. *Adm. 25p, Chd. 5p. Sun. July 20
(2.30–6.30)*

¶**Berwick House**⊕ (Mrs T. G. Hedley)
Lympne, 3 m. NW of Hythe. Via A261 from
Hythe; at junction with A20 (opp. Royal Oak
Motel, Newingreen) turn sharp left signposted
Lympne; garden ½ m. along on left. A medley
of small gardens within confines of mediumsized garden; unique bedded garden under
glass; good collection of fuchsias; potager
fleurs also a feature. Plant stall (June 22
only). NO DOGS. *Adm. 30p, Chd. over 5, 10p.
Sun. June 22 (2–6), Mon. June 23 (11–5)*

Bilting House⋆⅃⊕ (J. C. W. S. Erle-Drax
Esq) A28, 5 m. NE of Ashford, 9 m. from
Canterbury. Wye, 1½ m. An old-fashioned
garden with ha-ha; rhododendrons, azaleas;
shrubs, collection of conifers in plantation. In
beautiful part of Stour Valley. NO DOGS.
TEAS 25p. *Adm. 25p, Chd. under 15, 15p.
Sun. Aug. 17 (2.30–6)*

¶**Bog Farm***⊕ (Mr & Mrs K. J. Hewett) Brabourne Lees, 4 m. E of Ashford. Via A20 Ashford–Folkestone; turn left 3 m. from Ashford; proceed ½ m. to Woolpack Inn; bear right & continue 700 yds following sign to garden on right down single track lane. 1-acre garden, planned & planted by owners since 1959 around small Kentish farmhouse (not open); good collection of shrubs, trees, species plants, ferns & bulbs arranged to give some interest to each season; mixed borders; moisture plants; old roses & herb garden. NO DOGS. *Adm. 40p, Chd. 10p. Wed. July 9 & Wed. Aug. 13 (2–7)*

Bradbourne House Gardens*†⚘⊕ (East Malling Research Station) East Malling, 4 m. W of Maidstone. Entrance to Bradbourne House is E of New Road, East Malling. (New Road runs from Larkfield A20 to East Malling village.) Hatton Fruit Garden, Bradbourne House, consists of demonstration fruit gardens of particular interest to amateur fruit growers occupying walled garden, formerly kitchen garden of Bradbourne House. Gardens include various intensive tree forms of apples & pears together with model fruit gardens of tree, bush & cane fruits. Members of staff available for questions. TEAS (or West Malling 2 m.). *Adm. 25p, Chd. 5p. Sun. May 11 (2–6)*

Brenchley Manor⊕ (Mr & Mrs R. T. Gardiner-Hill) Brenchley, 8 m. SE of Tonbridge. Bus: MD 296 or 297; alight Brenchley, ½ m. Medium-sized garden; ornamental yew hedge; floribunda roses, herbaceous borders; Domesday oak. Use of SWIMMING POOL 10p extra. Early Tudor timber-framed house with fine Renaissance gateway. NO DOGS. Home-made TEAS. *Adm. 30p, Chd. 5p. Sun. June 22 (2–6)*

36 Campion Close (Mr & Mrs G. Olsen) Walderslade, 3 m. S of Chatham. From M2 leave by Exit 3 on to A229 Maidstone–Chatham; follow Walderslade signs; turn left into Tunberry Ave, then right into York Ave, left along Chestnut Ave & right into King George Ave; Campion Close on left. Bus: 184 from Chatham Pentagon to Chestnut Ave. Colourful small rockery garden with wide range of interesting plants & shrubs; greenhouses & conservatory specializing in geraniums & pelargoniums. NO DOGS. TEA. *Adm. 20p, Chd. 10p. May 4–Aug. 24 every Sun. (2–6)*

Chevening†⚘⊕ (By permission of H.R.H. The Prince of Wales & The Administrative Trustees of Chevening Estate) 4 m. NW of Sevenoaks. Turn N off A25 at Sundridge traffic lights on to B2211; after 1½ m. turn at Chevening X-rds turn left. 27 acres with lawns & woodland garden, lake, formal rides, parterre. Garden in course of restoration. NO DOGS. Tea Sevenoaks or Westerham. *Adm. 30p, Chd. 10p. Wed. June 25 (11–7; last adm. 6.30)*

Cobham Court†⚘ (Mrs Walter Whigham) Bekesbourne. 3 m. SE of Canterbury. From A2

Canterbury–Dover turn 1st left on Bridge bypass (signposted Bekesbourne); follow this rd for about 1 m.; just before railway arch turn right (signposted Adisham); house ¾ m. along this rd. Medium-sized interesting well stocked garden; herbaceous borders, shrub roses bounded by old walls; good collection of trees, many planted since 1963 inc. one of the oldest robinia trees in the country, supposedly planted by Charles Tradescant; kitchen garden. C14 house (not open) adjoining Norman church which is open. (*Share to Rheumatism & Arthritis Assn.*) Picnics allowed in meadow. Plant & produce stall depending upon availability. TEA & biscuits. *Adm. 40p, Chd. free. Sun. July 6 & Wed. July 9 (2–6)*

Coldham*⊕ (Dr J. G. Elliott) Little Chart Forstal, 5 m. NW of Ashford. Leave A20 at Charing by B2077; 1st left in 1½ m. right in 200 yds, signposted Little Chart; left in village & left at top of hill in ¼ m. Or leave A20 at Hothfield signposted Little Chart, Pluckley, Smarden & right in 2 m. Small garden developed since 1970 in setting of old walls; good collection of rare plants, bulbs, alpines, mixed borders, shrub roses, etc. Plant stall. C16 Kent farmhouse (not open). NO DOGS please. TEA & biscuits. *Adm. 40p, Chd. 20p. Sun. May 25 & Sun. July 13 (2–6)*

Congelow House*⚘⊕ (Mr & Mrs D. J. Cooper) Yalding, 8 m. SW of Maidstone. Approx. mid-way between Tonbridge & Maidstone & S of Yalding. 4-acre garden newly planted, created from an orchard since 1973; backbone of interesting ornamental trees planted about 1850; walled garden supplying vegetables to house; pleasure gardens inc. rhododendrons, azaleas, iris, roses & shrub roses. NO DOGS. TEAS. *Adm. 30p, Chd. 10p. Sun. June 8 (2–6)*

Court Lodge*†⚘ (Mr & Mrs G. F. Bedford) Groombridge, SW of Tunbridge Wells. Lawns, shrubs & roses. C15 house (not shown) of special interest from outside only as house was moved in 1909 from Udimore, Sussex. Photos on view showing demolition & reconstruction, also article giving history of house. TEAS. *Adm. 25p, Chd. 15p. Sun. July 20 (2–7)*

Crittenden House*⊕ (B. P. Tompsett Esq) Matfield, SE of Tonbridge. Station: Paddock Wood, 3 m. Bus: MD 6 or 297, alight Standings Cross, Matfield, 1 m. Garden around early C17 house completely planned & planted since 1956 on labour-saving lines. Featuring spring shrubs (rhododendrons, magnolias), roses, lilies, foliage, waterside planting of ponds in old workings. (*Share to CPRE (Kent Branch)*) Tea Cherrytrees, Matfield Green. Free car park. *Adm. 25p, Chd. under 12, 10p. Sun. & Mon. April 6 & 7; Sun. April 20; Sun. & Mon. May 4 & 5; Suns. June 1 & July 6 (2–7)*

Croach's⊕ (Mr & Mrs John A. Deed) Ide Hill, SW of Sevenoaks. Between Sevenoaks & Edenbridge; ¼ m. S of village on B2042. A few cars can park in drive; alternative parking at Village Hall, Ide Hill. Station: Sevenoaks, 4½ m. 4 acres of lawns, woodland with bulbs & flowering shrubs & trees (inc. rhododendrons, camellias, azaleas & cherries) with views to Ashdown Forest. (*Share to Ide Hill Church Fabric Fund*) NO DOGS please. *Adm. 25p, Chd. over 5, 10p. Sun. April 20 & Sun. May 18 (2–7)*

Crown Point Nursery*⚘ (Messrs G. Reuthe Ltd) nr Ightham. Car parking facilities by tarmac rd in entrance. Access to Nursery from A25 by drive through woodland. Station: Kemsing, 1½ m.; Sevenoaks, Bat & Ball, 2 m. Bus: MD 8 or 9 Maidstone–Sevenoaks, alight nr Sir Jeffry Amherst Arms. Woodland garden of 8 acres for culture of rhododendrons, azaleas & other shrubs. (*Share to Kent Trust for Nature Conservation*) Plants for sale. NO DOGS please. Tea Ightham. *Adm. 25p, Chd. 10p. Sun. May 11 (2–6)*

Denton Court⚘⊕ (Mr & Miss Gostling) Denton, 8 m. SE of Canterbury on A260. Bus: EK 616 Canterbury–Folkestone. Large garden; fine trees & shrubs; spring bulbs; clipped yews. (*Share to The National Trust*). *Adm. 30p, Chd. 15p. Sun. April 20 (2–5)*

Doddington Place⚘⊕ (John Oldfield Esq) 6 m. SE of Sittingbourne. From A20 turn N opp. Lenham or from A2 turn S at Teynham; both turnings signposted 'Doddington 4½ m.' Large garden, landscaped with wide views; trees & yew hedges; woodland garden with azaleas & rhododendrons, rock garden. (*Share to Kent Assn for the Blind*) Light TEAS. *Adm. 30p, Chd. 5p. Sun. May 18 & Sun. June 1 (2–6.30)*

Doghouse Farm⊕ (Peter M. Godden Esq) on Stone St (B2068), 6½ m. S of Canterbury. 1½ acres; small informal garden with shrubs & foliage plants. (*Share to Upper Hardres Stained Glass Appeal*) Plants for sale when available. NO DOGS. *Adm. 30p, Chd. 15p. Suns. April 20, May 4, 25, June 15; Sun. & Mon. July 6 & 7; Sun. July 27 (2–6)*

¶Elbridge House†⚘ (L. R. Colborn Esq). Between Sturry & Littlebourne; 4 m. NE of Canterbury. Via A257 from Canterbury towards Sandwich; turn left at Stodmarsh Rd. 6-acre garden, S facing, on 3 terraced slopes; oval lake with island; orchid houses & aviaries; many trees & shrubs. TEA & biscuits. *Adm. 50p, Chd. 20p. Suns. April 6, May 25, June 29, Aug. 31 (2–6)*

Foxhole (Mr & Mrs Vere Collins) Sandling, 2 m. NW of Hythe. From A20 turn off at signpost to Saltwood. ¼ m. S of Sandling station. Small informal garden (1½ acres) on different levels overlooking stream; spilling over with wide variety of foliage plants, climbers & flowering shrubs; kitchen garden. Entire garden created & maintained by owners.

C16 cottage with modern additions (not open). Aviary with homing budgerigars. (*Share to Kent Voluntary Service Council*) Picnics permitted (under cherry trees). NO DOGS. TEAS. *Adm. 30p, Chd. 5p. Suns. July 6 & 13 (2–7)*

Foxwold⚘⊕ (Mr & Mrs J. Pym & Mrs Cobb) Brasted Chart, 3 m. E of Westerham, 5 m. W of Sevenoaks. From A25 at Brasted turn S opp. King's Arms pub; ½ m. to drive entrance on right & ½ m. along drive. Or from Edenbridge take B2027; keep left for Toy's Hill & sign to Brasted; ¾ m. N of Fox & Hounds pub turn left Pipers Green Rd. 3 acres, terraced garden in woodland setting; azaleas, rhododendrons planted C19; vegetable garden. TEAS. *Adm. 30p, Chd. 15p. Sun. May 25 (2.30–7)*

2 Gentian Close* (Mr & Mrs J. Hamblett) Walderslade, 3 m. S of Chatham. See **Bali-Hai** for directions (gardens 150 yds apart). Small alpine garden, 15 ft x 20 ft, with many unusual & rare plants inc. large collection of dwarf conifers, & rare shrubs & rare dwarf bulbs; troughs; pool & waterfall. NO DOGS. *Adm. 20p, Chd. 5p. April 27–June 29 every Sun. (2–6)*

Godinton Park⚘⊕ (Alan Wyndham Green Esq) Entrance 1½ m. W of Ashford at Potter's Corner on A20. Bus: MD/EK 10, 10A, 10B Folkestone–Ashford–Maidstone, alight Hare & Hounds, Potter's Corner. Formal & wild gardens. Topiary. Jacobean mansion with elaborate woodwork. Unique frieze in drawing room depicting arms drill of Kent Halbardiers 1630. Tea Swan Hotel, Charing. *Adm. garden only 30p; house & garden 60p, Chd. under 16, 30p. △Sun. April 6 (2–5)*

Goodnestone Park⚘⊕ (The Lady Fitz-Walter) nr Wingham, Canterbury. Village lies S of B2046 rd from A2 to Wingham. Coming from Wingham signposted 1st left says Goodnestone. Coming from A2 1st signpost right after Adisham Station. Village st is 'No through rd', but house & garden at the terminus. Bus: EK 13, 14 Canterbury–Deal; bus stop: Wingham, 2 m. 5–6 acres; good trees; collection of old-fashioned roses; attractive views; walled garden. Plants for sale if available. Connections with Jane Austen who often stayed here. (*Share to N.S.P.C.C.*) Picnics allowed. NO DOGS please. TEAS. *Adm. 25p, Chd. 5p. Suns. April 20, May 25, June 8, 15, 22, July 6 (2–7)*

The Grange, Benenden*⚘⊕ (Capt. Collingwood Ingram). Own hybrid rhododendrons & special strain of polyanthus; big collection of rare trees, many of them unique specimens, inc. largest eucalyptus in England. Hot or cold snacks, Royal Oak, Iden Green, ¼ m. (open 12–2). *Adm. 30p. Sun. May 4 & Sun. May 11 (11–7)*

The Grange, Plaxtol (Mrs Robin Johnston) 5 m. SE of Sevenoaks. Just E of A227 Tonbridge–Wrotham. At Plaxtol church take Tree Lane; after 200 yds turn right down Grange Hill; house 200 yds down on right. Medium-sized garden; lawns, herbaceous borders, kitchen garden, lovely views. House (not shown) built 1702. (*Share to West Kent Marriage Guidance Council*) NO DOGS. TEAS. *Adm. 30p, Chd. free. Sun. June 29 & Sun. July 6 (2–6)*

Great Comp*⊕ (Mr & Mrs R. Cameron) 2 m. E of Borough Green. A20 at Wrotham Heath, proceed down Seven Mile Lane, B2016; at 1st X-rds turn right; garden on left about ½ m. Bus: MD 9; alight Platt Memorial Hall, ¾ m. Garden skilfully designed & constructed by present owners with virtually no assistance since 1956; whole area of 7 acres now fully developed, combining spacious setting of well-maintained lawns & paths with plantsman's collection of trees, shrubs, heathers & herbaceous plants. Good autumn colour. Early C17 house (not shown). (*Share to Tradescant Trust*) NO DOGS. Home-made TEAS (*3.30–5*). (In addition to dates shown below for NGS, garden open May 1–Oct. 15 every Fri., Sun. & Bank Hol.). *Adm. 50p, Chd. 20p. Sat. & Sun. Aug. 9 & 10 (11–6)*

Groombridge Place† (S. W. Mountain Esq) Groombridge, SW of Tunbridge Wells. Station: Groombridge. Bus: MD 291 Tunbridge Wells–East Grinstead, alight nr gates. Walled gardens, herbaceous borders, C17 moated house. *Adm. 25p, Chd. 15p. Sun. July 20 (2–6.30)*

Hales Place*†&⊕ (Mr & Mrs Michael Robson) Tenterden. Gates adjoin Tenterden Police Station in Oaks Rd, Tenterden, off E end of High St. Bus stop: Tenterden, High St, 800 yds. A Tudor setting *c*. 1544 with walled garden terraces, gazebos, well house & C15 tythe barn surrounding historic Tudor mansion. Spring garden & 25 acres of orchard walks. Tea Tenterden. *Adm. 25p, Chd. 10p, Cars 10p (free if total occupants exceed 60p). Sun. May 25 (2.30–6.30)*

Hall Place Gardens*&⊕ (The Lord Hollenden) Leigh, 4 m. W of Tonbridge. From A21 Sevenoaks–Tonbridge; at Hildenborough turn W on to B2027 & on 2½ m. to Leigh. Large outstanding garden with 11-acre lake, the lakeside walk crossing over picturesque bridges; garden contains many interesting trees & shrubs, well labelled. (In addition to dates below in aid of N.G.S., the garden is open every Sun. May 4 to June 15 inc.) DOGS must be kept on leads. TEAS. Free car park. *Adm. 50p, Chd. under 14, 10p. Sun. May 11 & Sun. June 1 (2.30–6.30)*

Hearts of Oak Benefit Society Convalescent Home*& (Hearts of Oak Benefit Society) Callis Court Rd, Broadstairs. From Broadstairs Broadway take St Peter's Park Rd; turn right under railway arch into Baird's Hill; join Callis Court Rd & garden entrance on right, 100 yds beyond Lanthorne Rd turning. 10½ acres; lawns, flowering trees & shrubs; formal flower beds; perennial borders; rose & water gardens; well-maintained kitchen gardens; spring bedding—displays of wallflowers, tulips, polyanthus. Herbaceous borders with wide variety of plants & shrubs especially suited to coastal conditions. NO DOGS. No picnics. Tea Broadstairs 1 m. *Adm. 25p, Chd. 10p. Sun. May 11 & Sun. Aug. 10 (2–5.30)*

● **Hever Castle**†&⊕ (The Lord & Lady Astor of Hever) 5 m. SE of Edenbridge midway between London & S coast, off B2026. Bus: MD 234 (not Sunday) Tunbridge Wells–Langton–Edenbridge. Formal Italian & landscaped garden with statuary, sculpture & topiary; lake. Moated castle, once the home of Anne Boleyn, also open. No adm. to castle without prior payment for adm. to gardens. On Tues. & Fris. (Special Days) extra rooms in castle are shown. Party rates available for gardens only (except on Bank Hol. Suns. & Mons.) 25 or more people. Refreshments available. Free car & coach park. NO DOGS in castle; on lead only in garden. *Adm. inc. VAT, gardens only, 80p, Chd. under 12, 30p; party rate for garden 50p, Chd. 25p. Castle £1 extra, Chd. under 12, 50p; castle on Tues. & Fris. £1.50 (adults & chd.).* **Hours:** *garden 1–7, no adm. after 6 when entrance gates close; castle 1.30–7, no adm. after 6.15 or 5.15 on Tues. & Fris.* **Dates:** *March 30 to Sept. 28, every Tues., Wed., Fri. (except Good Friday), Sun. & Bank Hol.*

Holden House&⊕ (P. A. Godfrey Phillips Esq) Southborough, 2½ m. S of Tonbridge. Leave Sevenoaks–Tonbridge bypass at Tunbridge Wells exit; turn right at first zebra crossing opposite Imperial Hotel, garden 300 yds. 10 acres with lawns, bulbs, rhododendrons, azaleas, kalmias, heathers, camellias, largest tulip tree in SE. (*Share to Royal Nat. Lifeboat Institution*) NO DOGS. *Adm. 30p, Chd., if accompanied, 5p. Fri. April 4; April 6–June 8 every Sun.; also Mon. April 7, May 5 & 26; Suns. Aug. 24, 31, Sept. 7, 14; also Mon. Aug. 25 (2–6); also by appt. (for parties only)*

Hole Park&⊕ (D. G. W. Barham Esq) Rolvenden. Bus: MD 12 Maidstone–Hastings; 97 Ashford–Tunbridge Wells; alight gates. Set in beautiful parkland; formal garden with herbaceous borders, roses, extensive yew hedges & many fine trees; natural garden containing rhododendrons, azaleas, spring bulbs, daffodils, conifers, dell & water garden; bluebell wood; October openings: autumn colour. NO DOGS. Light TEAS (Suns. only). *Adm. 30p, Chd. under 12, 10p. Sun. April 20. Wed. April 30, Suns. May 4, 18, Weds. May 28, June 4 (2–7); Suns. Oct. 12 & 19 (2–6)*

Holwood†&⊕ (Seismograph Service (England) Ltd) Keston. Bus: Green Line 704 or

705 Windsor—Sevenoaks; alight Fishponds, Keston. Mansion (not open) in neo-classical style (architect Decimus Burton), picturesquely sited in extensive woodland with fine views across Kent; flowering shrubs; greenhouses. One-time home of William Pitt. Historical Wilberforce & Pitt oaks. Iron Age fort & medieval tile kiln. TEA & biscuits available. Free car park. *Adm. 30p, Chd. 10p. Sun. Sept. 7 (2–6)*

Horton Priory★†ȹ⊕ (Mrs A. C. Gore) Sellindge, 6 m. SE of Ashford. From A20 Ashford—Folkestone, 1 m. from Sellindge, turn E along Moorstock Lane, signposted Horton Priory. Bus: EK/MD 10, 10A, 10B Maidstone—Ashford—Folkestone; alight Sellindge, 1 m. Parking for cars in front of house & along drive & garage areas. Herbaceous & rose border, lawn, pond & rock garden. Priory dates back to C12; church itself was destroyed in reign of Henry VIII, but remains of west doorway & staircase to south aisle of nave can be seen by front door; all Norman buttresses along whole of west front are genuine; all windows in west front C14 (some restored); one genuine small Norman window. Outer hall only open to visitors. *Adm. 30p, Chd. 5p. Sun. July 6 & Sun. Sept. 7 (2–6)*

Hush Heath Manor★†ȹ (Dr & Mrs Stanley Balfour-Lynn) 3 m. NE of Goudhurst. E of B2079. From Goudhurst Church take 1st turn left for Blantyre House; at Blantyre House, turn sharp left downhill for ½ m., 3 m. SE of Marden, via Marden Thorn. Station: Marden. Bus stop: Curtisden Green. Italian style garden; fine yew hedges, terraces, flowering shrubs, bog garden, old-fashioned roses & climbing roses cascading over trees. Tudor house (not open), 1534. (*Share to Gardeners' Sunday*) NO DOGS. Tea Goudhurst. *Adm. 30p, Chd. 15p. Sun. May 18 & Sun. June 22 (2–7)*

Ilam★⊕ (Mr & Mrs R. Stapylton-Smith) Horns Rd, Hawkhurst. 1 m. SW of Hawkhurst via A265 (towards Hurst Green) on left side of rd. Labour-saving garden, designed & created since 1973; variety of shrubs & herbaceous plants, all clearly labelled & some rarely seen in Kent; foliage & other plants of interest to the floral arranger. NO DOGS. TEAS. *Adm. 30p, Chd. 10p. Sat. & Sun. June 28 & 29 (2–7)*

Knole †ȹ⊕ (The Lord Sackville; The National Trust—see Nat. Trust, p. ix) Sevenoaks. Station: Sevenoaks. Bus: 402 Bromley—Sevenoaks or 483 West Croydon—Sevenoaks, alight Bus Station; Green Line 704 from Victoria, alight Sevenoaks school. Pleasaunce, deer park, landscape garden, herb garden. NO DOGS. Tea Sevenoaks. *Adm. £1 per car on entering park; garden 50p, Chd. under 14, 25p; house £1.20, Chd. under 14, 60p. △Wed. June 4 & Wed. Aug. 6 (11–5, last adm. 4.30)*

Kypp Cottage★ (Mr & Mrs R. Grant) Biddenden. 3½ m. NW of Tenterden. At Woolpack Corner on A262. Biddenden is picturesque & historical village with many beautiful old houses (inc. a row of Grade I). Cottage garden started about 1964 from rough ground; well stocked with extensive collection of interesting plants; new & old shrub roses & ground cover plants a feature. (*Share to N.S.P.C.C.*) Tea available in High St at Claris's (*3–6*) or Country Crafts (*2.30–5*). *Adm. 25p, Chd. 5p. Sun., Mon. & Tues. June 15, 16, 17; Sun., Mon. & Tues. July 6, 7, 8 (2–6)*

Laddingford House★ȹ⊕ (Mr & Mrs A. V. D. Cochrane) Laddingford, 7½ m. SW of Maidstone. From B2015 at Blue Bell Inn turn off left (E) & continue over Beltring railway halt; house is immediately opp. rd junction at the bridge (1¼ m. from Blue Bell Inn). 2 acres; an old garden replanted since 1972 on labour-saving lines & maintained by owners; walled garden, spring bulbs, unusual shrubs & mixed borders. Picnics allowed (but no fires & no dogs). Plants for sale when available. NO DOGS. TEAS, June 29 only, by Laddingford Village Assn. *Adm. 25p, Chd. 15p. Thurs. April 24 & Thurs. May 22 (11–4); Sun. June 29 (2–6); Mon. June 30 & Thurs. Sept. 25 (11–4)*

Ladham House★ȹ (Betty, Lady Jessel) Goudhurst. On NE edge of village, off A262. Buses: 26 Maidstone—Goudhurst; 297 Ashford—Tenterden—Hawkhurst—Goudhurst—Tunbridge Wells. Flowering shrubs, rhododendrons, camellias, azaleas & magnolias; heather gardens, spring & autumn; kitchen garden. July opening: flowering shrubs, mixed borders & roses; bog garden. Garden was subject of articles in *County Life and House & Garden*. Picnic area at garden. Tea Goudhurst. Car park free. *Adm. 40p, Chd. 10p. Suns. April 20 (11–6); May 25, July 20 (11–7); Oct. 5 (11–6); also by appt.*

43 Layhams Road⊕ (Mrs Dolly Robertson) West Wickham. The semi-detached house can be recognised by a small sunken flower garden in the front. Opp. Wickham Court Farm. A raised vegetable garden, purpose-built for the disabled with easy access to wide terraced walkways. The owner, who maintains the entire 24 ft x 70 ft area herself, would be pleased to pass on her experiences as a disabled gardener so that others may share her joy & interest. *Collecting box. Garden open by appt. only all year (Tel. 01-462 4196)*

Long Barn★† (Mr & Mrs W. S. Martin) Weald, 2 m. S of Sevenoaks. From Sevenoaks bypass (A21) take exit marked 'North Tonbridge'; follow sign to Weald, pass village green on left & Long Barn is at S end. Medium-sized garden, created by the late V. Sackville-West & Harold Nicolson who lived here from 1915–1930, prior to moving to Sissinghurst

Castle; terraced lawns, box hedges, yew trees & Lombardy poplars; raised flower beds designed by Lutyens who also supervised the conversion of the C14–15 house. (*Share to Sevenoaks & District Assn for Mental Health*) NO DOGS. *Adm. 35p, Chd. 15p. △Sun. May 11 & Sun. July 13 (2–6)*

¶**Luton House***⅃⊕ (Mr & Mrs John Swire) Selling, 4 m. SE of Faversham. From A2 (M2) or A251 make for Selling Post Office, drive gates 50 yds E of P.O., & on same side of rd. 4 acres; C19 landscaped garden; ornamental pond, arboretum recently underplanted with fine collection of azaleas, camellias & woodland plants. NO DOGS. *Adm. 25, Chd. 5p. Sun. April 27 & Sun. June 8 (2–6)*

Marle Place⊕ (Mr & Mrs Gerald Williams) nr Brenchley, 8 m. SE of Tonbridge. On B2162, 1 m. S of Horsmonden & 1½ m. N of Lamberhurst. From Tonbridge via A21; at AA box fork left for Goudhurst, then turn left on to Horsmonden Rd. 5 acres; Victorian gazebo; shrub borders & lawns; walled rose garden. House (not shown) C17, listed Grade II. Nature trail. NO DOGS. TEAS. *Adm. 30p, Chd. 15p. Sun. June 1 & Sun. July 6 (2–7)*

Mere House⊕ (John J. Wells Esq, M.P.) Mereworth, 7 m. W of Maidstone. From A26 Maidstone–Tonbridge turn on to B2016 & then into Mereworth village. Bus: MD 7 Maidstone–Tonbridge; alight Mereworth village, ¼ m. Medium-sized garden; ornamental shrubs, lake, lawns. (*Share to Army Benevolent Fund (Eastern Region)*) Picnics allowed (but no fires). NO DOGS except on lead. *Adm. 25p, Chd. 15p. Suns. April 20, June 15, July 13 (2–7)*

Mereworth Castle†⅃ (His Excellency, Sayed Mohamed Mahdi Al-Tajir) 7 m. W of Maidstone. A26 mid-way between Maidstone & Tonbridge. Beautiful landscape garden surrounding famous Palladian mansion (not open). NO DOGS. *Adm. 30p, Chd. 10p. Sun. June 15 (2–6)*

Mount Ephraim*⅃⊕ (Mr & Mrs C. A. W. Dawes) Hernhill, 3 m. E of Faversham. From A2 turn N in Boughton; or from M2 & A299 take turning for Hernhill at Duke of Kent inn. Bus: EK/MD 3 Canterbury–Faversham, alight Woodman's Hall, ¾ m. Herbaceous border; topiary; daffodils & rhododendrons; terraces leading to a small lake; Japanese rock garden with pools. Picnicking permitted. *Adm. 30p, Chd. 5p. Sun. & Mon. April 20 & 21 Mon. & Tues. May 26 & 27; Sun. & Mon. June 29 & 30 (2–7)*

Northbourne Court*† (The Lord Northbourne) W of Deal. Direction sign at N end of Northbourne village. Barfreston Church (Norman) 4½ m. Richborough Castle (Roman) 5½ m. Station: Deal, 4 m. Bus: EK 14 hourly, Deal–Canterbury via Eastry, alight Northbourne X-rds, ¼ m. Great brick terraces,

originally related to an earlier Elizabethan mansion, provide a picturesque setting for a wide range of shrubs & plants on chalk soil; geraniums, fuchsias & grey-leaved plants. Elizabethan Great Barn. (*Share to Gardeners' Sunday*). Tea Deal or Sandwich. *Adm. 40p, Chd. 20p. Suns. May 4, 25, June 15, July 6, 27, Aug. 24 (2–7)*

Oldbury Place⅃⊕ (Mr & Mrs P. H. Byam-Cook) Ightham, E of Sevenoaks. ½ m. from Ightham; on A25 at Oldbury X-rds. Approx. 7 acres; fine old trees, lawns & shrubs. Picnics allowed. Light TEAS. *Adm. 30p, Chd. 10p. Sun. July 6 (2–7)*

¶**The Old Parsonage** † (Dr & Mrs Richard Perks) Sutton Valence, 6 m. SE of Maidstone. A274 from Maidstone or Headcorn, turn E into village at King's Head Inn & proceed on upper rd through village; climb Tumblers Hill & entrance at top on right. 2 acres planted since 1959 as labour-saving garden; ground-cover is essence; many trees, shrubs & mixed borders; cranesbills & shrub roses a speciality; ancient nut plat being developed as a wild garden. Fine views over Low Weald. In grounds is Sutton Castle, C12 ruined keep (under restoration by D.O.E.). NO DOGS. *Adm. 30p, Chd. 10p Suns. June 22 & 29 (2–6)*

The Old Vicarage⅃⊕ (Mrs H. W. Backhouse) Ide Hill, 4½ m. SW of Sevenoaks. 3-acre woodland with flowering shrubs & beautiful view; rhododendrons, azaleas, camellias, magnolias, etc. Some of garden suitable for wheelchairs, inc. the view. Plants for sale if available. *Adm. 25p, Chd. 10p (under 5, free). Sun. April 20 & Sun. May 18 (2–7.30); also by appt.*

Otham Gardens, 4 m. SE of Maidstone & 15 m. SW of Ashford. From A2020 or A274 follow signs for Otham 1 m.; at Otham Green turn E down lane by monument & signs to Car Park & Stoneacre. Small village comprising number of fine old timbered houses; surrounded by orchards & beautiful sweeping views to N Downs. NO DOGS. TEA & Coffee available at Stoneacre, also tickets & map of gardens. *Combined charge 75p, Chd. 20p, admits to all 7 following gardens. Sun. June 22 (2–6)*

¶**Greenhill House** (Dr & Mrs Hugh Vaux) Colourful garden at height of summer with many interesting plants

¶**Homestead**⊕ (Mr & Mrs James Betts) Farmhouse garden with herbaceous borders & roses

¶**The Limes**⊕ (Mr & Mrs John Stephens) Well-established garden with roses, herbaceous borders, wisteria pergola

¶**Little Squerryes**⊕ (Mr & Mrs Gerald Coombe) Church Rd. Established garden; modern roses, herbaceous borders, landscaped & solar-heated swimming pool

¶**The Old School**⊕ (Mr & Mrs D. Marchant) Converted school playground; interesting plants

¶**White Cottage**⊕ (Mr & Mrs John Chambers) Small garden set among old buildings in restricted area for planting, transformed into beauty spot and blaze of colour in summer

¶**Stoneacre** (Mr & Mrs Cecil Thayer-Turner; The National Trust) Restoration of garden in progress to match period of house; intimate Shakespeare/herb garden enclosed by yew hedges & walls; herbaceous borders; raised terrace with rare plants; rockery. Small timber-framed Hall House dated 1480. House will also open to the public as June 22 will be last day of 3-day **Flower Festival marking the 500th anniversary of Stoneacre.** *Entrance to house 40p extra, Chd. 20p (free to Nat. Trust members)*

Oxon Hoath†&⊕ (Mr & Mrs Henry Bayne-Powell) nr Hadlow, 5 m. NE of Tonbridge. 2½ m. N of Hadlow; 4 m. S of Borough Green; 3 m. SW of Mereworth. Car *essential*. Via A20, turn off S at Wrotham Heath on to Seven Mile Lane (B2016); at Mereworth X-rds turn right & through West Peckham. Or via A26, in Hadlow turn off N along Carpenters Lane. 10 acres; landscaped with fine trees, rhododendrons & azaleas; woodland walk; cedar avenue; formal rose garden; peacocks. Large Kentish ragstone house (not shown) principally Georgian but dating back to C14; Victorian additions by Salvin. At one time owned by Culpeppers, grandparents of Catherine Howard. View over C18 lake to Hadlow Folly. NO DOGS. TEA & cakes in picnic area if fine. *Adm. 30p, Chd. 15p. Sun. May 25 (2–7)*

The Postern (Mr & Mrs John Phillimore) Postern Lane, Tonbridge. On E side of Tonbridge. Postern Lane runs between B2017 (1 m. from its junction with A21) & Vale Rd (the Tonbridge 'inner relief rd'); house approx. ½ m. from either end. Bus: MD 7, Maidstone—Tunbridge Wells, alight The Mitre, Hadlow Rd, Tonbridge, 1 m. 4 acres with lawns, flowering shrubs & roses (inc. old & new shrub roses); apple & pear orchards. Georgian house (not open) built 2nd half of C18. NO DOGS. TEAS (Suns. only). *Adm. 30p, Chd. 15p. Suns. June 29 & July 6 (2–6); also by appt. for parties only*

The Red House&⊕ (K. C. L. Webb Esq) Crockham Hill, 3 m. N of Edenbridge. Limpsfield–Crockham Rd, B269. Formal features of this large garden are kept to a minimum; rose walk leads on to 3 acres of rolling lawns flanked by imposing trees; interesting collection of fine trees & shrubs inc. rhododendrons, azaleas & magnolias. Fine views over the Weald & Ashdown Forest. NO DOGS. *Adm. 25p, Chd. 15p. Sun. May 25 (2–6)*

Ringfield&⊕ (Prof. Sir David Smithers) Knockholt. Via A21 London–Sevenoaks; from London turn at Pratts Bottom (Stone's Timber); from Sevenoaks at Dunton Green (Rose & Crown). Over 4,000 roses & much new tree planting; walled tennis court. Flint Queen Anne house (not open) with additions. *Adm. 30p, Chd. 10p. Sun. July 6 (2–7)*

Rock Farm* (Mr & Mrs P. A. Corfe) Nettlestead. 6 m. W of Maidstone. Turn S off A26 on to B2015 & then 1 m. S of Wateringbury turn off right. Garden of 1½ acres skilfully set out around old farmhouse & buildings; planned & planted since 1968 & maintained by owner; plantsman's collection of shrubs, herbaceous plants, ornamental pond. Plants for sale at Nursery on the premises. (*Share to Cancer Research*) NO DOGS. Tea West Malling, Teston. *Adm. 30p, Chd. under 12, 15p. Sats. May 17, 24, 31; Mon. & Wed. May 26 & 28; Sats. June 14, 21, 28; Weds. June 4, 11, 25; July every Sat., Weds. July 2, 16, 30 (11–5)*

¶**St Clere**&⊕ (Mr & Mrs Ronnie Norman) Kemsing, 6 m. NE of Sevenoaks. Take A25 from Sevenoaks towards Ightham; 1 m. past Seal turn left signposted Heverham & Kemsing; in Heverham take rd to right signposted Wrotham & West Kingsdown; in 75 yds continue straight ahead marked Private Rd; take 1st left & follow rd to house. 4-acre garden with herbaceous borders, shrubs, rare trees, kitchen garden. C17 mansion (not open). NO DOGS. TEAS. *Adm. 25p, Chd. 10p Sun. June 29 (2–6)*

● **Saltwood Castle** †&⊕ (The Hon. Alan Clark, M.P.) 2 m. NW of Hythe, 4 m. W of Folkestone; from A20 turn S at sign to Saltwood. Medieval castle, subject of quarrel between Thomas à Becket & Henry II. C13 crypt & dungeons; armoury; battlement walks & watch towers. Lovely position with fine views; spacious lawns & borders; courtyard walls covered with roses in summer. Picnics allowed. TEAS. Car park free. *Adm. 50p, Chd. 25p. Sun. & Mon. May 25 & 26; June & July every Sun.; Aug. daily except Sats. & Mons. but open on Aug. 25 (2–5.30)*

¶**The Salutation** (Mrs Peter Dixon) The Quay, Sandwich. House & garden designed by Sir Edward Lutyens; original planting by Miss Jekyll; well-maintained formal garden with herbaceous borders, roses, heather garden & wild garden. *Adm. £1, Chd. under 14 free if accompanied by an adult. (OAPs 50p; groups of 20 or more 75p). Sun. July 6 (11–4.30)*

Sandling Park*& (Maj. A. E. Hardy) NW of Hythe. Entrance off A20 *only*. Station: Sandling Junction, ¼ m. Bus: EK/MD 10, 10A, 10B Folkestone–Ashford–Maidstone; alight New Inn Green, 1 m. Large garden with good views & fine trees. Rhododendrons, azaleas, magnolias & big collection of primulas in a woodland setting. Large walled vegetable garden. NO DOGS. *Adm. 50p, Chd. under 12, 10p. Suns. May 4, 11, 18, 25, June 1 (10–6)*

● **Scotney Castle***†&. (Mrs Christopher Hussey; The National Trust) On A21 London–Hastings, 1¼ m. S of Lamberhurst. Bus: Nat. 037 London–Hastings, alight Chequers Inn, Lamberhurst; or MD 250 Tunbridge Wells–Hawkhurst (not Suns.), alight Lamberhurst Down. Famous picturesque landscape garden, surrounding moated C14 Castle, which was created ·by the Hussey family in the 1840s. House (not open) by Salvin built in 1837. Special Exhibition in old Castle May 26–Aug. 31 (same days & times as garden). Gift Shop. NO DOGS. Picnic area in car park. **May 26: TEA & biscuits in house** (**this date only**); other days, Tea Goudhurst. *Adm. 80p, Chd. 40p (during period of Exhibition (May 26–Aug. 31) 90p, Chd. 50p). Dates: April 2–Oct. 31 daily except Mons. & Tues., but open Bank Hol. Mons. Hours: April & Oct. 2–5; May–Sept. 2–6 (last adm. ½ hr before closing)*

Sea Close* (Maj. & Mrs R. H. Blizard) Cannongate Rd, Hythe. 5 mins walk to sea. 100 yds from bus stop. Via A259 Hythe–Folkestone; from Classic Cinema after ½ m. turn left into Cannongate Rd; 1st drive on right. 1¼ acres; small well-kept garden on steep slope facing S with sea view; developed & landscaped by present owners since 1966; large personal collection of interesting plants & shrubs planted for visual effect & labelled. (*Share to Royal Signals Assn*) Plants for sale if available. Regret NO DOGS. Tea Hythe. *Adm. 30p, Chd. 15p. Suns. June 1, July 6, Aug. 3 (2–6)*

Selling Gardens. 4 m. SE of Faversham. From A2 (M2) or A251 make for Selling Church (C13). Gardens are opp. each other in Vicarage Lane (½ m. N of church). NO DOGS. *Combined charge for both gardens 40p, Chd. 20p. Wed. April 16 (11–4)*

¶**Brook's Croft**&.⊕ (Mr & Mrs G. Forsman) 5 acres; C19 landscaped garden surrounded by cherry orchards; fine old trees; camellias, rhododendrons, large specimen of Magnolia Veitchii; garden replanted in late 1930s. Airedales & Dobermanns in Kennels

¶**Trafalgar House**†⊕ (Alan Neame Esq) Small garden (¾ acre) rectangular & semi-formal; replanting started in 1978. House (not open) built with prize-money from Battle of Trafalgar 1805

Sissinghurst Castle Garden*†&.⊕ (Nigel Nicolson Esq; The National Trust) Cranbrook. Station: Staplehurst. Bus: MD 5 from Maidstone, 14 m.; 297 Tunbridge Wells (not Suns.) 15 m.; 5 Hastings, 23 m. Garden created by the late V. Sackville-West. Spring garden, herb garden. Tudor buildings & tower, partly open to public. Moat. (In addition to dates below in aid of N.G.S., the garden is open daily April 1 to Oct. 13; weekdays 12–6.30; Sats., Suns. &

Bank Hols. 10–6.30.) NO DOGS. Lunches & TEAS. *Adm. £1.10 (pre-arranged parties Mon., Tues., Thurs., Fri., 70p each), Chd. 50p.* △*Weds. May 14, June 11, July 9 (12–6.30)*

Sissinghurst Place&.⊕ (Lt-Gen. Sir Napier & Lady Crookenden) Cranbrook. At E end of Sissinghurst on A262. 16 m. from Ashford; 15 m. from Tunbridge Wells. Bus: MD 5 from Maidstone. 3 acres; mostly lawns & flowering shrubs; some fine trees inc. a Durmast oak said to be 700 yrs old & the largest in England; lime avenue. Lunch & tea available in Sissinghurst. DOGS on leads only. *Adm. 25p, OAPs and Chd. 10p Sat. June 7 (10–6)*

Sprivers*&.⊕ (M. C. Dibben Esq) Horsmonden, 10 m. SE of Tonbridge. From A21 turn off N nr AA box on to B2162 for Horsmonden. Bus: 297, alight Shirrenden, ½ m. Garden ornaments in a natural setting; fine trees, yew hedges, flowering & foliage shrubs, herbaceous borders, spring & summer bedding, old walls; woodland walks. DOGS must be kept on lead. *Adm. 35p, Chd. 20p. Sun. June 1 (2–6)*

Stonewall Park*&. (V. P. Fleming Esq) Chiddingstone Hoath, 5 m. SE of Edenbridge. Chiddingstone Hoath is ½-way between Mark Beech & Penshurst. Tea Penshurst, 2 m. Large garden; wooded dell featuring rhododendrons & azaleas; wandering paths; lake. (*Share to Gardeners' Sunday*) Cups of TEA. DOGS on leads please. Tea Penshurst, 2 m. *Adm. 30p, Chd. 5p. Sat. & Sun. May 17 & 18 (2–5.30)*

Street End Place&.⊕ (Lt-Col John Baker White) Street End. 3 m. S of Canterbury on Canterbury–Hythe rd (Stone St). Drive gates at Granville Inn. Long-established garden, inc. wall garden, in pleasant setting; large area of naturalised daffodils with lawns & flowering shrubs; fine trees. DOGS on lead only. *Adm. 25p, Chd. over 10, 5p. Suns. April 13 & 20 (2–7)*

Tanners*&.⊕ (Mr & Mrs M. P. Nolan) Brasted, 2 m. E of Westerham. A25 to Brasted; in Brasted turn off alongside the green & up the hill to the top (1st drive on right opp. to Coles Lane). Bus stop: Brasted Green or White Hart, 200 yds. 5 acres; mature trees & shrubs; maples, magnolias, rhododendrons & foliage trees. Plants for sale if available. NO DOGS. TEAS. *Adm. 25p, Chd. 5p. Sun. May 18 (2–6) & Sun. Oct. 26 (12–5)*

¶**Updown Farm***⊕ (Mr & Mrs M. E. Willis-Fleming) Betteshanger, 3 m. S of Sandwich. From A256 Dover–Sandwich, ¾ m. S of Eastry turn off E signposted to Northbourne, take 1st left off this rd; house 1st on left. 3-acre garden started 1975 & still in the making, around Tudor & C18 farmhouse, inc. one of the most extensive figgeries in East Kent; cherry & plum orchards filled with old roses & climbers; terrace garden; herbaceous borders, inc. unusual grasses. NO DOGS.

TEAS. *Adm. 25p, Chd. 10p. Sun. May 25 & Sun. July 6 (2–7)*

Updown House⚬⊕ (Maj. Arthur James) Betteshanger, W of Deal. From A256 Dover–Sandwich rd, ¾ m. S of Eastry turn E on to C221 Eastry–Northbourne–Deal rd. Bus: EK 614 passes entrance (request stop). 2 acres of garden; also lawns; walled garden; old-fashioned roses, flowering shrubs, borders; cedars. Tea Updown Farm. *Adm. 25p, Chd. 10p. Sun. May 25 & Sun. July 6 (2–6)*

Warders*⊕ (Mr & Mrs R. D. Cooper) East St, Tonbridge. Off High St & N of R. Medway bridge. Room for few cars only. Public car parks off High St. About 2 acres; mostly flowering shrubs & ground cover; many unusual attractive plants; dwarf shrubs a feature; everything labelled. NO DOGS. *Adm. 30p, Chd. 10p. Sun. May 25 & Thurs. May 29 (2–6)*

Watergate House⊕ (Nicholas Graham Esq) Fordwich, 2½ m. NE of Canterbury. Via A28 Canterbury–Margate, to Sturry & at Welsh Harp public house turn right at signpost to Fordwich. Garden in centre Fordwich, a picturesque village, & next door to C16 Town Hall. Small walled garden designed by present owner for year-round interest; mixed borders with emphasis on ground cover & foliage plants. Plants for sale if available. NO DOGS. Tea Canterbury. *Adm. 30p (no reduction for Chd.). Sun. & Mon. May 18 & 19; Sun. & Mon. July 20 & 21 (1.30–5)*

Waystrode Manor†⊕ (Mr & Mrs Peter Wright) Cowden, 4½ m. S of Edenbridge. From B2026 Edenbridge–Hartfield, turn off at Cowden Pound. Station: Cowden, 1½ m. 8 acres; large lawns, small grey garden; borders, ponds, bulbs, shrub roses & clematis. House (not open) an Ancient Monument, 500 yrs old. (*Share to Gardeners' Sunday (June 29)*). Plant stall. NO DOGS. Picnics allowed. TEA. *Adm. 45p, Chd. 15p. Sun. May 25 (2–6); Wed. June 11 (2–5); Sun. June 29 (2–6); also by appt. for parties*

¶Weeks Farm⊕ (Mrs Pamela Milburne) Bedlam Lane, Egerton Forstal, 3½ m. E of Headcorn. From Headcorn follow signs for Smarden; in 2 m. take left turn signposted Egerton; house 1½ m. along Bedlam Lane. 1½-acre garden on heavy Weald clay showing varied adaptation of badly drained site; wide, double mixed borders flanking gateway; vista a particular feature; great horticultural interest (early July) fantastic display of Madonna lilies. NO DOGS. TEAS. *Adm. 50p, Chd. 25p. Suns. June 29, July 6 & 13 (2–6)*

West Farleigh Hall⊕ (Mrs C. W. Norman) 4½ m. W of Maidstone. Turn S off A26 Maidstone–Tonbridge Rd at Teston Bridge. Roses, irises & herbaceous borders, vegetables; woodland walk. (*Share to S.S.A.F.A.*)

Picnic area available, but no fires please. *Adm. 20p, Chd. 5p. Sun. June 22 & Wed. July 23 (2–7)*

West Studdal Farm⊕ (Mr & Mrs Peter Lumsden) West Studdal, N of Dover. Farm is just off A256 on E side. From Dover area via Whitfield & on approx. 1½ m. passing High & Dry pub on right, after which take 2nd rd on right. From Sandwich area via Eastry & on 2 m., passing Plough & Harrow pub on right, after which take 2nd rd on left; follow rd to 1st X-rds & turn right, then on 500 yds, at entrance on left is pair of yellow cottages. Medium-sized garden around old farm house set by itself in small valley; herbaceous borders, roses & fine lawns protected by old walls & beech hedges. Duodecagonal folly (in which teas will be served). Plants for sale. TEAS. *Adm. 30p, Chd. 15p. Sun. Aug. 17 (2–6.30)*

Withersdane Hall*⊕ (Wye College) Wye, NE of Ashford. A28 take fork signposted Wye. Bus: EK 601 Ashford–Canterbury via Wye. Well-labelled garden of educational & botanical interest; several small gardens carefully designed within main garden; flower borders & alpines; spring flowering bulbs; collection of early flowering shrubs especially suited to chalk; herb garden. NO DOGS. Tea Wye. *Adm. 30p, Chd. 15p. Sun. July 6 & Sun. Sept. 7 (2–6)*

Woodlands Manor⚬⊕ (Mr & Mrs Colin B. George) Adisham, 5 m. SE of Canterbury. From A2 Canterbury–Dover, 2 m. from Canterbury take the Bridge bypass (dual carriageway); *ignore* the sign to Adisham; after 1 m. leave bypass at sign to Elham B2065; at bottom of exit rd turn sharp left; follow signs marking 6' 6" rd to house, 1 m. Approaching from the E, from Adisham village turn right at end of 'The Street'; at Woodlands Farm, ¾ m., follow signs. Station: Adisham. Bus: 16 or 17 Canterbury–Folkestone & 15 Canterbury–Dover; alight Bishopsbourne turn (request stop), pass under concrete bridge; signs to house, 1 m. Ample car park. Small Georgian house of architectural interest (not open) set in old walled gardens with herbaceous borders, flower beds, rockery, rose garden; pleached lime walk; statuary; gazebo; warm corners; shady gardens. Woodland walks; good vistas; sheltered park. NO DOGS. Light TEAS (June 29 only). *Adm. 30p, Chd. 15p. Sun. April 20 (2–5); Sun. June 29 (2–6)*

Woolton Farm*⚬⊕ (Lady Mount) Bekesbourne, 3½ m. SE of Canterbury. Station: Bekesbourne, 1 m. Bus: EK 13, 14 or 130 Canterbury–Deal, alight farm signpost. Garden of trees & shrubs (the heathers, rhododendrons, azaleas, flowering cherries a feature) with lawns. Plants for sale if available. NO DOGS. TEAS. *Adm. 30p, Chd. 10p. Suns. May 18 & 25 (2–6)*

Yeomans †⊕ (Mr & Mrs L. V. Chater) Great Chart, 2 m. SW of Ashford. On A28 in centre of Great Chart village. Medium-sized garden overflowing with colourful borders; roses, perennials, annuals; large well-planted vegetable garden; vines. Fine example of C15 house (not open). NO DOGS please. TEAS (in pool house). *Adm. 50p, Chd. 5p. Sun. Aug. 3 (2–6)*

LANCASHIRE, NORTH MERSEYSIDE & GREATER MANCHESTER

Hon. County Organiser:
THE LADY PILKINGTON, Windle Hall, St Helens

DATES OF OPENING
APRIL daily
    CRANFORD, Aughton, nr Ormskirk
April Sunday 27
    WINDLE HALL, St Helens
MAY daily
    CRANFORD, Aughton, nr Ormskirk
MAY Saturday 17 & Sunday 18
    191 LIVERPOOL ROAD SOUTH, Maghull
MAY Sunday 25 & Monday 26
    STONESTACK, 283 Chapeltown Rd, Turton, nr Bolton
JUNE & JULY daily
    CRANFORD, Aughton, nr Ormskirk
JULY Sunday 6
    WINDLE HALL, St Helens
AUGUST daily
    CRANFORD, Aughton, nr Ormskirk
AUGUST Sunday 10
    GREYFRIARS, nr Preston
AUGUST Sunday 17
    WYNFIELD, Burscough, nr Ormskirk
AUGUST Sunday 24 & Monday 25
    STONESTACK, 283 Chapeltown Road, Turton, nr Bolton
SEPTEMBER daily
    CRANFORD, Aughton, nr Ormskirk
SEPTEMBER Sunday 7
    WINDLE HALL, St Helens
OCTOBER daily to mid-October
    CRANFORD, Aughton, nr Ormskirk

DESCRIPTIONS OF GARDENS
Cranford (T. J. C. Taylor Esq) Formby Lane, Aughton, 2 m. SW of Ormskirk. Route A59. Station: Town Green. Bus: Ribble 101, Liverpool–Ormskirk–Preston; 311, Liverpool–Ormskirk–Chorley–Blackburn, alight Turnpike Rd. ½-acre 25-yr-old garden unusually planted & planned for labour saving; shrubs, small trees, roses. *Collecting box. April 1 to mid-Oct. daily (10–dusk)*

Greyfriars⊕ (Mr & Mrs William Harrison) Walker Lane, Fulwood, 2 m. N of Preston. Junc. 32 off M6 (M55); 1st turn to Preston; 1 m. on Lightfoot Lane (Walker Lane on left). 8 acres; lawns & gardens, 2,000 various

heathers; over 1,000 rose trees; 1,500 fuchsias & geraniums, greenhouses; banks of rhododendrons & bulbs. TEAS. *Adm. 25p, Chd. 10p. Sun. Aug. 10 (2–6)*

191 Liverpool Road South⊕ (Mr & Mrs D. Cheetham) Maghull. A59 Liverpool–Preston Rd; from Ormskirk or Liverpool take B5422 & garden about ½ m. along this rd. ⅓-acre suburban garden planted with rhododendrons, azaleas & a variety of shrubs, bulbs & trees suitable for all-year colour in the smaller garden. TEA or coffee. *Adm. 15p, Chd. 5p. Sat. & Sun. May 17 & 18 (11–7)*

Stonestack (Mr & Mrs Frank Smith) 283 Chapeltown Rd, Turton; 4½ m. N of Bolton, via A666 leading to B6391. Bus: 563 or 565; alight Turton Towers. 1½-acre garden; shrubs, rhododendrons, azaleas; herbaceous border; rockeries, waterfall, ornamental fishpond, fountain; rose borders; bog garden; fuchsias a special feature; greenhouses. *Adm. 20p. Sun. & Mon. May 25 & 26; Sun. & Mon. Aug. 24 & 25 (2–6)*

Windle Hall⊕ (The Lord & Lady Pilkington) N of E Lancs Rd, St Helens. 5 m. W of M6 via E Lancs Rd, nr Southport junction. Entrance *now only* from St Helens side, by bridge over E Lancs Rd. Bus: St Helens No. 6 to Abbey Rd, ¼ m. 200-yr-old walled garden surrounded by 5 acres of lawns & woodland full of spring flowers; (part to be re-landscaped owing to ravage of Dutch Elm disease); a rockery with stream & tufa stone grotto; herbaceous borders, new pergola & rose gardens containing exhibition blooms, all named; ornamental pheasants; greenhouses. Winner of Poignard in Wilkinson Sword Charity Award, Aug. 1979. TEAS. *Adm. 25p, OAPs & Chd. 15p. Suns. April 27. July 6, Sept. 7 (2–6); also by appt. for coach parties*

¶**Wynfield*** (Mr & Mrs B. Aughton) Flax Lane, Burscough, NE of Ormskirk. Travelling W from Parbold to Burscough (via B5239), ¼ m. past Briars Hall Hotel, on left down Square Lane. 2½ acres; lawns, herbaceous borders, small rose garden; 2 rockeries with waterfalls; rare conifers & mixed heathers; miniature lake full of carp. TEA & biscuits. *Adm. 25p, OAPs & Chd. 15p. Sun. Aug. 17 (2–6)*

LEICESTERSHIRE & RUTLAND

Hon. County Organisers:
(Leicestershire) MRS GEORGE JOHNSON, Long Close, Woodhouse Eaves, Loughborough, LE12 8RZ
(Rutland) MRS K. SYMINGTON, Godfrey's House, Belton, Uppingham, LE10 9JU

DATES OF OPENING
APRIL to SEPTEMBER by appointment
    9 MERE RD, Upper Bruntingthorpe, nr Lutterworth

LEICESTERSHIRE & RUTLAND—
continued

APRIL to OCTOBER by appointment
  STONE COTTAGE, Hambleton, nr Oakham
APRIL Sunday 20
  ROCKYFIELD, Ulverscroft, nr Markfield
APRIL Saturday 26
  NOSELEY HALL, nr Billesdon
MAY Sunday 11
  SEDGEMERE, Market Bosworth
MAY Sunday 18
  GUNTHORPE, nr Oakham
MAY Sunday 25
  LONG CLOSE, Woodhouse Eaves,
    nr Loughborough
JUNE Sunday 1
  BELTON GARDENS, nr Uppingham
  EXTON PARK, nr Oakham
JUNE Sunday 8
  THE CEDARS, Kegworth
  HOLLY HAYES, Birstall, nr Leicester
  ROCKYFIELD, Ulverscroft, nr Markfield
JUNE Sunday 15
  HOLLY HAYES, Birstall, nr Leicester
  SWAN HOUSE, Lyddington, nr Uppingham
JUNE Sunday 22
  ‡BELVOIR LODGE, nr Grantham
  THE OLD RECTORY, Teigh, nr Oakham
  ‡RESERVOIR COTTAGE, Knipton,
    nr Grantham
JUNE Sunday 29
  BARKBY HALL, Barkby, nr Syston
  PRESTON GARDENS, nr Uppingham
  SEATON OLD RECTORY, nr Uppingham
JULY Saturday 5
  HOLYWELL HALL, nr Stamford
JULY Sunday 6
  ASHWELL LODGE, nr Oakham
  THE BELL HOUSE, Lyddington,
    nr Uppingham
  FRIARS WELL, nr Melton Mowbray
JULY Sunday 13
  BROOKSBY AGRICULTURAL COLLEGE,
    nr Melton Mowbray
  LITTLE DALBY HALL, nr Melton
    Mowbray
JULY Sunday 20
  BISBROOKE HALL, nr Uppingham
  PRESTWOLD HALL, Loughborough
  STONE HOUSE, Blaston, nr Market
    Harborough
  THORPE LUBENHAM HALL, nr Market
    Harborough
JULY Sunday 27
  UNIVERSITY OF LEICESTER BOTANIC
    GARDEN, Stoughton Drive South,
    Leicester
AUGUST Sunday 3
  GADDESBY HALL, Gaddesby
AUGUST Monday 25 (Bank Hol.)
  ROCKYFIELD, Ulverscroft, nr Markfield

DESCRIPTIONS OF GARDENS

Ashwell Lodge⊕ (Mrs Stephen Eve)
Ashwell, 3 m. N of Oakham. From A1, 10 m.

N of Stamford, turn off W through Greatham
& Cottesmore; at far end of Cottesmore turn
right for Ashwell. Cars must park in village st.
Medium-sized garden; herbaceous borders,
paved rose garden, shrubs, greenhouse.
Plants for sale if available. NO DOGS. TEAS.
Adm. 40p. Sun. July 6 (2.30–6)

Barkby Hall★†⅄⊕ Mr & Mrs A. F. Pochin)
Barkby, nr Syston, 5 m. NE of Leicester.
Woodland garden, azaleas, rhododendrons,
ericas, conifers, roses, herbaceous, shrubs;
mature trees, interesting church nr grounds.
NO DOGS. *Adm. 25p, Chd. 12p. Sun. June 29
(3–7)*

The Bell House★ (Mrs R. Borgerhoff
Mulder) Lyddington, 1½ m. S of Uppingham;
between A6003 & B672. Small old-world
walled garden with roses & other good plants.
Close to C12 Bede House, Lyddington. *Adm.
25p, Chd. 10p. Sun. July 6 (2–6)*

Belton Gardens. 3 m. W of Uppingham;
½ m. N of A47 Uppingham–Leicester Rd; at
bottom of Wardley Hill turn N for Belton.
TEAS Westbourne House. *Combined charge
for following 3 gardens 40p, Chd. 5p. Sun.
June 1 (2–6)*
  36 Main Street⊕ (David Willmott Esq)
  Small rockery garden; heathers; conifers
  Westbourne House★†⅄⊕ (D. M. Burke
  Esq) Walled garden; herbaceous borders;
  water garden & conservatory; NO DOGS
  Godfrey's House (Mrs Symington) Small
  cottage garden

Belvoir Lodge⊕ (The Dowager Duchess of
Rutland) 7 m. W of Grantham. Between A52
& A607, ½ m. from Belvoir Castle. Medium-
sized garden; roses & delphiniums. Tea
Reservoir Cottage. *Adm. 15p, Chd. 5p. Sun.
June 22 (2–7)*

Bisbrooke Hall★⅄⊕ (Mr & Mrs G. H. Boyle)
Glaston, 3 m. E of Uppingham. On A47 on
western edge of Glaston Village. Large garden;
lawns, roses & shrubs of botanical interest;
fine trees in parkland. *Adm. 30p, Chd. under 12
free. Sun. July 20 (2–6)*

Brooksby Agricultural College★†⅄ (by
permission of Leicestershire County Council)
6 m. SW of Melton Mowbray. From A607
(9 m. from Leicester or 6 m. from Melton
Mowbray) turn at Brooksby; entrance 100 yds.
Bus: MR Leicester–Melton Mowbray–Grantham; alight Brooksby turn, 100 yds. Grounds
inc. extensive lawns, lake, ornamental brook,
flowering shrub borders, heather bed, large
collection young trees & other ornamental
features; glasshouses & advisory desk. Church
built 1220 open. *Adm. 25p, Chd. (accompanied) 10p. Sun. July 13 (2-6)*

The Cedars★†⅄ (Mrs H. B. Taylor) London
Rd, Kegworth. 6 m. NW of Loughborough on
A6. Loughborough end of Kegworth. 1-acre,
mixed, old walled garden with interesting
selection of trees & shrubs. House dates from

1. WESTWICK COTTAGE, Hertfordshire

Mrs Sheila Macqueen

A garden which specialises in plants for the flower arranger ; one of the group opening in Laverstock Green (see page 65)

Photograph : Country Life
(Jonathan M.Gibson)

2.
ROOKSNEST,
Berkshire

Miss M. V. Tufnell

A garden of particular
botanical interest with
emphasis on shrubs
and ornamental trees
(see page 6)

Photograph::
Oxford Mail & Times

3.
FAIRFIELD HOUSE,
Hampshire

Mr & Mrs Peter Wake

Very good collection
of plants with fine
trees ; and an
interesting conversion
of an old walled
garden (see page 54)

4.

**ADWELL HOUSE,
Oxfordshire**

*Mr & Mrs W. R. A.
Birch Reynardson*

In addition to the
water garden and
ornamental lakes there
are fine trees and
lawns (see page 98)

Photograph:
Oxford Mail & Times

5.

CARROG, Dyfed

Mr & Mrs Geoffrey Williams

A garden reclaimed, replanted and maintained entirely by owners, in a setting of mature trees (see page 32)

(see page 32)

Photograph:
Country Life
(Jonathan M. Gibson)

6.

MALTHOUSE FARM, Surrey

Mr & Mrs C. Kahn

A garden with flowering trees and shrubs, flowing into the landscape of the South Downs (see page 123)

Photograph:
Sheila J. Orme

7.

UNIVERSITY OF BRISTOL BOTANIC GARDEN, Somerset & South Avon

At Bracken Hill is this garden of over 3,000 species grown to display the diversity of the plant kingdom (see page 116)

Photograph:: Bristol United Press

8. WAYSTRODE MANOR, Kent

Photograph: Derek Tilley

Mr & Mrs Peter Wright

Beyond the borders and grey garden near to a 500-yrs-old house are
spacious lawns and a pond (see page 78)

1700 (not open); Thomas Moore once lived here. TEAS. *Adm. 25p, Chd. 5p. Sun. June 8 (2.30–5.30)*

Exton Park✭♿⊕ (The Rt Hon. The Earl of Gainsborough) NE of Oakham. Turn N off A606 Oakham–Stamford Rd at Barnsdale Ave. Bus stop: Exton, ½ m. Extensive park of great beauty; lakes, lawns, rare specimen trees & shrubs. *(Share to N.S.P.C.C.)* TEAS (3–5). Car park free. *Adm. 30p, Chd. (12–16) 15p; free under 12. Sun. June 1 (2–6)*

¶Friars Well⊕ (Sir John & Lady King) Wartnaby, 4 m. NW of Melton Mowbray. From A606 turn W in Ab Kettleby; from A46 at Durham OX turn E on to A676. Medium-sized garden; shrubs, herbaceous borders & roses. Plants for sale. TEAS. *Adm. 25p, Chd. 5p. Sun. July 6 (2–6)*

Gaddesby Hall♿⊕ (Mr & Mrs Gerrit van Ravenzwaay) in Gaddesby village, NE of Leicester. From A607, Leicester–Melton Mowbray, at Rearsby turn off E for Gaddesby. Approx. 6 acres; roses & dahlias, extensive lawns, ornamental pond; fine cedar trees, Wellingtonia, maple. Interesting church in adjoining ground. *Adm. 30p, Chd. 10p. Sun. Aug. 3 (2–6)*

Gunthorpe✭♿⊕ (A. T. C. Haywood Esq) 2 m. S of Oakham. Via Uppingham Rd; entrance by 3 cottages, on right going S. Medium-sized garden; flowering trees in a good setting. TEAS. *Adm. 40p (but maximum charge per car load £1). Sun. May 18 (2.30–6)*

Holly Hayes♿⊕ (Mr & Mrs H. Murphy) Birstall, N of Leicester. On Birstall Rd, ½ m. from A6. Leicester–Loughborough. Bus: LCT service from Leicester, alight at gates. Azaleas & rhododendrons. *(Share to RSCPA (Leicester Branch).) Adm. 25p. Sun. June 8 & Sun. June 15 (2–dusk)*

Holywell Hall†♿⊕ (Mr & Mrs W. P. Lockwood) N of Stamford. 4 m. E of A1. Large garden; lawns sloping down to water; large trees in park, an attractive setting in secluded valley. C18 house & church, orangery & summerhouse. TEA & home-made cakes. *Adm. 30p, Chd. 5p. Sat. July 5 (2–6)*

Little Dalby Hall†♿⊕ (Lady Martin) Little Dalby, 3 m. SE of Melton Mowbray. From A606, Melton Mowbray–Oakham, 3 m. from Melton, turn W at signpost to Somerby. Large garden beautifully landscaped with lawns & trees; fine cedar trees; Wellingtonia in wood. *(Share to Mental Health Research).* Tea Anne of Cleaves, Melton Mowbray. *Adm. 30p, Chd. 15p. Sun. July 13 (2–7)*

Long Close✭†♿ (Mrs George Johnson) Main St, Woodhouse Eaves, S of Loughborough. From A6 turn W in Quorn B591. Bus: Leicester–Loughborough, alight at gates (nr playing fields) 5 acres rhododendrons (many varieties), azaleas & flowering shrubs; old

shrub roses; many rare shrubs & trees; heathers, conifers, forest trees; lily pools; fountain; terraced lawns. TEA & biscuits. *Adm. 30p, Chd. accompanied 5p. Sun. May 25 (2–7)*

¶9 Mere Road✭ (Mr & Mrs W. A. Evitt) Upper Bruntingthorpe, NE of Lutterworth. Leave A50 at X-rds just E of Shearsby signposted between Bruntingthorpe & Walton; or from Lutterworth via A426, opp. Shell Garage turn E signposted Walton, Kimcote & Bruntingthorpe. Small garden for alpine enthusiasts; dwarf bulbs & conifers, ponds & stream; extensive collection of alpines all clearly marked. Best months April–June but interesting all year. NO DOGS or children. *Adm. 25p, Garden open by appt. only April to Sept. (Tel. Peatling Magna 531)*

Noseley Hall†⊕ (Lord Hazlerigg) S of Billesdon, SE of Leicester. From A47 Leicester–Uppingham Rd, turn S on to B6047 & then E for Noseley. Large garden; good show of daffodils; lawns & lakes; C13 chapel in grounds. *(Share to Noseley Chapel Fund).* TEA & biscuits. *Adm. 30p, Chd. 10p. Saturday April 26 (2–5.30)*

The Old Rectory✭⊕ (Mr & Mrs D. B. Owen) Teigh, 5 m. N of Oakham. Between Wymondham & Ashwell; or from A1 via Thistleton & Market Overton. Medium-sized garden; great variety of herbaceous & shrub borders. House (not open) C18. Attractive & unusual C18 church next door. *(Share to Mental Health Foundation (Rutland Branch).)* NO DOGS. TEAS. *Adm. 30p, Chd. free. Sun. June 22 (2–6.30)*

Preston Gardens. 2 m. N of Uppingham. On A6003 between Uppingham & Oakham. TEAS at Preston Hall. *Combined charge for following 2 gardens 30p, Chd. 10p. Sun. June 29 (2–6)*

The Dower House⊕ (Lt-Col & Mrs F. G. Norton-Fagge) Small garden; herbaceous, flowering shrubs & specie roses; collection of clematis

Preston Hall⊕ (Mrs R. M. Micklethwait) 2½ acres; extensive views, lawns, roses, inc. collection of shrub roses

Prestwold Hall✭♿ (Mr & Mrs Simon Packe-Drury-Lowe) 3 m. E of Loughborough. A6 or M1 to Loughborough; A60 to Hoton. Between Hoton & Burton-on-the-Wolds. Large gardens; terraced lawns with large rose garden; wild garden; cedars; conservatory with temperate trees & plants. House (not open) C19 & earlier, home of the Packe family for over 300 yrs. Church with fine monuments. Free car park in attractive surroundings open from 12.30 for picnicking. TEA & biscuits (afternoon only). *Adm. 30p, Chd. 5p. △Sun. July 20 (2–7)*

Reservoir Cottage⊕ (Lord & Lady John Manners) Knipton, 7 m. W of Grantham.

LEICESTERSHIRE & RUTLAND—
continued

W of A1 ; between A52 & A607; nr Belvoir Castle. Medium-sized country garden with lovely views over the lake. TEAS. *Adm. 25p, Chd. 5p. Sun. June 22 (2–7)*

Rockyfield*⚬⊕ (Mr & Mrs P. B. Heslop) Priory Lane, Ulverscroft, 1½ m. N of Markfield, NW of Leicester. From M1 (junc. 22) take A50 towards Leicester; turn 1st left, 1st right & 1st right again. 6¼ acres; informal garden in lovely Charnwood forest area; extensive collection of unusual trees, flowering shrubs & heathers; woodland walks; naturalised daffodils; magnificent views. Cottage (not open) designed by Ernest Gimson, noted architect & furniture designer. Plants for sale. Tea Newtown Linford. *Adm. 25p, Chd. free. Sun. April 20 & Sun. June 8; Mon. Aug. 25 (11–dusk)*

Seaton Old Rectory⚬ (Maj.-Gen. & Mrs R. E. Coaker) 3 m. SE of Uppingham. Turn S off A47 at Uppingham or Glaston. Medium-sized garden ; fine view, copper beeches. shrubs, roses, herbaceous border. TEAS. *Adm. 30p, Chd. 5p. Sun. June 29 (2.30–6.30)*

Sedgemere*⚬⊕ (G. H. Ratcliffe Esq) Station Rd, Market Bosworth, NE of Nuneaton. Pleasant informal garden with herbaceous borders, lawns, specimen trees & shrubs, rockeries overlooking lake—all in wooded setting. TEA & biscuits. *Adm. 20p. Sun. May 11 (2.30–7.30)*

Stone Cottage*⊕ (John Codrington Esq) Hambleton, 3 m. E of Oakham. Turn S off A606 for Hambleton. Small garden with interesting plants, shrubs, herbs, etc. Views of new Rutland Water. *Collecting box. Garden open by appt. only, April to Oct. (Write or Tel. Oakham 2156)*

Stone House⊕ (Mrs Pen Lloyd) Blaston, NE of Market Harborough. From A6, Leicester–Market Harborough, at Kibworth Harcourt turn E for Hallaton, Blaston. From B664 turn W for Blaston. Medium-sized gardens; lily ponds, rose gardens, herbaceous borders, Japan bronzes, small lake. TEAS. *Adm. 30p, Chd. 5p. Sun. July 20 (2.30–6.30)*

Swan House⊕ (Mr & Mrs Anthony Weston) Lyddington, 2 m. S of Uppingham, between A6003 & B672. 1½-acre garden, recently landscaped with shrubs, young trees, lawns & water garden. NO DOGS. TEAS. *Adm. 30p, Chd. 10p. Sun. June 15 (2–6); also by appt. (Tel. Uppingham 3388)*

Thorpe Lubenham Hall⚬⊕ (The Viscount & Viscountess Kemsley) 2 m. W of Market Harborough. From A50 at Husbands Bosworth turn E on to A427 to Market Harborough. From A6 Leicester–Market Harborough turn W on to A427 for Lubenham. Bus stop: ¼ m. from garden. Large garden; lawns, herbaceous borders, shrubs & roses (all named); green-

houses; accessible island with moat; bog garden. *(Share to Council of Order of St John (Leicestershire Branch).)* TEA & biscuits. *Adm. 30p, Chd. 5p. Sun. July 20 (2–7)*

University of Leicester Botanic Garden*⚬⊕ (by permission of the Council of the University of Leicester) Stoughton Drive South, Leicester (incorporating grounds of Beaumont Hall, Southmeade House, Hastings House & The Knoll) On SE outskirts of Leicester, nr Oadby Race Course. Bus: LCT services to Stoneygate Terminus. Turn left for Stoughton Drive South, opp. Oadby Race Course. 16 acres; trees; rose, rock, water & sunken gardens; botanical order bed; botanical greenhouses; herbaceous borders; heather garden. *Adm. 25p, Chd. 5p. Sun. July 27 (2–7)*

LINCOLNSHIRE

Hon. County Organiser:

WILLIAM KOCHAN ESQ, The Old Hall, Sausthorpe, nr Spilsby, PE23 4JL

DATES OF OPENING

MARCH 16 to JUNE 8 every Sunday
  WHEELABOUT, Mavis Enderby, nr Spilsby
MAY Sunday 11
  DODDINGTON HALL, nr Lincoln
MAY Sunday 25
  HARRINGTON HALL, nr Spilsby
JULY Sunday 6
  GUNBY HALL, Burgh-le-Marsh
  STRAGGLETHORPE HALL, Brent
    Broughton, nr Newark
AUGUST Sunday 24
  SAUSTHORPE OLD HALL, nr Spilsby
SEPTEMBER Sunday 7
  MARSTON HALL, nr Grantham

DESCRIPTIONS OF GARDENS

Doddington Hall*⚬ (Anthony Jarvis Esq) 5 m. SW of Lincoln. From Lincoln via A46, turn W on to B1190 for Doddington. Superb walled gardens; thousands of spring bulbs; Wild gardens; mature trees; Elizabethan mansion Free car park. Jointly with other charities. Home-made Cream TEAS. *Adm. house & garden 90p, Chd. 45p; garden only ½-price.* △*Sun. May 11 (2–6)*

Gunby Hall (Mr & Mrs J. D. Wrisdale; The National Trust—see p. ix) 2½ m. NW of Burgh-le-Marsh; S of A158. Walled gardens full of flowers & roses. House built by Sir William Massingberd 1700. *Adm. house & garden 60p, Chd. 30p. Sun. July 6 (2–6)*

Harrington Hall*†⊕ (Lady Maitland) 6 m. NW of Spilsby. Turn off A158, Lincoln–Skegness, at Hagworthingham, 2 m. from Harrington. C18 garden; roses, herbaceous borders, broom borders. House rebuilt 1678; porch tower Elizabethan; old walls; high terrace mentioned in Tennyson's *Maud*.

Interesting plants & shrubs for sale. TEAS.
*Adm. house & garden 80p, School Chd. 40p
garden only 40p, Chd 20p.* △*Sun. May 25
(2–7)*

Marston Hall†& (The Rev. Henry Thorold)
6 m. N of Grantham. Turn off A1, 4½ m. N of
Grantham & on 1½ m. to Marston. Station:
Grantham. Notable trees; wych elm &
laburnum of exceptional size. House C16 continuously owned by the Thorold family since
C14; interesting pictures & furniture. *Adm.
house & garden 40p, Chd. 20p.* △*Sun. Sept.
7 (2–6)*

Sausthorpe Old Hall†& (W. F. Kochan Esq)
Sausthorpe, NW of Spilsby. A158 Lincoln–
Skegness. Old garden; lawns; shrubberies;
trees, vistas of Lincolnshire Wolds. Associa-
tions with Tennyson. TEAS. *Adm. house &
garden 40p, Chd. 20p. garden only 30p, Chd.
15p. Sun. Aug. 24 (2–6)*

Stragglethorpe Hall (Maj. Alan Rook) Nr
Brant Broughton, 7 m. E of Newark. From A17
Newark–Sleaford turn off S for Stragglethorpe.
2 acres of old English country garden around
Elizabethan house (not open) beautifully
restored; lawns, roses & shrubs, also 2-acre
vineyard, the most northerly in Europe. *Adm.
25p, Chd. 10p. Sun. July 6 (2–6)*

Wheelabout*&⊕ (Mr & Mrs R. G. T.
Wakeling) Mavis Enderby, 2 m. W of Spilsby.
From A16 turn off at East Keel & follow signs.
42 acres; masses of daffodils in woodland
with rare trees & shrubs. Partially suitable for
wheelchairs. DOGS on leads only. Jointly
with another charity. TEAS. *Adm. 50p, Chd.
25p. March 16–June 8 every Sun. (2–6)*

LONDON
(Greater London Area)

Hon. County Organiser:
MRS I. O. CHANCE

Asst. County Organiser:
MISS RACHEL CRAWSHAY

c/o THE NATIONAL GARDENS SCHEME
57 Lower Belgrave St
London SWIW, OLR
(Tel 01-730 0359)

DATES OF OPENING

APRIL Sunday 20
CHISWICK MALL, W4 (Walpole House
& Strawberry House)

MAY Sunday 4
CANFORD, 13 Daleham Gardens,
Swiss Cottage, NW3
SUDBROOK COTTAGE, Ham Common,
nr Kingston

MAY Sunday 11
17 PARK PLACE VILLAS, Little
Venice, W2

SUDBROOK COTTAGE, Ham Common,
nr Kingston
MAY Thursday 15
12 LANSDOWNE ROAD, Holland Park,
W11
MAY Sunday 18
61 CLEAVER SQUARE, Kennington, SE11
SUDBROOK COTTAGE, Ham Common,
nr Kingston
MAY Thursday 22
13 SELWOOD PLACE, South
Kensington, SW7 (entrance in
Onslow Gdns)
MAY Sunday 25
HIGHWOOD ASH, Mill Hill, NW7
36 STAVELEY ROAD, Chiswick, W4
SUDBROOK COTTAGE, Ham Common,
nr Kingston
JUNE Sunday 1
CHISWICK MALL, W4 (Walpole
House & Strawberry House)
JUNE Wednesday 4
4 HOLLAND VILLAS ROAD,
West Kensington, W14
JUNE Sunday 8
21 SELWOOD TERRACE, South
Kensington, SW7 (entrance adjacent to
92 Onslow Gardens)
JUNE Saturday 14
KENSINGTON, W8 (7 St Albans Grove
& 1 & 13 Cottesmore Gardens)
JUNE Sunday 15
15 CHEPSTOW VILLAS, Notting Hill
Gate, W11
HIGHGATE VILLAGE, N6 (6 The Grove,
79 & 82 Highgate West Hill)
SWISS COTTAGE, NW3 (1 Lower
Merton Rise & 15a Buckland Crescent)
JUNE Sunday 22
15 CHEPSTOW VILLAS, Nottingham
Hill Gate, W11
HIGHWOOD ASH, Mill Hill, NW7
21 SELWOOD TERRACE, South
Kensington, SW7 (entrance adjacent to
92 Onslow Gardens)
JULY Saturday 5
10 WILDWOOD ROAD, Hampstead,
NW11
JULY Sunday 6
HAMPSTEAD, NW3 (65 Frognal,
69 Redington Road, 37 Heath Drive
& 4 Lower Terrace)
2 MELINA PLACE, St. John's Wood,
NW8
21 SELWOOD TERRACE, South
Kensington, SW7 (entrance adjacent to
92 Onslow Gardens)
JULY Sunday 13
HIGHGATE, N6 (70 Talbot Road &
40 Hampstead Lane)
JULY Sunday 20
61 CLEAVER SQUARE, Kennington,
SE11
JULY Tuesday 22
2 CLIFTON HILL, St. John's Wood,
NW8

LONDON—continued

JULY Sunday 27
  2 CLIFTON HILL, St. John's Wood,
  NW8
AUGUST Sunday 10
  25 BERRY WAY, Rickmansworth, Herts
AUGUST Sunday 17
  96 GREENFIELD GARDENS,
  Cricklewood, NW2
OCTOBER Sunday 5
  HIGHGATE VILLAGE, N6 (7 The Grove
  & The Summit, Fitzroy Park)

DESCRIPTIONS OF GARDENS

Canford* (Mr & Mrs J. W. Rees) 13 Daleham Gardens, Swiss Cottage, NW3. Daleham Gardens runs parallel with Fitzjohns Avenue at the Swiss Cottage end. Station: Swiss Cottage or Finchley Rd. 2 gardens made into one, surrounded by trees; lawns, herbaceous borders, rockery, roses & raised water garden with statuary; speciality is shrubs for all seasons. NO DOGS. *Adm. 25p, Chd. 10p. Sun. May 4 (2-7)*

¶25 Berry Way (Mr & Mrs Frank Pinder) Rickmansworth. A412 Uxbridge Rd, Honeyhill Parade, turn into Field Way to top of rd, turn right into Berry Lane, which takes sharp left turn; Berry Way is 2nd turning on right. Small garden (approx. one-sixth of an acre) winning Top Gardener of 1979 contest (Woolworth's & TV Times); 3 ponds; very colourful bedding display; vegetable garden; 2 greenhouses (one with Black Hamburg grapevine). NO DOGS. *Adm. 20p, Chd. 10p. Sun. Aug. 10 (2-7)*

¶15 Chepstow Villas (W. J. Hopper Esq) Notting Hill Gate, London W11. Nr Notting Hill Gate underground station. Garden 60 ft x 40 ft; example of how small garden planted mostly with perennials & shrubs can be provided with unusually interesting features on several different levels. Japanese-style. TEAS. NO DOGS. *Adm. 25p, Chd. 10p. Sun. June 15 & Sun. June 22 (2-7)*

Chiswick Mall, W4. On April 20 & June 1 the following 2 gardens will be open. Station: Stamford Brook (District Line). Bus: 290 to Commodore Cinema. By car turn off Gt West Rd at Eyot Gardens or at Hogarth roundabout & Church St for Chiswick Mall. *Adm. to each garden 25p (minimum), Chd. 10p. Sun. April 20 (2-6) & Sun. June 1 (2-7)*

  Walpole House*† (Mr & Mrs J. H. Benson) Interesting collection of plants; water garden; spring flowers. Mid C16 to early C18 house, once home of Barbara Villiers, Duchess of Cleveland. Seeds & plants for sale. *(Share to Wemyss Memorial Hall, Stanway, Glos)*

  Strawberry House* (Beryl Countess of Rothes) Small garden with camellias & magnolias. Plants for sale

61 Cleaver Square*⊕ (Mr & Mrs Godfrey Royle) Kennington, SE11. At junction of Kennington Rd & Kennington Lane turn S into Cleaver St (entrance from Kennington Park Rd closed). Station: Kennington. Bus: 3, 95, 109, 133, 159, 172. Unusual small walled garden of 60 sq. yds (15 ft x 40 ft) designed with great variety of perennial plants & shrubs to give all-year-round interest. *(Share to The Tradescant Trust)* There are seats adjacent in tree-lined Georgian square. NO DOGS. Light refreshments. *Collecting box. Sun. May 18 & Sun. July 20 (2.30-6.30)*

2 Clifton Hill⊕ (Lt-Col & Mrs F. Jankel) St John's Wood, NW8. Clifton Hill crosses Abbey Rd; on corner of Clifton Hill & Loudoun Rd. Miniature town garden growing a variety of shrubs, flowers, fruit & vegetables; all space utilized. NO DOGS. Light refreshments available. *Adm. 30p (minimum), Chd. 10p. Tues. July 22 & Sun. July 27 (2-7)*

96 Greenfield Gardens (Terry Makepeace Esq) Cricklewood, NW2. W of Hendon Way between Cricklewood Lane & The Vale. Station: Golders Green or Willesden Green, both ¾ m. Bus: 260 from Golders Green or Willesden, alight Hendon Way (nr top of rd). Garden 100 ft x 30 ft, sweet peas, roses, dahlias, large variety of annuals; pond & greenhouses. Plants for sale *(Share to Cancer Research. NO DOGS. Adm. 25p. Chd. 15p. Sun. Aug. 17 (11-7)*

Hampstead, NW3. On July 6 the following 4 gardens will be open. Station: Hampstead (Northern Line, Edgware trains). Bus: 210 to Heath St stop, then via Holly Hill or Mount Vernon into Frognal; or Finchley Rd buses 2 & 2A to West End Lane, up Frognal Lane & turn left at top. TEA & biscuits (69 Redington Rd). *Combined charge 70p or 20p each garden. Sun. July 6 (2-6.30)*

  65 Frognal* (Miss W. B. Acworth) House faces junction of Frognal with Church Row. Lawns, roses, herbaceous border; interesting trees & shrubs

  69 Redington Rd⊕ (Mr & Mrs A. M. Gear) Medium-sized informal garden designed to be fairly simple to work; paved terrace with roses, steps & ramp to lower level; lawn with trees & shrubs. TEA & biscuits

  ¶37 Heath Drive (Mr & Mrs C. Caplin) Some uncommon plants; paths, lawn; interesting pruning; unusual arrangement of fruit trees, bushes & vegetables

  4 Lower Terrace (Mr & Mrs David Dent) Medium-sized garden on 3 levels with herbaceous border, roses, evergreens & good ground cover; interesting treatment of very shady walled front garden

Highgate Village, N6. On June 15 the following 3 gardens will be open. The Grove is between Highgate West Hill & Hampstead Lane. Stations: Archway or Highgate (Northern Line, Barnet trains). Bus: 210, 271 to Highgate Village. (*Share to The Tradescant Trust*). *Combined charge for 3 gardens 50p (Chd. 20p); or 20p each garden (Chd. 10p). Sun. June 15 (2–6)*

6 The Grove⊕ (Mrs Malcolm Horsman) Walled garden with beautiful views over Hampstead Heath; spring bulbs, camellias, flowering shrubs; lawn & rockery

79 Highgate West Hill (Mrs E. K. H. Whipple) 1½ acres with fine view over London; water garden with small pools & waterfalls

82 Highgate West Hill (Mrs T. Kingsley Curtis) Small garden on 2 levels, herbaceous borders above & kitchen garden below. View over London

Highgate Village, N6. On Oct. 5 the following 2 gardens will be open. The Grove is between Highgate West Hill & Hampstead Lane. Stations: Archway or Highgate (Northern Line, Barnet trains). Bus 210, 271 to Highgate Village. *Combined charge 35p. Sun. Oct. 5 (2–5)*

7 The Grove*⊕ (The Hon. Mrs Judith Lyttelton) ½-acre garden designed for maximum all-year-round interest with minimum upkeep

¶**The Summit,** (Mr & Mrs N. B. Mason) Fitzroy Park (leading off The Grove) Town garden on different levels. Plants for sale

Highgate, N6. On July 13 the following 2 gardens will be open. Tea Kenwood House, Hampstead Lane. *Adm. to each garden 25p (minimum), Chd. under 10, free. Sun. July 13 (2–6)*

70 Talbot Rd (Mr J. Daumiller & Miss E. Daumiller) From Archway Rd (A1) turn into Church Rd (Highgate Police Station on corner) then 1st right. From North Hill turn into Church Rd, then 1st left into Talbot Rd. Colourful garden, approx. 30 ft 80 ft; herbaceous border with delphiniums, phlox, etc; roses & begonias

Kenwood Gate⊕ (Mr & Mrs K. D. Brough) 40 Hampstead Lane. Immediately opp. Highgate entrance to Kenwood on Hampstead Lane. Bus 210 passes gate; Compton Ave stop. Medium-sized garden with herbaceous borders, roses & pool

Highwood Ash (Mr & Mrs Roy Gluckstein) Highwood Hill, Mill Hill, NW7. From London via A41 (Watford Way) to Mill Hill Circus; turn right up Lawrence St; at top bear left up Highwood Hill; house at top on right. Station: Burnt Oak (Northern Line). Bus: 251 from Burnt Oak Station to Rising Sun stop (outside gate). 3¼-acre garden inc. rose garden, shrub & herbaceous borders, rhododendrons & azaleas; a mixture of formal & informal. *Adm. 30p, Chd. 15p. Sun. May 25 & Sun. June 22 (1.30–6)*

4 Holland Villas Rd*⊕ (The Marquis & Marchioness of Dufferin & Ava) West Ken-

sington, W14. From Holland Park Ave, between Holland Park & Shepherd's Bush, turn S via Addison Rd into Holland Villas Rd; from Holland Rd (north-bound traffic only) turn right into Holland Villas Rd. Station: Shepherd's Bush or Holland Park. Bus: 12, 88; GL 711, 715 along Holland Park Ave, alight Royal Cres., or 49 along Holland Rd, alight Addison Cres. (request). Garden with rare shrubs, full of exciting combinations of shapes & colours, of particular interest to the artist. NO DOGS. *Adm. 25p. Wed. June 4 (2–7)*

Kensington, W8. On June 14 the following 3 gardens will be open. From Gloucester Rd turn into Victoria Grove, continuing into St Albans Grove. From Kensington High St turn into Victoria Rd. Stations: Kensington High St or Gloucester Rd. Bus stop: Milestone for 9, 46, 52, 72; Gloucester Rd for 49, 74. TEAS at Wychwood. *Combined charge for 3 gardens 65p or 25p each. Sat. June 14 (2.30–6)*

7 St Albans Grove* (Mrs Edward Norman-Butler) Off Victoria Rd. Small walled garden designed for 1 pair of hands & for all seasons

Wychwood (Mrs Edward Streator) 1 Cottesmore Gardens. Large walled garden in the Italian manner. TEA, cold drinks & biscuits (payment by donation)

13 Cottesmore Gardens (Mrs David *McCosh*) Family garden, well-designed for herbaceous borders with particular emphasis on foliage

Christ Church Garden, Eldon Rd, may also be visited free of charge. Bulbs & shrub border 56 yds long

12 Lansdowne Rd⊕ (The Lady Amabel Lindsay) Holland Park, W11. Turn N off Holland Park Ave nr Holland Park Station; or W off Ladbroke Grove ½-way along. Bus: 12, 88; GL 711, 715. Bus stop & station: Holland Park, 4 mins. Medium-sized garden; border, climbing roses, shrubs; fairly wild garden; mulberry tree 200 yrs old. *Adm. 25p, Chd. 10p. Thurs. May 15 (2–6)*

¶**2 Melina Place**⊕ (Mr & Mrs G. A. Yablon) St. John's Wood, NW8. Melina Place is small cul-de-sac off Grove End Rd at back of Lords Cricket Ground. Totally walled garden of Regency house with unusual entrance, good roses. NO DOGS. TEA, biscuits & scones. *Adm. 15p, Chd. 10p. Sun. July 6 (2–6)*

17 Park Place Villas (H. C. Seigal Eqs) Little Venice, W2. Park Place Villas is off Maida Ave which runs alongside Regent's Canal from Maida Vale to Warwick Ave. Station: Warwick Ave. Garden (⅛ acre) is one of an internal square of small gardens each belonging to a single house. Rhododendrons & azaleas; raised alpine bed & grass. NO DOGS. *Adm. 25p. Sun. May 11 (2–6.30)*

13 Selwood Place (Mrs Anthony Crossley) South Kensington, SW7. Entrance to garden is adjacent to 92 Onslow Gardens (cul-de-sac). Long green & white border & pink border in L-shaped walled garden; collection of roses, peonies, camellias, euphorbias, lilies, saxifrages; terrace; 12 ft rose stands in border; 2 vegetable beds. Garden suitable for wheelchairs only if dry. *Adm. 30p. Thurs. May 22 (2–6.30)*

21 Selwood Terrace (Mr & Mrs J. E. MacSwiney) South Kensington, SW7. Entrance to garden adjacent to 92 Onslow Gardens. Attractive town garden of special interest; lawns, herbaceous borders, roses; fan-shaped fig, flowering shrubs & climbers. Garden awarded certificate of merit All London Championships & winner of Lockwood Challenge Cup. *(Shared with Gardeners Sunday). Adm. 30p, Chd. 10p. Suns. June 8 & 22, July 6 (2–7)*

¶36 Staveley Road (J. G. Luke Esq) Chiswick, W4. Staveley Rd runs parallel with SW boundary of Chiswick House grounds; off Gt Chertsey Rd (A316). A shrub garden overlooked by trees of adjacent Chiswick House grounds. NO DOGS. Tea in adjacent grounds (Chiswick House). *Adm. 25p, Chd. 10p. Sun. May 25 (2–6)*

Sudbrook Cottage*⊕ (Beverley Nichols Esq) Ham Gate Avenue, Ham Common, nr Kingston. *Road subsidence at foot of Star & Garter Hill (Petersham Rd); therefore only possible approach* is from Kingston; or through Richmond Park & out by Ham Gate into Ham Gate Avenue. Station: Kingston; bus 65 Kingston–Ham Common (New Inn stop); LC 714, 716 to Ham Common (Hand & Flower Stop). Garden made famous by the owner's books; azaleas, rhododendrons & flowering shrubs. Jointly with another charity. *Adm. 30p, Chd. free. Suns. May 4, 11, 18, 25 (2.30–5)*

Swiss Cottage, NW3. On June 15 the following 2 gardens will be open. Stations: Swiss Cottage or Finchley Rd. TEAS. *Adm. 25p each garden, Chd. 10p. Sun. June 15 (2–6)*

1 Lower Merton Rise (Mr & Mrs P. H. D. Findlay) On edge of Elsworthy Conservation Area (Willett Estate, *c.* 1895). Lower Merton Rise runs between Adelaide Rd & Elsworthy Rd (E of Avenue Rd). Small informal, cottage-style garden with roses & herbaceous plants. TEAS

15A Buckland Crescent (Mrs M. Stein) Buckland Crescent runs off College Crescent. Parking near house barred by double yellow lines. Walled garden in Belsize Conservation Area; mixed planting for all-year-round effects; vegetable & nursery plots; metasequoia; pond; circular greenhouse. Plants for sale. TEAS

10 Wildwood Rd*⊕ (Dr J. W. McLean) Hampstead, NW11. Wildwood Rd runs between Hampstead Golf Course & N end of Hampstead Heath. From North End Rd turn by Manor House Hospital into Hampstead Way, then fork right. Garden planned & maintained by owner; herbaceous border, pond; HT roses; owner-grown delphiniums & seedlings, both prize-winners. NO DOGS. *Adm. 20p. Sat. July 5 (2–7)*

NORFOLK

Hon. County Organiser:
MRS M. A. BUXTON, Mill House, Westacre, King's Lynn, PE32 1UF

DATES OF OPENING

APRIL Easter Sunday 6 & Monday 7 & then every Tuesday, Wednesday & Thursday
SANDRINGHAM HOUSE & GROUNDS

MAY every Sunday, Monday, Tuesday, Wednesday & Thursday
 SANDRINGHAM HOUSE & GROUNDS
APRIL Sunday 27
 CREAKE ABBEY, nr Fakenham
MAY Sunday 4
 SHERINGHAM HALL, Sheringham
 WEST LEXHAM HALL, nr King's Lynn
MAY Sunday 11
 MANNINGTON HALL, nr Saxthorpe
MAY Sunday 18
 ELMHAM HOUSE GARDENS, nr East Dereham
 RYSTON HALL, nr Downham Market
MAY Sunday 25
 MILL HOUSE, Westacre, nr Swaffham
MAY Monday 26 (Bank Hol.)
 WICKEN HOUSE, Castle Acre, nr Swaffham
JUNE every Sunday, Monday, Tuesday, Wednesday & Thursday
 SANDRINGHAM HOUSE & GROUNDS
JUNE Sunday 1
 ERPINGHAM LODGE, nr Aylsham
JUNE Sunday 8
 HANWORTH HALL, nr Cromer
 HEYDON GARDENS, nr Aylsham
JULY every Sunday, Monday, Tuesday, Wednesday & Thursday to July 20
 SANDRINGHAM HOUSE & GROUNDS
 (grounds only open to July 24)
JULY Sunday 6
 EASTON LODGE, Easton, nr Norwich
 LETHERINGSETT GARDENS, nr Holt
JULY Sunday 13
 ALBY HALL, Erpingham
 WESTACRE HIGH HOUSE, Castleacre
JULY Friday 18
 BLICKLING HALL, nr Aylsham
JULY Sunday 20
 GAYTON HALL, nr King's Lynn
JULY Thursday 24
 QUARLES HOUSE, Wells
JULY Thursday 31
 HOLKHAM HALL, nr Wells
AUGUST from August 10 every Sunday, Monday, Tuesday, Wednesday & Thursday
 SANDRINGHAM HOUSE & GROUNDS
 (grounds only from August 3)
AUGUST Sunday 24
 BARNINGHAM HALL, Matlaske, nr Aylsham
 RAINTHORPE HALL, nr Newton Flotman
SEPTEMBER every Sunday, Monday, Tuesday, Wednesday & Thursday to September 25
 SANDRINGHAM HOUSE & GROUNDS
SEPTEMBER Friday 12
 FELBRIGG HALL, nr Cromer

DESCRIPTIONS OF GARDENS

Alby Hall⊕ (Mrs David Cargill) Erpingham, 5 m. S of Cromer. On A140 Cromer–Norwich Rd, 5 m. N of Aylsham. Small garden; shrub & species roses (over 300 different varieties); large amount of recent replanting & new layout. TEAS. *Adm. 25p, Chd. 10p. Sun. July 13 (2–6)*

Barningham Hall (Sir Charles & Lady Mott-Radclyffe) Matlaske, NW of Aylsham. Medium-sized garden, vistas, lake. TEAS. *Adm. 20p. Sun. Aug. 24 (2–6.30)*

Blickling Hall★†⅋⊕ (The National Trust—see p. ix) 1½ m. NW of Aylsham on N side of B1354 (which is 15 m. N of Norwich on A140). Bus: 401 King's Lynn–Gt Yarmouth; passes entrance. Large garden; parterre garden & crescent lake. Historic Jacobean house (not open this date). (*Share to The National Trust*) NO DOGS (except guide dogs). Tea Aylsham. *Adm. (garden only) 70p. Chd. 35p. △Fri. July 18 (2–6)*

Creake Abbey †⊕ (Brig. & Mrs P. Stewart-Richardson) North Creake, NW of Fakenham via B1355 Fakenham–Burnham Market rd. Medium-sized garden with shrubs & bulbs, walled garden & C12 Abbey ruins. TEAS. *Adm. 25p, Chd. 10p. Sun. April 27 (2–6)*

Easton Lodge (J. M. Rampton Esq) Easton, W of Norwich. A47 from Norwich; white gates in centre of Easton village. Bus: EC 34/34C Norwich–East Dereham–Swaffham–King's Lynn; alight Easton Dog. Medium-sized garden; azaleas in attractive setting with river at foot. Late Georgian house with Jacobean centre portion. TEAS. *Adm. 25p, Chd. 10p. Sun. July 6 (2.30–6)*

Elmham House Gardens⊕ (R. S. Don Esq) Elmham, 5 m. N of East Dereham. On B1110; entrance opp. Elmham Church. Medium-sized garden; views of park & lake; wild garden; commercial apple orchards, outdoor wine vineyards & blackberries. (*Share to St Mary's Church (North Elmham) Restoration Fund*) TEA & biscuits. *Adm. 25p, Chd. 5p. Sun. May 18 (2–6)*

Erpingham Lodge⅋⊕ (Mr & Mrs David Clarke) nr Ingworth, 2 m. N of Aylsham. From A140 Norwich–Cromer rd, turn off at Ingworth Church; then 1st turn left & Erpingham Lodge is on right. Bus: Norwich–Cromer, alight Erpingham X-rds, ½ m. Medium-sized garden; rhododendrons & mainly shrub garden; lake. Georgian house (not open). TEAS. *Adm. 40p, Chd. 10p. Sun. June 1 (2–6)*

Felbrigg Hall ★†⅋⊕ (The National Trust—see p. ix) Roughton, 2½ m. SW of Cromer. Just S of A148; main entrance from B1436; signed from Felbrigg village. Large pleasure gardens; mainly lawns & shrubs; orangery with camellias; rare, large walled garden recently restored & restocked as a fruit, vegetable & flower garden; vine house & dovecote; dahlias; wooded park. (*Share to The National Trust*) NO DOGS (except guide dogs).

TEAS. *Adm. 60p, Chd. 30p.* △*Fri. Sept. 12 (2–6)*

Gayton Hall⅃⊕ (Julian Marsham Esq) 6 m. E of King's Lynn. B1145 through Gayton village; turn right on to B1153 & immediately right again; gates 150 yds on left. 20 acres; wild woodland, water garden. TEAS. *Adm. 40p, Chd. 20p. Sun. July 20 (2–6)*

Hanworth Hall⅃⊕ (H. M. Barclay Esq) S of Cromer. From A140 Cromer–Aylsham Rd, 5 m. S of Cromer turn W for Hanworth, which is 1 m. from main rd. Medium-sized garden with famous old chestnut tree; walled garden; rhododendrons. (*Share to Hanworth Church*) TEAS. *Adm. 30p, Chd. 10p. Sun. June 8 (2–6)*

Heydon Gardens*⅃⊕ 8 m. W of Aylsham; 14 m. N of Norwich. Between Corpusty & Cawston, 1 m. W of B1149. Interesting, old, informal gardens. Home-made TEAS. *Combined charge for following 3 adjacent gardens 40p, Chd. 10p. Sun. June 8 (2.30–6)*
  The Grange (Brig. & Mrs Bulwer-Long)
  The Dower House (Mr & Mrs H. Phelps)
  The Old Cottage (The Misses Tindal & Fletcher)
  '**Heydon Hall** (Capt. & Mrs W. Bulwer-Long) also open, ¼ m. away. *Adm. 25p extra*

Holkham Hall*†⅃ (The Viscount Coke) 2 m. W of Wells. S of A149, Wells–Hunstanton. Bus: EC 36 Hunstanton–Wells–Cromer; alight Victoria Hotel or Holkham village, 1 m. Arboretum with many rare specimens, both trees & shrubs; large formal C19 terraced garden with polyantha roses & fountains. Hall & Exhibition of By-gones & Pottery also open. NO DOGS. TEAS. *Adm. to house 70p, OAPs in parties 40p each, Chd. 40p; Arboretum only 15p, car park 30p, coaches free.* △ *Thurs. July 31 (11.30–5)*

Letheringsett Gardens⊕ 1 m. W of Holt on A148. Tea & car park King's Head, Letheringsett. Following 4 gardens will be open. *Combined charge 30p, Chd. 10p. Sun. July 6 (2–6)*
  Old Rectory (Mrs M. E. B. Sparke) Small garden
  The Glebe (The Hon. Beryl Cozens-Hardy) Small riverside garden
  Hall Cottage (Mr David Mayes) Small riverside garden
  Letheringsett Hall (Mr & Mrs Mitchell) Home for the elderly. Large garden with river & lake

'**Mannington Hall** †⅃⊕ (The Hon. Robin Walpole) 2 m. N of Saxthorpe; 18 m. NW of Norwich via B1149 towards Holt. At Saxthorpe (junction of B1149 & B1354) turn off NE at signpost to Mannington. 20 acres inc. gardens featuring shrubs, roses & woodland; walled garden with borders; new scented garden planted for 1980; lake. C15 moated manor house (not open). In grounds ruined Saxon church with C19 follies. NO DOGS. TEAS. *Adm. 40p, Chd. 10p* △Sun. May 11 *(2–6)*

Mill House (M. A. Buxton Esq) Westacre, 5 m. N of Swaffham. Attractive millhouse garden on R. Nar & lakeside walk. TEAS. *Adm. 25p, Chd. 10p. Sun. May 25 (2–6)*

Quarles House⊕ (Mr Bryan & Lady Carey Basset) 4 m. SW of Wells-on-Sea. From Fakenham take King's Lynn Rd & turn right on to B1355 signposted Burnham Market; after 4 m. turn right at signpost to Waterden; next turn left, after 2 m. then right at signpost marked Quarles. Small garden with good herbaceous border at its best in late July. Tea Holkham Hall nearby. *Adm. 20p, Chd. 10p. Thurs. July 24 (2–6)*

Rainthorpe Hall*†⅃⊕ (G. F. Hastings Esq) 8 m. S of Norwich & 1 m. SW of Newton Flotman. From Norwich take A140 for 7 m.; at Newton Flotman, by garage, fork right & on 1 m. to red brick gates on left. Large garden with fine trees; botanical interest, inc. a collection of bamboos. Elizabethan house (not open) connected with Amy Robsart. NO DOGS. Tea Little Chef. *Adm. 50p, Chd. 25p. Sun. Aug. 24 (2.30–6)*

Ryston Hall*⅃⊕ (Mr & Mrs E. R. M. Pratt) 2 m. SE of Downham Market. From A10 turn off in Denver. Medium-sized garden; rhododendrons, azaleas, rock garden, lawns & ornamental trees. TEAS. *Adm. 20p, Chd. 10p. Sun. May 18 (2–6)*

Sandringham Grounds: by gracious permission of H.M. The Queen, the House & Grounds at Sandringham will be open to the public (except when H.M. The Queen or any member of the Royal Family is in residence). Donations are given from the Estate to various charities. For further information see p. xiii. *Adm. house & grounds £1, OAPs 80p, Chd. 50p; grounds only 70p, OAPs 50p, Chd. 40p. Sun. & Mon. April 6 & 7 & then every Tues., Wed., Thurs., from April 8; May to Sept. every Sun., Mon., Tues., Wed. & Thurs. except house closed July 21–Aug. 9, & grounds closed July 25–Aug. 2 inc. (Hours: House 11 (Sun. 12 noon) to 4.45; Grounds 10.30 (Sun. 11.30) to 5)*

Sheringham Hall† ⅃ ⊕ *(Thomas Upcher Esq)* Bus: EC 226 Holt–Sheringham–Cromer–Overstrand stops at gate & in Upper Sheringham village, both 1 m. from garden. Cars can drive through wood from entrance at top of Holt Hill at junction of Sheringham–Cromer Rds. Medium-sized garden planted with varied collection of flowering shrubs. Regency house (not shown) by Humphrey Repton, beautifully situated in landscape setting with sea views. *Adm. 25p, Chd. 10p. Sun. May 4 (2–6)*

Westacre High House *†&⊕ (Capt. H. Birkbeck) nr Castleacre, 6 m. N of Swaffham. E of King's Lynn via B1145; 2 m. E of Gayton turn right (S) for Westacre. 3-acre garden; herbaceous borders in walled garden; lawns; large park; interesting trees. (*Share to Deaf & Dumb Assn., Norfolk Branch*). TEAS. *Adm. 30p, Chd. (school age) 10p. Sun. July 13 (2–6)*

West Lexham Hall &⊕ (Mrs H. Olesen) E of King's Lynn, 6 m. N of Swaffham; A1065 signposted West Lexham. Large garden; beautiful setting with water, lawns, trees; kitchen garden. Farm buildings & round-tower church. TEA & biscuits. *Adm. 30p, Chd. free. Sun. May 4 (2–6)*

Wicken House †⊕ (Lord & Lady Keith) Castle Acre, 5 m. N of Swaffham. A1065 from Swaffham on Fakenham Rd; turn W at Newton to Castle Acre; then 2 m. N off Massingham Rd. Medium-sized garden; flowering shrubs; greenhouses. Part of house dates from 1700. NO DOGS. TEAS. *Adm. 25p, Chd. 5p. Mon. May 26 (2–5)*

NORTHAMPTONSHIRE

Hon. County Organiser:
MRS JOHN BOUGHEY, Butts Close, Farthinghoe, Brackley, NN13 5NY

DATES OF OPENING

APRIL Good Friday 4 & Wednesday 9
COTON MANOR, nr Northampton
APRIL Sunday 13
LILFORD HALL, nr Oundle
APRIL Sunday 20
CASTLE ASHBY HOUSE, nr Northampton
GREAT ADDINGTON MANOR,
nr Kettering
APRIL Sunday 27
BARNWELL MANOR, nr Peterborough
BOUGHTON HOUSE & THE DOWER
HOUSE, nr Kettering
KELMARSH HALL, nr Market Harborough
MAY Sunday 4
CHIPPING WARDEN GARDENS,
nr Banbury
MAY Sunday 11
EYDON HALL, nr Banbury
MAY Sunday 18
BADBY GARDENS, nr Daventry
MAY Monday 19
BADBY GARDENS, nr Daventry
JUNE Sunday 1
COTTESBROOKE HALL, nr Northampton
JUNE Sunday 15
EDGCOTE, nr Banbury
RAVENSTHORPE GARDENS,
nr Northampton
JUNE Sunday 22
BOUGHTON HOUSE & THE DOWER
HOUSE, nr Kettering
HOLDENBY HOUSE, nr Northampton

JUNE Sunday 29
GEDDINGTON GARDENS, nr Kettering
JULY Sunday 6
CHARLTON GARDENS, nr Banbury
EASTON NESTON, Towcester
FRIARS WELL, Anyho, nr Banbury
WEEKLEY GARDENS, nr Kettering
JULY Sunday 13
‡BRACKLEY GRANGE, Brackley
‡STEANE PARK, nr Brackley
JULY Sunday 27
PYTCHLEY HOUSE, nr Kettering
AUGUST Sunday 3
DEENE PARK, nr Corby
SEPTEMBER Sunday 7
LITTLE HOUGHTON GARDENS,
nr Northampton
SEPTEMBER Sunday 14
CASTLE ASHBY HOUSE, nr Northampton
SEPTEMBER Thursday 18
COTON MANOR, nr Northampton
SEPTEMBER Sunday 21
COTTESBROOKE HALL, nr Northampton

DESCRIPTIONS OF GARDENS

Badby Gardens. 3 m. S of Daventry; on E side of A361 Daventry–Banbury. Close to Badby Woods & Fawsley Park (suitable for walking & picnics). Following 4 gardens will be open, all designed & maintained by their owners. Plants for sale. TEAS. *Combined charge 50p, Chd. 10p. Sun. & Mon. May 18 & 19 (2–7)*

Barehill Farm (Mr & Mrs W. G. Jones) Medium-sized garden with flowering trees, shrubs, conifers & heathers. Picnic area available. Fine views of Northamptonshire uplands

Church Hill (Mr & Mrs C. M. Cripps) After turning off A361 through village, garden lies in fork between Church Hill & Bunkers Hill. Small informal garden, started in 1969 with all-year interest in mind; old shrub roses & some interesting plants. NO DOGS please

Church Hill Farm (Maj. & Mrs J. B. Jenkins) Through village & up hill to Church; garden opp. behind high laurel hedge. ½-acre garden with old & modern roses; orchard with unusual varieties; herbaceous border. Good views. Pet donkeys

Home Farm (Mrs G. Jones) Medium-sized country garden with old shrub roses & climbing plants

Barnwell Manor †⊕ (T.R.H. Princess Alice Duchess of Gloucester & The Duke & Duchess of Gloucester) nr Peterborough. 2 m. S of Oundle; 4½ m. NE of Thrapston on A605. Bus: UC 266 Kettering–Peterborough; EC 312; alight 200 yds from garden. Pleasant grounds, spring flowers. C13 castle ruins. Light Refreshments. Car park free. *Adm. 30p, Chd. 10p. Sun. April 27 (2.30–6.00)*

Boughton House *†&⊕ (His Grace The Duke of Buccleuch & Queensberry) N of

Kettering. Boughton House is on A43, 3 m. N of Kettering between Weekley & Geddington; follow special signs. Beautiful grounds with avenues & lakes of historical interest; large walled vegetable garden; greenhouses; daffodils; lily pond, rose garden, herbaceous borders. Also open within the grounds, (no extra charge), the garden of **The Dower House**∗ (Sir David & Lady Scott (Valerie Finnis)). 2 acres; an informal plantsman's garden with wide variety of trees, shrubs & hardy plants; spring flowers & bulbs; walled garden with 200 yds of raised rock plant borders; sink gardens. Unusual plants for sale. ADVENTURE PLAYGROUND free for children. NO DOGS. TEAS. *Adm. 50p, Chd. 10p.* △ *(Boughton House) Sun. April 27 & Sun. June 22 (2–6)*

Brackley Grange⊕ (Mr & Mrs K. Bailey) 2½ m. NW of Brackley. A43 Oxford–Northampton; up main st in Brackley; turn left by Brackley Motors Garage signposted Halse, Marston St Lawrence; continue for 1 m. & turn left at lodge gate down ½ m. drive. 1½ acres; shrubs & herbaceous borders & rose garden; magnificent weeping lime tree. *(Share to St. Peter's Church, Brackley)* NO DOGS. Tea Steane Park Garden; chapel open & service in evening. *Adm. 25p, Chd. free. Sun. July 13 (2–5)*

Castle Ashby House†⅄⊕ (The Marquess of Northampton) 6 m. E of Northampton· 1½ m. N of A428 Northampton–Bedford; turn off between Denton & Yardley Hastings. Parkland setting inc. avenue first planted at suggestion of King William III in 1695; lakes etc by Capability Brown; Italian gardens with orangery; extensive lawns & trees. Elizabethan house open. TEAS. *Adm. 40p, Chd. 20p.* △ *Sun. April 20 & Sun. Sept. 14 (2–5)*

Charlton Gardens.⊕ 7 m. SE of Banbury, 5 m. W of Brackley. From A41 turn off N at Aynho; or from A422 turn off S at Farthinghoe. The following 2 gardens will be open. Home-made TEAS at The Cottage. *Combined charge 20p, Chd. 5p. Sun. July 6 (2–6.30)*

    The Cottage⊕ (The Countess of Birkenhead) Flowering shrubs, roses, lawns, stream, lakes & newly-planted woodland walk. House in village street

    Holly House⊕ (The Hon. Nicholas Berry) Small garden with beautiful views & walled garden. C18 house

Chipping Warden Gardens 6 m. NE of Banbury on A361 Banbury-Daventry Rd, Bus stop in Chipping Warden 100 yds from the Manor. The following 2 gardens will be open. *(Share to Chipping Warden Church)* TEA, biscuits and home-made cakes at The Manor. *Combined charge 50p (Chd. 10p) or 30p each garden (chd. 5p). Sun. May 4 (2.30–6)*

Chipping Warden Manor† (Mr T. & The Hon. Mrs Sergison-Brooke) Medium-sized garden; formal garden, herbaceous border, water garden; Kitchen garden. Carolean house (not open)

    The Spring House⅄ (Mr & Mrs Shepley-Cuthbert) In Mill Lane (leave Church on right for Mill Lane). 2½ acres; mainly woodland garden; many spring bulbs & blossom; fine old trees & recent plantings; tapestry hedge; shrub roses; bog garden being re-conquered

Coton Manor∗⊕ (Cdr & Mrs H. Pasley-Tyler) 10 m. N of Northampton. 11 m. SE of Rugby nr Ravensthorpe Reservoir. From A428 & A50 follow AA signs. C17 stone manor house with water gardens, herbaceous borders, rose garden, old holly & yew hedges; interesting variety of foliage plants; sub-tropical house. Large collection of ornamental waterfowl, cranes & flamingoes. Unusual plants for sale. Home-made TEAS. *Adm. 70p, Chd. 30p.* △ *Fri. April 4, Wed. April 9, Thurs. Sept. 18 (2–6) (see also p. 146)*

Cottesbrooke Hall⊕ (Maj. Sir Reginald & the Hon. Lady Macdonald-Buchanan) 10 m. N of Northampton. Nr Creaton on A50 Northampton–Welford–Leicester Rd; nr Brixworth on A508 Northampton–Market Harborough–Leicester Rd. Bus: UC to Bricklayers' Arms, Creaton, 2 m. Large garden; formal & wild gardens; herbaceous borders, fine old cedars. Parties shown round greenhouses & kitchen garden. Early C18 house (not shown). Cottesbrooke Church was featured in Donald Sinden's TV programme 'Discovering English Churches'. Brixworth Church, 2½ m. away, dates back to C7 & is well worth a visit) TEA. Car park free. *Adm. 30p, Chd. 10p. Sun. June 1 & Sun. Sept. 21 (2–6)*

Deene Park∗†⅄ (Edmund Brudenell Esq) 6 m. N of Corby. A43 Kettering–Stamford Rd. Medium-sized garden; long borders, old-fashioned roses, rare trees & shrubs, large lake. Interesting church; fine tombs. TEA & biscuits. *Adm. 30p, Chd. 15p.* △ *Sun. Aug. 3 (2–6)*

Easton Neston⅄⊕ (The Lord Hesketh) Towcester. Entrance on A43. Bus: to 2nd lodge, Easton Neston, ¼ m. Large garden; formal garden; ornamental water, clipped yew hedges, arboretum, walled kitchen garden. C14 church; interesting family tombs. TEA & biscuits. *Adm. 35p, Chd. 5p. Sun. July 6 (2–6)*

Edgcote†⅄⊕ (Edward Courage Esq.) 6 m. NE of Banbury. On E side of A361, Banbury–Daventry; from Banbury turn off right in Wardington village. Unspoilt Georgian house (not open) set in grounds of mature trees & lawns with 8 acres of lake; small formal garden. *(Share to Foscote Court (Banbury) Charitable Trust)* TEA & biscuits. *Adm. 25p, Chd. 5p. Sun. June 15 (2–6)*

Eydon Hall⬥⊕ (Sir Edward & the Hon. Lady Ford) Eydon, 8 m. NE of Banbury. A361 Banbury–Daventry; B4036 at Chipping Warden or Byfield, turn off E for Eydon. Large garden with beautiful views & fine trees. House (not open) Palladian style 1791. Church part C13 across park. (*Share to St Nicholas Church*) TEA & biscuits. *Adm. 30p, Chd. 10p. Sun. May 11 (2–6.30)*

Friars Well⊕ (The Viscount & Viscountess Ward) Aynho, 6 m. SE of Banbury Entrance on A41 in village of Aynho, on corner by turning to Deddington (white criss-cross gates). Bus: Banbury–Bicester, alight Aynho, 100 yds. Small garden started in 1963, on top of hill with magnificent view; divided into sections with mixed hedges & stone walls; pleached limes & hornbeams, unusual shrubs & roses. Subject of article by Lanning Roper in 'Country Life'. Tea The Cottage, Charlton. *Adm. 20p, Chd. 5p. Sun. July 6 (2–7)*

Geddington Gardens, 3½ N of Kettering. On A43 Northampton–Stamford. Parking on White Lion car park (opp. 7 New Rd) and at Village Hall, Queen St. The following 6 gardens will be open. TEAS at 40 West St. *Combined Charge for all 6 gardens 50p, Chd. 10p. Sun. June 29 (2–6)*
¶**7 New Road** (Mr & Mrs R. Woodcock) Garden of ¼-acre; mixed borders, alpines, vegetables and fruit. NO DOGS
¶**15 New Rd** (Mr & Mrs C. R. Hough) L-Shaped, informal garden, of ¼-acre; rockery, heather beds, pool, greenhouse, fruit trees, soft fruit and vegetable plot
¶**19 New Rd** (Mr & Mrs G. Hopkins) Garden of ¼-acre with roses, greenhouse, fruit and vegetables
¶**17 Queen Street** (Rev. & Mrs W. N. C. Murray) Garden of ¼-acre with shrubs, mixed beds and pool.
¶**30 West Street** (Mr & Mrs J. Palmer) Small cottage garden, mainly vegetables and greenhouse; general interest. Cottage Grade II listed building
¶**40 West Street** (Mr & Mrs P. Spence) Garden ¼-acre, created since 1975 from old farm yard; mostly raised beds of general interest; newly-established fruit and vegetable garden

Great Addington Manor*†⊕ (Miss Breitmeyer) Addington. 7 m. SE of Kettering. Turn left at Wellingborough on to Thrapston–Kettering Rd, A604, left again for Addington. Medium-sized garden; blossom, yew hedges, shrubs. Elizabethan house shown. NO DOGS in house. Tea & biscuits in Village Hall adjoining (3.30–6). *Adm. garden 25p, Chd. 5p; house 20p extra, Chd. 10p. Sun. April 20 (2–6.30)*

Holdenby House†⊕ (James Lowther Esq) 7 m. W of Northampton. A50; after level crossing turn left for East Haddon & Holdenby. Remains of Elizabethan terraced gardens with Elizabethan arches. Interesting historical site of Holdenby Palace. (In addition to date shown below for NGS, garden open April 6–Sept. 28 every Sun. & Bank Hol.) TEAS (June 22 only). *Adm. 60p, Chd. 30p. Sun. June 22 (2–6)*

Kelmarsh Hall⬥ (Miss Lancaster) On A508, 5 m. S of Market Harborough, 12 m. N of Northampton. 4-acre garden with topiary; woodland walks; daffodils, primroses, lilacs & cyclamen. Georgian house (not open) 1732. TEA & biscuits. *Adm. 30p, Chd. 10p. Sun. April 27 (2–6)*

Lilford Hall, †⬥⊕ S of Oundle; 17 m. NE of Kettering. On A605 mid-way between Oundle & Thrapston (AA signposted). 240 acres; large area of daffodils, rock gardens, aviaries, animals. Elizabethan house. NO DOGS. Café in park. (In addition to date shown below for NGS, open April 5–Nov. 30 daily; Suns. 80p, Chd. 40p; Weekdays 60p, Chd. 30p). *Adm. 80p, Chd. 40p. △Sun. April 13 (10–6)*

Little Houghton Gardens, 4 m. E of Northampton. A428 Northampton–Bedford; turn off Little Houghton By-pass at sign to Little Houghton. NO DOGS. TEAS at the Grange. *Combined charge for 2 gardens 40p, Chd. 10p. Sun. Sept. 7 (2–6)*
¶**Little Houghton House**⬥⊕ (C. V. Davidge Esq) In middle of village (white gates in stone wall). 10 acres; late Georgian house (not open) set in garden of mature trees and lawns; lake
¶**Little Houghton Grange** (Mr & Mrs Christopher Davidge) 2 acres; walled garden; lawns, sunken rosebeds. House mainly Jacobean/Queen Anne (1687–1710). TEAS served in old restored barn

Pytchley House⬥⊕ (Sir Gerald & Lady Glover) Pytchley, 3 m. S of Kettering. Between A43 & A509. Bus: UC 408, alight Pytchley, ¼ m. Rose garden, lawns, fine trees & topiary, swimming pool Temple of Zeus. House 1633. Please no pushchairs or wheelchairs on lawns. *Essential* dogs kept on leads. TEA & biscuits (Yew Tree Cottage, adjacent to Pytchley House). *Adm. 25p, Chd. 10p. Sun. July 27 (3–6.30)*

Ravensthorpe Gardens, 10 m. NW of Northampton. From A428 take turning off E for East Haddon. From A50 take turning off W for Teeton. The following 4 gardens in Ravensthorpe will be open. NO DOGS. Home-made TEAS at The Cottage. *Combined charge 40p, Chd. 10p. Sun. June 15 (2–6)*
¶**2 Chequers Lane** (Miss M. Gifford) Very small garden designed to give illusion of space; shrubs and plants for year-round interest, achieving minimum maintenance
¶**The Cottage** (Mr H. L. Batten & Mrs Barbara Batten) A Flower Arranger's garden. Visitors may also see a collection of hunting boots. Home-made TEAS

Little Lane (Mrs Hilda Roberts) Very small garden; interesting plants, shrubs, climbers, heathers, conifers, alpines

Wigley Cottages (Mr & Mrs Dennis J. Patrick) Garden of $\frac{1}{8}$ acre started 1976; island beds with mixed plantings of shrubs, herbaceous, silver foliage and groundcover plants; herb border; conservatory with passion flower, plumbago, jasmine etc. Outstanding view over Ravensthorpe Reservoir. Unusual plants for sale.

Steane Park★†✿⊕ (Capt. J. F. Norris) $2\frac{1}{2}$ m. NW of Brackley. A422 Brackley–Banbury Rd; Bus from Brackley or Banbury, alight Lodge gates. Medium-sized garden; park & lawns. Jacobean Chapel in grounds (Service at 6 pm). C16 house (not open). TEA & biscuits. *Adm. 25p, Chd. free. Sun. July 13 (2–7)*

Weekley Gardens, 3 m. N of Kettering. A43 Kettering–Stamford Rd. Church with fine tombs. TEAS at the Old Vicarage. The following 3 gardens plus 2 or 3 more will be open for a *combined charge of 40p, Chd. 5p. Sun. July 6 (2.30–6)*

    The Old Vicarage (Mrs Edward Butlin) $1\frac{1}{2}$ acres; mixed shrubs & perennials; shrubs & old-fashioned roses

    The Old Almshouse (Lord & Lady George Scott) Roses & herbaceous plants in garden dating back to 1611 when Lord Montagu of Boughton built the house originally called The Montagu Hospital for 6 worthy old men, who each had a vegetable plot in what was then the kitchen garden & orchard & kept pigs & chickens in the orchard where roses now climb the remaining trees

    Corner Thatch (Mrs M. Carling) Informal walled C17 cottage garden; roses, herbaceous plants & shrubs etc

NORTHUMBERLAND

DATES OF OPENING

ALL YEAR daily
    WALLINGTON GROUNDS, Cambo (House April to Sept. daily except Tues; Oct. Weds., Sats. & Suns.)

ALL YEAR daily
    CRAGSIDE COUNTRY PARK, Rothbury (House April to Sept. 30 daily except Mons. but open Bank Hols & closed Tues. after; also Oct. Weds., Sats. & Suns.)

APRIL to SEPTEMBER daily except Fridays (but open Good Fri.);
OCTOBER every Saturday & Sunday
    LINDISFARNE CASTLE, Holy Island

DESCRIPTIONS OF GARDENS

Cragside †✿⊕ (The National Trust) Rothbury, 13 m. SW of Alnwick (B6341) & 15 m. NW of Morpeth (B6344). Extensive grounds of over 900 acres on S edge of Alnwick Moor; famous for magnificent trees & rhododendrons & beautiful lakes. House designed by Richard Norman Shaw, famous Victorian architect, & built 1864–1895, contains much of original furniture designed by Shaw; also pictures & experimental scientific apparatus (it was 1st house in the world to be lit by electricity generated by water power). *Adm. Country Park 50p; house & Country Park £1.20. Country Park all year daily (10.30–6); Oct. Weds., Sats. & Suns. (2–5); house: summer to Sept. 30 daily except Mon. (but open Bank Hols. & closed Tues. after) (1–6); Oct. Sats. & Suns. (2–5)*

Lindisfarne Castle† (The National Trust) Holy Island, 5 m. E of Beal across causeway (which is closed for $5\frac{1}{2}$ hrs at height of tide each day); 6 m. E of A1. Tiny fort built *c.* 1550 in romantic situation on high rock overlooking sea; converted to private house in 1903 by Sir Edwin Lutyens. Tiny garden (on which Gertrude Jekyll is thought to have advised) can be viewed but not entered. *Adm. £1. April 1 to Sept. 30 daily except Fris. (but open Good Friday) (11–1, last adm. 12.30, & 2–5); Oct. Weds., Sats. & Suns. (2–5)*

Wallington★†✿ (The National Trust) Cambo. From N 12 m. W of Morpeth (B6343); from S via A696 from Newcastle, approx. 6 m. W of Belsay, B6342 to Cambo. Walled & terraced garden with fine shrubs & species roses; conservatory with magnificent fuchsias; 100 acres woodland & lakes. House dates from 1688 but altered and interior greatly changed *c.* 1740; exceptional rococo plasterwork by Francini brothers; fine porcelain, furniture, pictures & needlework, dolls' houses, museum & display of coaches. *Adm. grounds: 50p (April to Oct.; free rest of year); house & grounds £1.20. Grounds open all year; house open April 1 to Sept. 30 daily except Tues. (1–6); Oct. Weds., Sats. & Suns. (2–5)*

NOTTINGHAMSHIRE

Hon. County Organiser:
THE HON. MRS CHAWORTH MUSTERS, Felley Priory, Jacksdale

Assistant Hon. County Organiser:
MISS NORA WITHAM, Whip Ridding, Kirklington, Newark

DATES OF OPENING

APRIL Sunday 20
    FELLEY PRIORY, Underwood
APRIL Sunday 27
    WHIP RIDDING, Kirklington, nr Newark
MAY Sunday 4
    FLINTHAM HALL, nr Newark
MAY Sunday 11
    SKRETON COTTAGE, Screveton, nr Newark

MAY Sunday 18
  HOLME PIERREPONT HALL,
    Radcliffe-on-Trent
MAY Sunday 25
  PAPPLEWICK GARDENS, nr Nottingham
MAY Monday 26 (Spring Bank Hol.)
  MORTON HALL, nr Retford
  SOUTH COLLINGHAM HOUSE,
    nr Newark
JUNE Saturday 7
  7 BARRATT LANE, Attenborough,
    Beeston
JUNE Sunday 8
  7 BARRATT LANE, Attenborough,
    Beeston
  GREEN MILE, Babworth, nr Retford
  ST ANNE'S MANOR, Sutton Bonington
JUNE Sunday 22
  WOLLATON GARDENS, nr Nottingham
JUNE Sunday 29
  BISHOP'S MANOR, Southwell
  BRAMCOTE GARDENS, nr Nottingham
  BROOK HOUSE, Lowdham,
    nr Nottingham
  ‡CUCKNEY GARDENS, nr Mansfield
  GAMSTON GARDENS, nr Retford
  GONALSTON GARDENS, nr Southwell
  SOUTH COLLINGHAM HOUSE,
    nr Newark
  ‡WELBECK WOODHOUSE, nr Worksop
JULY Sunday 6
  7 BARRATT LANE, Attenborough,
    Beeston
  ‡MATTERSEY HOUSE, nr Retford
  ‡‡NOTTINGHAMSHIRE COLLEGE OF
    AGRICULTURE, Southwell
  ‡THORN HOUSE, Ranskill, nr Retford
  THRUMPTON HALL, Nottingham
  ‡‡THURGARTON GARDENS, nr Southwell
  WHATTON MANOR, nr Nottingham
JULY Sunday 13
  HALAM GARDENS, nr Southwell
  HILL HOUSE, Epperstone
  THE OLD HALL, Lowdham
JULY Sunday 20
  FLINTHAM HALL, nr Newark
AUGUST Sunday 17
  BURTON JOYCE GARDENS,
    nr Nottingham
SEPTEMBER Sunday 7
  THURGARTON GARDEN,
    nr Southwell; COLT HOUSE only

DESCRIPTIONS OF GARDENS

¶**7 Barratt Lane*** (Mr & Mrs D. J. Lucking) Attenborough, Beeston, 6 m. SW of Nottingham. Via A6005 turn left down Attenborough Lane (signposted Attenborough Nature Reserve); then 1st right into Barratt Lane. Bus: Barton's Nottingham–Derby, alight Attenborough Lane. ½-acre mature garden; flowering shrubs, clematis, alpines, fruit & vegetables; many labelled plants with some of botanical interest. Plant Stall. Refreshments available on **June 7 & 8 at Flower Festival in Attenborough Church.** *Adm.*

to garden 25p, Chd. 10p. Sat. & Sun. June 7 & 8; Sun. July 6 (2–7)

Bishop's Manor †⊕ (The Rt Rev the Lord Bishop of Southwell & Mrs Wakeling) in Southwell. Small garden with lawns, roses, shrubs & herbaceous border. Medieval ruins of Archbishop's Palace. NO DOGS. TEAS. *Adm. 25p, Chd. 5p. Sun. June 29 (2–6)*

Bramcote Gardens. On A52, 5 m. S of Nottingham; at Bramcote roundabout take A6007 towards Ilkeston; Stanley Drive is 2nd left. The following 2 gardens will be open. TEA & biscuits at No. 17. *Combined charge for 2 gardens 35p, Chd. 10p. Sun. June 29 (2–6)*
  17 Stanley Drive (Mr & Mrs John Widdison) Small suburban plot; intimate garden closely planted, mainly with hardy perennials
  ¶**1 Stanley Drive** (Mr & Mrs S. S. Randall) Flower arranger's garden; mixed shrubs, old roses, interesting plants

Brook House⊕ (Mrs Patience Pearson) Ton Lane, Lowdham, 8 m. NE of Nottingham. Medium-sized garden; mimosa tree; attractive terrace; shrubs & flower beds; roses; lawn. (*Share to Lowdham Church*) TEAS. *Adm. 25p, Chd. 10p. Sun. June 29 (2–6)*

Burton Joyce Gardens, NE of Nottingham on A612 to Newark-on-Trent. TEAS at 14, St. Helen's Grove. *Combined charge for following 3 gardens 35p, Chd. 10p. Sun. Aug. 17 (2–6)*
  136 Nottingham Road (Mr & Mrs J. M. Smeeton) On A612. Medium-sized garden, alpines, shrubs, trees, dahlias, herbaceous plants, ornamental greenhouse
  ¶**134 Nottingham Road** (Mrs H. Robeson) On A612 Small garden with roses, annuals, etc.
  14 St. Helen's Grove⊕ (Mr & Mrs H. L. J. Massey) On right if coming from Nottingham, nr church. Medium-sized mixed garden with lawns, interesting shrubs & trees, heathers, pond, etc.; terrace. TEAS

Cuckney Gardens, 6 m. N of Mansfield. Mid-way along A60 Worksop–Mansfield rd. Bus: Service 22. The following 2 gardens will be open. TEAS at Cuckney House. *Combined charge for both gardens 35p, Chd. 10p. Sun. June 29 (2–6)*
  ¶**Cuckney House**⊕ (Mr & Mrs N. E. Elliott) Large garden with lawns, roses & shrubs; rhododendrons, herbaceous border, roses
  ¶**Mill House**⊕ (Mr & Mrs E. A. Nicoll) In middle of Cuckney take A616 to Ollerton & house just off rd in village. 2 acres; old mill site; mill pond & unique river water garden; waterside & bog plants; heather garden; rockery; trees; all planted since 1969. NO DOGS

Felley Priory⊕ (Maj. R. P. Chaworth Musters) Underwood, 4 m. N of Hucknall.

Off A608 Hucknall–Heanor, ½ m. W of M1 junction No. 27, & ¼ m. E of Underwood. Medium-sized garden with daffodils, around old house. Plant stall. TEAS. *Adm. 25p, Chd. 10p. Sun. April 20 (2–6)*

Flintham Hall★†♿⊕ (Myles Thoroton Hildyard Esq) 6 m. SW of Newark. On A46. Bus: Newark–Nottingham, alight R.A.F. Station Syerston or village. Daffodils, bluebells, cherries in May. Border, walled garden, old-fashioned roses, new shrub garden; Regency pheasantry, unique conservatory; C18 park with lake, very fine trees, woodland walk. Picnics allowed. TEAS. *Adm. 30p, Chd. 10p. Sun. May 4 & Sun. July 20 (2–6)*

Gamston Gardens. 3 m. S of Retford; A638 Retford–Markham Moor Rd. The following 2 gardens will be open. TEAS at Gamston Manor. *Combined charge for 2 gardens 35p, Chd. 10p. Sun. June 29 (2–6)*

  Gamston Manor⊕ (Mr & Mrs Pat Roe) In middle of Gamston village. Approx. 1¼ acres with lawns, trees & roses
  Brewery House Cottage⊕ (C. M. D. Polhill Esq) In Gamston turn off main rd; across river bridge & 1st gateway on right; or from A614 turn off E through Bothamsall, over A1 & entrance 100 yds before river. Cottage garden with flowering shrubs & shrub roses

Gonalston Gardens⊕ ¾ m. NE of Lowdham; off A612 Southwell–Nottingham rd. About 6 gardens of various sizes will be open, inc. formal cottage gardens, larger landscaped areas of trees & grass (The Hall), roses & water gardens (Hall Farm House), colourful foliage (The Manor), etc. A diagram showing location of the various gardens will be displayed in village on opening day. TEAS at Hall Farm House. *Combined charge for all gardens (inc. the following) 50p, Chd. 10p. Sun. June 29 (2–6)*

  ¶**The Hall** (Cdr & Mrs Philip Francklin)
  ¶**Hall Farm House** (Mr & Mrs Ron Smith)
  ¶**The Manor House** (Mr & Mrs John Langford)
  Also other gardens

Green Mile♿⊕ (Mr & Mrs A. C. M. B. Scott) Babworth, 2½ m. W of Retford. Turn off A620 alongside the Prison; or off A638 at Barnby Moor; Green Mile on rd between Barnby Moor & Ranby Prison. Garden of 8 acres developed since 1950; some unusual trees & shrubs; old-fashioned & hybrid tea roses; woodland garden. Picnics allowed. TEA & biscuits. *Adm. 25p, Chd. 10p. Sun. June 8 (2–6)*

Halam Gardens W of Southwell. A612 Newark–Mansfield rd via the White Post (2 m. from Southwell). The following 2 gardens will be open. TEAS at Barn Cottage. *Combined charge for 2 gardens 30p, Chd. 10p. Sun. July 13 (2–6)*

  ¶**St Helen's Croft** (Mr & Mrs L. Ninnis) Medium-sized garden; alpine path; many troughs, silver foliage & flower arrangers' plants. Plants for sale. NO DOGS. Wheelchair available
  ¶**Barn Cottage** (Mrs Ewin) Radley Rd. Pleasant cottage garden. NO DOGS. TEAS

Hill House (Mrs F. H. Sketchley) Chapel Lane, Epperstone. 9 m. NE of Nottingham via A612; left at Lowdham roundabout on to A6097 (Epperstone By-Pass) & right into village & right again at church into Chapel Lane. Medium-sized garden; herbaceous border, rose garden, flowering shrubs. TEAS. *Adm. 25p, Chd. 10p. Sun. July 13 (2–6)*

Holme Pierrepont Hall★†⊕ (Mr & Mrs Robin Brackenbury) 4 m. E of Nottingham. Approach off A52 at the edge of West Bridgford past the National Water Sports Centre, following signs to Holme Pierrepont Hall. Medium-sized garden; courtyard garden laid out to original C19 design (illustrated in Gardens Exhibition at Victoria & Albert Museum), with a box parterre; tulips; herbaceous border; newly planted semi-formal garden. Owner-gardened. No Dogs. TEAS. *Adm. 25p, Chd. 10p. △Sun. May 18 (2–7)*

Mattersey House⊕ (Mr & Mrs T. P. O'Connor-Fenton) Mattersey, 6 m. N of Retford, 4 m. SE of Bawtry; from A636 at Ranskill turn E on to B6045 for Mattersey; house at X-rds in village. Buses from Retford & Bawtry. Medium-sized; walled garden; shrubs roses & herbaceous borders. Late Georgian house (not open). NO DOGS. TEAS. *Adm. 25p, Chd. 10p. Sun. July 6 (2–6.30)*

Morton Hall★♿⊕ (Lady Mason) Ranby, 4 m. W of Retford. Junction of A1 & A620, Worksop–Retford, at Ranby. Medium-sized woodland garden, spring flowers, flowering shrubs, rhododendrons, azaleas, specimen trees; pinetum in park, cedars & cypresses. Picnics allowed. TEAS. *Adm. 25p, Chd. 10p. Mon. May 26 (2–6)*

Nottinghamshire College of Agriculture★⊕ (Nottinghamshire Education Committee) Brackenhurst, 1 m. S of Southwell, on A612. Ornamental shrubs, lawns, rose & sunken gardens, walled garden, glasshouses, views. Tea at Thurgarton Gardens (not available at Brackenhurst). *Adm. 25p, Chd. 10p. Sun. July 6 (2–6)*

The Old Hall (Tony Etridge Esq) Church Lane, Lowdham, 9 m. NE of Nottingham. From A6097 (Epperstone By-Pass) turn off W towards Lambley; Church Lane is on right & Old Hall is only house on that lane. Approx. 7 acres; informal herbaceous, shrubberies, heathers, lawns, roses; good vegetable & soft fruit garden. House, also open, dates from C16, being an Elizabethan small house to which extensions have been made. NO DOGS. TEAS. *Adm. to garden 25p, Chd. 10p; house 30p extra, Chd. 15p. Sun. July 13 (2–7)*

Papplewick Gardens, 7 m. N of Nottingham. On NW outskirts of Papplewick village (junction of B683 & B6011). Bus: 141, Mansfield–Nottingham; alight nr gates. TEA & biscuits at Papplewick Hall. *Combined charge for following 2 gardens 35p, Chd. 10p. Sun. May 25 (2–6)*

Papplewick Hall*†&⊕ (Mrs Claude Chadburn). Rhododendrons, rose garden. Path to church. Georgian house (not shown) *c.* 1789; designed by Adam brothers; built by the Rt Hon. Frederick Montagu, friend of poet Thomas Gray (*Gray's Elegy*) & of Wm Mason, who wrote part of his *English Gardens* here.

Altham Lodge⊕ (Mr & Mrs C. G. Hill) Beautiful small garden

St Anne's Manor*&⊕ (Sir Charles & Lady Buchanan) Sutton Bonington, 5 m. NW of Loughborough N of B5324. Fair-sized garden with much colour & many interesting plants & shrubs, roses & mixed borders. (*Share to St Michael with St Anne's Church, Sutton Bonington*). *Adm. 25p, Chd. 10p. Sun. June 8 (2–6)*

Skreton Cottage⊕ (Mr & Mrs J. S. Taylor) Screveton, 8 m. SW of Newark. 12 m. E of Nottingham. From A46, Fosse Rd, turn off E to Car Colston; at Green turn left & on for 1 m. Bus: Nottingham–Newark; alight Red Lodge Inn, then 1 m. walk. 1¾ acres of landscaped gardens of general interest, a young garden with lawns & specimen trees; paved silver garden; mixed plantings of roses, shrubs & herbaceous plants. (*Share to Camphill Village Trust for Mentally Handicapped*) TEAS. *Adm. 25p, Chd. 10p. Sun. May 11 (2–6)*

South Collingham House*⊕ (Mr & Mrs P. R. Allen) 3 m. N of Newark. A46 from Newark, turn left on to Gainsborough Rd (A1133) to Collingham. Easy parking. Medium-sized garden; clipped yews, shrub roses, shrubs, herbaceous border, established herb garden; (the late Mrs Fitzherbert's collection of thymes; kitchen garden; bluebell wood. (*Share to Collingham (Notts) Scouts, Guides, Cubs & Brownies (May 26); Notts Marriage Guidance Council (June 29)*). Plant stall. TEAS. *Adm. 25p, Chd. 10p. Mon. May 26 & Sun. June 29 (2–6)*

Thorn House⊕ (Col & Mrs Denis Brown) Ranskill, 6 m. N of Retford. Via A638 Retford–Ranskill; at X-rds in Ranskill turn W on to B6045. 1½-acre garden with Long Walk; herbaceous & shrub borders with rose arches; rose-covered pergola; copper beech, walnut & sycamore trees. Car Park. Picnics allowed. Tea Mattersey House. *Adm. 25p, Chd. 10p. Sun. July 6 (2–6)*

Thrumpton Hall†&⊕ (George Seymour Esq) 8 m. SW of Nottingham. W of A684; 3 m. from M1 at Exit 24 junction. C17 larches,

cedars, planted to commemorate historic events since George III. Lake. Early Jacobean house shown, in 3 parties at 3.0, 4.0 & 5.0 only. NO DOGS in house. TEAS. *Adm. to garden 25p, Chd. 10p; house 45p extra, Chd. 25p.* △*Sun. July 6 (2–6)*

Thurgarton Gardens. 2½ m. S of Southwell on A612 to Lowdham. The following 2 gardens will be open. NO DOGS. TEA & biscuits at Colt House. *Combined charge 35p, Chd. 10p. Sun. July 6 (2–6)*

Colt House*⊕ (Mr & Mrs R. A. Grout) Garden at High Cross 1 m. N of Thurgarton, travelling towards Southwell, take turn left (W) marked Magadales Farm, entrance 100 yds. ½-acre informal garden with island beds, pool & rockery; one of the most comprehensive collections of variegated & foliage plants in the country. Plant stall. *This garden also open Sun. Sept. 7 (2–6). Adm. 25p, Chd. 10p*

Mount Pleasant& (Mrs N. Cooper) From A612 turn off E along Bleasby Rd. Medium-sized garden; many interesting trees inc. excellent specimen of ginkgo biloba (the Maidenhair tree); shrub roses, ground cover plants, shrubs etc. Plant stall

Welbeck Woodhouse⊕ (Her Grace The Duchess of Portland) 4 m. S of Worksop. Only entrance on A6009, between Worksop & Budby, well-marked. Bus: Nottingham–Worksop service; bus stop Lion gates, 2½ m. Medium-sized garden; woodland & flower. *Adm. 25p, Chd. 10p. Sun. June 29 (2–6)*

Whatton Manor*&⊕ (Miss E. M. Player) 12 m. E of Nottingham 2½ m. SE of Bingham (on A52). Bus: Nottingham-Grantham, alight Whatton village, ½ m. Garden of much interest; lawns, walled garden, roses, formal bedding, glasshouses; begonia & fuchsia collection. NO DOGS. *Adm. 25p, Chd. 10p. Sun. July 6 (2–7)*

Whip Ridding (Miss Nora Witham) nr Kirklington, W of Newark 5 m. N of Southwell. From A617 Newark–Mansfield Rd turn off N at sign to Eakring; garden 1½ m. along on right. Small garden with spring flowers, flowering shrubs & rhododendrons; woodland walk. Apiary. Plant stall. NO DOGS. TEAS. *Adm. 25p, Chd. 10p. Sun. April 27 (2–6)*

Wollaton Gardens, W of Nottingham. 4 m. along A52 Nottingham–Derby rd, turn right by Wollaton Park into Parkside; nr top fork left into Brookhill Drive. The following 2 small suburban gardens, specialising in hardy plants etc., will be open. Access between the 2. TEAS. *Combined charge for both gardens 35p, Chd. 10p. Sun. June 22 (2–6)*

10 Brookhill Drive (Miss D. T. Hogg & Miss J. L. M. Eyden)

¶**12 Brookhill Drive** (Mr & Mrs J. S. Dunning)

OXFORDSHIRE

(including Vale of the White Horse)

Hon. County Organisers:
MRS DAVID HODGES, Brook Cottage,
Alkerton, nr Banbury, OX15 6NL and
(Vale of the White Horse) MRS R. H.
WHITWORTH, The Old Manor House,
Letcombe Regis, Wantage, OX12 9LP

DATES OF OPENING

APRIL by appointment
23 BEECHCROFT RD., Oxford
BROOK COTTAGE, Alkerton, nr Banbury
APRIL, from April 2, every Wednesday,
Thursday, Sunday & Bank Hol.
weekend
PUSEY HOUSE nr Faringdon
APRIL Easter Sunday 6
CORNWELL MANOR, Kingham,
nr Chipping Norton
THE OLD RECTORY, Cuxham,
nr Watlington
APRIL Easter Monday 7
KINGSTON HOUSE, Kingston Bagpuize,
nr Abingdon
APRIL Saturday 12
FARINGDON HOUSE, Faringdon
APRIL Sunday 13
‡BAMPTON MANOR, Bampton
‡WEALD MANOR, Bampton
‡‡BUCKLAND, nr Faringdon
‡‡FARINGDON HOUSE, Faringdon
KINGSTONE LISLE PARK, nr Wantage
‡‡‡QUARRY BANK HOUSE, Tackley, nr
Woodstock
‡‡‡STONESFIELD MANOR, nr Woodstock
APRIL Sunday 20
BROUGHTON POGGS & FILKINS
GARDENS, nr Burford
GAUNT MILL, Standlake, nr Witney
LADY MARGARET HALL COLLEGE,
Oxford
LIME CLOSE, Drayton, nr Abingdon
SWIFTS HOUSE, nr Bicester
APRIL Sunday 27
BROADWELL & KENCOT GARDENS,
nr Lechlade
BRUERN ABBEY, Churchill, nr
Chipping Norton
EPWELL MILL, Epwell, nr Banbury
WATLINGTON PARK, Watlington
WHEATLEY GARDENS, nr Oxford
MAY by appointment
23 BEECHCROFT RD., Oxford
BROOK COTTAGE, Alkerton, nr Banbury
LAUND, Peppard Lane, Henley-on-Thames
MANOR FARM, Salford, nr Chipping
Norton
MAY Every Wednesday, Thursday,
Sunday & Bank Hol. weekends
PUSEY HOUSE, nr Faringdon
MAY Sunday 4
BURFORD GARDENS, Burford

THE MANOR HOUSE, Sutton Courtenay,
nr Abingdon
‡SARSDEN GLEBE, Churchill, nr Chipping
Norton
TROY, Ewelme, nr Wallingford
WATERPERRY HORTICULTURAL
CENTRE, nr Wheatley
‡WILCOTE MANOR, nr Charlbury
MAY Monday 5 (May Day Hol.)
KINGSTON HOUSE, Kingston Bagpuize,
nr Abingdon
TROY, Ewelme, nr Wallingford
WILCOTE MANOR, nr Charlbury
MAY Sunday 11
‡DENTON HOUSE, Denton, nr Oxford
‡GARSINGTON MANOR, Garsington,
nr Oxford
HIGHWOOD COTTAGE, Upper Bolney,
Harpsden, nr Henley-on-Thames
MARTEN'S HALL FARM, Longworth,
nr Abingdon
‡ROCK HOUSE, 14 Westfield Rd., Wheatley
WESTWELL MANOR, nr Burford
MAY Sunday 18
THE MALT HOUSE, 59 Market Place,
Henley-on-Thames
ROCK HOUSE, 14 Westfield Rd.,
Wheatley
STANTON HARCOURT MANOR,
nr Oxford
MAY Sunday 25
ADWELL HOUSE, Tetsworth, nr Oxford
CLIFTON HAMPDEN, THE MANOR
HOUSE, Clifton Hampden, nr
Abingdon
THE MILL HOUSE, Sutton Courtenay,
nr Abingdon
SHOTOVER HOUSE, Wheatley, nr Oxford
MAY Monday 26 (Spring Bank Hol.)
KINGSTON HOUSE, Kingston Bagpuize,
nr Abingdon
‡SHERWOOD LODGE, Bagley Wood Rd.,
Kennington, Oxford
‡SILVER TREES, Bagley Wood Rd.,
Kennington, Oxford
JUNE by appointment
23 BEECHCROFT RD., Oxford
BROOK COTTAGE, Alkerton, nr Banbury
LAUND, Peppard Lane, Henley-on-Thames
MANOR FARM, Salford, nr Chipping
Norton
JUNE Every Wednesday, Thursday &
Sunday
PUSEY HOUSE, nr Faringdon
JUNE Sunday 1
‡EPWELL MILL, Epwell, nr Banbury
LAUND, Peppard Lane, Henley-on-Thames
‡WARDINGTON MANOR, nr Banbury
JUNE Sunday 8
‡JOYCE GROVE, Nettlebed, nr
Henley-on-Thames
‡NUFFIELD PLACE GARDEN, Nuffield,
nr Henley-on-Thames
WIGGINTON GARDENS, nr Chipping
Norton

JUNE Saturday 14
  BROOK COTTAGE, Alkerton, nr Banbury
JUNE Sunday 15
  ASHBROOK HOUSE, Blewbury, nr Didcot
  ‡BROOK COTTAGE, Alkerton, nr Banbury
  ‡HOOK NORTON MANOR, nr Banbury
JUNE Saturday 21
  TADMARTON GARDENS, nr Banbury
JUNE Sunday 22
  ‡HOOK NORTON MANOR, nr Banbury
  KIDDINGTON HALL, nr Woodstock
  KINGSTONE LISLE PARK, nr Wantage
  ‡‡LONGWORTH MANOR, nr Kingston
    Bagpuize
  MANOR FARM, Old Minster Lovell,
    nr Witney
  THE OLD RECTORY, Coleshill, nr
    Faringdon
  ‡‡THE OLD RECTORY, Longworth,
    nr Abingdon
  ‡TADMARTON GARDENS, nr Banbury
JUNE Saturday 28
  TACKLEY GARDENS, Tackley, nr
    Woodstock
JUNE Sunday 29
  BAMPTON MANOR, Bampton
  ‡COURT FARM, Little Haseley, nr Oxford
  ‡HASELEY COURT & COACH HOUSE,
    Little Haseley, nr Oxford
  THE GRANGE, East Hanney, nr Wantage
  ‡‡THE GLEBE FARM, Hinton Waldrist,
    nr Faringdon
  ‡‡THE GRANGE, Hinton Waldrist,
    nr Faringdon
  ‡‡HINTON MANOR, Hinton Waldrist,
    nr Abingdon
  MARNDHILL, Ardington, nr Wantage
  TACKLEY GARDENS, Tackley,
    nr Woodstock
  WILCOTE HOUSE, nr Charlbury
JUNE Monday 30
  MARNDHILL, Ardington, nr Wantage
JULY by appointment
  23 BEECHCROFT RD., Oxford
  BROOK COTTAGE, Alkerton, nr Banbury
  LAUND, Peppard Lane, Henley-on-Thames
  MANOR FARM, Salford, nr Chipping
    Norton
**JULY from July 2 daily except
  Mons. & Fris.**
  PUSEY HOUSE, nr Faringdon
JULY Sunday 6
  ADWELL HOUSE, Tetsworth, Oxford
  CAULCOTT GARDENS, Heyford,
    nr Bicester
  COMPTON BEAUCHAMP,
    nr Shrivenham
  ‡DOWER HOUSE, Stonor,
    nr Henley-on-Thames
  ‡WHITE COTTAGE, Shepherds Green,
    Rotherfield Greys, nr Henley-on-Thames
  STANTON HARCOURT MANOR,
    nr Oxford
  ‡‡SWINBROOK HOUSE, nr Burford
  ‡‡SWINBROOK MANOR, nr Burford

JULY Saturday 12
  BROOK COTTAGE, Alkerton,
    nr Banbury
JULY Sunday 13
  BROOK COTTAGE, Alkerton, nr Banbury
  ‡DOWER HOUSE, Stonor,
    nr Henley-on-Thames
  ‡NETTLEBED GARDENS,
    nr Henley-on-Thames
  OXFORD COLLEGE GARDENS, Oxford
JULY Saturday 19
  BEGGARS BARN, Shutford, nr Banbury
  CHECKENDON COURT, Checkendon
JULY Sunday 20
  ‡BEGGARS BARN, Shutford, nr Banbury
  CHECKENDON COURT, Checkendon
  ‡POST COTTAGE, Milton, nr Banbury
JULY Sunday 27
  ‡THE OLD MANOR, Letcombe Regis,
    nr Wantage
  ‡WHITE'S FARM HOUSE, Letcombe
    Bassett, nr Wantage
AUGUST by appointment
  23 BEECHCROFT RD., Oxford
  BROOK COTTAGE, Alkerton, nr Banbury
  LAUND, Peppard Lane, Henley-on-Thames
  MANOR FARM, Salford, nr Chipping
    Norton
**AUGUST daily except Mons. & Fris.
  (but open Aug. 25)**
  PUSEY HOUSE, nr Faringdon
AUGUST Sunday 3
  BARTON ABBEY, Steeple Barton
AUGUST Sunday 10
  BLENHEIM PALACE, Woodstock
AUGUST Sunday 17
  WESTWELL MANOR, nr Burford
AUGUST Sunday 24
  WROXTON COLLEGE (WROXTON
    ABBEY), nr Banbury
**AUGUST Monday 25 (Summer Bank
  Hol.)**
  KINGSTON HOUSE, Kingston Bagpuize,
    nr Abingdon
  WROXTON COLLEGE (WROXTON
    ABBEY), nr Banbury
AUGUST Sunday 31
  THE YEWS, Swerford
SEPTEMBER by appointment
  23 BEECHCROFT RD., Oxford
  BROOK COTTAGE, Alkerton, nr Banbury
  MANOR FARM, Salford, nr Chipping
    Norton
**SEPTEMBER daily (except Mons. &
  Fris.)**
  PUSEY HOUSE, nr Faringdon
SEPTEMBER Saturday 6
  GREYS COURT, Rotherfield Greys, nr
    Henley-on-Thames
SEPTEMBER Sunday 7
  CLIFTON HAMPDEN, THE MANOR
    HOUSE, Clifton Hampden,
    nr Abingdon
  SPARROW HALL, Swalcliffe, nr Banbury

SEPTEMBER Sunday 14
  BROUGHTON POGGS & FILKINS
    GARDENS, nr Burford
  WHEATLEY GARDENS, nr Oxford

SEPTEMBER Sunday 21
  ‡BECKLEY GARDENS, nr Oxford
  BROUGHTON CASTLE, nr Banbury
  ‡RECTORY FARM, Stanton St John,
    nr Oxford

SEPTEMBER Sunday 28
  THE OLD RECTORY, Coleshill,
    nr Faringdon
  ST CATHERINE'S COLLEGE, Manor
    Road, Oxford

OCTOBER daily (except Mons. & Fris.)
  to October 19
  PUSEY HOUSE, nr Faringdon

OCTOBER by appointment
  BROOK COTTAGE, Alkerton, nr Banbury

OCTOBER Sunday 5
  ‡EPWELL MILL, Epwell, nr Banbury
  THE MILL HOUSE, Sutton Courtenay,
    nr Abingdon
  ‡TADMARTON GARDENS, nr Banbury

OCTOBER Saturday 18
  BROOK COTTAGE, Alkerton, nr Banbury

OCTOBER Sunday 19
  BROOK COTTAGE, Alkerton, nr Banbury

DESCRIPTIONS OF GARDENS

Adwell House*⚘⊕ (Mr & Mrs W. R. A. Birch Reynardson) Tetsworth, 4 m. SW of Thame. From London leave M40 at exit 6, turning left in Lewknor. From Oxford A40, turning right in Tetsworth. Roses, formal garden, water garden, ornamental lakes, fine trees & lawns; new tree & shrub planting. TEAS. *Adm. 30p, Chd. 5p. Sun. May 25 & Sun. July 6 (2.30–6.30)*

Ashbrook House*⚘⊕ (Mr & Mrs R. J. B. Walker) Blewbury, 4 m. S of Didcot. At W end of Blewbury, off A417. Medium-sized garden on chalk; pond & stream; small early Georgian house (not open). Medieval thatched chalk walls in village. TEAS. *Adm. 25p, Chd. 10p. Sun. June 15 (2–7)*

Bampton Manor*⚘⊕ (The Countess Munster) At entrance to Bampton on Witney–Faringdon Rd. Medium-sized garden; interesting layout; walled spring & herb garden; roses & good trees. Plants for sale. Tea Weald Manor (April 13 only). *Adm. 40p, Chd. under 14 free. Sun. April 13 & Sun. June 29 (2.30–6)*

Barton Abbey⚘⊕ (Mrs P. Fleming) Steeple Barton, nr Steeple Aston N of Oxford. Junction of A423 & B4030. Approx. 4 acres lawns & 3 acres of lake; fine trees; kitchen garden & glasshouses; Shetland pony stud & prize rosette display. Picnics permitted. TEA & biscuits. *Adm. 25p, Chd. 5p. Sun. Aug. 3 (2–7)*

Beckley Gardens, 4 m. NE of Oxford; A40 from either direction to Cowley-Headington roundabout & take sign to Beckley. 2 small

gardens in unspoilt village; also interesting church with recently discovered C14 murals now restored. Tea Rectory Farm, Stanton St John. *Adm. 20p (Chd. 5p) each garden or 40p (Chd. 10p) with Rectory Farm. Sun. Sept. 21 (2–6)*

  4 Church Street (Lady de Villiers) Picturesque cottage garden on hillside with open views

  Manor Farm House (The Hon. Mrs Holland-Hibbert) 1-acre garden made since 1976 around old farmhouse. Superb views over Otmoor

23 Beechcroft Road* (Mrs Anne Dexter) Oxford. A connoisseur's garden; a 23 yd by 7 yd, south facing, paved garden of a terraced house has been made secluded by planting evergreen shrubs, roses & clematis all round the brick walls; the 2 herbaceous, 2 alpine & 2 shady beds all contain many interesting & unusual plants, shrubs & ferns & troughs filled with small alpines. NO DOGS or push-chairs. *Adm. 50p. Garden open by appt. only (April to Sept. 30); (Tel. Oxford 56020*

Beggars Barn⊕ (Mr & Mrs A. E. Shipton) Shutford, 5 m. W of Banbury. A422 Stratford-on-Avon–Banbury; 4 m. W of Banbury turn to Shutford. 2-acre garden made in lovely open country, since 1976 when a barn was converted into a house; rose garden, shrubs, young trees & summer bedding; also spring-fed trout pool. NO DOGS. Tea Post Cottage, Milton (July 20 only). *Adm. 25p, Chd. 5p. Sat. & Sun. July 19 & 20 (2–7)*

Blenheim Palace†⚘ (His Grace the Duke of Marlborough) Woodstock, 8 m. N of Oxford. Bus: 44 Oxford–Chipping Norton–Stratford, alight Woodstock. Original grounds & garden plan by Henry Wise. Some additions later by Capability Brown. Refreshments available. *Adm. gardens 20p (Car park & Palace tour extra charge). △Sun. Aug. 10 (11.30–5)*

Broadwell & Kencot Gardens, 5 m. NE of Lechlade, E of A361 Lechlade–Burford. 2 charming adjoining Cotswold villages both with interesting churches. Plants for sale. TEAS Broadwell House. *Adm. 50p (Chd. 20p) admits to all, or 15p (Chd. 5p) each garden. Sun. April 27 (2–6)*

  Broadwell House*†⚘⊕ (Brig & Mrs Charles Cox) 1½-acre garden; large cedar tree entwined with wisteria climbing from an old well; Wellingtonia & Walnut; topiary; magnolias, flowering cherry & maples; many grey-leafed plants & various euphorbias & herbaceous border; limestone soil but some azaleas, grown in special earth. Listed house & old barn

  Broadwell Old Manor⊕ (Mrs P. E. Morley) Old-fashioned ½-acre garden considerably replanned & replanted since 1976 with spring, herbaceous & shrub borders; Italian-style courtyard with stone troughs & many climbers on the house

Kencot House (Mr & Mrs Andrew Patrick) 2-acre garden with lawns, trees, borders; quantities of daffodils and other spring bulbs; notable Ginkgo tree. Also interesting carved C13 archway

Kencot Cottage (Mrs Molly Foster) Very small garden with spring bulbs & bedding; also Bonzai trees

The Old Rectory (Mr & Mrs Alan Lamburn) 1¼-acre family garden with lawns, trees and bulbs

Brook Cottage* (Mr & Mrs David Hodges) Alkerton, 6 m. W of Banbury. From A422, Banbury–Stratford; turn W at signpost to Alkerton & left opp. Alkerton War Memorial. 4-acre garden, mostly formed since 1964, surrounding C17 house (not open); bulbs, roses, shrubs, water garden, white border, yellow border. TEAS (on dates shown below & for parties by prior arrangement). Ploughman's lunch on Oct. 18 & 19 only. *Adm. 40p, Chd. 5p. Sat. & Sun. June 14 & 15; Sat. & Sun. July 12 & 13 (2–7); Sat. & Sun. Oct. 18 & 19 (11–6); also by appt. April 1 to Oct. 31 (Tel. Edgehill 303 or 445)*

Broughton Castle †⊕ (Lord Saye & Sele) 2½ m. W of Banbury on Shipston-on-Stour road (B4035). 1-acre garden; shrub & herbaceous borders, walled garden, roses & climbers seen against background of C13-C16 castle surrounded by moat in open parkland. House also open, extra charge. TEAS. *Adm. 25p, Chd. 10p. Sun. Sept. 21 (2–5)*

Broughton Poggs & Filkins Gardens. Enchanting limestone villages between Burford & Lechlade, just E of A361. A number of gardens varying in size from the traditional cottage garden to over 2 acres and growing a wide variety of plants. TEAS on both days at Barn Corner (weather permitting). *50p ticket admits to all, from The Court House & Broughton Hall, Broughton Poggs & Filkins Mill, Filkins, Chd. ½ price. Sun. April 20 & Sun. Sept. 14 (2–6.30)*

Broughton Poggs:

Broughton Hall (Mr & Mrs C. B. S. Dobson)

Corner Cottage (Mr & Mrs C. Clark) (*April 20 only*)

The Court House (Richard Burls Esq)

The Old Rectory (Mrs E. Wansborough) (*April 20 only*)

Rectory Cottage (Mr & Mrs Watkins) (*April 20 only*)

Filkins:

Abbeystones (E. P. Foster Esq) (*Sept. 14 only*)

Barn Corner (Mrs C. Ede) (*April 20 only*)

St Peter's House (Mr & Mrs D. Barnett) (*April 20 only*)

Cotswold (G. Swinford Esq)

Filkins Mill (Mr & Mrs R. Hobbs)

Bruern Abbey⊕ (Hon. Mr & Mrs Michael Astor) Churchill, 5 m. SW of Chipping Norton. From A424 turn off E, 3 m. N of Burford, & follow signpost to Bruern; or from A361 between Chipping Norton & Shipton-under-Wychwood turn off N, go past Lyneham & turn left at signpost to Bruern. Medium-sized garden, part formal & part lake & water garden; blossom & early spring flowers; walks, wild flowers & views. TEAS. *Adm. 30p, Chd. 5p. Sun. April 27 (12–6)*

Buckland †⅃ (Mr & Mrs Richard Wellesley) NE of Faringdon. Turn N off A420 at Buckland X-rds. Bus: 66 Oxford–Swindon, 67 Oxford–Faringdon, alight Buckland X-rds Beautiful lakeside walk; fine trees; daffodils & shrubs. House also open (no period furniture). Norman church adjoins garden. TEAS. *Adm. 30p; house 20p extra. Sun. April 13 (2–7)*

Burford Gardens, 10 m. W of Oxford. Just N of A40 Oxford–Cheltenham. 10 m. S of Chipping Norton (A361). 10 m. E of Stow-on-the-Wold (A424). 2 gardens within easy walking distance in one of the most beautiful & famous of Cotswold villages with fine C11–15 church. TEAS. Free car park. *Combined charge 30p, Chd. 5p. Sun. May 4 (2–6)*

The Countryman⅃ (Mr & Mrs Crispin Gill) Sheep St. 1½-acre stone terraced town garden, with lawns, bulbs, shrubs, large walnut, mulberry & medlar, & spring flowers

Pytts Piece*⊕ (Lady Burder) High St. ¾-acre garden designed & planted since 1970 with wide selection of trees, flowering cherries & many bulbs

Caulcott Gardens, Heyford, 6 m. W of Bicester. Turn off B4030 Bicester–Enstone rd. 2 m. W of Middleton Stoney. NO DOGS. TEAS. *Adm. 30p, Chd. 10p. Sun. July 6 (2–7)*

Caulcott Lodge (Mr & Mrs E. J. Lane-Fox) Garden of approx. 1 acre; herbaceous & shrub borders; a pond; swimming pool surrounded by stone walls; all created since 1969 to combine ease of upkeep & year-round colour

Caulcott School House* (Mr & Mrs R. Cropley) ¼-acre cottage-style family garden of botanical interest; many hardy bulbs which enjoy a hot dry soil; flowering shrubs, shrub roses & interesting climbers

Checkendon Court⅃⊕ (Lt-Col Harold Phillips) Checkendon, NW of Reading. 2 m. NE of Woodcote on B479; house nr Checkendon Church. 4-acre garden, attractively laid out with yew hedges, large herbaceous borders, roses, kitchen garden; the whole backed by beech woods. NO DOGS. TEAS. (*Share to village charities*). *Adm. 40p, Chd. 5p (extra charge for other small Checkendon gardens open in aid of village charities). Sat. & Sun. July 19 & 20 (2–7)*

Clifton Hampden, The Manor House⅃⊕ (D. C. L. Gibbs Esq) Clifton Hampden, 4 m. E of Abingdon. A415 Abingdon–Dorchester (Oxon.). Medium-sized garden; river bank along Thames; borders. Plant stall. Share to

Relief for Dominica (West Indies). *Adm. 25p, Chd. 10p (under 5 free). Sun. May 25 & Sun. Sept. 7 (2.30–6)*

Compton Beauchamp⊕ (E. Penser Esq) 2 m. SE of Shrivenham, 7 m. W of Wantage. From B4057 turn N, 1½ m. W of White Horse Hill. 4 acres; partly walled garden, lawns, flowering shrubs, weeping willows, magnolias; herbaceous border & rose garden; many specimen trees; moat & monks' walk. Compton Beauchamp was a medieval manor house; present house (not open) C16 with 1710 classical facade. The moated grange of Tom Brown's Schooldays. NO DOGS. TEAS. *Adm. 30p, Chd. 10p. Sun. July 6 (2–7)*

Cornwell Manor⭑⚭ (The Hon. Mrs Peter Ward) Kingham, 3 m. W of Chipping Norton. Turn S off A44, 2 m. W of Chipping Norton. Large grounds, about 9 acres, with formal terrace adjacent to Manor House; water gardens leading to woodland areas & lakes; spring garden; many specimen trees & thousands of spring bulbs. NO DOGS. TEAS. *Adm. 40p, Chd. 10p. Sun. April 6 (2–6)*

Court Farm⭑⊕ (Mr & Mrs Desmond Heyward) Little Haseley, SE of Oxford. M40 from London & turn left at exit 7; then 1st turning left to Great Haseley & straight down main road to Little Haseley. 5-acre garden started in 1971; unusual trees & shrubs; bog garden & small walled silver & grey foliage garden. TEAS. Share to Invalid Children's Aid Assn. *Adm. 30p (Chd. 5p) or 50p (Chd. 10p) with Haseley Court & Coach House. Sun. June 29 (2–7)*

Denton House†⚭⊕ (Mr & Mrs J. Luke) Denton, SE of Oxford. Between A40 (Wheatley turn-off) & B480; 1 m. E of Garsington. 3-acres; walled garden enclosing large lawns & many mature trees & shrubs; spring bulbs include fritillaria; wild garden; walled vegetable garden; interesting stable yard. Gothic windows from Brazenose Chapel set in high stone wall which surrounds garden. Pony rides. NO DOGS. TEAS. Share to Cuddesdon Church & village hall funds. *Adm. 20p, Chd. 5p. Sun. May 11 (2–7)*

Dower House ⊕ (The Dowager Lady Camoys) Stonor, 4 m. N of Henley-on-Thames. Leave Henley on A423 towards Oxford; after 1 m. take B480 to Stonor; 100 yds. past Stonor Arms white house on right with green shutters. Approx. 2-acres; basically an old garden recently refurbished; interesting design with many H.T. & old-fashioned shrub roses; vegetable garden; enormous clipped yew; the whole is backed by Stonor Park with its fine trees & deer. NO DOGS. Tea Nettlebed Gardens (July 13 only). *Adm. 50p, Chd. under 14 free. Suns. July 6 & 13 (2–7)*

Epwell Mill (Mrs F. Couse) Epwell, 7 m. W of Banbury, between Shutford & Epwell.

Medium-sized garden, interestingly landscaped in open country based on disused water-mill; terraced pools; bulbs; azaleas. TEAS. *Adm. 25p. Suns. April 27, June 1, Oct. 5 (2–7)*

Faringdon House †⚭⊕ (R. Heber-Percy Esq) Faringdon. Medium-sized garden; bulbs; park; lake & orangery. Adjoining church. Tea in market place. *Adm. 25p, Chd. 10p. Sat. & Sun. April 12 & 13 (2–6)*

Garsington Manor †⚭ (Lady Wheeler-Bennett) SE of Oxford. N of B480. Bus: Oxford–Garsington. House of architectural interest (not shown) on site of earlier monastery; C14 monastic fish ponds & columbarium; Elizabethan flower garden now bedded with tulips; Italian garden made by Lady Ottoline Morrell. Tea Denton House. *Adm. 40p, Chd. 5p. Sun. May 11 (2–7)*

Gaunt Mill⭑ (Brig. F. R. L. & Mrs Goadby) Standlake, 6 m. SE of Witney; 300 yds. E of village on B4449. 3-acre garden created out of wilderness since 1949 on background of 1,000-year-old mill site with 2 arms of R. Windrush & mill pool, inc. 2-acre island with some unusual trees & shrubs; naturalised bulbs. *Adm. 25p, Chd. 10p. Sun. April 20 (2–6)*

The Glebe Farm⊕ (Mr & Mrs J. C. Lewis) Hinton Waldrist, 7 m. E of Faringdon. 1 m. N of A420 Oxford–Faringdon Rd, between Kingston Bagpuize & Faringdon. Small (1-acre) garden with roses & shrubs. NO DOGS. Tea The Grange, Hinton Waldrist. *Adm. 20p, Chd. 5p. Sun. June 29 (2–6)*

The Grange East Hanney⊕ (Dr & Mrs R. Scott Russell) 3½ m. NE of Wantage on A338 Wantage–Frilford rd. 2-acre garden made by owners since 1950; roses, shrubs & herbaceous plants; small kitchen garden, orchard. Listed C17 house (not open) & barns. NO DOGS. TEAS. *Adm. 25p, Chd. 5p. Sun. June 29 (2–7)*

The Grange Hinton Waldrist⊕ (Mr & Mrs Antony Davenport) 5 m. E of Faringdon. 1 m. N of A42 Oxford–Faringdon Rd, between Kingston Bagpuize & Faringdon. 1½-acre garden around C16 farmhouse & thatched barn; semi-wild garden; trees & shrubs. Listed house & barn. Wantage Silver Band playing. TEAS. *Adm. 20p, Chd. 5p. Sun. June 29 (2–6)*

Greys Court †⚭⊕ (Sir Felix & Lady Brunner; The National Trust) Rotherfield Greys, 3 m. NW of Henley-on-Thames on rd to Peppard. 8-acre garden largely situated amongst ruined walls & buildings of original house includes rose, cherry, white wisteria, wild & kitchen gardens; lawns, herbaceous borders. Jacobean house with C18 alterations on site of original C13 house fortified by Lord Grey in C14. Donkey wheel & tower. Henley Town Band playing. NO DOGS. TEAS. *Adm. 60p, Chd. 30p. △Sat. Sept. 6. (2.15–6)*

Haseley Court & Coach House★ (Viscount & Viscountess Hereford & Mrs C. G. Lancaster) Little Haseley, SE of Oxford. 6 m. SW of Thame. A40 London–Oxford; from London at Milton Common turn left, or from Oxford turn right; at Gt Haseley signpost turn left. 10 acres; 'Chess Garden' in box & yew & Portugal laurel; moat; walled garden; fruit garden; orchard; roses a feature. Tea Court Farm. *Adm. 30p (Chd. 10p) or 50p (Chd. 10p) with Court Farm. Sun. June 29 (2–7)*

Highwood Cottage⊕ (W. S. White Esq) Upper Bolney, 3 m. S of Henley-on-Thames. 2 m. S of Henley, on A4155, turn right at Shiplake War Memorial into Woodlands Rd; after ½ m. turn first left. Easy parking. Medium-sized garden featuring bluebell woodland, outstanding wisteria, splendid willow, & a quantity of well-established woodland & ornamental trees & shrubs inc. magnolias & rhododendrons. (*Share to Ockenden Venture (Lifeline)*). TEAS. PLANTS. NO DOGS. *Adm. 25p, Chd. 5p. Sun. May 11 (2–7)*

Hinton Manor†♿⊕ (Mrs Nicholas Davenport) Hinton Waldrist, 7 m. W of Abingdon. Just off N side of A420. 4 acres; C17 box garden & fountain; Roman walk and statues; roses & geraniums; moat & Norman earthworks. *Adm. 30p, Chd. 5p. Sun. June 29 (2–6)*

Hook Norton Manor (Lt-Col & Mrs Philip Fielden) SW of Banbury. From A361 Chipping Norton–Banbury Rd, 1 m. from Chipping Norton turn off N & follow signs to Hook Norton village. Medium-sized garden; terraced lawns & shrubs, leading down to stream, small bog garden & wild garden. Picnics permitted. Tea Brook Cottage (June 15), Tadmarton Gardens (June 22). Share to village church repair fund. *Adm. 25p, Chd. 5p Suns. June 15 & 22 (2–6.30)*

¶**Joyce Grove**♿⊕ (Nettlebed Home, Sue Ryder Foundation) Nettlebed, 5 m. NW of Henley-on-Thames; entrance on B481, 300 yds. from intersection with A423 Oxford–Henley rd. 26 acres; fine trees, rhododendrons, orchard, woodland walks & open views. Edwardian mansion (not open) built by grandfather of Peter & Ian Fleming. TEAS. Share to Sue Ryder Foundation. *Adm. 30p, Chd. 10p. Sun. June 8 (2–7)*

Kiddington Hall†♿ (Mr L. W. Robson & Lady Robson) 4 m. NW of Woodstock. From A34, Oxford–Stratford, turn right at X-rds in Kiddington & down the hill; entrance on left. Large grounds with lake & parkland designed by Capability Brown: terraced rose garden beside house designed by Sir Charles Barrie; C12 church & C16 dovecot. TEAS. Share to Kiddington Church Restoration Fund. *Adm. 30p, Chd. 10p. Sun. June 22 (3–7)*

Kingston House★†♿⊕ (Lady Grant) Kingston Bagpuize, at junction of A415 & A420, 5½ m. W of Abingdon. Flowering shrubs & bulbs (early openings). Woodland garden; herbaceous plants & shrubs; hydrangeas. (*Share to Kingston Bagpuize Parish Church & Village Hall Committee.* NO DOGS. *Adm. 50p, Chd. 25p.* △*Mons. April 7, May 5 & 26, Aug. 25 (2–6)*

Kingstone Lisle Park★♿⊕ (Capt T. L. Lonsdale) 5 m. W of Wantage; 1 m. from White Horse Hill B4507. April opening: daffodils; June opening: delphiniums, peonies, roses, herbaceous border. Plants for sale. On June 22 Wantage Silver Band playing. TEAS (home-made cakes). *Adm. 25p, Chd. 5p. Cars free. Sun. April 13 & Sun. June 22 (2–6)*

Lady Margaret Hall College⊕ (Principal & Fellows) Norham Gardens, Oxford. 1 m. N of Carfax from St Giles fork right into Norham Rd, 2nd right into Fyfield Rd. Approx. 8 acres of formal & informal gardens; daffodils & water meadows by R. Cherwell. College 100 yrs old includes listed buildings. *Adm. 25p, Chd. free. Sun. April 20 (2–6)*

Laund♿⊕ (Mr S. A. & Miss M. P. Walden) Peppard Lane, Henley-on-Thames. 1 m. from town centre; M4 from London, over bridge to traffic lights; turn left on to Reading Rd; turn right into St Andrews Rd; after ¼ m. turn left into Berkshire Rd & leave car in this road; continue into Peppard Lane. 1-acre garden mostly created since 1974 but already well established; fine specimens of trees & shrubs, interplanted with lilies, delphiniums, phlox & numerous annuals. NO DOGS. TEAS & plants for sale if fine. Share to Gardeners' Sunday. *Adm. 25p, Chd. 10p. Sun. June 1 (2–6); also by appt. May 1–Aug. 31 (Tel. Henley-on-Thames 4715)*

Lime Close★⊕ (Miss C. Christie-Miller) Henley's Lane, Drayton (2 m. S of Abingdon); on E side of A34 in Drayton (by Rogowski, newsagent). 3 acres with choice shrubs, bulbs (rare Fritillaries, dwarf and large narcissus, dwarf iris) raised beds of alpines and an alpine house. TEAS. *Adm. 25p, Chd. 5p. Sun. April 20 (2–7)*

Longworth Manor⊕ (Lt-Col & Mrs John Walton) nr Kingston Bagpuize, 7 m. W of Abingdon. N of A420 Oxford (10 m.)–Faringdon (7 m.) Rd. Medium-sized garden with roses & borders. Plants for sale. Good view to Cotswolds over R. Thames Valley. Dogs on leads only. TEAS. *Adm. 25p, Chd. 5p. Sun. June 22 (2–6.30)*

¶**The Malt House**★ (D. F. K. Welsh Esq) 59 Market Place, Henley-on-Thames. Close to Henley Town Hall. ½-acre unusual, imaginatively-designed town garden, featuring 16 cent. malt-house, lawn & beds of less common plants & shrubs. (Unsuitable for pushchairs or young children.) NO DOGS. Teashops in town. *Adm. 25p, Chd. 5p. Sun. May 18 (2–6)*

¶**Manor Farm, Old Minster Lovell** †⊕ (Sir Peter & Lady Parker) 1½ m. NW of Witney on A40 towards Burford; turn right at sign to Old Minster Lovell; in ¼ m. cross Windrush bridge, right at old Swan; stop at car park at top of street; follow sign to church & ruins. 5-acre garden made since 1974 around small Cotswold farm-house adjoining churchyard & ruins of Minster (open); large medieval barns divide garden into various sections still being planted; grass & informal herbaceous areas; shrub & specie roses. C14 dovecot. Plant & produce stalls & craft display (under cover if wet). (*Share to C.P.R.E.*) TEAS. *Adm. 25p, Chd. 10p. Sun. June 22 (2-7)*

Manor Farm (Col Sir Andrew Horsbrugh-Porter, Bt & Lady Horsbrugh-Porter), Salford 2 m. W of Chipping Norton. Take A44 Oxford–Worcester Rd; from Chipping Norton take 2nd right turn into Salford; drive straight ahead into yard. Small plantsman's garden made since 1964; small trees, shrubs, perennials & wall climbers. Tea Chipping Norton. *Adm. 25p. Garden open by appt. only May–Sept. (Tel. Chipping Norton 2597*

The Manor House, Sutton Courtenay⊕ (The Hon. F. D. L. Astor) S of Abingdon. Bus: Oxford–Milton, alight Cross Trees, 2 mins. Large garden with R. Thames running through it. NO DOGS. TEAS. *Adm. 20p, Chd. 5p. Sun. May 4 (2-7)*

Marndhill*⚲⊕ (Lord & Lady Chelsea) Ardington, 1½ m. E of Wantage; S of A417 Wantage–Reading. 3½-acre garden; green, herbaceous & shrub borders; herb garden; walled kitchen garden; fine trees with extensive & recent replanting. NO DOGS. *Adm. 25p, Chd. 10p. Sun. June 29 (2.30–6.30), Mon. June 30 (10–5)*

Marten's Hall Farm*⊕ (Mr & Mrs John Parker-Jervis) Longworth, 7 m. W of Abingdon. 2 m. NW of Kingston Bagpuize (at junction of A415 & A420). Garden of ¾-acre, mostly replanted since 1970; many uncommon plants & shrubs, inc. fritillaries & peonies. Listed farmhouse (not open). Plants for sale. NO DOGS please. TEA & biscuits. *Adm. 30p, Chd. 15p. Sun. May 11 (2-7)*

The Mill House*†⚲⊕ (Mrs Peter Laycock) Sutton Courtenay, S of Abingdon. Bus: Oxford–Abingdon–Milton, alight village, 100 yds. Approx. 6 acres; garden on two islands, dissected by mill stream & mill pond. Shrubs, roses. Tea Abingdon or Steventon. *Adm. 30p, Chd. 5p. Sun. May 25 (2-7) & Sun. Oct. 5 (2-6)*

Nettlebed Gardens, 5 m. NW of Henley-on-Thames. 4 gardens in charming historical village where bricks have been made since 1300. On A423, Henley–Oxford. Bus: Reading–Nettlebed; Henley–Nettlebed–Oxford; bus stop Nettlebed. TEAS at The Leaze. *Adm. 50p, Chd. 20p. Sun. July 13 (2-7)*

The Malt House⊕ (Mr & Mrs J. A. Brymer) Medium-sized garden, mostly roses; walled garden with pond & waterfall

Waterpits⊕ (Mr & Mrs L. Sims) Crocker End. 2 cottage gardens joined into one with pleasant view over typical Chiltern dry valley & woods

The Leaze⊕ (Mr & Mrs S. Seligman) Crocker End. ¾-acre garden divided into 3 small gardens, one walled; one mainly roses & herbaceous plants; one more open with shrubs & shrub roses. TEAS

¶**Field House**⊕ (Miss Cooper-Dean) Crocker End. 1-acre garden; well kept lawns surrounded by herbaceous borders & rose beds; various flowering trees & shrubs; also fruit trees, grape vine & large kitchen garden. Lovely views

¶**Nuffield Place** †⚲⊕ (Nuffield College) Nuffield, 6 m. NW of Henley; 6 m. SE of Wallingford. Off A423; from Henley turn right, from Oxford left, at sign for Huntercombe Pl. 4-acre garden laid out during & after first world war; many mature trees, shrubs, rhododendrons & borders; lawns, pond & rockery; beechwoods. The home of Lord & Lady Nuffield from 1933–63. NO DOGS. Tea Joyce Grove, Nettlebed. *Adm. 30p, Chd. 10p. Sun. June 8 (2-6)*

The Old Manor, Letcombe Regis*†⚲⊕ (Maj.-Gen. & Mrs Rex Whitworth) 1½ m. SW of Wantage. Letcombe Regis signposted from B4507 Wantage–Swindon Rd. 1½-acre garden surrounds C17 manor house & runs down to Letcombe brook; old granary & dovecot frame the lawns. Plants for sale. NO DOGS. Tea White's Farmhouse, Letcombe Bassett. *Adm. 25p, Chd. 5p. Sun. July 27 (2-6)*

The Old Rectory, Coleshill⊕ (Mr & Mrs Martin) 3 m. W of Faringdon. Coleshill (a Nat. Trust village) is on B4019, approx. midway between Faringdon & Highworth. Medium-sized garden; lawns & informal shrub beds; wide variety of shrubs, inc. old-fashioned roses; 30-yr-old standard wisteria. Distant views of Berkshire & Wiltshire Downs. House (not open) dates from late C14. TEAS. *Adm. 20p, Chd. 5p. Sun. June 22 (2-7) & Sun. Sept. 28 (2-6)*

The Old Rectory, Cuxham*†⚲⊕ (Miss M. E. Edwards) 1½ m. W of Watlington. Via B480 from Oxford. Between M40 (exit 6) and A423. 2-acre garden surrounding late Georgian house (not open) in medieval village with interesting church; many good plants, spring bedding & kitchen garden; wild garden a feature with naturalized small daffodils, primroses, fumitory (Corydalis bulbosa), anemones & other miniature bulbs. NO DOGS. Simple TEAS (in the bungalow with fire). *Adm. 25p, Chd. 5p. Sun. April 6 (2-6)*

The Old Rectory, Longworth⊕ (Mrs P. E. Rolt) W of Abingdon. N of A420 Oxford (10 m.)–Faringdon (7 m.) Rd; in Longworth village at W end. 1-acre garden with borders. House (not open) Queen Anne & Georgian. Tea Longworth Manor. *Adm. 15p, Chd. 5p. Sun. June 22 (2–6)*

Oxford College Gardens. 4 private gardens not normally open to the public. All within easy walking distance. NO DOGS. TEAS New College Hall. *Adm. 50p, Chd. 20p admits to all. Sun. July 13 (2–6)*

¶**New College: Warden's garden**†⊕ Entered from New College Lane, off Catte St. Small garden enclosed among College buildings

¶**Queen's College: Provost's garden***† Entered from High Street. ½-acre; has been a garden continuously from 14 cent. when Queen's was founded. E side beautiful facade of early 18 cent. library. 8 lovely statues; succession of flowering trees & shrubs; many interesting & unusual herbs

¶**Queen's College: Fellows' garden** Entered from High St. ½-acre with splendid herbaceous borders seen against high old stone walls; large ilex tree

¶**Wadham College: Fellows' garden** Entered from Park's Rd. 5-acre garden best known for trees. In the Fellows' Main Garden, a superb purple beech, a fine magnolia acuminata, etc; in the Fellows' Private Garden, a very large quercus lucombeana, a ginkgo with curious ascending branches, a young tulip tree, & other recent plantings

Post Cottage⊕ (Mr & Mrs W. G. Bamford) Milton, 4 m. S of Banbury, between (& 1 m. from) villages of Bloxham (A36) & Adderbury (A423); 20 m. N of Oxford. Small walled garden of nearly ½ acre, landscaped with shaped flowerbeds amongst lawns to give cottage character; massed with herbaceous plants & shrubs for ground cover & to give colour March to Sept. NO DOGS. TEAS. Share to Milton Church. *Adm. 25p, Chd. 5p. Sun. July 20 (2–6)*

● **Pusey House***⚬⊕ (Mr & Mrs Michael Hornby) 5 m. E of Faringdon; 12 m. W of Oxford; ½ m. S of A420. Large garden; herbaceous borders; walled gardens & water garden; large collection of shrubs & roses; many fine trees. Plants for sale. Free car park. TEAS for organized parties (Tel. Buckland 222). *Adm. 70p, Chd. under 10 free (parties by appt. 50p each). April 2 to June 29, every Wed., Thurs., & Sun.; July 2 to Oct. 19 daily (except Mons. & Fris.); also open Bank Hol. weekends (2–6)*

Quarry Bank House⊕ (Mr & Mrs D. J Smith) Tackley, 2 m. N of Woodstock. From A423 take A4095 turn to Bicester; entrance at bottom of Gibraltar Hill on sharp bend of river bridge. 4¾-acre garden with abundance of early spring flowers in sheltered situation on R. Cherwell; lawns, fine cedar, orchard &

newly planted bank of trees & shrubs; attractive walks in natural quarry setting. NO DOGS. TEAS. *Adm. 25p, Chd. 5p. Sun. April 13 (2–6)*

Rectory Farm (Lord & Lady Stanley of Alderley) Stanton St John, 5 m. NE of Oxford. From A40 at Headington roundabout take turning for Stanton St John just off B4027. Mature garden of unusual layout about 1 acre with shrub roses a speciality; interesting mixed borders & vegetable garden. TEAS. *Adm. 30p (Chd. 10p) or 40p (Chd. 10p) with Beckley Gardens. Sun. Sept. 21 (2–6)*

Rock House*† (Mrs C. R. S. Harris) 14 Westfield Rd, Wheatley, 6 m. E of Oxford on A40. Alpines & rock plants in natural quarry setting, on 4 levels; interesting old well. House part C17, part early C19 (not open). NO DOGS please. Tea Denton House (May 11 only). *Adm. 25p, Chd. 5p. Suns. May 11 & 18 (2–7)*

¶**St Catherine's College***⚬⊕ (The Master & Fellows of St Catherine's College) Manor Rd, Oxford. From Magdalen Bridge entrance to Oxford turn right immediately over bridge into Holywell; then first right again by St Cross church. From north Oxford branch off Banbury Rd into Parks Rd; left into South Parks Rd & continue until next left turn which is Manor Rd. Garden planted around new college 1963–65, both designed by late Prof. Arne Jacobsen. Garden designed to link modern architecture with river meadow site; water garden & very wide range of trees & shrubs. NO DOGS. TEAS (3–5.30). Large free car park. *Adm. 30p, Chd. 10p includes entrance to part of college. Sun. Sept. 28 (2–6)*

Sarsden Glebe†⚬ (Miss Judy Hutchinson) Churchill; 3 m. SW of Chipping Norton. Via B4450 to Churchill; from Burford via A361 & turn W for Churchill. Medium-sized garden, probably by Repton; trees, anemones & bulbs. Tea Wilcote Manor. *Adm. 25p, Chd. 5p. Sun. May 4 (2.30–6)*

¶**Sherwood Lodge**⚬⊕ (Mr & Mrs William Osborn-King) Bagley Wood Rd, Kennington, Oxford, 3 m. SW of Oxford, 3 m. N of Abingdon on A4183 (old A34). Bagley Wood Rd signposted Kennington. 7-acre woodland garden; naturalised bulbs, flowering shrubs, azaleas & rhododendrons. Tea Silver Trees. *Adm. 25p (Chd. 5p) or 40p (Chd. 10p) with Silver Trees. Mon. May 26 (2–7)*

Shotover House⚬⊕ (Maj. A. A. Miller) Wheatley, 6 m. E of Oxford on A40. Bus: Oxford–Thame or Oxford–High Wycombe– London; alight Islip turn. Landscape garden with lawns, fine trees & lake. TEAS (in arcade). *Adm. 30p, Chd. 5p. Sun. May 25 (2–7)*

Silver Trees*⚬⊕ (Dr & Mrs P. F. Barwood) Bagley Wood Rd, Kennington, S of Oxford. From A34 Oxford–Abingdon turn off at sign to Boars Hill, then left on to A4183 to Abingdon; next left into Bagley Wood Rd. Approx. 3

acres; woodland garden with informal shrub beds, camellias & naturalized daffodils; wild garden; also some alpines. Plants for sale. TEAS. *Adm. 25p (Chd. 5p) or 40p (Chd. 10p) with Sherwood Lodge. Mon. May 26 (2–7)*

Sparrow Hall⊕ (Mr & Mrs J. Panks) Swalcliffe, W of Banbury. Village on B4035, ½-way between Banbury & Shipston-on-Stour. ¾-acre garden started in 1967 from derelict farmyard, chicken run & small field, planned to make as much use of colour as possible with shrubs, perennials, rock plants & bulbs. Converted farmhouse backs large patio with stone troughs & other containers filled with plants for seasonal display. TEAS. Share to Swalcliffe Village Hall. *Adm. 25p, Chd. 5p. Sun. Sept. 7 (1.30–5.30)*

Stanton Harcourt Manor★†⊕ (Mr Crispin & The Hon. Mrs Gascoigne) W of Oxford; B4449. Formal, woodland & water gardens. C15 Chapel & kitchen in grounds. Plants for sale. TEAS. Share to St Michael's Church. *Adm. 40p, Chd. 10p. Sun. May 18 & Sun. July 6 (2–6.30)*

Stonesfield Manor⅃⊕ (Mr & Mrs Christopher Eastwood) 3 m. W of Woodstock. 1 m. N of Woodstock on A34 turn W; after ¼ m. fork left. From Charlbury go S on Witney Rd (B4022) for ½ m. then turn left. 3 acres; daffodils & fine trees; walled garden with vegetables & herbaceous border. Interesting old cockpit. Share to DGAA. *Adm. 25p, Chd. 5p. Sun. April 13 (2–6.30)*

Swifts House⅃⊕ (Maj. & Mrs B. G. Barnett) 3½ m. NW of Bicester. On A41 Bicester–Banbury. 3 acres; great numbers of naturalised daffodils first planted in 1900 & added to yearly ever since; mature trees; walled kitchen garden. NO DOGS. TEA & biscuits. *Adm. 30p, Chd. 10p. Sun. April 20 (2–5.30)*

Swinbrook House⊕ (Mrs Duncan Mackinnon) nr Burford. 2 m. E of Burford turn N off A40. ½-way between Swinbrook & Shipton-under-Wychwood. Medium-sized garden; herbaceous borders; shrubs & shrub roses; large kitchen garden; fine views Picnics allowed. *Adm. 30p (Chd. 5p), or 40p (Chd. 10p) with Swinbrook Manor. Sun. July 6 (2–7)*

Swinbrook Manor⊕ (Mrs S Freund) 2½ m. E of Burford. From A40 Burford–Witney, 2 m. E of Burford turn for Swinbrook. Small garden, near interesting church. Tea Burford. *Adm. 20p (Chd. 5p), or 40p (Chd. 10p) with Swinbrook House. Sun. July 6 (2–7)*

Tackley Gardens, 9 m. N of Oxford. Turn off A423 Oxford–Banbury at Sturdy's Castle. Plants for sale & TEAS. *Adm. 30p, Chd. 10p admits to both. Sat. & Sun. June 28 & 29 (2–7)*

Hill Court (Dame Felicity Peake) C16 walled garden, 2 acres, with fine views of

partly Norman church & restored Manor House (not open) overlooking Park laid out in 1787 by Sir John Whalley Smythe; terraced rose garden inc. C16 pigeon house

16 Balliol Close★ (Mr & Mrs S. Boorne) Small garden (¼ acre) on calcareous soil constructed since 1968; shrubs, many of which are dwarf or unusual varieties, underplanted with bulbs; terraced rock garden on 4 levels with miniature waterfall & planted with many varieties of alpine and dwarf plants. NO DOGS

Tadmarton Gardens, 5 m. SW Banbury on B4035. TEAS (June 21 & 22 only) Tea Epwell Mill (Oct. 5). Share to Tadmarton Village Hall Fund. *Adm. 30p, Chd. 10p. Sat. & Sun. June 21 & 22; Sun. Oct. 5 (2–6)*

The Manor⊕ (Mr & Mrs R. K. Asser) Medium-sized garden with beautiful views of unspoilt countryside; fine trees; shrubs; C15 barn & C18 dovecot

Yeomans★ (Mr & Mrs A. E. Pedder) Small cottage-style garden with iris, peonies, shrub roses & a wide selection of other plants including climbers. Plants for sale

Troy⊕ (Mr & Mrs T. Ruck Keene) Ewelme, 3 m. NE of Wallingford. From A423 take turning signposted Ewelme & R.A.F. Benson. Between Nettlebed & Crowmarsh. Grey & silver garden, herb garden, daffodils & narcissi. Summer houses mentioned by Jerome K. Jerome (to whom the house once belonged). Plants for sale. Flock of Jacobs Sheep with lambs. DOGS on leads only. Home-made TEAS. Share to Nat. Soc. for Autistic Children. *Adm. 30p, Chd. 5p. Sun. & Mon. May 4 & 5 (2–7)*

Wardington Manor★†⊕ (The Lord Wardington) 5 m. NE of Banbury, A361. 5 acres with topiary, rock garden, flowering-shrub walk to pond. Jacobean manor house (not shown) 1665. TEAS. *Adm. 30p, Chd. 10p. Sun. June 1 (2–6)*

Waterperry Horticultural Centre,★†⅃⊕ nr Wheatley, E of Oxford. Cars turn off A40 at Wheatley, 2 m. Bus: alight Waterstock turn on A418, 20 mins. walk. An estate of more than 80 acres. Plants for sale. Church of Saxon origin, with famous old glass, brasses & woodwork, in grounds. TEAS. *Adm. 40p, Chd. under 14, 20p. △Sun. May 4 (2–6)*

Watlington Park⅃⊕ (The Hon. C. L. B. Brett) 2 m. SE of Watlington. 3½ m. S of M40, Exit 5; entrance just beyond Christmas Common. Large garden with lawns, fine trees & parkland surrounding C18 house (not open) with beautiful views over Oxfordshire plain; large areas of naturalised daffodils & walled kitchen garden. Plants & home produce for sale. TEAS. Share to The League of Pity. *Adm. 30p, Chd. 10p. Sun. April 27 (2–7)*

Weald Manor†⅃⊕ (Maj. & Mrs R. A. Colvile) Bampton. At W end of Bampton, entrance off A4095. Medium-sized, old garden with many daffodils; fine trees & small lake. Also includes garden of **Stables Cottage** (Mr & Mrs R. Franks) made from stable yard. DOGS on leads only. TEAS. *Adm. 25p (Chd. 10p) or 50p (Chd. 10p) with Bampton Manor. Sun. April 13 (2.30–6.30)*

¶**Westwell Manor** (Mr & Mrs T. H. Gibson) 2 m. SW of Burford, just off A40 Oxford–Cheltenham. 6-acre garden surrounding beautiful old Cotswold Manor House (not open); many spring bulbs, both naturalized & in formal borders; cherry blossom; water garden; herbaceous borders; topiary. Also museum of craftsmen's tools (donations in aid of church). *(Share to Westwell Church).* Simple TEAS. *Adm. 30p, Chd. 10p. Sun. May 11 & Sun. Aug. 17 (2–7)*

Wheatley Gardens On April 27 the following 4 gardens will be open. 6 m. E of Oxford just off A40. TEAS at The Old House. *Combined charge for 4 gardens 50p, Chd. 10p; or 20p each garden, Chd. 5p. Sun. April 27 (2–6)*

¶**5 Anson Close** (Mr & Mrs G. Northcote) Unusual-shaped, small water garden in Japanese manner (black & red timber studio substitutes for the traditional teahouse); flowering shrubs & plants; terraced lawns, stream & cascades. Ceramics for sale. NO DOGS.

Chestnuts⊕ (Mrs D. E. W. Morgan) Park Hill. Small garden designed to maximise width & minimize length; 2 raised beds of alpines; spring flowers & shrubs. DOGS on leads please. Share to British Red Cross Oxfordshire Branch

The Doctor's House⊕ (Dr & Mrs R. Flury) 16 Church Rd. 1-acre cottage-style garden, interestingly landscaped with rockery, bulbs & shrubs

The Old House†⊕ (Mr & Mrs N. Minty) 17 Kiln Lane. Approx. 2 acres; stream, small lake; bulbs, shrubs & roses. TEAS

Wheatley Gardens. On Sept. 14 the following 3 gardens will be open. 6 m. E of Oxford just off A40. TEAS at The Old House. *Combined charge for 3 gardens 40p, Chd. 10p; or 20p each garden, Chd. 5p. Sun. Sept. 14 (2–6)*

5 Anson Close (see previous entry)

The Old House (see previous entry). TEAS

The Walled Cottage⊕ (Mr & Mrs John Prest) 8 Church Rd. Small, enclosed family garden, aiming at a scene of rest for parents, places to play & hide for children, room to stretch a large dog, some flowers & foliage all year round & space for fruit & vegetables

White Cottage*⊕ (Harold E. Johnston Esq) Shepherds Green, Rotherfield Greys, 4 m. W of Henley-on-Thames. Approaching from Thames Bridge, at main traffic lights in centre of Henley-on-Thames go straight across & up hill past Town Hall (signposted Peppard); follow this un-numbered rd for 3½ m., cross Greys Green & fork right (signposted Shepherd's Green); in ¼ m. turn right at telephone kiosk, pass 'Green Tree' P.H. & bear right. ¾ acre garden of horticultural interest; yew and box hedges serve as background to flowering shrubs, roses & herbaceous plants, inc. good display of delphiniums of unusual colours. *(Share to Gardeners' Sunday).* Plants for sale. *Adm. 25p, Chd. 5p. Sun. July 6 (2–7)*

White's Farm House*⊕ (Mr & Mrs Michael Shone) Letcombe Bassett. 3 m. SW of Wantage. Letcombe Bassett signposted from B4507 Wantage–Swindon Rd. Medium-sized, wild garden planted 1961, & small enclosed water garden. Garden illustrates problems of growing trees & shrubs on chalk. Wantage Silver Band playing. TEAS (served in repaired C17 barn). *Adm. 25p, Chd, 5p. Sun. July 27 (2–7)*

Wigginton Gardens, 6 m. SW of Banbury, 1 m. W of A361 Banbury–Deddington Junction. NO DOGS please. TEAS at Sunbiggin. Share to W.I. *Adm. 25p, Chd. 5p. Sun. June 8 (2–6)*

Buddleia Cottage* (Miss M. J. Bartlett) Small plantsman's garden with all-year interest & ground cover plants to minimise work; scented shrubs, climbers, bulbs, alpines. Unsuitable wheel and pushchairs

Sunbiggin⊕ (Miss M. Allison) 1-acre garden with beautiful views over open countryside. Lawns, shrubs, herbaceous plants & vegetables

Wilcote House⊕ (The Hon. C. E. Cecil) Finstock, 3 m. S of Charlbury. NW of Oxford between Northleigh & Finstock; E of B4022. Roses, herbaceous borders. *Adm. 25p, Chd. 5p. Sun. June 29 (2–6)*

Wilcote Manor †&⊕ (Sir Mark Norman, Bt & Lady Norman) 5 m. SW of Charlbury. E of B4022, by Finstock & Ramsden. Old yew hedges with topiary; naturalised daffodils; herbaceous borders; rose garden; fine old trees, lawns & magnolias. Very early Elizabethan manor house; early small church in Decorated style. TEAS. Share to Thames Valley Police Benevolent Fund. *Adm. 30p, Chd. 5p. Sun. & Mon. May 4 & 5 (2–6)*

Wroxton College (Wroxton Abbey) †&⊕ (Fairleigh Dickinson University) Wroxton, 4 m. W of Banbury. A422 Banbury–Stratford. Bus: Banbury–Tysoe; alight Wroxton village, 3 mins. 56 acres of lawns, woodlands & lakes originally laid out in 1733–48 by Francis North, 1st Earl of Guildford surrounding manor house commenced in 1217. Cream TEAS. Conducted tours of Abbey extra charge. *Adm. 30p, Chd. 5p Sun. & Mon. Aug. 24 & 25 (2–6.30)*

The Yews&⊕ (Mr & Mrs Frederick W. Timms) Swerford 5 m. NE of Chipping Norton. Just off A361 between Banbury & Chipping Norton; turning ¼ m. from Masons Arms, signposted Swerford. Garden (approx. 2 acres) recently reconstructed after building new house in grounds; walled garden with mature trees & shrubs; water garden & swimming pool. NO DOGS. TEAS. *Adm. 25p, Chd. 10p. Sun. Aug. 31 (2–7)*

POWYS

Hon. County Organisers:

North (Montgomery District) MRS DENISE HATCHARD, Maenllwyd Isaf, Abermule

South (Brecknock & Radnor Districts) MISS ELIZABETH YOUNGHUSBAND, Neuadd, Crickhowell

DATES OF OPENING

By appointment all year
MAENLLWYD ISAF, Abermule
TYNEWYDD, Cwm Goleu, nr Welshpool
APRIL to DECEMBER daily
GLIFFAES COUNTRY HOUSE HOTEL, nr Crickhowell
APRIL Sunday 20
GLEBE HOUSE, Guilsfield, nr Welshpool
MAY Sunday 4
ABERCYNRIG, Llanfrynach, nr Brecon
MAY Sunday 25
LLANSTEPHAN HOUSE, Llyswen, nr Brecon
MAY Monday 26
VAYNOR PARK, Berriew
MAY Saturday 31
OLD RECTORY, Boughrood, nr Hay-on-Wye
JUNE Sunday 1
GREGYNOG, Tregynon, nr Newtown
LLYSDINAM, Newbridge-on-Wye
JUNE Saturday 7
TRAWSCOED HALL, nr Welshpool
JUNE Sunday 8
FFRWDGRECH, Brecon
TRAWSCOED HALL, nr Welshpool
JUNE Sunday 15
MAENLLWYD ISAF, Abermule
JULY Sunday 6
THE DINGLE, Welshpool
JULY Saturday 26 & Sunday 27
GLEBE HOUSE, Guilsfield, nr Welshpool
SEPTEMBER Sunday 14
POWIS CASTLE, Welshpool
SEPTEMBER Saturday 20 & Sunday 21
DOLFORGAN GARDENS, Kerry

DESCRIPTIONS OF GARDENS

¶**Abercynrig** †⊕ (William Lloyd Esq) Llanfrynach, 3 m. SE of Brecon. From A40 turn on to B4558 1½ m. E of Brecon; thereafter signed. Medium-sized garden, owner-maintained; C17 manor house (part shown) with small lake surrounded by daffodils in spring. Cider Mill in out-buildings. Bus: Brecon—

Llanfrynach; alight Llanfrynach Pond, ½ m. Tea White Swan Inn, Llanfrynach. *Adm., inc. part-house, 30p, Chd. 10p. Sun. May 4 (2–7)*

The Dingle*⅃⊕ (Mr & Mrs D. R. Joseph) 3 m. N of Welshpool. Via A490 towards Llanfyllin for 1 m.; then turn left for Groespluan; go straight on for 1¾ m. then fork left & garden is immediately on left. 2 acres; unusual shrubs & trees in south-facing garden with large banks leading down to a big pool. Nursery attached to garden. *Adm. 25p, Chp. 10p. Sun. July 6 (2–7); also open by appt. all year (tel. Welshpool 2587)*

¶**Dolforgan Gardens** (Mr & Mrs Noel Jerman) Kerry, E of Newtown. On W edge of Kerry on A489 (going towards Newtown) on N side of rd. New, mainly heather, garden made since 1970 in an area surrounded by mature shrubs & trees, showing what can be achieved in retirement. *Adm. 25p, Chd. 10p. Sat. & Sun. Sept. 20 & 21 (2–5.30)*

Ffrwdgrech*⅃ (Mr & Mrs W. D. D. Evans) 1 m. S of Brecon. From A40 turn S opp. Drover's Arms along Ffrwdgrech Rd; entrance lodge ¾ m. on left. Bus: Merthyr—Brecon; alight Drover's Arms, ¾ m. Medium-sized garden, owner maintained; flowering shrubs; forest garden with stream; fine trees; 2 acres of lawns; pond. Good views of Beacons. Dogs on leads. TEAS. *Adm. 30p, Chd. 10p. Sun. June 8 (2–7); also by appt. for parties only (April–June)*

Glebe House*⊕ (Mrs Jenkins & Mrs Habberley) Guilsfield, 3 m. N of Welshpool. A490 (Llanfyllin) rd from Welshpool for 2 m; fork right for Guilsfield. 1½ acres; magnificent spring bulb display; unusual clematis & climbing roses; several gardens within a garden. Plant stall. TEAS. *Adm. 25p, Chd. 10p. Sun. April 20, Sat. & Sun. July 26 & 27 (2–6)*

Gliffaes Country House Hotel*⅃⊕ (Mr & Mrs Brabner) NW of Crickhowell. Station: Abergavenny, 8 m. Bus: Newport—Abergavenny—Brecon, alight Penmyarth. Large garden; shrubs; ornamental trees; fine maples; rhododendrons. Fine position high above R. Usk. TEAS. *Collecting box. April 1– Dec. 31 (all day)*

Gregynog* †⅃⊕ (University of Wales) Tregynon, 7 m. N of Newtown. A483 Welshpool—Newtown Rd, turn W at B4389 for Betws Cedewain, 1 m. through village gates on left. Large garden; fine banks, rhododendrons & azaleas; dell with specimen shrubs; formal garden; short nature trail starting from car park. Early C19 black & white house on site inhabited since C12. TEAS. *Adm. 25p, Chd. 10p. Sun. June 1 (2–7)*

¶**Llanstephan House** (The Hon. Hugo Philipps) Llyswen, 9 m. SE of Builth Wells. E from A479, approx. 2 m. NW of Llyswen, turn off E at Llanstephan Bridge, over R. Wye

& on for ½ m. 4-acre garden; shrubs, rhododendrons, azaleas; rhododendron-planted hill behind house; view of Wye Valley & Black Mountains. TEA & biscuits. *Adm. 30p, Chd. 10p. Sun. May 25 (2–7)*

Llysdinam*&⊕ (Lady Delia Venables-Llewelyn & Llysdinam Charitable Trust) Newbridge-on-Wye, SW of Llandrindod Wells. Turn W off A479 at Newbridge-on-Wye; turn right immediately after crossing R. Wye; entrance ¼ m. up hill. Medium-sized garden; azaleas, rhododendrons; fine view of Wye Valley. TEA & biscuits. *Adm. 30p, Chd. 10p. Sun. June 1 (2–7)*

Maenllwyd Isaf*&⊕ (Mrs Denise Hatchard) Abermule, 5 m. NE of Newtown & 10 m. S of Welshpool. On B4368 Albermule–Much Wenlock Rd, 1½ m. from Abermule. 3-acre garden with interesting shrubs, goldfish pool, aviary, a peacock, mallard ducks on a 'wild' pool (homemade), wood, & R. Mule. House built about 1580 & scheduled as of historical or architectural interest, farm buildings of same era being used as minuscule museum. Plant stall of home-grown plants. Raffles for wine & cake. TEAS. *Adm. 25p, Chd. 10p. Sun. June 15 (2–6.30); also by appt. all year (W.I.s especially welcome)* (*Tel. Abermule 204*)

¶**Old Rectory**⊕ (The Hon.Gwenllian Philipps) Boughrood, on B4350; 8 m. SW of Hay-on-Wye, 10 m. NE of Brecon. Turn off A470 in Llyswen between Bridge End pub & school; over bridge & straight through Boughrood village & 1st gate on right. 1-acre garden, owner-maintained, on banks of R. Wye; good views. *Adm. 20p, Chd. 5p. Sat. May 31 (11–7)*

Powis Castle Gardens*†&⊕ (The National Trust) Welshpool. Turn off A483 ¾ m. out of Welshpool & up Red Lane for ¼ m. Gardens were laid out in 1720 & have the most famous hanging terraces in the world, enormous yew hedges, lead statuary & a large wild garden. There will be a musical period in the Orangery or on the terrace outside at around 3 o'clock. Plant stall & raffles. TEAS. *Adm. castle & garden £1.10; garden only 70p; Chd. ½-price. Sun. Sept. 14 (2-6)*

Trawscoed Hall*&⊕ (Mr & Mrs J. G. K. Williams) 3 m. N of Welshpool. From Welshpool take the A490 towards Llanfyllin & continue for 3 m. Approx. 4 acres; fine trees, lovely view & interesting plants surrounding a Georgian house (not open). Granary dating from 1772. Plant stall. TEAS. *Adm. 25p, Chd. 10p. Sat. & Sun. June 7 & 8 (2–7)*

Tynewydd*&⊕ (Mr & Mrs R. W. Parr) Cwm Goleu, 6 m. W of Welshpool. From Welshpool via A458 towards Llanfair Caereinion & Dolgelly; garden lies off B4385 between Castle Caereinion & Llanfair Caereinion (telephone for instructions with appt.) Young

garden, approx. 3 acres; trees & shrubs inc. rhododendrons & magnolias; heathers & conifers; many uncommon plants. Autumn colour. Fine views. NO DOGS. *Collecting box. Garden open by appt. all year.* (*Tel. Llanfair Caereinion 724*)

Vaynor Park †& (Col. & Mrs Corbett-Winder) Berriew, 6 m. SW of Welshpool. A483 from Welshpool, turn W after 5 m. on to B4390 for Berriew; left in village; lodge ½ m. on right. Lovely village with black & white buildings. Medium-sized garden, entirely owner-maintained; rhododendrons, shrubs, fine trees, some planted by present owners; magnificent views. Plant stall. TEAS. *Adm. 25p, Chd. 10p. Mon. May 26 (11–6); also open all year by appt.* (*Tel. Berriew 204*)

SHROPSHIRE
(Salop)

Hon. County Organisers:
MRS P. TREVOR-JONES, Preen Manor,
  Church Preen, nr Church Stretton
MRS B. JENKINSON, Chetton Grange,
  Bridgnorth

DATES OF OPENING

APRIL Sunday 20
  ‡ATTINGHAM PARK, nr Shrewsbury
  ‡CRONKHILL, Cross Houses,
    nr Shrewsbury
MAY Thursday 1
  CHYKNELL, nr Bridgnorth
  RYTON GARDENS, nr Shifnal
MAY Monday 5
  PITCHFORD HALL, nr Shrewsbury
MAY Sunday 11
  GATACRE PARK, Six Ashes, nr Bridgnorth
  THE WOOD, Codsall Wood,
    nr Wolverhampton
MAY Saturday 17
  THE DAIRY HOUSE, Ludstone,
    Claverley, nr Wolverhampton
MAY Sunday 18
  GATACRE PARK, Six Ashes, nr Bridgnorth
  SWALLOW HAYES, Albrighton,
    nr Wolverhampton
MAY Sunday 25
  BROCKTON FARM, nr Much Wenlock
  BRONCROFT CASTLE, Craven Arms
  ‡GREAT NESS HOUSE, nr Shrewsbury
  LUDSTONE HALL, nr Claverley
  ‡OAK COTTAGE, Nesscliffe, nr Shrewsbury
  UPPER SHELDERTON HOUSE,
    Clungunford, nr Craven Arms
MAY Monday 26 (Spring Bank Hol.)
  ‡GREAT NESS HOUSE, nr Shrewsbury
  ‡OAK COTTAGE, Nesscliffe, nr Shrewsbury
JUNE Sunday 1
  BURWARTON HOUSE, nr Bridgnorth
  HATTON GRANGE, Shifnal
  PEPLOW HALL, Hodnet, nr Market
    Drayton

SWALLOW HAYES, Albrighton,
nr Wolverhampton
UPPER SHELDERTON HOUSE,
Clungunford, nr Craven Arms

JUNE Monday 2
HATTON GRANGE, Shifnal

JUNE Thursday 5
THE DAIRY HOUSE, Ludstone,
Claverley, nr Wolverhampton
RYTON GARDENS, nr Shifnal

JUNE Sunday 8
ADCOTE SCHOOL, Little Ness,
nr Shrewsbury

JUNE Saturday 14
BURFORD HOUSE GARDENS,
Tenbury Wells

JUNE Sunday 15
GLAZELEY GARDENS, nr Bridgnorth

JUNE Saturday 21
THE DAIRY HOUSE, Ludstone,
Claverley, nr Wolverhampton

JUNE Sunday 22
MILLICHOPE PARK, Munslow,
nr Craven Arms

JUNE Saturday 28
‡THE DOWER HOUSE, Great Ness,
nr Shrewsbury
‡THE GROVE, Kinton, Nesscliffe,
nr Shrewsbury

JUNE Sunday 29
DAVID AUSTIN ROSES, Albrighton
‡THE DOWER HOUSE, Great Ness,
nr Shrewsbury
GLAZELEY GARDENS, nr Bridgnorth
‡THE GROVE, Kinton, Nesscliffe,
nr Shrewsbury
LOWER HALL, Worfield, nr Bridgnorth
MAWLEY HALL, nr Cleobury Mortimer
MEADOW HOUSE, Oldbury, nr Bridgnorth
PLAISH GARDENS, nr Church Stretton

JULY Thursday 3
THE DAIRY HOUSE, Ludstone,
Claverley, nr Wolverhampton
RYTON GARDENS, nr Shifnal

JULY Sunday 6
DAVID AUSTIN ROSES, Albrighton
‡BECKBURY GARDENS, nr Shifnal
‡BECKBURY HALL, nr Shifnal
‡‡CORFTON GARDENS, nr Ludlow
‡‡THE OLD PARSONAGE, Munslow,
nr Craven Arms
RUDGE HALL, Pattingham,
nr Wolverhampton
THE WEIR HOUSE, Bucknell
WRENTNALL HOUSE, Pulverbatch

JULY Sunday 13
GLAZELEY GARDENS, nr Bridgnorth
GOLDING, Pitchford, nr Shrewsbury

JULY Saturday 19
THE DAIRY HOUSE, Ludstone,
Claverley, nr Wolverhampton

JULY Sunday 20
THE OLD VICARAGE, Cardington,
nr Church Stretton

WENLOCK ABBEY, Much Wenlock

JULY Sunday 27
LINLEY HALL, nr Bishops Castle

AUGUST Saturday 2
BURFORD HOUSE GARDENS,
Tenbury Wells

AUGUST Thursday 7
THE DAIRY HOUSE, Ludstone,
Claverley, nr Wolverhampton

AUGUST Sunday 10
DUDMASTON, nr Bridgnorth

AUGUST Saturday 16
THE DAIRY HOUSE, Ludstone,
Claverley, nr Wolverhampton

AUGUST Sunday 17
WILLOWBROOK, Roughton,
nr Bridgnorth

SEPTEMBER Thursday 4
THE DAIRY HOUSE, Ludstone,
Claverley, nr Wolverhampton

SEPTEMBER Saturday 6 & Sunday 7
MORVILLE HALL, nr Bridgnorth

SEPTEMBER Sunday 14
LIMEBURNERS, Ironbridge, Telford

SEPTEMBER Saturday 20
THE DAIRY HOUSE, Ludstone,
Claverley, nr Wolverhampton

SEPTEMBER Sunday 21
LIMEBURNERS, Ironbridge, Telford

DESCRIPTIONS OF GARDENS

¶**Adcote School**†⅃ (Adcote School Educational Trust Ltd) Little Ness; 8 m. NW of Shrewsbury. From Shrewsbury via A5 to Montford Bridge & then turn off NE following signs to Little Ness. 20 acres; fine trees inc. beeches, tulip trees, oaks (American & Evergreen); atlas cedars, Wellingtonia etc; rhododendrons & azaleas; small lake; landscaped garden. House (part shown) designed by Norman Shaw R.A.; Grade 1 listed building; William Morris windows; De Morgan tiles. NO DOGS. Cups of TEA. *Adm., inc. part house, 40p, Chd. 20p. Sun. June 8 (2–6)*

Attingham Park†⅃⊕ (The National Trust) 4 m. SE of Shrewsbury. Turn off A5 at Atcham. Bus: MR on A5 routes alight Atcham at gates of drive. Large garden; park, landscaped by Repton in 1797; deer park, long riverside walk with daffodils. Magnificent house designed in 1785 by George Steuart. TEAS. *Adm. to garden 30p, Chd. 15p; house 50p extra, Chd. 25p. △Sun. April 20 (2–6; house 2–5.30)*

Beckbury Gardens,⊕ 4 m. S of Shifnal. From A464 Wolverhampton–Shifnal turn off left at Whiston Cross & follow signs to Beckbury. From A424 Bridgnorth–Telford turn right at Norton & follow signs to Beckbury. Parking by kind permission of the Seven Stars in car park adjacent to Inn, opp. entrance to Higford Lane. Approx. 1 acre of private cottage gardens maintained entirely by owners; flowers, vegetables & old roses. NO DOGS. Teas by Beckbury & Ryton W.I. in Village Hall.

Combined charge 20p, Chd. free. Sun. July 6 (2–5.30)

1–4 Higford Lane (Mr & Mrs I. N. Bridge; Dr & Mrs P. Hutton; Mr & Mrs J. Meredith)

Beckbury Hall⊕ (Sir Humphrey Browne) 4 m. S of Shifnal. A464 Wolverhampton–Shifnal, turn left Whiston Cross, 1st right for Ryton, 1st left for Beckbury. Bus: Wolverhampton–Shifnal–Shrewsbury, alight Whiston Cross, 3 m. Simple garden; old roses. Teas by Beckbury & Ryton W.I. in Village Hall. *Adm. 30p, Chd. free. Sun. July 6 (2–5.30)*

Brockton Farm*⊕ (Mr & Mrs E. Geoffrey Jones) 5 m. SW of Much Wenlock. Situated in the Corvedale, close to Wenlock Edge. B4378 Much Wenlock–Craven Arms Rd at Brockton X-rds. Approx. 2 acres; designed & constructed by owners, with labour-saving shrub planting to show colour all year round; ornamental pool, with wild fowl, surrounding a Roman camp; small lily pond. House (not open) c. 1700, built from local limestone, with later additions. TEAS. *Adm. 25p, Chd. 10p. Sun. May 25 (2.30–6)*

Broncroft Castle†⊕ (Mr & Mrs C. T. C. Brinton) Craven Arms. 14 m. SW of Bridgnorth on Craven Arms Rd, B4368, turn left at Beambridge, then right. Large garden; herbaceous borders, waterside garden, many spring shrubs & trees. Picnics allowed. *Adm. 50p, Chd. 15p. Sun. May 25 (12–7)*

Burford House Gardens*†⚘⊕ (John Treasure Esq) 1 m. W of Tenbury Wells. 400 yds S of A456. Bus: CM Ludlow–Tenbury Wells. Medium-sized garden designed in 1954 by owner, in beautiful surroundings on R. Teme. Flowering shrubs, herbaceous plants, extensive lawns. Georgian house 1726 on site of former residence of Cornwall family. Ground floor of Burford House (no extra charge): Flower arrangements displayed on period furniture & complemented by other articles of fine art, completing horticultural theme of house & gardens. Fine church adjacent containing Cornwall monuments. Nursery gardens adjoining specialising in clematis & shrubs. NO DOGS. TEAS. *Adm. 70p, Chd. 40p. △Sat. June 14 & Sat. Aug. 2 (2–5)*

Burwarton House*⚘⊕ (The Viscount Boyne) Burwarton, 10 m. SW of Bridgnorth. Approx. 10 m. from both Bridgnorth & Ludlow on B4364. 35 acres; woodland garden with fine trees & specimen conifers; rhododendrons & azaleas in natural surroundings. Plants for sale. TEAS. *Adm. 30p, Chd. 10p. Sun. June 1 (2–6)*

Chyknell⊕ (W. S. R. Kenyon-Slaney Esq) 4 m. E of Bridgnorth. From A454 turn S at The Wheel, Worfield; from A458 turn N for Claverley. Bus: Wolverhampton–Bridgnorth, alight The Wheel, Worfield; garden 1½ m. Medium-sized garden; collection of lilacs &

other flowering shrubs; roses & clematis. TEA & biscuits. *Adm. 25p, Chd. 10p. Thurs. May 1 (2–6)*

Corfton Gardens⊕ 7 m. N of Ludlow. B4368, between Bridgnorth & Craven Arms, nr Diddlebury. From Much Wenlock take B4378 towards Craven Arms. The following 4 gardens will be open. Picknickers welcome at Lower House. *Collecting box at each garden. Sun. July 6 (2–7)*

    Lower House (Mr & Mrs N. Forbes) Small walled garden; swimming available; also ices & squash. DOGS on leads please

    Orchard Cottage (Miss G. M. Wheeler) Small cottage garden

    8 Lower Corfton (Mr & Mrs H. Davies) Attractive cottage garden

    ¶**5 Lower Corfton** (Mr & Mrs I. Davies) Attractive cottage garden

Cronkhill†⊕ (Mrs L. Motley; The National Trust) Cross Houses, 4 m. SE of Shrewsbury, ¾ m. from Atcham (on A5 Shrewsbury–Wellington) & ½ m. from Cross Houses (on A458 Shrewsbury–Much Wenlock). Small spring garden; extensive views of Shrewsbury countryside. Nash house (not open) Italianate style built 1802. TEA & biscuits. *Adm. 20p, Chd. free. Sun. April 20 (2–6)*

The Dairy House* (Miss N. E. Wood) Ludstone, nr Claverley, 7 m. W of Wolverhampton. S of A454. Bus: MR 890 Wolverhampton–Bridgnorth; alight Red Hill, ¾ m. 3-acre garden developed by owner on waterside setting of much natural beauty; heaths, woodland, flowering shrubs & roses, bulbs, lilies. Plants for sale if available. Picnics permitted (no tea at garden). *Adm. 25p, Chd. 10p. Sat. May 17, Thurs. & Sats. June 5, 21, July 3, 19, Aug. 7, 16, Sept. 4, 20 (2–5.30)*

David Austin Roses*⚘⊕ (Mr & Mrs David Austin) Bowling Green Lane, Albrighton, 8 m. NW of Wolverhampton. A464 Wolverhampton–Shifnal, 4 m. from Shifnal, turn at entrance to Bowling Green Lane marked 'David Austin Roses'. Large rose garden with over 500 different varieties; one of the most extensive collections of old roses, shrub roses, specie roses & climbing roses; rose breeding houses; new roses on trial; nursery rosefields. Also private garden with hardy plants, shrubs & sculpture. Roses for sale. TEAS. *Adm. 30p, Chd. free. Sun. June 29 & Sun. July 6 (2–7)*

The Dower House⊕ (Col. & Mrs J. M. Flint) Great Ness, 9 m. NW of Shrewsbury. From A5 Shrewsbury–Oswestry, 3½ m. N of Montford Bridge, turn right (E) at X-rds just before Nesscliffe. Small garden with roses, herbaceous borders, small lake & fine views; many new shrubs planted since 1970 when garden was re-made, partly walled. Attractive house (not open) early 1800s. TEAS. *Adm. 25p, Chd. 5p. Sat. & Sun. June 28 & 29 (2–6)*

Dudmaston★†⅃⊕ (Sir George & Lady Labouchere; The National Trust) 4 m. SE of Bridgnorth on A442. Bus stop at gates (½ m.). Large garden with fine trees, shrubs & lovely views over Dudmaston Pool & surrounding country. TEAS. *Adm. 30p, Chd. 15p. Sun. Aug. 10 (2–5.30)*

Gatacre Park★⅃⊕ (Sir Edward & Lady Thompson) Six Ashes, 6 m. SE of Bridgnorth on A458. Stourbridge–Bridgnorth Rd. 8 acres; flowering shrubs & fine trees, inc. magnolias, 80-ft tulip tree & manna ash; topiary walk; large woodland garden with pieris, azaleas & rhododendrons inc. many interesting species. Magnificent views over Park. Plants for sale. TEA & biscuits. *Adm. 30p, Chd. 5p. Sun. May 11 & Sun. May 18 (2–6)*

Glazeley Gardens★ (Mrs C. H. Taylor) 3½ m. S of Bridgnorth. On B4363 Bridgnorth–Cleobury Mortimer Rd. Medium-sized garden with nursery adjoining; largely herbaceous borders with a heather bed, cottage garden beds, shade garden, bulb bed, roses, shrubs, peonia, small scree bed, iris bed; moisture garden; about 600 different varieties of hardy plants; some shrubs of unusual interest. Very beautiful, natural setting. TEAS. *Adm. 30p, Chd. 20p. Suns. June 15, 29, July 13 (12–6)*

Golding† (Mr & Mrs H. A. Hartley) nr Pitchford, 7 m. S of Shrewsbury. From A458 turn off W for Cound & Acton Burnell. From A49 turn off E for Longnor & Acton Burnell. 1¼-acre garden; renaissance period terraced garden, rockery, shrubs, herbaceous plants & lilies; kitchen garden. Golding mentioned in Domesday Book. Manor house 1668 (not open) of early red brick with sandstone quoins. Cruck barn. NO DOGS. TEAS. *Adm. 35p, Chd. 20p. Sun. July 13 (2–6)*

Great Ness House†⅃⊕ (Mr & Mrs C. M. Livesey) 9 m. NW of Shrewsbury. From A5, 3½ m. N of Montford Bridge, turn right (E) at X-rds just before Nesscliffe. Medium-sized garden with scheduled cobbled courtyard; sandstone walls; orchard; famous Nesscliffe oaks. Tea Oak Cottage Herb Farm. *Adm. 25p, Chd. 10p. Sun. & Mon. May 25 & 26 (2–6)*

¶**The Grove**★⊕ (Mr & Mrs Philip Radcliffe Evans) Kinton, nr Nesscliffe; 10 m. NW of Shrewsbury; 10 m. SE of Oswestry. From A5, 1 m. N of Nesscliffe, turn off W at signpost to Kinton ¾ m; in village, opp. tithe barn, turn right; parking by barn. Medium-sized garden; informal mixed borders, largely shrubs & old-fashioned roses; permanent planting (no bedding out). Fine views to Breiddens. Attractive house (not open) c. 1800 on earlier base. NO DOGS. Plants for sale if available. Tea The Dower House, Great Ness. *Adm. 25p, Chd. 5p. Sat. June 28 (11–7); Sun. June 29 (2–6)*

Hatton Grange⅃⊕ (R. I. Kenyon-Slaney Esq) Shifnal. Lodge gate entrance on A464,

2 m. S of Shifnal. 1 m. up drive. Large dingle with pools, rhododendrons, azaleas & fine old trees. Plants for sale if available. TEAS. *Adm. 40p, Chd. 20p. Sun. June 1 & Mon. June 2 (2–7)*

Limeburners⊕ (Mr & Mrs J. E. Derry) Lincoln Hill, on outskirts of Ironbridge, Telford. Turn off B4380 at W edge of Ironbridge up Lincoln Hill; garden is nr top of hill on left-hand side, below The Beeches Hospital. 9½ acres; wild garden & light woodland, formerly site of a rubbish tip developed by owners as a Nature Garden to attract wild life & particularly butterflies and moths. Former limestone workings; fossils. NO DOGS. Tea shops in town. *Adm. 25p, Chd. 10p. Suns. Sept. 14 & 21 (2–6)*

Linley Hall⊕ (Sir Jasper & Lady More) 3 m. NE of Bishop's Castle. Turn E off A488 nr Lydham. Parkland; lawns, lake, temple, rose garden, herbaceous border. *Adm. 25p, Chd. 5p. Sun. July 27 (2–7)*

Lower Hall★ (Mr & Mrs C. F. Dumbell) Worfield, E of Bridgnorth, ½ m. N of A454 Wolverhampton–Bridgnorth, in centre of Worfield village. 4-acre garden on R. Worfe with stream & pool; shrub & woodland garden; walled garden of interest to new gardeners. Tudor half-timbered house (not open). TEAS. *Adm. 35p, Chd. 10p. Sun. June 29 (2–6)*

Ludstone Hall★†⅃⊕ (Mr & Mrs George Ferguson) Claverley, 7 m. W of Wolverhampton. S of A454. Bus: MR 890 Wolverhampton & Bridgnorth, alight Red Hill, ¾ m. Large garden; early Stuart house; moat & fishpond of several centuries earlier; Knott garden. Plants for sale. TEAS. *Adm. 25p, Chd. 10p. Sun. May 25 (2–6.30)*

Mawley Hall★†⅃ (Mr & Mrs Anthony Galliers-Pratt) 2 m. NE of Cleobury Mortimer. On A4117 Bewdley–Ludlow Rd. Bus: X 92, alight at gate. Medium-sized garden situated in beautiful country with magnificent views; newly created garden; fine trees; spring bulbs, herbs, roses, interesting flowering shrubs. TEA. *Adm. 30p, Chd. 10p. Sun. June 29 (2–6)*

Meadow House⊕ (Mr & Mrs R. Sidaway) Oldbury, 1 m. SW of Bridgnorth off Cleobury Mortimer Rd. 3-acre garden with shrubs, trees, vegetables, roses, clematis & general interest. Plants for sale. TEAS. *Adm. 25p, Chd. 10p. Sun. June 29 (11–6)*

Millichope Park⅃ (Mr & Mrs L. Bury) Munslow, 8 m. NE of Craven Arms. From Ludlow (11 m.) turn left off B4368, ¾ m. out of Munslow. Large garden; informal woodland lakeside garden with very fine specimen trees. TEAS. *Adm. 30p, Chd. 10p. Sun. June 22 (2–6)*

Morville Hall †⊕ (Miss A. P. Bythell: The National Trust) 3 m. W of Bridgnorth. A458

Bridgnorth–Shrewsbury; at fork with B4368 to Craven Arms & Ludlow. Bus: Bridgnorth–Shrewsbury, alight Morville, 200 yds. Medium-sized garden; roses & flowering shrubs; pool garden; yew avenues; Georgian house. TEA & biscuits on Sept. 6. TEAS (by Morville WI) on Sept. 7. Flower Festival in adjacent Morville Parish Church (in aid of Church Restoration Fund). *Adm. (inc. part-house) 30p, Chd. 15p. Sat. & Sun. Sept. 6 & 7. (2–6.30)*

¶**Oak Cottage Herb Farm** (Mrs Ruth Thompson) Nesscliffe, 7 m. NW of Shrewsbury A5. Entrance 100 yds down lane opp. Nesscliffe Hotel. Car park in farmyard opp. white cottage. Cottage garden ($\frac{1}{3}$ acre) based on herbs & old cottage garden plants & scented geraniums. Nursery with plants for sale. NO DOGS. TEAS. *Adm. 25p, Chd. 5p. Sun. & Mon. May 25 & 26 (2–6)*

The Old Parsonage*† (Mrs Ann F. Porges) Munslow, Craven Arms. 10 m. from Ludlow; 12 m. from Bridgnorth. B4368, turn at War Memorial in Munslow & on $\frac{1}{4}$ m. to Church & Parsonage. 2-acre garden; roses, azaleas, flowering shrubs, herbaceous border, large pool. Adjacent to house is St Michael's church, of historical & architectural interest. TEAS. *Adm. 25p, Chd. 10p. Sun. July 6 (2–7); visitors welcome to come other days (always an answer at the house)*

The Old Vicarage&⊕ (Mr & Mrs W. B. Hutchinson) Cardington, 6 m. NE of Church Stretton. 3 m. N of B4371 Church Stretton–Much Wenlock Rd, signposted. $2\frac{1}{2}$-acre garden re-designed for easy maintenance; trees, shrubs, roses, heathers, primulas, alpines, water & wild garden. TEAS. *Adm. 30p, Chd. 5p. Sun. July 20 (2–6)*

Peplow Hall*&⊕ (Hon. R. V. Wynn) 3 m. S of Hodnet via A442; turn off E. Large garden with lawns, azaleas, rhododendrons, etc.; roses & bedding out; walled kitchen garden; lake. TEAS. *Adm. 50p, Chd. 10p. Sun. June 1 (10–5)*

¶**Pitchford Hall†**⊕ (Mr & Mrs Oliver Colt-hurst) $6\frac{1}{2}$ m.S of Shrewsbury. A5/A449 junction (roundabout) signposted to Pitchford & Acton Burnell. 4 acres; $\frac{1}{2}$-timbered treehouse in lime tree built *c.* 1700. Queen Victoria stayed here in 1832 (aged 13). St Michael's Church. Natural bitumen well. *Adm. 30p, OAPs & Chd. 10p. Mon. May 5 (2–5)*

Plaish Gardens, 6 m. NE of Church Stretton 3 m. N of B4371 Church Stretton–Much Wenlock Rd. TEAS. *Combined charge for following 2 gardens 30p, Chd. 5p. Sun. June 29 (2–6)*

  Plaish Cottage (Mr & Mrs M. C. Vaughan) Shrub & tree garden with fine views; pool & woodland walk (necessary to wear wellingtons); planted courtyard surrounded by C17 stone house

Garden Cottage (Mr & Mrs J. S. Senior) Intimate cottage garden with pool, fruit, vegetables & bog garden

Rudge Hall⊕ (Mr & Mrs Alan Henn) Pattingham, 7 m. W of Wolverhampton. Between A464 & A454. Bus: WM 16 Wolverhampton–Pattingham, 1 m. Medium-sized garden; 2 small formal gardens. TEAS. *Adm. 25p, Chd. 10p. Sun. July 6 (2–7)*

Ryton Gardens, 4 m. S of Shifnal. A464 Wolverhampton–Shifnal; turn off left (S) at Whiston Cross; then 1st right, signed Beck-bury & Ryton; continue straight on (passing turn for Beckbury) to Ryton. Bus: Wolver-hampton–Shifnal–Shrewsbury (Midland Red); alight at Whiston Cross, $2\frac{1}{2}$ m. *Combined charge for following 2 gardens 35p, Chd. 10p. Thurs. May 1, June 5, July 3 (2–7)*

¶**Ryton House**⊕ (Mr & Mrs P. E. J. White) Simple garden, $1\frac{1}{4}$ acres, mainly roses

¶**Ryton Grove**⊕ (Dr & Mrs W. S. A. Allan) 6-acre garden; shrubs, rock garden, vegetable garden, woodland

Swallow Hayes*⊕ (Mr & Mrs Michael Edwards) Rectory Rd, Albrighton, 7 m. NW of Wolverhampton. At Albrighton on A41 turn off into Rectory Rd (garden $\frac{1}{2}$ m. from Albrighton). $1\frac{1}{2}$-acre garden planted since 1968 with emphasis on all-the-year interest & colour & ease of maintenance; wide range of shrub varieties. TEAS. *Adm. 25p, Chd. 10p. Sun. May 18 & Sun. June 1 (2–6)*

Upper Shelderton House*⊕ (Mr & Mrs G. Rollason) Clungunford, 3 m. SW of Craven Arms. From A49 turn W at Craven Arms, or at Bromfield, signposted. From Clungunford, on B4367, turn E. Medium-sized garden; large collection of species & woodland rhododendrons, azaleas, rare trees & shrubs, bedding out; landscaped lake. Beautiful views. TEAS. *Adm. 25p, Chd. 10p. Suns. May 25 & June 1 (2–7)*

The Weir House (Mrs P. G. Eccles) Bucknell, 14 m. W of Ludlow, N of A4113, nr junction with B4367. Small garden; mixed shrub & herbaceous borders; topiary. NO DOGS. TEA & biscuits. *Adm. 30p, Chd. 10p. Sun. July 6 (2–6)*

Wenlock Abbey†⊕ (C. S. Motley Esq) Much Wenlock. Bus: MR 963 Bridgnorth–Shrewsbury, alight Much Wenlock, 200 yds. Medium-sized garden. Great historic interest. Ruins of Cluniac monastery; walled rose garden. Tea Malthouse Cafe, Much Wenlock. *Adm. 30p, Chd. 15p. Sun. July 20 (2–6)*

Willowbrook (Mr & Mrs H. J. Marshall) Roughton, 3 m. E of Bridgnorth. From Bridgnorth via A454 & fork right at signpost Roughton & Barnsley. From Wolverhampton via A454 for 10 m., then fork left, $\frac{1}{2}$ m. beyond Wheel Inn, Worfield. Bus: MR 889 Wolver-hampton–Bridgnorth. Medium-sized attractive garden with natural pool, herbaceous border &

well-established flowering shrubs & trees; mature well-stocked vegetable & soft fruit garden. TEA & biscuits. *Adm. 30p, Chd. 10p. Sun. Aug. 17 (2–6.30).*

The Wood (Maj. & Mrs F. J. Yates) Codsall Wood, 9 m. NW of Wolverhampton. 2 m. E of Albrighton on A41. From A5 turn off S at Bradford Arms Hotel. Bus: Wolverhampton–Albrighton. Medium-sized garden; rose garden; herbaceous border & yew hedges. NO DOGS. *Adm. 25p, Chd. 10p. Sun. May 11 (2–6.30)*

Wrentnall House⊕ (Cdr Michael Holcroft) Pulverbatch, 8 m. SW of Shrewsbury. From Shrewsbury By-pass turn left at roundabout 'Longden Road'; through Longden about 8 m. from roundabout turn right at Wrentnall. Bus: MR Shrewsbury–Pulverbatch, alight 200 yds from house. 1 acre of nice herbaceous borders, interesting collection of plants & shrubs; beautiful view. TEA & biscuits. *Adm. 20p, Chd. 10p. Sun. July 6 (2–6)*

SOMERSET & SOUTH AVON

Hon. County Organisers:
MRS PAUL HOBHOUSE, Hadspen House, Castle Cary
MRS PATRICK TAYLOR, West Compton House, nr Shepton Mallet

Asst. Hon. County Organisers:
MISS P. DAVIES-GILBERT, Coombe Quay, West Monkton, Taunton
COUNTESS CHARLES DE SALIS, Yarlington House, Wincanton
MRS CHARLES MARROW, Kingsdon, Somerton

Hon. Treasurer:
MRS BASIL NICHOLSON, Boxbushe Farm, Batcombe

DATES OF OPENING

JANUARY to DECEMBER every Tuesday & Thursday
HADSPEN HOUSE, Castle Cary
MARCH from March 23 daily except Saturdays
CLAPTON COURT, nr Crewkerne
APRIL daily except Saturdays
CLAPTON COURT, nr Crewkerne
APRIL every Tuesday, Thursday & Sunday
HADSPEN HOUSE, Castle Cary
APRIL Easter Sunday 6
SAMPFORD ARUNDEL GARDENS, nr Wellington
WOOTTON HOUSE, Butleigh Wootton, nr Glastonbury
APRIL Saturday 12
BARLEY WOOD, Wrington

APRIL Sunday 13
FAIRFIELD HOUSE, Stogursey, nr Bridgwater
APRIL from April 20 every Tuesday, Thursday & Sunday
WEATHERHAM, Brompton Regis, Dulverton
APRIL Sunday 20
PARISH'S HOUSE, Timsbury, nr Bath
SAMPFORD ARUNDEL GARDENS, nr Wellington
APRIL Sunday 27
WAYFORD MANOR, nr Crewkerne
MAY daily except Saturdays
CLAPTON COURT, nr Crewkerne
MAY daily except Thursdays & Fridays
BRYMPTON d'EVERCY, Yeovil
MAY every Tuesday, Thursday & Sunday
HADSPEN HOUSE, Castle Cary
WEATHERHAM, Brompton Regis, Dulverton
MAY Sunday 4
CROWE HALL, Widcombe, nr Bath
SAMPFORD ARUNDEL GARDENS, nr Wellington
MAY Saturday 10
STOWELL HILL, Templecombe, nr Sherborne
MAY Sunday 11
GREENCOMBE, Porlock, nr Minehead
RAYNE THATCH, Leigh Woods, nr Bristol
STOWELL HILL, Templecombe, nr Sherborne
MAY Sunday 18
BARRINGTON COURT, nr Ilminster
BRACKENWOOD NURSERIES, Portishead
INWOOD, Hewstridge, Templecombe
SOMERSET COLLEGE OF AGRICULTURE & HORTICULTURE, Cannington, nr Bridgwater
MAY Saturday 24
STOWELL HILL, Templecombe, nr Sherborne
MAY Sunday 25
COURT HOUSE, East Quantoxhead
STOWELL HILL, Templecombe, nr Sherborne
WAYFORD MANOR, nr Crewkerne
WEACOMBE HOUSE, West Quantoxhead
JUNE daily except Saturdays
CLAPTON COURT, nr Crewkerne
JUNE daily except Thursdays & Fridays
BRYMPTON d'EVERCY, Yeovil
JUNE every Tuesday, Thursday & Sunday
HADSPEN HOUSE, Castle Cary
WEATHERHAM, Brompton Regis, nr Dulverton
JUNE Sunday 1
MILTON LODGE, Wells
JUNE Sunday 8
ORCHARDLEIGH PARK, nr Frome
WESTHOLME HOUSE, Pilton, nr Shepton Mallet

JUNE Sunday 15
  MILTON LODGE, Wells
  ORCHARD HOUSE, Claverton, Bath
JUNE Sunday 22
  GAULDEN MANOR, Tolland, nr Taunton
JUNE Saturday 28
  BARLEY WOOD, Wrington
  MIDELNEY MANOR, Drayton, nr Langport
JUNE Sunday 29
  THE BABYCHAM GARDENS, Shepton
    Mallet
  ‡BRATTON FARM HOUSE, Bratton
    Seymour, nr Wincanton
  CROWE HALL, Widcombe, nr Bath
  LITTLE NORTON MILL NURSERY,
    Norton sub Hamdon, nr Crewkerne
  ‡YARLINGTON HOUSE, nr Wincanton
JULY daily except Saturdays
  CLAPTON COURT, nr Crewkerne
JULY daily except Thursdays & Fridays
  BRYMPTON d'EVERCY, Yeovil
JULY every Tuesday, Thursday & Sunday
  HADSPEN HOUSE, Castle Cary
  WEATHERHAM, Brompton Regis,
    Dulverton
JULY Sunday 6
  BARROW COURT, Galhampton, nr Yeovil
  MILTON LODGE, Wells
  STAPLETON MANOR, Martock
JULY Sunday 13
  UNIVERSITY OF BRISTOL BOTANIC
    GARDEN, Leigh Woods, Bristol
JULY Sunday 20
  COMPTON CASTLE, Compton Pauncefoot,
    nr Yeovil
JULY Sunday 27
  BARRINGTON COURT, nr Ilminster
  TINTINHULL HOUSE, nr Yeovil
AUGUST daily except Saturdays
  CLAPTON COURT, nr Crewkerne
AUGUST daily except Thursdays & Fridays
  BRYMPTON d'EVERCY, Yeovil
AUGUST every Tuesday, Thursday & Sunday
  HADSPEN HOUSE, Castle Cary
  WEATHERHAM, Brompton Regis,
    nr Dulverton
AUGUST Sunday 24
  STAPLETON MANOR, Martock
  TINTINHULL HOUSE, nr Yeovil
SEPTEMBER daily except Saturdays
  CLAPTON COURT, nr Crewkerne
SEPTEMBER daily except Thursdays & Fridays, to September 24
  BRYMPTON d'EVERCY, Yeovil
SEPTEMBER every Tuesday, Thursday & Sunday
  HADSPEN House, Castle Cary
  WEATHERHAM, Brompton Regis,
    nr Dulverton
SEPTEMBER Sunday 7
  THE PILTON MANOR VINEYARD,
    Pilton, nr Shepton Mallet

OCTOBER daily except Saturdays, to October 19
  CLAPTON COURT, nr Crewkerne
OCTOBER every Tuesday, Thursday & Sunday
  HADSPEN HOUSE, Castle Cary
  WEATHERHAM, Brompton Regis,
    nr Dulverton (to Oct. 19 only)
NOVEMBER & DECEMBER every Tuesday & Thursday
  HADSPEN HOUSE, Castle Cary

DESCRIPTIONS OF GARDENS

The Babycham Gardens (Showerings Ltd) Kilver St, Shepton Mallet. Very fine rock garden, waterfalls, lake, shrubs & roses. TEAS. *Adm. 40p, Chd. 10p. Sun. June 29 (2–6)*

¶**Barley Wood**†⚹ (H.A.T. Group Limited) Wrington, 10 m. SW of Bristol. From Bristol take A38 (S); go past Lulsgate Airport & on approx. 1 m. to Redhill; at top of Redhill follow sign to Wrington; continue for 1½ m. & garden is on right. 600 acres; magnificent displays of wild spring bulbs, terraced gardens, yew hedges, walled gardens, greenhouses & immaculately kept large vegetable gardens & orchards surrounded by well-maintained farms, woodland & parks. House at one time home of Hannah More. Magnificent view of Wrington Vale & Mendips. NO DOGS. *Adm. 50p, Chd. under 12, free. Sat. April 12 & Sat. June 28 (2–6)*

Barrington Court⋆†⊕ (A. I. A. Lyle Esq); The National Trust—see p. ix) NE of Ilminster. Lily, iris & rose gardens. Wall shrubs & borders. Regret NO DOGS. *Adm. Garden 30p. House 30p △ Sun. May 18 & Sun. July 27 (2–6)*

¶**Barrow Court**⚹⊕ (Mr & Mrs Richard Longman) Galhampton, 3½ m. SW of Castle Cary, 3 m. N from Sparkford (A303) towards Castle Cary. 2-acre garden; lawns & flower borders; sunken garden with numerous bedding plants; variety of shrubs. NO DOGS. TEA & biscuits. *Adm. 30p, Chd. 10p. Sun. July 6 (2–6)*

Brackenwood Nurseries⋆⚹ (John Maycock Esq) 131 Nore Rd, Portishead. Motorway over Avon Bridge at Bristol; leave at Portbury—Gordano interchange; take A369 to Portishead (2 m.); Nore Rd is coast road to Clevedon. 4-acres of woodland garden on steeply sloping site overlooking Bristol Channel; rhododendrons, azaleas, pieris, embothriums etc. Waterfowl enclosure; ornamental water lily pools situated at rear of Brackenwood Nurseries. Ornamental Ducks, Pheasants, Parrakeets. NO DOGS. *Adm. 20p, Chd. 10p. Sun. May 18 (10–5)*

Bratton Farm House (Mr & Mrs A. J. Brock) Bratton Seymour 3 m. N of Wincanton. A371 Wincanton–Castle Cary; turn right

SOMERSET & SOUTH AVON—continued

signposted Bratton Seymour; after ¼ m. on right grey stone wall with cattle grid. 2-acres; small enclosed garden with various features; interesting plants. NO DOGS. Tea Yarlington House. *Adm. 20p, Chd. 10p. Sun. June 29 (2–7)*

● **Brympton d'Evercy**†⊕ (Charles E. B. Clive-Ponsonby-Fane Esq) 2 m. W of Yeovil. Via A3088 (Montacute Rd) & follow signs. 10-acres; up to 1976 these once-famous gardens were on the slippery slope to oblivion; since then & virtually single-handed Judy Clive-Ponsonby-Fane has started to recreate some of their former glory. The 10 acres inc. daisy; potpourri; herbaceous & shrub beds; extensive lawns; vineyard. Parish church nearby. NO DOGS. Cream TEAS. Free parking. *Adm. charges not available at time of going to press. May 3–Sept. 30 daily except Thurs. & Fris. (2–6)*

● **Clapton Court**★♿⊕ (Capt. S. J. Loder) 3 m. S of Crewkerne on B3165. 9 acres; one of Somerset's most beautiful gardens; fine collection of rare & unusual trees & shrubs of botanical interest in formal & woodland settings; outstanding display of spring bulbs; park-like surroundings with many fine mature trees. Unusual shrubs, alpines & ferns for sale all year daily (except Sats.). NO DOGS. Coaches welcome. Parties weekdays & meals available by arrangement (Tel. Crewkerne 73220 or 72200). Home-made cream TEAS (Suns. & Bank Hols.). *Adm. 50p, Chd. 25p. March 23–Oct. 19 daily except Sats. (2–5)*

¶**Compton Castle**♿⊕ (Mrs A. A. Showering) Compton Pauncefoot, 5 m. W of Wincanton. 1 m. S of A303 between Wincanton & Sparkford. 30 acres; picturesque landscaped garden with lawns, trees & lakes. NO DOGS. TEAS. *Adm. 75p, Chd. free. Sun. July 20 (2–7)*

Court House (Col. & Mrs Walter Luttrell) East Quantoxhead, 12 m. W of Bridgwater. A39 signposted East Quantoxhead; on right from Bridgwater House at end of village past duck pond. 3-acre garden; shrubs, roses; some herbaceous. Views to sea & Quantocks. Tudor House (not open). *Adm. 40p, Chd. 10p. Sun. May 25 (2–6)*

Crowe Hall♿⊕ (John Barratt Esq) Widcombe, 1 m. SE of Bath. Turn left up Widcombe Hill, off A4, leaving White Hart pub on right. Large garden of variety; fine trees, lawns, many spring bulbs, walled gardens etc; on steep hillside with Italianate terracing & Victorian grotto; summer: old-fashioned roses & shrubs; display of flowers in tubs & hanging baskets a speciality. *Adm. 40p, Chd. 20p. Sun. May 4 & Sun. June 29 (2–6)*

Fairfield House★†♿⊕ (Sir Michael & Lady Gass) Stogursey, 11 m. NW of Bridgwater. From A39 Bridgwater–Minehead, turn off N; garden approx. 1 m. W of Stogursey. Woodland garden with bulbs & shrubs. Elizabethan house (not open). DOGS if on leads. TEA & biscuits. *Adm. 40p. Sun. April 13 (2–6)*

Gaulden Manor⊕ (J. H. N. Starkie Esq) Tolland, nr Lydeard St Lawrence, 9 m. NW of Taunton. A358, Taunton–Minehead, just N of Bishop's Lydeard turn off W, signposted Tolland (4 m.). Medium-sized garden with bog plants, primulas & herb garden. Plants for sale. NO DOGS. TEAS. *Adm. to garden 30p. △Sun. June 22 (2–6)*

Greencombe★♿⊕ (Miss Joan Loraine) ½ m. W of Porlock, off road to Porlock Weir. Woodland garden overlooking Porlock Bay; camellias, rhododendrons, azaleas & peat-loving shrubs. NO DOGS. *Adm. 50p, Chd. 25p. Sun. May 11 (2–7)*

● **Hadspen House**★ (Mr & Mrs Paul Hob-House & Trustees of the late Sir Arthur Hobhouse) 2 m. SE of Castle Cary on A371 to Wincanton. 6-acre Edwardian garden with C18 background & house (not open); sheltered, S-facing, on neutral soil with some mature trees; but mainly new planting of trees for bark & foliage interest; shrubs, shrub roses & tender wall plants. Shrubs & unusual plants for sale. Regret NO DOGS. Tea George Hotel, Castle Cary. *Adm. 40p, Chd. 20p. All year every Tues. & Thurs. (10–5); also Suns. April 1 to Oct. 30 (2–5); also by appt. (Tel. Castle Cary 50200)*

¶**Inwood**♿⊕ (Count & Countess Guy de Pelet) Henstridge, 7 m. E of Sherborne. On A30 before Henstrige X-rds (coming from Shaftesbury); iron gates on left. 7 acres with beautiful trees & extensive lawns; gazebos bulbs, cherry trees, lilac, shrubbery, woodland, statuary. Peacocks. TEAS. *Adm. 25p, Chd. 10p. Sun. May 18 (2–6)*

Little Norton Mill Nursery (Mr & Mrs J. McClintock) Norton sub Hamdon, 4½ m. NE of Crewkerne. Village just E of junction of B3165 with A3088 & A303. From Yeovil take A3088 through Montacute & W of Stoke turn left for Norton sub Hamdon. Medium-sized garden developed during last 10 yrs; includes old mill pond & variety of interesting shrubs & plants. Plants for sale. *Adm. 20p, Chd. 10p. Sun. June 29 (2–7)*

Midelney Manor†⊕ (Maj. R. Cely Trevilian) Drayton, 3 m. SW of Langport. Signposted on A376 Langport–Taunton by Bell Hotel, Curry Rivel. 3 acres; wall gardens, rose garden, wild garden. House, Elizabethan & Queen Anne, part shown. Heronry & falcons mews. (*Share to British Red Cross*) NO DOGS. House not suitable for wheelchairs. TEAS. *Adm., house & garden, 75p, Chd. 30p. Sat. June 28 (2–5.30)*

Milton Lodge★♿ (D. C. Tudway Quilter Esq) ½ m. N of Wells. From A39 Bristol–Wells, turn

N up Old Bristol Rd; car park first gate on left. Bus: B376 Bristol–Wells, alight Wells (Old Bristol Rd). Medium-sized mature terraced garden; arboretum. Outstanding views of Cathedral & Vale of Avalon. (*Share to Wells Cathedral Preservation Trust*) Tea Wells, ½ m. *Adm. 40p, Chd. 20p. Suns. June 1, 15, July 6 (2–7)*

Orchard House★ (Rear Adm. & Mrs Hugh Tracy) Claverton, 3½ m. from centre of Bath on A36; turn off at signpost to Claverton Village. Or ½ m. down hill from American Museum, Claverton. Bus stop Claverton. 2½-acres; plantsman's garden in which owners have tried to combine botanical interest with attractive & informal layout; collections of herbs, alpines, ground-cover & silver plants; rock gardens, herbaceous borders, lawns, shrubs, views. Hand list of shrubs supplements labelling. Plants for sale. Small (wholesale) Nursery. Regret NO DOGS. TEA & biscuits, soft drinks. *Adm. 30p, Chd. 10p. Sun. June 15 (2–6)*

Orchardleigh Park†♿⊕ (Arthur Duckworth Esq) 3 m. N of Frome. A362 Frome–Radstock; Lodge gates on main road. A36 Frome–Bath turning at Woolverton. Bus: Frome–Bath, alight Oldford. Beautiful terraced gardens & C18 stonework surrounding Victorian mansion; views over park & lake; old walled kitchen garden. Plants for sale. C13 island church at head of lake; fine stained glass. Tea Frome. *Adm. 30p, Chd. 10p. Sun. June 8 (2–6.30)*

Parish's House⊕ (B. G. S. Cayzer Esq) Timsbury, SW of Bath. Bus: B 179, 367 to Timsbury, alight in village. Medium-sized garden. *Adm. 20p. Sun. April 20 (11–7)*

The Pilton Manor Vineyard★†♿⊕ (Nigel de Marsac Godden Esq) The Manor House, Pilton, 2½ m. SW of Shepton Mallet. On A361 Shepton Mallet–Glastonbury Rd; Manor nr Pilton Church. From A37 Fosseway turn W for Pilton. Vineyard & winery; wine on sale. Manor house & original vineyard date back to 1235. Small garden; grounds with stream, Inc. weir & waterfall & very large chestnuts; avenue of fine lime trees. Historical & rare square-built dovecote. For wheelchairs, vineyard only suitable. Light snack lunch available in wine bar & garden (12–2 only). Vineyard shop. English Mustard, herbs, etc. TEAS. *Adm. 50p, Chd. 25p. Sun. Sept. 7 (12–6)*

Rayne Thatch (Mr & Mrs A. Thompson) North Rd, Leigh Woods, 2½ m. W of centre of Bristol. From Clifton–Bristol cross Clifton suspension bridge; turn 1st right; garden 400 yds on right opp. Bristol University Botanic Gardens. 1¼-acre woodland garden on edge of Leigh Woods (Nat. Trust) with landscaped pools & rocks. (*Share to St Peter's Hospice*) NO DOGS. Tea Bristol. *Adm. 25p, Chd. 10p. Sun. May 11 (2–7)*

Sampford Arundel Gardens. 3 m. W of Wellington. M5 junction 26. From A38, 2 m. W of Wellington, turn off S at Beam Bridge Hotel signposted White Ball & follow signs to Marlands. The following 2 gardens will be open. (*Share to Sampford Arundel Parish Rooms Improvement Fund*) TEA & biscuits (at Broadleigh on April 6 & May 4; at Marlands on April 20). *Combined charge for 2 gardens 50p, Chd. under 14 free. Suns. April 6, 20, May 4 (2–6)*

Marlands★♿⊕ (Mr & Mrs Peter Etherton) 11½ acres; streams and small lake; small waterwheel; thousands of bulbs; azaleas and rhododendrons; woodland walks; about 40 beds being progressively restored. Adventure playground for small children under construction (use at parents' risk)

Broadleigh Court★♿ (Mr & Mrs R. D. Kathro) 4-acre garden; spring bulbs, rockery, rhododendrons, azaleas, flowering shrubs. NO DOGS

Somerset College of Agriculture & Horticulture★†⊕ Cannington, 3 m. NW of Bridgwater. On A39 Bridgwater–Minehead Rd. Bus: 215, alight at entrance. Old College: Benedictine Priory 1138; fine Elizabethan W front; 7 old sandstone walled gardens protect wide range of plants, inc. many less hardy subjects, ceanothus, fremontias, wistarias, etc; 10 very large greenhouses recently built containing exceptionally wide range of ornamental plants, also bananas, oranges, sugar, tea, pawpaws, passion fruit, etc. New College (built 1970): magnificent views to Quantocks; tree & shrub collections; ground-cover plantings; rose garden, spring bedding in formal garden; lawn grass collection & trials; horticultural science garden; one of the largest collections of ornamental plants in SW England, planted for landscape effect & arranged for ease of identification (most labelled). Tea Ye Old Willow Tree, nr entrance. *Adm. for both college grounds 40p, Chd. 20p (organized parties of O.A.P.s 10p if arranged in advance). Sun. May 18 (2–6)*

Stapleton Manor†♿⊕ (Mr & Mrs G. E. L. Sant) Martock. 6 m. NW of Yeovil. From A303, approx. 4 m. SW of Ilchester, turn W through Ash to Stapleton Cross; at Stapleton Cross turn right; garden ¼ m. along on right. Bus: WN 472 Yeovil–Martock; alight Stapleton Cross, ¼ m. 1½-acre garden surrounding Georgian Hamstone house (not open) scheduled as of historic interest; lily pond; roses; shrubs; herbaceous borders. Tea Spinning Wheel, Martock. *Adm. 20p, Chd. free. Sun. July 6 & Sun. Aug. 24 (11–7)*

Stowell Hill (Lady McCreery) Templecombe, NE of Sherborne. Turn at Stowell, ½ m. from Templecombe on A357. Bus: WN 468 Yeovil–Gillingham (not Suns.); alight Royal Hotel, Templecombe. Spring bulbs. Collection of flowering shrubs, inc. rhododendrons, azaleas,

SOMERSET & SOUTH AVON—
continued

magnolias, Japanese cherries. *Adm. 25p, Chd. 5p. Sats. & Suns. May 10 & 11, 24 & 25 (Sats. 11–7; Suns. 2–7)*

Tintinhull House*⊕ (Miss M. Ware; The National Trust—see p. ix) NW of Yeovil. ½ m. S of A303, W of Ilchester, National Trust signposts. Semi-formal garden with mixed shrub & herbaceous borders & pool garden. House (not shown) C17 & C18. NO DOGS. *Adm. 40p. △Sun. July 27 & Sun. Aug. 24 (2–6)*

University of Bristol Botanic Garden*⊕ Bracken Hill, North Rd, Leigh Woods, 2 m. W of Bristol. From Bristol via Clifton; after crossing the suspension bridge North Rd is first turn to right. 5-acre garden with about 3,000 species grown to display the diversity of the plant kingdom; special collections of hebe, cistus, salvia, sempervivum, etc., & many British plants are grown; 5,000 sq. ft. of glass & large rock garden. Plants for sale. NO DOGS. *Adm. 25p, Sun. July 13 (2–6)*

Wayford Manor*⚲ (Robin L. Goffe Esq) SW of Crewkerne. Turning on B3165 at Clapton; or on A30 between Chard & Crewkerne. 3-acre garden, noted for magnolias & acers. Bulbs; flowering trees & shrubs; rhododendrons. Beautiful views. Fine Elizabethan manor house dating from C13 (not shown). Plants for sale. TEAS. *Adm. 30p Chd. 10p. Sun. April 27 & Sun. May 25 (2–6)*

Weacombe House⚲ (Mr & Mrs A. J. Greswell) West Quantoxhead, E of Williton. Bus: 218 Taunton–Minehead, alight Woolston Moor, ½ m; 215 from Bridgewater, alight St Audries, ½ m. Medium-sized garden; shrubs, mainly rhododendrons & azaleas; lake & lawns. (*Share to Dodington Parish Church*) Children's playground. Plant stall & cake stall. TEAS. *Adm. 40p, Chd. 20p. Sun. May 25 (2–7)*

Weatherham*† (Mr & Mrs T. Sutcliffe) Brompton Regis, 4½ m. N of Dulverton. From A396 take secondary rd signposted Brompton Regis (turning by larch trees opp. turning into B3222); keep left at fork by large beech tree (2 m. from turn off); Weatherham is 2nd farm on left (ring for directions if in doubt). 4-acres under development; typical cottage garden around traditional Somerset Farm House & buildings; hardy & old-fashioned plants, primulas, woodland garden, pond, moorland views; much to interest those planning a garden as this one has been made since 1975 & is still being developed & enlarged. (*Share to Kew Guild*) Small nursery (Tel Brompton Regis 253); variety of plants for sale. DOGS on leads. *Collecting box. April 20–Oct. 19 every Tues. Thurs. & Sun. (2–5.30)*

Westholme House⚲⊕ (Brig. & Mrs N. S. E. Maude) Pilton, SE of Wells. From E via A361

Glastonbury–Pilton downhill through village to sharp corner & turn off right (keeping Pilton Stores on right) signposted North Wootton & Wells; up narrow rd out of village for ¼ m. & straight on at small X-rds, follow wall to house, on left over cattle grid. Large garden; fine Georgian house (not open) of Bath stone in unique setting with terraced garden overlooking lake, woodland & park with outstanding views to Glastonbury Tor. TEAS. *Adm. 30p, Chd. 10p. Sun. June 8 (2–6)*

Wootton House*†⚲⊕ (The Hon. Mrs John Acland-Hood) Butleigh Wootton, 3 m. S of Glastonbury. Herbaceous borders; rose garden; shrubs, trees, bulbs; rock garden; woodland garden. C17 house (not open). (*Share to S.S.A.F.A. (Wells & Glastonbury Branch)*). TEA & biscuits. *Adm. 40p, Sun. April 6 (2–6)*

Yarlington House⊕ (Countess Charles de Salis) 3½ m. from both Wincanton & Castle Cary; signposted Yarlington off A303 between Wincanton & Sparkford. Signposted Sherborne, Milborneport & Yarlington off A371 between Wincanton & Castle Cary. New garden being developed; pleached limes, statuary, rose garden, walled garden, recently planted laburnum walk; woods. C18 house (not open) & park. Use of swimming pool 20p extra. (*Share to Home Farm Trust for Mentally Handicapped*) NO DOGS. TEAS. *Adm. 20p, Chd. 10p. Sun. June 29 (2–7)*

STAFFORDSHIRE & part of WEST MIDLANDS

Hon. County Organiser:
MRS R. MARTIN, The Field, The Wergs, nr Wolverhampton

DATES OF OPENING

ALL YEAR daily (except December 25)
TRENTHAM GARDENS, nr Stoke-on-Trent
ALL YEAR every Thursday, Friday, Saturday & Sunday
IZAAK WALTON COTTAGE, Yarnfield, nr Stafford
Mid-MARCH to Mid-OCTOBER daily except Mondays (but open Bank Hols.)
SHUGBOROUGH, nr Stafford
APRIL Easter Sunday 6
WIGHTWICK MANOR, nr Wolverhampton
MAY Sunday 18
THE FIELD, The Wergs, nr Wolverhampton
MAY Sunday 25
LITTLE ONN HALL, Church Eaton, nr Stafford
JUNE Sunday 29
MOSELEY OLD HALL, nr Wolverhampton
JULY Saturday 12
UPMEADS, Stafford

JULY Sunday 13

‡COPEHALE, Coppenhall, nr Stafford

‡YEW TREE COTTAGE, Dunston Heath, nr Stafford

STRETTON HALL, nr Stafford

AUGUST Sunday 24

CAGLIARI, Upper Longdon, nr Rugeley

DESCRIPTIONS OF GARDENS

¶**Cagliari***&⊕ (Mr & Mrs C. P. How) Lower Way, Upper Longdon, 2½ m. S of Rugeley. A51 mid-way between Rugeley & Lichfield, turn off W at High St, Longdon, for Upper Longdon; garden is 1 m. from turning, nr The Gate Inn. 2-acre garden created since 1959; informal borders and beds; chiefly specimen trees, shrubs, rhododendrons, azaleas and heathers. Car park, tea and refreshments at nearby Gate Inn. *Adm. 40p, Chd. 20p. Sun. Aug. 24 (2–7)*

¶**Copehale** (G. Ramage Esq) Coppenhall, 2½ m. S of Stafford. Via A449 Stafford–Wolverhampton Rd going S, cross railway bridge; then right (and immediately left) just before main rd turns sharply left; under motorway and follow rd to X-rds (Coppenhall); right and entrance 100 yds on left. From Penkridge turn off A449 W signed Coppenhall. 1¼-acre garden designed to take advantage of extensive views S over Staffordshire plain; tall trimmed Leylandii hedges. NO DOGS. *Adm. 30p, Chd. 10p. Sun. July 13 (2–6)*

The Field&⊕ (Mr & Mrs R. Martin) The Wergs, 3 m. NW of Wolverhampton. A41 Wolverhampton–Albrighton; turn, by Crown Inn, at The Wergs N to Codsall. Medium-sized garden, bulbs, flowering trees, shrubs, rhododendrons, wallflowers & bedding plants; vegetables, greenhouses; fine wych elms. TEAS. *Adm. 30p, Chd. 10p. Sun. May 18 (2–7)*

●**Izaak Walton Cottage** †⊕ (Staffordshire County Council) Shallowford, nr Yarnfield, 6 m. NW of Stafford. A5013 from Stafford; turn right (N) to follow signposted route. Garden of ½ acre established recently to contain plants that were cultivated in Izaak Walton's lifetime up to 1683. In cottage small exhibition illustrating Walton's life & history of the cottage. *Adm. 5p. All year, every Thurs.–Sun. (10–1 & 2–5)*

Little Onn Hall*&⊕ (Mr & Mrs I. H. Kidson) Church Eaton, 6 m. SW of Stafford. A449, Wolverhampton–Stafford; at Gailey roundabout turn W on to A5 for 1½ m. turn right to Stretton; 200 yds turn left for Church Eaton; or Bradford Arms–Wheaton Aston & Marston; garden 1½ m. 6 acres; herbaceous lined drive; abundance of rhododendrons; formal paved rose garden with pavilions at front; large lawns with lily pond around house; old moat garden with fish tanks & small ruin; fine trees; walkways around. Paddock open for picnics (orange juice & ice-cream on sale). *Adm. 40p, Chd. 10p. Sun. May 25 (2–6)*

Moseley Old Hall*†⊕ (The National Trust—see p. ix) Brookhouse Lane, Fordhouses, 3½ m. N of Wolverhampton, West Midlands. Between A460 & A449 follow signposts. Small garden, a modern reconstruction of C17 garden with formal box parterre; so far as possible only plants grown in England before 1700 are included; old roses, herbaceous plants, small herb garden, arbour. Late Elizabethan house of historic interest with secret hiding places; refuge of Charles II after battle of Worcester. NO DOGS. TEAS. *Adm. garden 20p, Chd. 10p; house 50p extra, Chd. 25p. Sun. June 29 (2–6)*

●**Shugborough** †&⊕ (The National Trust—see p. ix; Staffordshire County Council) 5 m. SE of Stafford. From A513 Stafford–Rugeley Rd turn off N at Milford. House dating from 1693 & enlarged by Samuel Wyatt 1790–1806. Park contains a group of monuments by James 'Athenian' Stuart which are among earliest neo-Grecian buildings in this country. TEAS. Farm also open at weekends (adm. 25p extra, Chd. 20p) but by party appt. only during week. *Adm. garden & museum only 50p Chd. 25p; house 50p extra, Chd. 25p. Mid-March to mid-Oct. daily except Mons., but open Bank Hols. (Hours: Tues.–Fri. 10.30–5.30; Sats., Suns. & Bank Hol. Mons. & Tues. 2–5.30)*

Stretton Hall*†&⊕ (Mrs Monckton) 10 m. S of Stafford; 10 m. N of Wolverhampton. From M6 leave by exit 12 on to A5, going W & after 3 m. turn off N for Stretton. Coming from W along A5, pass Bellfields Reservoir & on 2 m., then turn off N for Stretton. Approx. 6 acres; terrace garden with roses, lawns with flowering shrubs & herbaceous border; fine forest trees; old walled kitchen garden; vegetables & small vineyards. Lovely old house (not open). Pre-Reformation church with fixed stone altar. NO DOGS. TEAS. *Adm. 30p, Chd. 10p. Sun. July 13 (2–6.30)*

●**Trentham Gardens***†&⊕ (Trentham Gardens Ltd) 3 m. S of Stoke-on-Trent. A34 & exit 15 from M6. 700 acres; formal Italian garden; rose, rock, peat block & herbaceous gardens. Special displays for Townswomen's Guild & Flower A..angers; blind garden & clematis walk; 12 demonstration plots; dwarf conifer display. 2 Garden Centres & Nursery. Miniature railway, swimming pool; caravan site, boating etc. Full catering facilities. *Adm. charges not available at time of going to press. All year daily (9–dusk)*

▪**Upmeads**⊕ (Mr & Mrs C. D. Lingwood) Newport Rd. 1 m. W of Stafford. On A518 Stafford–Newport rd; on right hand (N) side of rd, opp. junction with Westway. 1-acre formal garden; Dutch garden; small gardens on different levels; foliage, shrubs, sunken rose garden, clematis. House (not open) by Edgar Wood 1908; described by Pevsner as 'one of the most interesting houses of that date'. NO

STAFFORDSHIRE—continued

DOGS. *Adm. 40p, Chd. 10p. Sat. July 12 (2–6)*

Wightwick Manor*†⅍⊕ (The National Trust—see p. ix) Compton, 3 m. W of Wolverhampton, West Midlands. A454, Wolverhampton–Bridgnorth, just to N of rd, up Wightwick Bank, beside Mermaid Inn. 17-acre, Victorian-style garden laid out by Alfred Parsons; yew hedges & topiary; terraces; 2 pools; remarkable row of Irish yews & golden hollies; terrace by T. H. Mawson with stone fragments from bombed Houses of Parliament. Daffodils & blossom. William Morris house; many treasures of period. △*Sun. April 6 (2.30–5.30)*

¶**Yew Tree Cottage**⊕ (Mr & Mrs H. W. Rogers) Dunston Heath, 3½ m. S of Stafford. M6 junction 13. A449, 400 yds to Dunston and turn right for Dunston Heath; after 1 m. turn right again and after 500 yds left. Cottage garden (1½ acres) designed for round-the-corner surprises; trees, shrubs, roses, herbaceous borders, rockeries and pools, summer bedding; heather and conifer section; vegetable garden. 400 Exhibition Fantails; prize-winning stud. NO DOGS. *Adm. 30p, Chd. 10p. Sun. July 13 (2–6)*

SUFFOLK

Hon. County Organisers:
(East) MRS B. A. JENKINS, SRN, SCM, Paigles, 6 The Street, Holton St Peter, Halesworth
(West) MRS MARTIN FORREST, Smallbridge House, Cockfield, Bury St Edmunds

DATES OF OPENING

By appointment
  LANEHEAD, Garboldisham, nr Diss (weekdays only)
  PAIGLES, Holton-St-Peter, nr Halesworth
MARCH to OCTOBER daily
  PRIESTS HOUSE GARDENS, Flixton
APRIL Easter Sunday 6 to SEPTEMBER 28 every Sunday & Thursday & Bank Hol (also every Tuesday & Wednesday, July & August)
  SOMERLEYTON HALL, nr Lowestoft
APRIL Easter Sunday 6
  WEST WOOD, Walberswick, nr Southwold
  WHEPSTEAD HALL, nr Bury St Edmunds
APRIL Sunday 20
  VENNS, Middlewood Green, Earl Stonham, nr Stowmarket
MAY Sunday 25
  MAGNOLIA HOUSE, Yoxford
  VENNS, Middlewood Green, Earl Stonham, nr Stowmarket

MAY Monday 26
  MAGNOLIA HOUSE, Yoxford
JUNE Sunday 1
  BEARES, Saxtead, nr Framlingham
JUNE Sunday 8
  NORTH COVE HALL, nr Beccles
JUNE Sunday 15
  GABLE HOUSE, Redisham, nr Beccles
JUNE Sunday 22
  HOLTON-ST-PETER GARDENS, nr Halesworth
  PAIGLES, Holton-St-Peter, nr Halesworth
JUNE Sunday 29
  BARNINGHAM HOUSE, nr Bury St Edmunds
  EUSTON HALL, nr Thetford
  NEDGING HALL, Nedging, nr Hadleigh
JULY Sunday 6
  EUSTON HALL, nr Thetford
  GIFFORD'S HALL, Wickhambrook
JULY Sunday 13
  ELM GREEN FARMHOUSE, Bradfield St Clare
  REDISHAM HALL, nr Beccles
JULY Sunday 20
  GREAT THURLOW HALL, nr Haverhill
JULY Sunday 20 & daily to Saturday 26
  1 PARK LANE, Charsfield, nr Woodbridge
JULY Friday 25
  HEVENINGHAM HALL, nr Halesworth
AUGUST Sunday 31, SEPTEMBER Sundays 7 & 21, OCTOBER Sundays 5 & 19
  BEARES, Saxtead, nr Framlingham

DESCRIPTIONS OF GARDENS

Barningham House⊕ (Mr & Mrs W. Martineau) Barningham. 11 m. NE of Bury St Edmunds, via A143 to Stanton, then turn N on to B111 (towards Garboldisham) & along 2 m. to Barningham. 2-acre garden, small lake with woodland walk, walled garden with shrub borders. NO DOGS. TEAS. *Adm. 25p, Chd. 10p. Sun. June 29 (2.30–6.30)*

Beares*⅍⊕ (Mr & Mrs S. A. Notcutt) Saxtead. Just off A1120 between Saxtead Green (& windmill) & Dennington. 3 m. NW of Framlingham (with castle). Garden has been developed around Suffolk pink farmhouse & its ancient ponds; over 1,000 different trees, shrubs & perennials; all clearly labelled. *(Share (except on June 1) to Suffolk Heritage Trust).* Uncommon plants for sale. TEAS (June 1 only). *Adm. 40p, Chd. free. Suns. June 1, Aug. 31, Sept. 7, 21, Oct. 5, 19 (2–6)*

¶**Elm Green Farmhouse*** (Dr & Mrs J. W. Litchfield) Bradfield St Clare, 7 m. SSE of Bury St Edmunds. Via A134 (going towards Sudbury), 1 m. after Sicklesmere turn left (E) & follow signposts to Cockfield Green for 2½ m.; lane to Elm Green Farm is 1 m. before Cockfield *Great* Green. 1-acre garden created & maintained by owners, surrounding thatched

C17 farmhouse (not open) in open farmland; wide variety of shrubs, herbaceous plants, alpines & bulbs inc. many lilies. NO DOGS. *Adm. 30p, Chd. 10p. Sun. July 13 (2-5.30)*

Euston Hall †♿⊕ (His Grace The Duke of Grafton) 3 m. SE of Thetford. From Thetford take A1088 to Euston & Ixworth. From Newmarket take A11 to Elveden, then turn right for Barnham & Euston. Large garden: herbaceous & shrub borders, C17 pleasure grounds & lake. C18 house open (July 6 only); famous collection of paintings. C17 church & temple by William Kent. (*Shared with St John Ambulance (July 6)*) NO DOGS. TEAS in old kitchens. *Adm. garden only (June 29) 30p, OAPs & Chd. 15p; house & garden (July 6 only) 60p, Chd. 30p.* △*Sun. June 29 & Sun. July 6 (2.30–5.30)*

Gable House⊕ (Mr & Mrs John Foster) Redisham 3½ m. S of Beccles. Mid-way between Beccles & Halesworth on Ringsfield–Ilketshall St Lawrence Rd. Garden of 1 acre; mixed borders inc. Irises & primulas; fruit & vegetables. Some plants should be available for sale (perennials etc.). NO DOGS. TEAS. *Adm. 25p, Chd. 10p. Sun. June 15 (2–6)*

Gifford's Hall⊕ (R. Gardner Esq) Wickhambrook. ¾ m. from Plumbers' Arms, Wickhambrook on B1063, nr junction with A143; 10 m. SW of Bury St Edmunds, 10 m. NE of Haverhill. Medium-sized garden; roses; herbaceous borders. Moated C15 house of architectural interest shown, NO DOGS. TEA available. *Adm. 25p, Chd. 10p; House 25p extra, Chd. 10p. Sun. July 6 (2–6.30)*

Great Thurlow Hall⊕ (R. A. Vestey Esq) N of Haverhill. Great Thurlow village on B1061 from Newmarket; 3½ m. N of junction with A143 Haverhill–Bury St Edmunds Rd. Very large garden (20 acres); walled kitchen garden, greenhouses, herbaceous borders, shrubs, roses, spacious lawns, river walk & trout lake. *Adm. 25p, Chd. (accompanied) 5p. Sun. July 20 (2–7)*

Heveningham Hall*†♿⊕ (Department of the Environment) 5 m. SW Halesworth; Lodge entrance on Peasenhall–Walpole Rd; other entrance on B1117; 13 acres; lawns, shrubs, cedars, herbaceous borders, rose garden, walled garden with crinkle-crankle wall, new clematis area; Orangery (by Wyatt); Capability Brown park & lake. Georgian mansion (not open this date). NO DOGS. TEAS. *Adm. to garden 40p, Chd. 20p (under 6, free).* △*Fri. July 25 (2–6)*

Holton St Peter Gardens.⊕ 1 m. NE of Halesworth; at junction of B1123 & B1124, 3 m. from Blythburgh (on A12). At least 6 gardens will be open in old part of village; also small modern gardens on Park Estate. Festival in church. Holton Windmill. (*Share to new village hall appeal & church fund*) TEAS. *Combined charge for all gardens, inc. the*

following: 40p, Chd. 10p, or 10p each garden. Sun. June 22 (2–6)
  Homestead (Dr & Mrs Pagan)
  Holton Lodge (Mr & Mrs Spindler)
  Mill View (Mr & Mrs Bacon)
  Lytton Cottage (Mr & Mrs Ridgewell)
  Paigles (Mr & Mrs Jenkins)
  ¶**60 Orchard Valley** (Mr & Mrs Carver)
  Also other gardens

Lanehead* (Mrs N. A. Laurie) Garboldisham, 8 m. W of Diss (Norfolk) Medium-sized garden with natural walks of shrubs, perennials, roses & ground cover; water garden; borders for all-year interest & colour. *Collecting box. Garden open by appt. only, on weekdays (Tel. Garboldisham 380)*

Magnolia House (Mark Rumary Esq) Yoxford, N of Saxmundham. In centre of Yoxford village on A1120. Small walled garden; flowering trees, mixed borders of shrubs, roses, hardy plants & bulbs; ancient mulberry tree. NO DOGS please. *Adm. 30p, Chd. 5p. Sun. & Mon. May 25 & 26 (2-6)*

Nedging Hall♿⊕ (Mr & Mrs R. Macaire) Nedging; 4 m. N of Hadleigh, via A1141 towards Bildeston; house on right (E) side of rd. 15 acres of park-like grounds with small lake & many fine trees. *Adm. 25p, Chd. 5p. Sun. June 29 (2–6)*

North Cove Hall *♿⊕ (Mr & Mrs Ben Blower) 4 m. E of Beccles. Just off A146 Beccles–Lowestoft Rd. 1½-acre garden; pond, walled garden, heathers & dwarf conifers; rare trees & shrubs; rose garden. TEAS. *Adm. 30p, Chd. free. Sun. June 8 (2.30–5.30)*

Paigles* (Mr & Mrs F. H. Jenkins) 6 The Street, Holton-St-Peter, 1 m. NE of Halesworth. Holton is at junc. of B1123 & B1124, 3 m. from Blythburgh on A12. Paigles is an end-of-terrace cottage on B1124 opp. school. Small garden started in 1975 with some work still to be done; main interest alpines, but always something of interest; two small greenhouses, one with specie cyclamen in flower Oct.–March; Hellebores in flower Jan.–March; specie crocus early spring; sink gardens, small pool & rockery. Plants for sale. Visitors welcome any time of year but *please telephone beforehand. Collecting box. Sun. June 22 (2–6); also open by appt., all year (Tel. Halesworth 3731)*

1 Park Lane⊕ (Mr & Mrs E. E. Cole) Charsfield, 6 m. N of Woodbridge. On B1078, 3 m. W of Wickham Market. Approx. ¼ acre; council house garden; vegetables, flowers for drying, 2 greenhouses; small fishpond with water wheel; many pot plants etc. In village of Charsfield (known to many readers & viewers as Akenfield). *Adm. 15p. Sun. July 20 daily to Sat. July 26 inc. (2–7)*

Priests House Gardens *♿⊕ (Mr & Mrs A. C. Toll) Flixton, 2½ m. S of Bungay. Off B1062 midway between Bungay & Homersfield (this road links with A143 from Bury St Edmunds at Homersfield & A144 Halesworth –Norwich at Bungay) 3 acres; established landscaped gardens in lovely peaceful setting in Waveney Valley; fine shrub borders of great interest to botanists & flower arrangers. NO DOGS. Choice selection of container-grown shrubs for sale. Picnic facilities, with adequate seating. Free car park. Organised parties welcome by appt. Tel. Bungay 2717. *Collecting box for Nat. Gardens Scheme. March 1 to Oct. 31 daily (11–dusk)*

Redisham Hall&⊕ (Mr & Mrs Palgrave Brown) SW of Beccles. From A145, 1½ m. S of Beccles, turn W on to Ringsfield–Bungay Rd. Beccles, Halesworth or Bungay, all within 6 m. 5 acres; parkland & woods 400 acres. Georgian house *c.* 1760 (not shown). TEAS (4–5 p.m. only). *Adm. 25p. Sun. July 13 (2.30–6.30)*

● **Somerleyton Hall***†&⊕ (The Lord & Lady Somerleyton) 5 m. NW of Lowestoft. Off B1074. Large garden; famous maze, beautiful trees & avenue. House C16, added to 1844. Grinling Gibbons' carving, library, tapestries. Mentioned in Domesday Book. Miniature railway. NO DOGS. *Adm. (charges not yet available). Easter to end of Sept. every Thurs., Sun. & Bank Hol; also every Tues. & Wed. July & Aug. (2–6)*

Venns*&⊕ (Evan Selwyn-Smith Esq) Middlewood Green, Earl Stonham, 4 m. E of Stowmarket. 1 m. off A140 Ipswich–Norwich Rd on Mendlesham–Stowupland Rd; travelling from Ipswich take 1st left past Magpie P.H. House opp. R 'T' junction to Mendlesham. A very old 3-acre farmstead being made into a garden by owner single-handed; being planned & planted for year-round interest & scent; garden now taking shape; many old roses, specimen trees & shrubs & wide variety of bulbs & herbaceous rarities. House C14 cruck hall under restoration; Elizabethan barn; 5 ponds with fish. Earl Stonham Church with fine hammer beam roof nearby. Visitors welcome to come & talk gardening any time. Plants for sale when available. NO DOGS please. TEAS. *Adm. 15p. Sun. April 20 & Sun. May 25 (2–7); also by appt., all year (Tel. Stonham 303)*

West Wood*† (Miss Mea Allan) Walberswick, S of Southwold. From A12 turn off E at Blythburgh on to B1387 & along 3 m. to Walberswick; after church fork right. Medium-sized garden; spring bulbs; primroses, alpine garden; pleached walk. Link with Tradescant family. *(Share to The Tradescant Trust)* NO DOGS. TEAS. *Adm. 25p, Chd. 5p. Sun. April 6 (2–6)*

Whepstead Hall⊕ (Mr A. T. U. Park & Miss E. M. M. Park) Whepstead, 4 m. S of Bury St Edmunds, via A143 (towards Haverhill) &

then turn off left (S) along B1066 towards Glemsford. In Whepstead village on B1066 adjacent to church. 5-acre garden, spring garden with lake & daffodils. Tea Angel Hotel, Bury St Edmunds. *Adm. 25p, Chd. 10p. Sun. April 6 (2–6)*

SURREY

Hon. County Organiser:
LADY HEALD, Chilworth Manor, nr Guildford

Assistant Hon. County Organiser:
MRS D. M. LIDDELL, Odd Cottage, West Clandon, Guildford, GU4 7TG

Buses AV: Alder Valley; GL: Green Line coaches; LC: London Country; LT: London Transport; TV: Tillingbourne Valley

DATES OF OPENING

MARCH Sunday 16
  PINKS HILL NURSERIES, Wood Street Village, nr Guildford
APRIL Thursday 3
  SUTTON PLACE, nr Guildford
APRIL Easter Monday 7
  GORSE HILL MANOR, Gorse Hill Road, Virginia Water
APRIL Saturday 12, Sunday 13, Monday 14, Tuesday 15, Wednesday 16
  CHILWORTH MANOR, nr Guildford
APRIL Sunday 20
  FEATHERCOMBE, Hambledon, nr Godalming
  GORSE HILL MANOR, Gorse Hill Road, Virginia Water
  VANN, Hambledon, nr Godalming
APRIL Monday 21
  VANN, Hambledon, nr Godalming
APRIL Thursday 24
  SUTTON PLACE, nr Guildford
APRIL Sunday 27
  DUNSBOROUGH PARK, Ripley, nr Woking
  FEATHERCOMBE, Hambledon, nr Godalming
  PARK LANE HOUSE, Farnham
  RAMSTER, Chiddingfold
MAY Sunday 4
  FEATHERCOMBE, Hambledon, nr Godalming
  PINEWOOD HOUSE, Worplesdon Hill
  RAMSTER, Chiddingfold
MAY Monday 5 (Bank Hol.)
  FEATHERCOMBE, Hambledon, nr Godalming
  GORSE HILL MANOR, Gorse Hill Road, Virginia Water
  VANN, Hambledon, nr Godalming
MAY Sunday 11
  FEATHERCOMBE, Hambledon, nr Godalming
  PINEWOOD HOUSE, Worplesdon Hill
  RAMSTER, Chiddingfold
  WINTERSHALL, Bramley

MAY Sunday 18
 FAIRWAY LODGE, South Drive,
  Wentworth, nr Virginia Water
 FEATHERCOMBE, Hambledon,
  nr Godalming
 PINEWOOD HOUSE, Worplesdon Hill
 POSTFORD HOUSE, Chilworth
 RAMSTER, Chiddingfold
 WESTBOURN, Virginia Water

MAY Sunday 25
 BELLASIS HOUSE, nr Dorking
 ‡FAIRWAY LODGE, South Drive,
  Wentworth, nr Virginia Water
 FEATHERCOMBE, Hambledon,
  nr Godalming
 MALTHOUSE FARM, Hambledon,
  nr Guildford
 PINEWOOD HOUSE, Worplesdon Hill
 RAMSTER, Chiddingfold
 ‡ROBIN HILL, Wentworth, Virginia Water

MAY Monday 26 (Spring Bank Holiday)
 FEATHERCOMBE, Hambledon,
  nr Godalming
 GORSE HILL MANOR, Gorse Hill Road,
  Virginia Water
 GRAYSWOOD HILL, Haslemere
 MALTHOUSE FARM, Hambledon,
  nr Godalming
 RAMSTER, Chiddingfold

MAY Wednesday 28
 POSTFORD HOUSE, Chilworth

MAY Saturday 31
 CLAREMONT LANDSCAPE GARDEN,
  Esher
 ABINGER MILL, Abinger Hammer

JUNE Sunday 1
 FEATHERCOMBE, Hambledon,
  nr Godalming
 RAMSTER, Chiddingfold
 SOUTH PARK, nr Blechingley
 1 YEW TREE COTTAGES, Esher

JUNE Sunday 8
 FEATHERCOMBE Hambledon,
  nr Godalming
 GRAYSWOOD HILL, Haslemere
 RAMSTER, Chiddingfold

JUNE Wednesday 11
 LIME TREE COTTAGE, Weybridge

JUNE Sunday 15
 LUCAS GREEN MANOR, West End,
  Woking
 MERRIST WOOD AGRICULTURAL
  COLLEGE, Worplesdon, nr Guildford
 VANN, Hambledon, nr Godalming

JUNE Monday 16
 VANN, Hambledon, nr Godalming

JUNE Saturday 21
 CHILWORTH MANOR, nr Guildford

JUNE Sunday 22
 CHILWORTH MANOR, nr Guildford
 1 YEW TREE COTTAGES, Esher

**JUNE Monday 23, Tuesday 24,
 Wednesday 25**
 CHILWORTH MANOR, nr Guildford

JUNE Saturday 28
 THE MOORINGS, Horley

JUNE Sunday 29
 DUNSBOROUGH PARK, Ripley,
  nr Woking
 GORSE HILL MANOR, Gorse Hill Road,
  Virginia Water
 HAZEL HALL, Peaslake, nr Guildford
 THE MOORINGS, Horley

JUNE Monday 30
 THE MOORINGS, Horley

JULY Saturday 5
 MANOR HOUSE, Headley, nr Epsom

JULY Sunday 6
 MANOR HOUSE, Headley, nr Epsom
 SOUTH PARK FARM, South Godstone
 WINKWORTH ARBORETUM, Godalming

JULY Monday 7
 SOUTH PARK FARM, South Godstone

JULY Saturday 12
 CHILWORTH MANOR, nr Guildford

JULY Sunday 13
 CHILWORTH MANOR, nr Guildford
 WOODYERS, Wonersh, nr Guildford

**JULY Monday 14, Tuesday 15 &
 Wednesday 16**
 CHILWORTH MANOR, nr Guildford

JULY Sunday 20
 DUNSBOROUGH PARK, Ripley,
  nr Woking
 ST MARY'S HOMES, Godstone

JULY Saturday 26
 ABINGER MILL. Abinger Hammer

JULY Sunday 27
 1 YEW TREE COTTAGES, Esher

AUGUST Sunday 3
 DUNSBOROUGH PARK, Ripley,
  nr Woking
 GRAYSWOOD HILL, Haslemere

AUGUST Saturday 9
 HOLDFAST COTTAGE, Haslemere

AUGUST Sunday 10
 HOLDFAST COTTAGE, Haslemere
 PINKS HILL NURSERIES, Wood Street
  Village, nr Guildford

AUGUST Sunday 24
 FEATHERCOMBE, Hambledon,
  nr Godalming

**AUGUST Monday 25 (Summer Bank
 Holiday)**
 FEATHERCOMBE, Hambledon,
  nr Godalming

SEPTEMBER Sunday 7
 ANNESLEY, nr Haslemere

SEPTEMBER Sunday 21
 PINKS HILL NURSERIES, Wood Street
  Village, nr Guildford

SEPTEMBER Sunday 28
 CLAREMONT LANDSCAPE GARDEN,
  Esher
 GRAYSWOOD HILL, Haslemere

OCTOBER Sunday 19
 GORSE HILL MANOR, Gorse Hill Road,
  Virginia Water

DESCRIPTIONS OF GARDENS

Abinger Mill⊕ (Mr & Mrs Donald Austen) Abinger Hammer. From A25 Dorking–Guildford, turn into Raikes Lane (Crossways Farm) & then 1st turn left & house is 1st on left. Bus: GL 425; alight Crossways Farm, short distance from house. Recent planting of interesting trees & shrubs in an old mill garden; waterfall & Tillingbourne stream. NO DOGS. *Adm. 25p, Chd. 5p. Sat. May 31 & Sat. July 26; (2–5.30) also open by appt.*

Annesley*⊕ (Capt. & Mrs Trechman) Three Gates Lane, ½ m. NE of Haslemere. Off A286 Haslemere–Godalming Rd. Bus: AV 18, alight end of Three Gates Lane, ¼ m. 3 acres; shrubs, roses, annuals & items of interest to the flower arranger. TEAS. *Adm. 20p, Chd. 10p. Sun. Sept. 7 (2–7)*

Bellasis Houseዿ (Paul Wates Esq) Box Hill, 2 m. NE of Dorking. A217 London-Reigate Rd; at Burgh Heath (at end of carriageway section) fork W (right) on to B2032 towards Dorking; after 2 m. turn right towards Leatherhead & Box Hill; after ¼ m. fork left into Box Hill Rd; after 1½ m. turn right into Headley Heath Approach & house on left. Fine trees, shrubs, rhododendrons, hydrangeas; woodland walks. NO DOGS. NO COACHES. Tea Fort Tea Rooms, Box Hill. *Adm. 30p, Chd. 5p. Sun. May 25 (2.30–6)*

Chilworth Manor†⊕ (Sir Lionel & Lady Heald) 3½ m. SE of Guildford. From A248, in centre of Chilworth village, turn up Blacksmith Lane. Bus: LC 425 Guildford–Dorking; alight Chilworth level crossing. Station: Chilworth. Garden laid out in C17; C18 walled garden added by Sarah, Duchess of Marlborough; spring flowers; flowering shrubs; herbaceous border. House C17 with C18 wing on site of C11 monastery recorded in Domesday Book; stewponds in garden date from monastic period. House open for Flower Arrangements on following dates (20p extra): April 12 & 13 (by St Catherine's Flower Arrangement Club); July 12 & 13 (by Horsley Floral Decoration Group). Free car park in attractive surroundings open from 12.30 for picnicking. TEAS (Sats. & Suns. only). *Adm. to garden 20p, Chd. free. House 20p extra. Open Sats.–Weds. April 12–16, June 21–25, July 12–16 (2–7); also open by appt.*

¶**Claremont Landscape Garden** †ዿ⊕ (The National Trust) ½ m. SE of Esher; on E side of A307 (No access from new A3 by-pass). Station: Esher. Bus: GL 715, alight at entrance gates. Earliest surviving English landscape garden; recently restored; begun by Vanbrugh & Bridgeman before 1720; extended & naturalized by Kent; lake, island with pavilion, grotto & turf ampitheatre, viewpoints & avenues. Refreshments available. *Adm. 20p, Chd. 10p.* △*Sat. May 31 & Sun. Sept. 28 (9–7; last adm. 6.30)*

Dunsborough Park*ዿ⊕ (C. F. Hughesdon Esq) Ripley; entrance across Ripley Green. Bus: GL 715 alight Ripley village. Spring flowers, rose garden, bedding, greenhouses inc. stove house with tropical plants & peach houses. Garden mainly suitable for wheelchairs. Tea Green Lantern Cafe, High St (opp. entrance to Ripley Green). *Adm. 20p, Chd. 5p. Suns. April 27, June 29, July 20, Aug. 3 (2–7)*

Fairway Lodge* (Cdr & Mrs Innes Hamilton) South Drive, Wentworth, Virginia Water. From A30 at Virginia Water opp. Wheatsheaf Restaurant, turn down B389; right at roundabout; follow yellow signs. 2½ acres; plantsman's garden made since 1969; trees, shrubs, woody plants, many home-propagated; primulas. Many mistakes (free, chatty leaflet). 1979 Year of the Garden Wilkinson Sword Award winner. (*Share to Gardeners' Sunday*) Plants for sale. Regret NO DOGS. TEAS. *Adm. 25p, Chd. 5p. Suns. May 18 & 25 (2–7)*

Feathercombe*⊕ (Mrs Wieler & Miss Parker) nr Hambledon, S of Godalming. 2 m. from Milford Station on Hambledon Rd, turn to Feathercombe off rd between Hydestile X-rds & 'Merry Harriers' P.H. Fine view; flowering shrubs & trees; heathers. Plants for sale. Picnic area at garden. Tea Winkworth Arboretum. *Adm. 20p, Chd. free. April 20–June 8 every Sun.; also Mons. May 5, 26, Aug. 25 & Sun. Aug 24 (2–6)*

Gorse Hill Manor* (Mrs E. Barbour Paton) Gorse Hill Rd, nr Virginia Water (10 mins walk). A30 turn off opp. Wheatsheaf Hotel; in 1 m. ('phone box on right) turn left, round hairpin bend; house is last on left at top of hill. 3 acres; over 450 different varieties of trees & shrubs, all identified, which are a speciality. Pit pony (which served 19 yrs in mines) & 2 donkeys. NO very young children & NO DOGS. Tea Tudor Rose Restaurant, Virginia Water village. *Collecting box. Mon. April 7, Sun. April 20, Mons. May 5 & 26; Sun. June 29 & Sun. Oct. 19 (2–5.30); also open by previous appt. for parties from gardens clubs (Tel. Wentworth 2101)*

Grayswood Hill*ዿ (Mr & Mrs J. W. Sutherland-Hawes) 1 m. N of Haslemere/ From Godalming via A286, turn left (E) just after Haslemere 40 mph sign. Large collection of trees & shrubs, inc. some rare specimens; rhododendrons, dwarf conifers & azaleas a speciality. Superb views of Weald of Sussex. Small nursery garden; plants for sale. Tea Wheatsheaf Hotel, Grayswood. *Adm. 25p, Chd. 15p. Mon. May 26; Suns. June 8; Aug. 3, Sept. 28 (2–6)*

Hazel Hall*†ዿ⊕ (Mr & Mrs Hugh Merriman) Peaslake, 6½ m. SE of Guildford. In Peaslake turn off into Pond Lane leaving the Hurtwood Inn on the left. 2½ acres; trees, shrubs & roses. Early Georgian House, Grade II. Also 2 Georgian miniature houses (scale 1 in. to 1 ft.) fully furnished in that period. NO DOGS. TEAS. *Adm. to garden 25p, Chd. free; house 25p extra (adults & chd.). Sun. June 29 (2.15–6.15)*

Holdfast Cottage⊕ (Brig A. D. McKechnie) Holdfast Lane, Haslemere. 1½ m. E of Haslemere; take Haslemere–Petworth Rd & after 1 m. turn left; garden 400 yds on left. 2–3 acres with herbaceous borders, roses & rock garden. *Adm. 25p. Sat. & Sun. Aug. 9 & 10 (2–7)*

¶**Lime Tree Cottage** (Mr & Mrs P. Sinclair) 25 Ellesmere Rd, 1½ m. from centre of Weybridge. Ellesmere Rd is a turning off Queen's Rd (A317) immediately west of its junction with Seven Hills Rd (B365). No. 25 is at top end of Ellesmere Rd. Very small plantswoman's garden on site 70 ft x 70 ft incl. house; excellent example of garden design with wide variety of plants showing what can be done in very limited space. Local pottery for sale by Mrs Wendy Stringer. NO DOGS. MORNING COFFEE & TEAS at **Pineholme** (Mr & Mrs P. Atkinson) next door. *Adm. 20p, Chd. 10p. Wed. June 11 (10.30–4)*

¶**Lucas Green Manor** (Mr & Mrs Ernest Bigland) Lucas Green Rd, West End, 5 m. W of Woking, 3 m. SW of Chobham. From A322 Bracknell–Guildford rd, turn off W between West End & Bisley for Lucas Green. 3½-acre garden with lawns & rhododendrons. C16 house listed Grade II (part shown) reputed to have been rest house for monks on way to Chertsey Abbey. *Adm., inc. part-house, 35p, Chd. 10p. Sun. June 15 (2–6)*

Malthouse Farm† (Mr & Mrs C. Kahn) Hambledon, 2½ m. S of Godalming. On Godalming–Witley Rd. 3 m. Hambledon Village or A283 going S turn left at bottom of hill past Witley marked Hambledon. Garden of 2–3 acres flowing into landscape of South Downs; rhododendrons, azaleas, flowering trees & shrubs; spring bulbs, roses, vegetables, small water garden. House (not open) C17 with later additions; C18 granary on stone mushrooms recently restored. NO DOGS. TEA & biscuits. *Adm. 25p, Chd. 10p. Sun. & Mon. May 25 & 26 (2–6)*

Manor House&⊕ (Sir Ronald Wates) Headley, S of Epsom, 3½ m. SE of Leatherhead; entrance off B2033 at point where this road joins Headley Heath (adjacent to Cricket Ground). 4-acre garden with lawns, formal summer bedding, herbaceous borders, rose garden, flowering shrubs, & trees, kitchen garden, greenhouses, yew hedges. Tea caravan on Headley Heath (1 min); Ample refreshment facilities Box Hill 2½ m. *Adm. 30p, Chd. 15p. Sat. July 5 & Sun. July 6 (2–6)*

Merrist Wood Agricultural College*&⊕ (Surrey County Council) Worplesdon, 4 m. NW of Guildford. On A321, 4 m. from Guildford. From Aldershot via A323; from Bagshot via A322. Over 10 acres of nursery ground with a library of plant genera for student education. Demonstration gardens constructed by students. Plants labelled. Natural oak & bluebell woodland & lovely views across farmland to the Hog's Back. NO DOGS. TEA & biscuits available. Free parking. *Adm. 25p, Chd. 15p. Sun. June 15 (2–6)*

The Moorings*⊕ (Dr & Mrs C. J. F. L. Williamson) Russells Cres., Horley. Nr town centre between A23 & B2036 & 400 yds from railway station. 1 acre of secluded country garden in centre of small town; contains all sorts of rare plants, interesting trees, many roses & pleasant vistas. An escapist's garden! TEA & biscuits, also plants for sale (both on June 28 & 29 only). *Adm. 25p, Chd. 10p. Sat. & Sun. June 28 & 29 (2–7); Mon. June 30 (2–5)*

Park Lane House*⊕ (Mrs R. McConnel) Castle Hill, Farnham. In Farnham turn up Castle St leading to Castle Hill. Cars may be parked in Old Park Lane. Station : Farnham, ¾ m. Bus stop : Castle St, 5 mins walk up hill. Medium-sized garden of horticultural interest; flowering shrubs, spring bulbs, rose garden, alpines, greenhouses & herbaceous borders. NO DOGS. *Adm. 25p, Chd. 10p. Sun. April 27 (2–7)*

Pinewood House*&⊕ (Jack Van Zwanenberg Esq) Heath House Rd, Worplesdon Hill, 3½ m. SW of Woking. A322 Guildford–Bagshot; turning opp. Brookwood Cemetery wall, clearly marked Heath House Rd. 7 acres of gardens & woodland; azaleas, rhododendrons, wistaria, lovely trees, water garden. Attractive house with large atrium. Superb plants for sale. NO DOGS. TEA & biscuits (15p). *Adm. house & garden 30p, Chd. free. Suns. May 4, 11, 18, 25 (2–6); also open by appt. (Tel. Brookwood 3241); group visits by arrangement*

Pinks Hill Nurseries Ltd*⊕ (D. Earl Bicknell Esq) Wood Street Village, 3 m. W of Guildford. Village of Wood Street is S of A323 (turning 2½ m. from Guildford Town Centre); Nursery near village school. Small & unique garden laid out in country setting, with heather beds, rockeries, pools & waterfalls, to demonstrate ideas which can be carried out in large & small gardens with labour-saving techniques. *Adm. 20p, Chd. 10p Suns. March 16, Aug. 10, Sept. 21 (10–1 & 2.30–5.30)*

Postford House⊕ (Mrs R. Litler-Jones) Chilworth, 4 m. SE of Guildford. Route A248. Bus: LC 425 Guildford–Dorking, alight nr entrance. 25 acres; rock garden; stream; rhododendrons, azaleas & shrubs. Swimming pool may be used by visitors (collecting box). Plants for sale. TEAS. *Adm. 15p, Chd. 10p. Sun. May 18 & Wed. May 28 (2–6)*

Ramster*⅃⊕ (Sir Aubrey & Lady Burke) Chiddingfold. On A283, ½ m. S of Chiddingfold; large iron gates on right. Large woodland garden of exceptional interest, with fine rhododendrons, azaleas, camellias, magnolias, trees & shrubs. *Adm. 25p, OAPs & Chd. 15p. Suns. April 27, May 4, 11, 18, 25, June 1, 8; Mon. May 26 (2–7)*

Robin Hill*⅃ (Mrs P. Galt) Heatherside Drive, Wentworth, Virginia Water. From A30 opp. Wheatsheaf Restaurant turn on to B389; then right into Wellington & right into East Drive. 9½ acre garden; sloping to stream & woods; azaleas & rhododendrons & many rare trees & shrubs; 1,000 species of roses; water garden; lovely vistas. NO DOGS. *Adm. 25p, Chd. 5p. Sun. May 25 (2–6)*

St Mary's Homes*† (St Mary's Homes) Church Lane, Godstone, 6 m. E of Redhill. Parish church & old area of Godstone Village, preservation area; Bay Pond (Surrey Naturalists Trust) 5 mins walk. A22 or A25 (M25) to Godstone; Church Lane connects both & garden is ¼ m. from each, next to Church. Old people's almshouses with Chapel (open) all of architectural interest. Attractive garden of traditional cottage type; wide variety of annual & perennial plants. TEA & cakes. *Adm. 15p, Chd. 10p. Sun. July 20 (2–7)*

South Park⅃ (Uvedale Lambert Esq) 2 m. SE of Blechingley. 2 m. SW of Godstone. Bus: LC 410, Reigate–Bromley; LC 411, Reigate–Croydon, alight Godstone Green or White Post, Blechingley, 2 m. Landscaping. C17 chapel. Victorian doll's house on view 10p extra, Chd. 5p. TEAS. *Adm. 25p, Chd. 5p. Sun. June 1 (2–7)*

South Park Farm †⅃⊕ (Mr & Mrs E. B. Stewart-Smith) South Godstone, 6 m. E of Redhill. 1 m. S of railway bridge over A22 at South Godstone; turn right into Private Road opp. Walkers' Garden Centre; follow signs for 1 m. Medium-sized garden; old-fashioned roses, small lake, herbaceous border, fine trees & landscape. C17 farm house (not open) & large C17 barn. Peacocks & horse drawn carriages. TEAS. *Adm. 25p, Chd. 5p. Sun. July 6 & Mon. July 7 (2–7)*

Sutton Place †⊕ (Sutton Place Property Co. Ltd) N of Guildford. Entrance on A3, left-hand side coming from Guildford just beyond Town boundary (where street lighting ends). Station: Woking or Guildford, 4 m. Bus: AV 290, 99A from Woking or Guildford, alight at Sutton Place, 1 m. Rose garden; Dutch garden; extensive lawns; wild garden. Tudor mansion (not open). NO DOGS. *Adm. 30p, Thus. April 13 & Thurs. April 24 (2.30–5.30)*

Vann*†⅃ (Mr & Mrs M. Caroe) Hambledon, 6 m. S of Godalming. A 283 to Chiddingfold; turn off at head of green, 1st left past P.O. signed 'Vann Lane'; house 2 m. along on right with post box on gate. Bus: AV 21, alight Chiddingfold or Hambledon Lane End, 2 m. 4½-acre garden surrounding Tudor & William & Mary house; later additions & alterations incorporating old farm buildings by W. D. Caroe 1907. Formal yew walks, ¼-acre pond, Gertrude Jekyll water garden, pergola, woodland, old cottage garden; spring bulbs, azaleas, roses. Featured *Country Life* May 26 1976; *The Field* June 9 1977. Surrey Magazine Sept. 1979. Maintained by family with 12 hours assistance per week. Plant & vegetable stall. Home-made TEAS in house (April 20, May 5, June 15 only). *Adm. 35p, Chd. 10p. Suns. April 20 & June 15, Mon. May 5 (2–7); Mons. April 21 & June 16 (10–6); also by appt. April–July (Tel. Wormley 3413)*

¶**Westbourn** (John Camden Esq) Pinewood Rd, Virginia Water. Via A30 through Egham & on 3 m. to Wheatsheaf Hotel; turn into Christchurch Rd (opp. Hotel); after 200 yds turn right into Wentworth Estate (Pinewood Rd); garden 50 yds along, opp. small roundabout. 4 acres on 2 levels, mainly rhododendrons & azaleas (outstanding collection) under a high shade canopy of Scots pine & oak trees. *Adm. 40p, Chd. 10p Sun. May 18 (2–6)*

Winkworth Arboretum*⅃ (The National Trust—see p. ix) Hascombe Rd, Godalming. Entrances with car parks; Upper—3 m. SE of Godalming on E side of B2130; Lower—2½ m. S of Bramley on Bramley–Hascombe Rd, turn right off A281 from Guildford by Bramley Grange Hotel, up Snowdenham Lane. Coaches (by arrangement) should use Upper car park on B2130. Station: Godalming, 3 m. 95 acres of hillside planted with rare trees & shrubs; 2 lakes; many wild birds; view over North Downs. Light refreshments available. *Adm. free but collecting box for Nat. Gardens Scheme.* △*Sun. July 6 (dawn–dusk)*

Wintershall*†⅃⊕ (Mr & Mrs Peter Hutley) 2½ m. S of Bramley village on A281 turn right, then next on right. Wintershall drive next on left. Bus: AV 33 Guildford–Horsham; alight Palmers Cross, 1 m. 2½-acre garden & 100 acres of park & woodland; bluebell walks in spring; banks of wild daffodils; rhododendrons; pheasantry, specimen trees, ornamental pools & ponds; several acres of lakes & flight ponds; Domesday yew tree. Tea Bramley Grange Hotel. *Adm. 20p, Chd. 10p. Sun. May 11 (2–6)*

Woodyers⊕ (Brig. & Mrs Fraser Scott) Wonersh, 4 m. S of Guildford. A281 Guildford–Horsham; at Shalford turn off E on to B2128 to Wonersh; in village centre (opp. car park of Grantley Arms) take road to Shamley

Green. Bus : AV 273 & 295 ; alight at Grantley
Arms. ¾ acre, traditional, owner-maintained,
walled garden ; lawns, roses, herbaceous,
bedding & shrubs ; kitchen garden ; greenhouses. Swimming. Plants for sale. Refreshments. *Adm. 25p. Sun. July 13 (2–6)*

1 Yew Tree Cottages (Mr & Mrs G. A.
Sinfield) Portsmouth Rd (Scilly Isles), Esher.
On A3 (½ m. from Esher town centre on
London side), close to Scilly Isles roundabout.
Cars must park at 'Marquis of Granby' close to
garden. Stations : Esher (main line), 1 min
walk & Hinchley Wood. Bus : Green Line 715,
alight 'Orleans Arms'. Small, charming old-
world cottage garden, designed & maintained
entirely by owners ; lawns & herbaceous
borders set off by clipped yews, box edging &
beautiful trees ; spring garden with peonies &
iris ; Italian-style walled garden, with pool &
fine old stonework, of special interest.
NO DOGS. TEAS. (Meals & refreshments
'Marquis of Granby'). *Adm. 25p. Suns. June
1, 22, July 27 (11–7); also open by appt. for
parties (Tel. 01-398 3871)*

SUSSEX

Hon. County Organisers:
(East Sussex & mid-Sussex) MRS E. JOAN
HORNIBLOW, White Fox Lodge, Udimore,
nr Rye TN31 6AE and CARL LUDWIG Esq,
The Cottage, 155 Western Rd,
Hurstpierpoint

(West Sussex) MRS NIGEL AZIS, Coke's
Cottage, West Burton, Pulborough

Hon. County Treasurers:
(East Sussex & mid-Sussex) T. F. FAULKNER
Esq, The Old Rectory Farm, Isfield,
nr Uckfield, TN22 5XR

(West Sussex) C. A. ROBERTS Esq,
Bury Gate House, Pulborough

DATES OF OPENING

By appointment
CHAMPS HILL, Coldwaltham,
  Pulborough (April, Sept.)
CHIDMERE, Chidham, nr. Chichester
  (March—Oct. ; parties only)
COKE'S COTTAGE, West Burton
  (April, June)
COOKE'S HOUSE, West Burton
  (April–July)
COX'S COTTAGE, West St, Selsey
  (All year)
THE HIGH BEECHES, Handcross
  (parties only)
LANE END, Midhurst (June–Sept.)
LITTLE COURT, Midhurst
TELEGRAPH HOUSE, North Marden,
  Chichester (June, July)

March every Saturday & Sunday
DENMANS, Fontwell

**MARCH, from March 15 every Saturday,
  Sunday, Wednesday & Thursday**
BORDE HILL, Haywards Heath
**APRIL daily except Mondays (but open
  Monday 7)**
GREAT DIXTER, Northiam
**APRIL every Saturday, Sunday,
  Wednesday & Thursday & Bank Hol.**
BORDE HILL, Haywards Heath
APRIL every Saturday & Sunday
DENMANS, Fontwell
APRIL daily except Saturdays
WEST DEAN GARDENS, nr Chichester
APRIL Good Friday 4
COKE'S COTTAGE, West Burton,
  nr Pulborough
APRIL Easter Saturday 5
‡AMBERLEY CASTLE, Amberley
‡COKE'S COTTAGE, West Burton,
  nr Pulborough
APRIL Easter Sunday 6
‡AMBERLEY CASTLE, Amberley
‡COKE'S COTTAGE, West Burton,
  nr Pulborough
RYMANS, Apuldram, nr Chichester
APRIL Easter Monday 7
HIGHDOWN, Goring-by-Sea
APRIL Saturday 12
CHURCH FARMHOUSE, East Lavant,
  nr Chichester
APRIL Sunday 13
CHIDMERE, Chidham
CHURCH FARMHOUSE, East Lavant,
  nr Chichester
COKE'S COTTAGE, West Burton,
  nr Pulborough
APRIL Monday 14
CHIDMERE, Chidham
COKE'S COTTAGE, West Burton,
  nr Pulborough
APRIL Saturday 19
CISSBURY, Findon
APRIL Sunday 20
BEECHES FARM, Buckham Hill,
  nr Uckfield
BIRCH GROVE HOUSE, Chelwood Gate
‡BURTON MANOR, nr Pulborough
CISSBURY, Findon
THE HIGH BEECHES, Handcross
MALT HOUSE, Chithurst, nr Rogate
NEWTIMBER PLACE, Newtimber,
  nr Hassocks
‡WARNINGCAMP HOUSE, Arundel
‡WEST BURTON HOUSE, nr Pulborough
APRIL Monday 21
WEST BURTON HOUSE, nr Pulborough
APRIL Sunday 27
BIRCH GROVE HOUSE, Chelwood Gate
‡COOKE'S HOUSE, West Burton,
  nr Pulborough
THE FOX & HOUNDS FARM, Bolney
‡HOUGHTON FARM HOUSE, Arundel
LEGH MANOR, Anstye, nr Cuckfield
MALT HOUSE, Chithurst, nr Rogate
SOUTH LODGE, Lower Beeding,
  nr Horsham

APRIL Monday 28
‡COOKE'S HOUSE, West Burton,
  nr Pulborough
‡HOUGHTON FARM HOUSE, Arundel

MAY daily except Mondays (but open Mondays 5 & 26)
GREAT DIXTER, Northiam

MAY every Saturday, Sunday, Wednesday, Thursday & Bank Hol.
BORDE HILL, Haywards Heath

MAY every Saturday & Sunday
DENMANS, Fontwell

MAY daily except Saturdays
WEST DEAN GARDENS, nr Chichester

MAY Saturday 3
JOAN NIGHTINGALE HOUSE, Haywards
  Heath

MAY Sunday 4
LANGNEY PRIORY, nr Eastbourne
MALT HOUSE, Chithurst, nr Rogate
OFFHAM HOUSE, nr Lewes
RYMANS, Apuldram, nr Chichester
SOUTH LODGE, Lower Beeding,
  nr Horsham

MAY Monday 5 (May Day Hol.)
MALT HOUSE, Chithurst, nr Rogate
ST ROCHE'S ARBORETUM, Singleton
  Hill

MAY Tuesday 6
NYMANS, Handcross
ST ROCHE'S ARBORETUM, Singleton
  Hill

MAY Wednesday 7, Thursday 8 & Friday 9
ST ROCHE'S ARBORETUM, Singleton
  Hill

MAY Saturday 10
‡PAXTONS, East Lavant, nr Chichester
‡ST ROCHE'S ARBORETUM, Singleton
  Hill
WEST SUSSEX COLLEGE OF
  AGRICULTURE, North Heath,
  nr Pulborough

MAY Sunday 11
CHARLESTON MANOR, West Dean,
  nr Seaford
DREWITTS, Warninglid
HEASELANDS, Haywards Heath
MALT HOUSE, Chithurst, nr Rogate
‡PAXTONS, East Lavant, nr Chichester
‡ST ROCHE'S ARBORETUM, Singleton
  Hill
STANDEN, East Grinstead

MAY Monday 12
DREWITTS, Warninglid

MAY Wednesday 14
CHAMPS HILL, Coldwaltham, Pulborough
HEASELANDS, Haywards Heath
SOUTH LODGE, Lower Beeding,
  nr Horsham

MAY Thursday 15
CHAMPS HILL, Coldwaltham, Pulborough

MAY Saturday 17
KING EDWARD VII HOSPITAL,
  nr Midhurst
ROOM OUTSIDE, Goodwood Gardens,
  nr Chichester
STILE HOUSE, Gay St, nr Pulborough

MAY Sunday 18
BURTON MANOR, nr Pulborough
CHIDMERE, Chidham
‡FAIRFIELD, Little Bognor, Fittleworth
FERNHURST GARDENS, Haslemere
HEASELANDS, Haywards Heath
‡‡MALT HOUSE, Chithurst, nr Rogate
MOUNTFIELD COURT, nr Robertsbridge
PORTUS, West Wittering, nr Chichester
‡STILE HOUSE, Gay St, nr Pulborough
‡‡TROTTON OLD RECTORY,
  nr Petersfield

MAY Monday 19
CHIDMERE, Chidham
FAIRFIELD, Little Bognor, Fittleworth
PORTUS, West Wittering, nr Chichester

MAY Wednesday 21
HEASELANDS, Haywards Heath

MAY Saturday 24
SOUTH LODGE, Lower Beeding,
  nr Horsham
TELEGRAPH HOUSE, North Marden,
  Chichester

MAY Sunday 25
CISSBURY, Findon
‡COLLIERS FARM, Fernhurst,
  nr Haslemere
COPLANDS, Northiam
‡COWDRAY PARK GARDENS, Midhurst
‡‡FITTLEWORTH GARDENS (The Grange,
  The Hazels, Lowerstreet House)
HEASELANDS, Haywards Heath
‡‡‡MALT HOUSE, Chithurst, nr Rogate
NEWICK PARK, Newick
PEANS WOOD, Robertsbridge
SOUTH LODGE, Lower Beeding,
  nr Horsham
‡‡‡TELEGRAPH HOUSE, North Marden,
  Chichester
‡‡THE UPPER LODGE, Stopham,
  nr Pulborough

MAY Monday 26 (Spring Bank Hol.)
‡CISSBURY, Findon
‡‡COLLIERS FARM, Fernhurst,
  nr Haslemere
FITTLEWORTH GARDENS (The Grange,
  The Hazels, Lowerstreet House)
‡HIGHDOWN, Goring-by-Sea
‡‡MALT HOUSE, Chithurst, nr Rogate

MAY Wednesday 28
HEASELANDS, Haywards Heath

MAY Saturday 31
BIGNOR PARK, Pulborough

JUNE daily except Mondays
GREAT DIXTER, Northiam

JUNE every Saturday, Sunday, Wednesday & Thursday
BORDE HILL, Haywards Heath

JUNE every Saturday & Sunday
DENMANS, Fontwell

JUNE daily except Saturdays
  WEST DEAN GARDENS, nr Chichester
JUNE Sunday 1
  COBBLERS, Crowborough
  DAMEREL, North Chailey, nr Lewes
  ‡BIGNOR PARK, Pulborough
  ‡UPPER HOUSE, West Burton
  ‡‡BUNDYS, Bolney, nr Horsham
  ‡‡THE FOX & HOUNDS FARM, Bolney
  ‡‡‡FAIR RIDGE, Robertsbridge
  ‡‡‡LITTLE PEANS, Robertsbridge
  ‡‡‡NEWHOUSE FARM, Robertsbridge
  ‡‡‡‡LANE END, Midhurst
  ‡‡‡‡MALT HOUSE, Chithurst, nr Rogate
  SOUTH LODGE, Lower Beeding,
    nr Horsham
JUNE Monday 2
  ‡BIGNOR PARK, Pulborough
  ‡‡LANE END, Midhurst
  ‡‡ST ROCHE'S ARBORETUM, Singleton
    Hill
  ‡UPPER HOUSE, West Burton
JUNE Tuesday 3 daily to Saturday 7
  ST ROCHE'S ARBORETUM, Singleton
    Hill
JUNE Sunday 8
  COKE'S COTTAGE, West Burton,
    nr Pulborough
  OFFHAM HOUSE, nr Lewes
  PARHAM PARK, nr Pulborough
  ST ROCHE'S ARBORETUM, Singleton
    Hill
  UPPARK, nr Petersfield
JUNE Monday 9
  COKE'S COTTAGE, West Burton,
    nr Pulborough
JUNE Tuesday 10
  NYMANS, Handcross
JUNE Wednesday 11 & Thursday 12
  PARHAM PARK, nr Pulborough
JUNE Friday 13
  DOWN PLACE, Harting, Petersfield
JUNE Saturday 14
  DOWN PLACE, Harting, Petersfield
  ROOM OUTSIDE, Goodwood Gardens,
    nr Chichester
JUNE Sunday 15
  COBBLERS, Crowborough
  ‡COLLIERS FARM, Fernhurst,
    nr Haslemere
  DANESACRE, Sidlesham, nr Chichester
  DOWN PLACE, Harting, Petersfield
  ‡ICI PLANT PROTECTION DIVISION,
    Fernhurst
JUNE Monday 16
  COLLIERS FARM, Fernhurst,
    nr Haslemere
  DOWN PLACE, Harting, Petersfield
JUNE Tuesday 17 & Wednesday 18
  COLLIERS FARM, Fernhurst,
    nr Haslemere
JUNE Saturday 21
  TREYFORD MANOR, nr Midhurst
JUNE Sunday 22
  ‡COKE'S COTTAGE, West Burton,
    nr Pulborough

  RYMANS, Apuldram, nr Chichester
  ‡‡TREYFORD MANOR, nr Midhurst
  ‡‡TROTTON OLD RECTORY, nr Petersfield
  ‡WEST BURTON HOUSE, nr Pulborough
JUNE Monday 23
  ‡COKE'S COTTAGE, West Burton,
    nr Pulborough
  ‡WEST BURTON HOUSE, nr Pulborough
JUNE Wednesday 25
  OLD LODGE, Nutley
JUNE Saturday 28
  COX'S COTTAGE, Selsey
  WHITEHOUSE COTTAGE, nr Haywards
    Heath
JUNE Sunday 29
  BEECHES FARM, Buckham Hill,
    nr Uckfield
  COBBLERS, Crowborough
  COWBEECH FARM, Cowbeech,
    Hailsham
  COX'S COTTAGE, Selsey
  FITTLEWORTH GARDENS (Lowerstreet
    House & The Mill House)
  FOLKINGTON GARDENS, nr Polgate
  HOUGHTON FARM HOUSE, Arundel
  KETCHES, Newick, nr Lewes
  THE OLD VICARAGE, Firle, nr Lewes
  ROGATE GARDENS, nr Petersfield
  STRAWBERRY HOUSE, Kingsley Green,
    nr Haslemere
  WESTBOURNE GARDENS, nr Emsworth
  WHITEHOUSE COTTAGE, nr Haywards
    Heath
JUNE Monday 30
  COX'S COTTAGE, Selsey
JULY daily except Mondays
  GREAT DIXTER, Northiam
**JULY every Saturday, Sunday,
Wednesday & Thursday**
  BORDE HILL, Haywards Heath
JULY every Saturday & Sunday
  DENMANS, Fontwell
JULY daily except Saturdays
  WEST DEAN GARDENS, nr Chichester
JULY Thursday 3
  LONG HOUSE, Cowfold
JULY Saturday 5
  TELEGRAPH HOUSE, North Marden,
    Chichester
JULY Sunday 6
  BANKS FARM, nr Lewes
  COATES MANOR, nr Fittleworth
  COPLANDS, Northiam
  COWBEECH FARM, Cowbeech,
    nr Hailsham
  HIGHDOWN, Goring-by-Sea
  PHEASANTS HATCH, Piltdown,
    nr Uckfield
  ROGATE GARDENS, nr Petersfield
  TELEGRAPH HOUSE, North Marden,
    Chichester
  UDIMORE GARDENS, nr Rye
JULY Monday 7 & Tuesday 8
  COATES MANOR, nr Fittleworth

**JULY Wednesday 9, Thursday 10 &
Friday 11**
  LITTLE COURT, Midhurst
JULY Saturday 12
  ‡LITTLE COURT, Midhurst
  ‡PAXTONS, East Lavant, nr Chichester
JULY Sunday 13
  ‡CASTERS BROOK, Cocking, nr Midhurst
  COBBLERS, Crowborough
  EASTHAM GRANGE, Guestling,
    nr Hastings
  ‡PAXTONS, East Lavant, nr Chichester
  RENBY GRANGE, Boars Head,
    nr Crowborough
  WINCHELSEA GARDENS, Winchelsea
JULY Sunday 20
  HEASELANDS, Haywards Heath
  RENBY GRANGE, Boars Head, nr
    Crowborough
  RYMANS, Apuldram, nr Chichester
JULY Sunday 27
  COBBLERS, Crowborough
**AUGUST daily except Mondays (but
open Monday 25)**
  GREAT DIXTER, Northiam
**AUGUST every Saturday, Sunday,
Wednesday, Thursday & Bank Hol.**
  BORDE HILL, Haywards Heath
AUGUST every Saturday & Sunday
  DENMANS, Fontwell
AUGUST daily except Saturday
  WEST DEAN GARDENS, nr Chichester
AUGUST Sunday 3
  COBBLERS, Crowborough
  LEGH MANOR, Anstye, nr Cuckfield
AUGUST Sunday 10
  UPPARK, nr Petersfield
AUGUST Wednesday 13 & Thursday 14
  CHAMPS HILL, Coldwaltham, Pulborough
AUGUST Sunday 17
  COBBLERS, Crowborough
AUGUST Sunday 24
  NEWTIMBER PLACE, Newtimber,
    nr Hassocks
  RYMANS, Apuldram, nr Chichester
  SOUTH CORNER HOUSE, Duncton,
    nr Petworth
**AUGUST Monday 25 (Summer Bank
Hol.)**
  PENNS IN THE ROCKS, Groombridge
  SOUTH CORNER HOUSE, Duncton,
    nr Petworth
AUGUST Sunday 31
  REYSON OASTS, Broad Oak, nr Rye
SEPTEMBER daily except Mondays
  GREAT DIXTER, Northiam
**SEPTEMBER every Saturday, Sunday,
Wednesday & Thursday**
  BORDE HILL, Haywards Heath
SEPTEMBER every Saturday & Sunday
  DENMANS, Fontwell
SEPTEMBER daily except Saturdays
  WEST DEAN GARDENS, nr Chichester

SEPTEMBER Sunday 7
  CHURCH HILL HOUSE, Midhurst
  FAIRFIELD, Little Bognor, Fittleworth
  GOATCHER'S NURSERIES, Washington
SEPTEMBER Monday 8
  FAIRFIELD, Little Bognor, Fittleworth
**OCTOBER daily except Mondays to
October 12 inc.**
  GREAT DIXTER, Northiam
OCTOBER every Saturday & Sunday
  DENMANS, Fontwell
OCTOBER Sunday 5
  STANDEN, East Grinstead
**OCTOBER Saturday 18, Sunday 19,
Saturday 25**
  GREAT DIXTER, Northiam
OCTOBER Sunday 26
  GREAT DIXTER, Northiam
  ST ROCHE'S ARBORETUM, Singleton
    Hill

DESCRIPTIONS OF GARDENS

Amberley Castle †⊕ (The Baroness Emmet
of Amberley) Amberley. Garden within C14
castle wall. Dogs only on leads. Tea Houghton
Bridge or Coke's Cottage (April 6 only).
Adm. 25p. Sat. & Sun. April 5 & 6 (2–6)

Banks Farm (Michael Warren Esq) Barcombe, 4 m. N of Lewes. Between A275 &
A26, well signposted from Barcombe. 7½
acres; shrubs, roses & lawns; 2 ponds &
water gardens; walled pool garden. TEAS.
Adm. 30p, Chd. 10p. Sun. July 6 (2–6)

Beeches Farm †&⊕ (Mr & Mrs Robert
Thomas) Buckham Hill, Uckfield; Uckfield—
Isfield Rd. TEAS. *Adm. 25p, Chd. 10p. △Sun.
April 20 & Sun. June 29 (2–6)*

Bignor Park &⊕ (The Viscount Mersey)
Pulborough, 5 m. from Petworth on West
Burton Rd. Nearest village: Sutton (Sussex).
Medium size garden. Walled herbaceous
garden, roses. Tea & biscuits Upper House
(June 1 & 2 only). *Adm. 20p, Chd. 10p. Sat.
May 31; Sun. & Mon. June 1 & 2 (2–6)*

Birch Grove House (Birch Grove Estates
Ltd) Chelwood Gate. Station: East Grinstead
7 m. (Southdown bus 170/176 to Red Lion,
Chelwood Gate); Haywards Heath, 8 m.
(Southdown bus 170/176 to Red Lion,
Chelwood Gate). Daffodils in spring wood-
land. *Adm. 50p, Chd. 20p; under 5, free. Sun.
April 20 & Sun. April 27 (2–6)*

● **Borde Hill Garden** *&⊕ (R. N. S. Clarke
Esq) 1½ m. N of Haywards Heath on Balcombe
Rd. Large garden of great botanical interest &
beauty; rare trees & shrubs; extensive views;
woodland walks; camellias, magnolias, rhododendrons, azaleas. NO DOGS. Picnic area in
delightful surroundings. TEAS; also luncheon
snacks. Free car park. *Adm. 60p, Chd. 30p;
organised parties of 12 or more 50p each.
March 15 to Sept. 28 every Wed., Thurs., Sat.,
Sun. & Bank Hol. (10–6)*

Bundys⚭⊕ (Mr & Mrs J. C. J. Clark) Colwood Lane, Bolney, 7 m. SE of Horsham. From A23, N of Bolney, turn off W; then 1st left at pillar box. 3 acres; camellias, azaleas, rhododendrons, handkerchief tree. NO DOGS. TEAS. *Adm. 30p, Chd. 10p. Sun. June 1 (2–6)*

¶**Burton Manor**⊕ (Mr & Mrs Bertram Butler) West Burton Lane, 5 m. SW of Pulborough. A29 going S, turn right at foot of Bury Hill, signposted West Burton & Bignor Roman Villa; house is down road on right. Park on one side of road only and walk up drive. 2-acre garden; lawns, bulbs, flowering trees, shrubs, azaleas; view of downs. NO DOGS. Share to West Sussex Assoc. for Care of the Disabled (Arundel & District Branch). *Adm. 40p, Chd. 20p. Sun. April 20 & Sun. May 18 (2–6)*

Casters Brook∗ (Mr & Mrs E. B. Owen-Jones) Cocking, 3 m. S of Midhurst. A286 Midhurst–Chichester Rd; at Cocking P.O. take sharp turn to E & garden is 100 yds on right (through farm entrance). Chalk garden of just under 2 acres made from neglected orchard since 1963; slopes down to old mill pond; interesting corners created on different levels all in beautiful downland setting. Next to C11 church. NO DOGS. Tea Midhurst. *Adm. 25p, Chd. (must be accompanied by adult) 10p. Sun. July 13 (2–6)*

Champs Hill (Mr & Mrs A. H. Bowerman) Coldwaltham, S of Pulborough. Coming from Pulborough on A29, in Coldwaltham turn right on to Fittleworth Rd; entrance 300 yds on right. 27 acres of wild garden on old sandpits; woodland walks; heathers; views of Arun Valley & S Downs. NO DOGS. *Adm. 25p. Wed. & Thurs. May 14 & 15; Wed. & Thurs. Aug. 13 & 14 (11–7); also by appt. April to Sept. (Tel. Bury (Sussex) 631)*

Charleston Manor∗†⚭⊕ (Lady Birley) West Dean, 7 m. W of Eastbourne, ¾ m. S of Litlington, B2108. Bus: SD 12 from Brighton & Eastbourne. Romantic garden, framed with yew hedges & old flint walls; flowering shrubs, bulbs, cyclamen, euphorbias. Earliest part of house 1080–1100. Notable tithe barn & Norman dovecote. Sorry, NO DOGS. Good walking on Downs nearby. Tea Drusilla's, nr Alfriston & Litlington Tea Gardens. *Adm. 50p. △Sun. May 11 (2–6)*

Chidmere∗⊕ (Thomas Baxendale Esq) Chidham, 6 m. W of Chichester. A27, 1 m. Bus: SD250 Chichester–Emsworth. Interesting garden; yew & hornbeam hedges; bulbs, rock garden & flowering shrubs bounded by large mere, now a private nature reserve. C15 house (not shown). *Adm. 25p, Chd. 15p. Sun. & Mon. April 13 & 14; Sun. & Mon. May 18 & 19 (2–7); also by appt., for parties only (Tel. Bosham 573096)*

Church Farmhouse⊕ (Mr & Mrs G. M. Burton) East Lavant, 3½ m. N of Chichester.

A286 Chichester–Midhurst Rd; turn E to East Lavant. Medium-sized garden; spring bulbs, walled area, orchard. NO DOGS. TEA & biscuits. *Adm. 15p. Sat. & Sun. April 12 & 13 (2–5.30)*

Church Hill House⊕ (Michael Riseley-Prichard Esq) Midhurst. In centre of town. Small walled garden with roses, geraniums, etc.; typical small family town garden; small orangery. Tea Spread Eagle Hotel, 50 yds. *Collecting box. Sun. Sept. 7 (2–6)*

Cissbury⊕ (Hon. Mrs R. J. P. Wyatt) Nepcote, Findon, 4 m. N of Worthing. From Worthing 4 m. via A24 to Findon & 1st turn right after derestriction sign at Nepcote. From N via A24; follow Findon bypass to end of dual carriageway; turn left immediately at Nepcote. Large garden with views of Downs & parkland; spring bulbs & some plants of interest. Light TEAS. *Adm. 25p, Chd. 10p. Sat. & Sun. April 19 & 20 (2.30–5.30); Sun. & Mon. May 25 & 26 (2.30–6)*

Coates Manor∗⊕ (Mr & Mrs G. H. Thorp) nr Fittleworth. From Fittleworth S for ½ m. along B2138 & turn at signpost marked 'Coates'. 1 acre, mainly shrubs & foliage of special interest. Elizabethan house (not shown) scheduled of historic interest. *Collecting box. Sun., Mon. & Tues. July 6, 7 & 8 (11–6.30)*

Cobblers∗ (Mr & Mrs Martin Furniss) Mount Pleasant, Jarvis Brook, Crowborough. A26 Tunbridge Wells–Uckfield Rd; at Crowborough Cross take B2100 signed Crowborough Station & Rotherfield; at 2nd X-rds (Green Lane & Tollwood Rd) turn right into Tollwood Rd to Mount Pleasant; entrance gate on right. Medium-sized garden (approx. 2 acres) on sloping site; designed & planted by present owners since 1968, in informal manner to display large range of herbaceous & shrub species, inc. water gardens, giving all-season colour. Subject of article in RHS Journal March '78 & of 2 BBC 2 gardening programmes, Aug. '78. NO DOGS. TEAS. *Adm. 50p, Chd. 30p. Suns. June 1, 15, 29; July 13, 27; Aug. 3, 17 (2,30–6)*

Coke's Cottage†⊕ (Mr & Mrs Nigel Azis) West Burton, 5 m. SW of Pulborough. Cottage garden, owner-maintained; bulbs, shrubs, herbaceous borders, roses; gravelled areas, new small water area, orchard, vegetable garden. Plant stall (early openings). NO DOGS. TEA & biscuits (Suns. only). *Adm. 20p, Chd. 10p. Fri., Sat. & Sun. April 4, 5, 6 (2–5); Suns. & Mons. April 13 & 14, June 8 & 9, June 22 & 23 (2–7); also open by appt. April, June (Tel. Bury 636)*

Colliers Farm (Mr & Mrs R. M. Hollis) Fernhurst, 4 m. S of Haslemere. A286 Haslemere–Midhurst Rd; S of Fernhurst, 300 yds beyond 30 mph decontrol sign on right. Medium-sized garden made since 1972;

lovely situation on S slope; shrubs & mixed borders inc. shrub roses; woodland walk with primulas, rhododendrons by stream & small pond. Few plants for sale if available. NO DOGS, please. TEAS (May 25 & June 15 only). *Adm. 20p, Chd. 5p. Suns. & Mons. May 25 & 26; June 15 & 16; Tues. & Wed. June 17 & 18 (2–6)*

Cooke's House* (Miss J. B. Courtauld) West Burton, 5 m. SW of Pulborough. 1 m. from Roman Villa, Bignor. Turn off A29 at White Horse, Bury, ¾ m. Medium-sized garden under the Downs, round Elizabethan house (not open); varied interest inc. spring flowers & topiary, old roses & herbs. Free car park. *Adm. 20p, Chd. 5p. Sun. & Mon. April 27 & 28 (2–6); also by appt. April to July (apply by letter with SAE)*

Coplands*⊕ (Mr & Mrs Hugh Saunders) Dixter Lane (nr Great Dixter), Northiam. Approx. 1 acre; established garden in course of being redesigned & restored; rhododendrons, azaleas, flowering shrubs & roses, mature trees & some rare plants. NO DOGS. Share to Dr Barnado's Homes. *Adm. 25p, Chd. 10p. Sun. May 25 & Sun. July 6 (2.30–6.30)*

Cowbeech Farm*†⅃ (Mrs M. Huiskamp) Cowbeech, 4 m. NE of Hailsham. A271 to Amberstone & then turn off N for Cowbeech. Medium-sized garden; natural dell & bog garden; small pond with island & ducks; waterfall; sculpture exhibition; lawns, choice shrubs & trees; rose beds & shrubberies; wild garden & small vegetable plot. NO DOGS. TEAS. Share to Gardeners' Royal Benevolent Society. *Adm. 20p, Chd. 10p. Suns. June 29 & July 6 (2–6)*

Cowdray Park Gardens⊕ (The Viscount Cowdray) Midhurst. Bus: 201, 261, Midhurst–Petworth–Worthing, alight Cowdray Park. Entrance by East Front. *Adm. 40p. Sun. May 25 (2–7)*

Cox's Cottage⊕ (Mrs P. C. May) West St, Selsey. Entrance to garden & parking is on Coxes Rd (*not* West St). From Chichester via A27 & turn on to B2145 & along 8 m. to Selsey; turn right into West St & after passing Cox's Cottage turn left & left again into Coxes Rd. Small, easily maintained series of gardens; grey & green foliages, old English roses, greenhouse, small vegetable garden, thyme & stone courtyard. Oil & water colour pictures, also pen & wash correspondence cards by owner will be on sale (proportion of sales to N.G.S.). NO DOGS. TEAS. *Adm. 25p, Chd. 10p. Sat., Sun. & Mon. June 28, 29 & 30 (2–5); also by appt. all year (Tel. Selsey 2131)*

Damerel⊕ (D. E. L. Parsons Esq) N Chailey, 6 m. E of Haywards Heath. 1 m. N of junction A272 (Haywards Heath–Maresfield) & A275

(Lewes–East Grinstead) Chailey X rds. 10-acre, open-landscaped, labour saving woodland garden. Plant stall. Home-made TEAS. *Adm. 25p, Chd. 10p. Sun. June 1 (2–6)*

Danesacre (Capt. & Mrs A. J. Petrie-Hay) Mill Lane, Sidlesham, 4½ m. S of Chichester. Chichester By-pass A27, turn S to Selsey; approx. 4 m. to Jolly Fisherman in Sidlesham turn left into Mill Lane; follow lane round Pagham Harbour, 4th house on left after leaving Old Quay. Small garden, mainly roses & shrubs; lily pond; small collection ornamental waterfowl. NO DOGS, please. Tea Bashead, opp. *Adm. 20p, Chd. 5p. Sun. June 15 (2–6)*

Denmans*⅃⊕ (Mrs J. H. Robinson) Denmans Lane, Fontwell. From A27 turn S at Denmans Lane, immediately W of Fontwell Racecourse. Bognor, Chichester & Arundel all 5 m. Walled gardens planned for year-round beauty; simple natural layout of trees, wall shrubs & climbers; gravel garden with plants & shrubs of interest; greenhouses; Denmans Plants for sale. NO DOGS. *Adm. 20p. March 1 to Oct. 31 every Sat. & Sun. (2–6)*

Down Place⅃ (Vice-Adm. Sir Geoffrey Thistleton-Smith) Harting, 5 m. SE of Petersfield, 11 m. NW of Chichester. ¼ m. below Harting Hill Picnic Site on B2141. 7-acre garden on chalk downland with extensive views. Partly landscaped, partly wild with trees & wild flowers. TEAS. Exhibition & sale of pictures by local artists. *Adm. (incl.) 40p, Chd. 20p. Fri., Sat., Sun. & Mon. June 13, 14, 15 & 16 (2–6)*

Drewitts (Maj. & Mrs Derek Wigan) Warninglid. Mid-way between Haywards Heath & Horsham. Warninglid, 1 m. Rock garden flanked by azaleas, rhododendrons. Fine views. TEAS. *Adm. 25p, Chd. 10p. Sun. & Mon. May 11 & 12 (2–7)*

Eastham Grange (Mr & Mrs Rufford Whitehead) Friars Hill, Guestling, 3 m. E of Hastings. From A259 at White Hart Inn, take Pett Rd. Charming owner-designed & maintained garden of nearly 1 acre with outstanding herbaceous border; old-established trees & shrubs; small water garden; fine views across Romney Marsh to Rye & Dungeness. NO DOGS. *Adm. 20p, Chd. 10p. Sun. July 13 (2.30–6.30)*

Fairfield⊕ (Mr & Mrs R. Constanduros) Little Bognor, Fittleworth. 3½ m. E of Petworth; A283 Petworth–Pulborough; turning to Little Bognor on Petworth side of Fittleworth; ½ m. up lane, 1st turning on left, house on right. Garden of ⅓ acre made since 1972; shrubs, herbaceous, clematis & roses; view of South Downs. NO DOGS. *Adm. 20p, Chd. 5p. Sun. & Mon. May 18 & 19, Sun. & Mon. Sept. 7 & 8 (2–5)*

¶Fair Ridge (Mr & Mrs J. O. Aveline), Bugsell Lane, 1 m. W of Robertsbridge. Turn off A21 in centre of Robertsbridge on road to Brightling for approx. 1 m.; right turn into Bugsell Lane nr top of hill. Parking in Brightling Rd & Langham Rd. 10-acre dell garden & bluebell wood; dwarf conifers, azaleas, heathers, acers & some specimen trees. *Adm. 20p, Chd. 5p. Sun. June 1 (2–6)*

Fernhurst Gardens. *✶⊕ On May 18 the following 5 gardens will be open. 4 m. S of Haslemere; A286 Haslemere–Midhurst; on entering Fernhurst gardens are on W side of road. Kingsley Green is 1½ m. S of Haslemere. (Look out for signs.) Bus route 219. Gardens of varying size & age, inc. a formal garden, a water garden in the making, rhododendrons, azaleas, shrubs, bulbs. Plants & cuttings for sale. TEAS. *Combined charge 40p, Chd. 10p. Sun. May 18 (2–6)*

- **Merryfield** (Mr & Mrs R. S. Emery)
- **Henley Gap** (Cdr & Mrs E. Ewing) Kingsley Green
- **Fernhurst Place** (Mr & Mrs R. Mann)
- **Woodpeckers** (Mr & Mrs E. D. Moller)
- **Summerfield** (Mr & Mrs C. H. Woodhouse) Square Drive, Kingsley Green

Fittleworth Gardens. On May 25 & 26 the following 3 gardens will be open. A283 midway between Petworth & Pulborough; in Fittleworth turn on to B2138. TEAS at The Grange. *Combined charge 40p, Chd. 10p. Sun. & Mon. May 25 & 26 (2–6.30)*

The Grange⊕ (Mr & Mrs P. F. Dutton) At The Swan in Fittleworth turn right & house 75 yds on left. 4-acre new garden made from paddock; spring flowering shrubs. Lovely views to river

The Hazels⊕ (M. C. Pratt Esq) At The Swan in Fittleworth turn right & garden is opp. General Stores close by. Approx. 1-acre; small collection of trees & shrubs planted since 1970; large collection of azalea seedlings; small heather garden; a few rhododendrons; informal garden

Lowerstreet House (L. J. Holloway Esq) Next to Swan Inn. Small garden with shrubs, bulbs, herbaceous, dahlias, & greenhouse

Fittleworth Gardens. On June 29 the following 2 gardens will be open. For directions see previous entry. TEAS at Mill House. *Combined charge 30p, Chd. 10p. Sun. June 29 (2–6.30)*

Lowerstreet House (L. J. Holloway Esq) Next to Swan Inn. Small garden with shrubs, bulbs, herbaceous, dahlias & greenhouse

The Mill House⊕ (P. Gilbert Esq) 1-acre garden with shrubs, old-fashioned roses; historic mill with R. Rother through garden

Folkington Gardens, 3 m. SW of Polegate. 5 m. NW of Eastbourne, S of A27 between Polegate & Wilmington. Bus stop on A27, 1 m. TEA & biscuits. *Combined charge for following 2 gardens 30p, Chd. 10p. Sun. June 29 (2–6)*

Folkington Place (Cmdr & Mrs H. J. Voorspuy) Medium-sized garden; collection of unusual plants

Old Rectory Cottage (Mr & Mrs T. G. Jennings) Small garden; herbaceous borders & roses in downland setting

The Fox & Hounds Farm (Mr & Mrs C. W. Reed) Bolney. Turn at Bolney Stage, main Brighton Rd, Broxmead Lane. Haywards Heath, 5 m. Daffodils, flowering shrubs, rhododendrons & azaleas. C16 house. TEAS. *Adm. 20p, Chd. 5p. Sun. April 27 & Sun. June 1 (2–5.30)*

Goatcher's Nurseries *✶⅋ (Messrs A. Goatcher & Son) Washington. ½ m. from Rock X rds on A24. 40-acres of hardy nursery stock, inc. perennials in bloom; vast range of conifers, trees & shrubs, inc. many mature & rare specimens. Adjoining garden, **Cedar Cottage** shows 'mixed borders' with plants for the connoisseur. Fine setting with views of S Downs. NO DOGS. *Collecting box. Sun. Sept. 7 (2–6)*

● **Great Dixter** *✶† (The Lloyd Family) Northiam. ½ m. N of Northiam, 8 m. NW of Rye. Bus: MD 12 Hastings–Tenterden; Rye–Northiam–Hastings, alight Northiam P.O., 500 yds. Topiary; wide variety of plants. Historical house shown (2–5). NO DOGS. Tea Mary Mason, Yew Tree Farm, Northiam. *Adm. garden 50p, Chd. 15p house 50p extra, Chd. 15p. April 1 to Oct. 12, daily except Mons., but open on Bank Hols.; also Sats. & Suns. Oct. 18 & 19, 25 & 26 (2–5, last adm. 5)*

Heaselands *✶⊕ (Mrs Ernest G. Kleinwort) Haywards Heath. 1 m. S of Haywards Heath Hospital on A273 to Burgess Hill. Bus: SD 82A (weekdays also 82, 83) Haywards Heath–Cuckfield, alight Butler's Green (Heaselands, 1 m.). Garden over 20 acres; flowering shrubs & trees rhododendrons & azaleas; water gardens; woodland; roses; aviaries; collection of wildfowl. Coaches by appt. only. TEAS available. Free car park. *Adm. 45p, Chd. 20p. Suns. May 11, 18, 25; Weds. May 14, 21, 28; Sun. July 20 (2–6.30)*

The High Beeches *✶†⅋ (The Hon. H. E. Boscawen) On B2110, 1 m. E of Handcross. 16 acres; woodland garden with trees, magnolias, rhododendrons & daffodils. Of great botanical interest; one of the three famous gardens in Sussex designed by members of the Loder family who later created Leonardslee & Wakehurst Place. Tea *not* available but picnic area provided. NO DOGS. *Adm. 50p, Chd. 20p. Sun. April 20 (10.30–6); also by appt. at other times for organised parties*

Highdown *✶ (Worthing Corporation) Littlehampton Rd (A259), Goring-by-Sea, 3 m. W of Worthing. Station: Goring-by-Sea, 1 m. Famous garden in chalk-pit. Tea Cissbury (May 26 only). *Collecting tin. Mon. April 7 & Mon. May 26; Sun. July 6 (2–6)*

Houghton Farm House (Mr & Mrs Michael Lock) 3 m. N of Arundel via A284 &

B2139. 1-acre garden with shrubs, bulbs & roses. Good views. NO DOGS. Tea The Tea Gardens, Houghton Bridge. *Adm. 20p. Sun. & Mon. April 27 & 28; Sun. June 29 (2–6)*

ICI Plant Protection Division,⬥⊕ Fernhurst, 3 m. S of Haslemere. From A286 Haslemere–Midhurst turn E at Fernhurst X-rds, signposted. 5½ acres; good lawns; fine trees, all about 100 yrs old; good shrubs, woodland walks; greenhouses with very good collection of decorative plants (all part of ICI Plant Protection's divisional HQ); also commercial glasshouses with tomatoes, chrysanthemums; commercial orchards. Nature trail. Interesting Victorian house. NO DOGS. Shop open. Refreshments available. Share to Gardeners' Sunday & Aldingbourne Centre for Handicapped Children. *Adm. per car £1. Sun. June 15 (10–6)*

Joan Nightingale House⊕ (The Little Black Bag Housing Assn Ltd) Bolnore Rd, Haywards Heath. ½ m. W of Haywards Heath, off A272 to Cuckfield, nr Munster Green. Bus stop 300 yds through Beechhurst. Small new formal garden; roses with mixed shrub borders. Part house shown (new flatlets & accommodation for district & other nurses). TEA & biscuits. *Silver collection. Sat. May 3 (2–6)*

Ketches⊕ (David Manwaring Robertson Esq) Newick, 5 m. W of Uckfield. From Newick on A272 take Barcombe Rd running S out of Newick & house is on right of rd, opp. turning to Newick Church. Medium-sized garden (1½ acres) with old-fashioned roses; shrub & herbaceous borders. NO DOGS. TEAS. *Adm. 30p, Chd. 10p. Sun. June 29 (2–6.30)*

King Edward VII Hospital, 3 m. NW of Midhurst. Bus: Alder Valley 219 Aldershot–Midhurst, alight at Hospital Drive, 1 m. Transport direct to Hospital leaves Haslemere Station at 1.45 & Midhurst Bus Station at 2.30. Large garden. DOGS allowed in grounds but NOT in hospital. TEAS (3–5 only). *Collecting box. Sat. May 17 (2–5.30)*

Lane End⊕ (Mr & Mrs C. J. Epril) Sheep Lane, Midhurst. Behind Public Library; from main rd (North St) turn left at Knockhundred Row, uphill to Lloyds Bank & left into Sheep Lane; at top of lane turn left for house, *but no entry for cars & no parking by house.* Car park by Church at bottom of hill; cars may also be parked in lane leading uphill towards house. Approx. 2 acres, inc. wild garden; alpine garden; rockery with pools; rhododendrons, azaleas & heath border. Below ramparts of original castle with lovely views over water meadows to ruins of Cowdray House. Tea Spread Eagle Hotel, Angel Hotel & teashops in Midhurst. *Adm. 25p, Chd. 10p. Sun. & Mon. June 1 & 2 (11–1 & 2–6); also by appt (June–Sept.).*

Langney Priory †⊕ (Mrs Fenwick-Owen) 3½ m. NE of Eastbourne. A259; turn on to Pevensey Rd & right into Priory Rd; next to St Richards Church. Walled garden & orchard surrounding a Priory, partly C12, daughter house of Cluniac Priory, Lewes. TEA & biscuits. *Adm. 20p, Chd. 5p. Sun. May 4 (2–5.30)*

Legh Manor (Mr & Mrs N. J. Teale & The Archaeological Society) Cuckfield Rd, Anstye, 2½ m. SW of Cuckfield. From A23 London–Brighton Rd, turn off at Bolney; take A272 to Anstye; at 'T' junction opp. Green Cross, turn right, then fork right on to Hurstpierpoint Rd; garden about ½ m. on right. Garden of about 5 acres; part designed by Gertrude Jekyll. Tudor house (not open) with later additions. NO DOGS. *Adm. 25p, Chd. 10p. Sun. April 27 & Sun. Aug. 3 (2–5)*

Little Court (D. E. L. Anderson Esq) Carron Lane, Midhurst. ½ m. from Midhurst; Carron Lane is 3rd turning on left from X-rds in Midhurst, about ¼ m. along A272 Midhurst–Petersfield. 1 acre, mature garden adjacent to Midhurst Common; fine trees & shrubs, flowers, vegetables & fruit; colourful paved courtyard. Tea Midhurst. *Collecting box. Wed., Thurs., Fri., Sat. July 9, 10, 11, 12 (2–6); also by appt. (Midhurst 2790.)*

Little Peans,⬥ (Mr & Mrs Stuart Oddy) Robertsbridge. Turn off A21 in centre of Robertsbridge on rd to Brightling for approx. 1 m. 7 acres with rhododendrons & azaleas. *Adm. 20p, Chd. 5p. Sun. June 1 (2–6)*

Long House⊕ (Michael Richardson Esq) Cowfold. ¾ m. N of A272, Cowfold–Bolney Rd; 1st turning left after Cowfold. Bus stop: 1st X-rds out of Cowfold towards Bolney, 1 m. Medium-sized & mainly formal garden; rose beds & herbaceous borders. TEAS. *Adm. 30p. Thurs. July 3 (12–6)*

Malt House *⬥ (Mr & Mrs Graham Ferguson) Chithurst, Rogate. From A272, 3½ m. W of Midhurst turn N at signpost to Chithurst; garden is 1½ m. on; or from A3, 2 m. S of Liphook, take turning SE to Milland & then follow signs to Chithurst for 1½ m. Approx. 4 acres; flowering shrubs inc. exceptional rhododendrons & azaleas, leading into 50 acres of lovely woodland walks. Few plants for sale. Tea Trotton Old Rectory (May 18 only). *Adm. 40p, Chd. 20p Suns. April 20, 27; Sun. & Mon. May 4 & 5; Suns. May 11, 18, 25; Mon. May 26; Sun. June 1 (2–7)*

Mountfield Court,⬥ (T. Egerton Esq) 2 m. S of Robertsbridge. On main London–Hastings Rd. ½ m. from Johns Cross. Bus: MD 5, 5A Hastings–Maidstone, alight Johns Cross. Tea Johns Cross Inn. *Adm. 20p, Chd. 10p. Sun. May 18 (2–6)*

Newhouse Farm (Mrs K. Wagstaff) 3 m. W of Robertsbridge; A21 turn W in Robertsbridge, following signpost for Brightling; 2½

m. beyond level crossing on right-hand side is private lane with signpost. 6-acre garden with rhododendron & azalea walks; heathers; bluebell wood; walk round semi-cultivated Sussex iron pit (pond). *Adm. 20p, Chd. 5p. Sun. June 1 (2–6).*

Newick Park★ (The Viscount Brentford) 1 m. S of Newick (which is on A272) towards Barcombe. Wild shrub garden featuring rhododendrons & azaleas; fine trees. TEAS. *Adm. 30p, Chd. 15p. Sun. May 25 (2–7).*

Newtimber Place⊕ (His Honour Judge & Mrs John Clay) Newtimber, nr Hassocks. 1 m. N of Pyecombe, turn W from A23 in dual carriageway. 7 m. N of Brighton. Bus: SD 170, 171, 172, 173. Brighton to Newtimber Rookery, 150 yds. Medium-sized garden. Old moated house. *Adm. 30p.* △*Sun. April 20 & Sun. Aug. 24 (2–6).*

Nymans★⊕ (Anne, Countess of Rosse; The National Trust—see p. ix) Handcross. On B2114 at Handcross signposted off M23/A23 London–Brighton Rd, SE of Handcross. Bus: SD 173 from Crawley & Haywards Heath; also Town & Country bus from Crawley. Rare trees & shrubs. Botanical interest. Wheelchairs are available at the garden. NO DOGS. Car park free. *Adm. 70p, Chd. 35p. Organised parties 50p each.* △*Tues. May 6 & Tues. June 10 (2–7).*

Offham House⊕ (Mr & Mrs H. S. Taylor; Mr & Mrs H. N. A. Goodman) Offham, 2 m. N of Lewes. On A275. Cooksbridge station ½ m. Fountains & flowering trees; double herbaceous border & long peony bed. TEAS. *Adm. 25p, Chd. 10p. Sun. May 4 & Sun. June 8 (2–6).*

Old Lodge (Eleanor, Countess Castle Stewart) Nutley. 5 m. NE of Nutley. W of B2026. Nearest landmark: Duddleswell Wireless Station. *Adm. 20p, Chd. 5p. Wed. June 25 (2–7).*

The Old Vicarage (Mr C. & the Hon. Mrs Bridge) Firle, 4 m. SE of Lewes. From A27 Lewes–Eastbourne rd, turn off S into Firle village. Medium-sized garden in valley on N side of Downs with view up to Downs; flint walls, yew hedges, pleached limes & combined vegetable & flower garden. TEA from 3 p.m. *Adm. 20p, Chd. 5p. Sun. June 29 (2–7).*

Parham Park★⊕ (Mr & Mrs P. A. Tritton & The Hon. Clive & Mrs Gibson) 4 m. SE of Pulborough. Main entrance on Pulborough–Storrington Rd, A283. 4 acres of walled garden, also pleasure grounds & lake. Cut flowers grown for house, greenhouses & wendy house. Plants for sale in shop. Beautiful Elizabethan house with fine collection of portraits, furniture, rare needlework, etc. (Also open other days; see local press). *Adm. house & garden £1, OAPs & Chd. 60p; garden only 25p.* △*Sun. June 8, Wed. & Thurs. June 11 & 12 (Garden 1–6; house 2–5.30).*

Paxtons (Mr & Mrs Richard T. Bett) E Lavant, 3½ m. N of Chichester. A286 Chichester–Midhurst Rd, turn E to East Lavant, follow yellow posters. 2½-acre village garden with lawns, walled formal garden, border, flowering shrubs, bulbs, vegetable garden; orchard; all owner-maintained. *Adm. 20p. Sats. & Suns. May 10 & 11, July 12 & 13 (2–6).*

Peans Wood⊕ (F. D. de Kok Esq) Brightling Rd, 1 m. W of Robertsbridge; turn off A21 in centre of Robertsbridge on rd to Brightling for approx. 1 m.; garden on left. 28 acres; rhododendrons & azaleas & specimen trees. *Adm. 20p, Chd. 5p. Sun. May 25 (2–6).*

Penns in the Rocks†☒ (Lord & Lady Gibson) Groombridge. 7 m. SW of Tunbridge Wells on Groombridge–Crowborough Rd just S of Plumeyfeather corner. Bus: MD 91 Tunbridge Wells–East Grinstead, alight Plumeyfeather corner, ¾ m. Large garden; wild garden with rocky outcrops of sandstone; lake; C18 temple; old walled garden. House (not shown) part C18. Home-made TEAS. *Adm. 30p, Chd. 10p. Car park 20p. Mon. Aug. 25 (2.30–6).*

Pheasants Hatch⊕ (Brig. & Mrs Thubron) Piltdown, W of Uckfield. Bus: SD 169 passes gate. Medium-sized garden; mixed borders & foliage border; rose garden. Peacocks. Home-made TEAS. *Adm. 30p, Chd. 15p. Sun. July 6 (2–7).*

Portus★ (Miss E. I. Caldwell) Roman Landing, West Wittering, 7 m. SW of Chichester, via A286 Chichester–West Wittering; take turning to sea car park, for 20 yds only; keep rightish & take very sharp right into Roman Landing. Garden of ¼ acre; azaleas, rhododendrons, acers, specialist alpines, peat blocks, tufa wall, troughs, alpine house, dwarf conifers, camellias. Display table of dwarf conifers. Some plants for sale. NO DOGS. *Adm. 20p, Chd. 10p. Sun. & Mon. May 18 & 19 (11–5).*

¶**Renby Grange**★⊕ (Mr & Mrs Ronald Carr), Boars Head, 2½ m. NE of Crowborough on A26. 1½ acres; interesting garden created by present owners since 1968 as foreground to magnificent views; emphasis on shrubs, foliage plants & ground cover for year-round beauty. Featured in *Harpers & Queen*. Plant stall. NO DOGS. TEAS. Share to East Sussex Assoc. for the Disabled. *Adm. 40p, OAPs & Chd. 20p. Suns. July 13 & 20 (2–7).*

Reyson Oasts★⊕ (A. R. Thorley Esq & R. D. Thorley Esq) Broad Oak, 5 m. W of Rye. From A28 at Broad Oak X-rds turn E along B2089 towards Rye for ½ m. & house on right. 6 acres; garden with rhododendrons, azaleas & lily pond. House (not open) converted from 3 oast houses. Tea in Rye. *Adm. 30p, Chd. 10p Sun. Aug. 31 (2–7).*

Rogate Gardens. On June 29 & July 6 the following 2 groups of gardens will be open.

5 m. E of Petersfield ; 5 m. W of Midhurst on A272. To reach Slade Lane : turn N off A272 in Rogate at small X-rds ; gardens are ½ m. up lane. To reach Fyning Lane : ¼ m. E of Rogate turn N off A272 up lane signposted Terwick Common ; gardens are 50 yds along. All gardens owner-maintained. NO DOGS. TEAS at Rogate village hall. Share to village hall extension fund. *Combined charge for gardens in Slade Lane 50p, Chd. 10p; further combined charge for gardens in North St & Fyning Lane 50p, Chd. 10p. Suns. June 29 & July 6 (2–6)*

Slade Lane:

¶1 & 2 Hale Cottages (Mrs N. Fifield, Mrs B. Piper), Slade Lane. Very small charming cottage gardens with lovely views

¶Hedge Lea (Mrs M. S. Mitchell), Slade Lane. Small garden with roses, shrubs, vegetables & small orchard

¶Hunters Cottage (Mrs R. Masters), Slade Lane. Charming small colourful garden

¶Hunters Lodge (Mr & Mrs S. Rimmer), Slade Lane. Small garden started in 1977 ; shrubs, conifers, heathers, vegetable & soft fruit garden ; lovely views

¶Slade House (Mrs H. Davey), Slade Lane. Medium-sized garden with herbaceous borders, vegetable & fruit garden

North Street & Fyning Lane:

¶Fyning Manor (Mr & Mrs R. Talbot). Medium-sized garden, shrubs, herbaceous borders & vegetable garden

¶Hambledon House (Mr & Mrs J. A. C. Greenwood), Fyning Lane. Medium-sized garden, shrubs, vegetable & soft fruit garden

¶Lower Lodge (Mrs G. M. Bodkin), North St. Small garden started in 1977

¶Pond House (Mr & Mrs G. M. Stroud), North St. Garden converted from farmyard ; pond, bog garden, shrubs, roses, small vegetable & soft fruit garden ; open views to South Downs

¶Old Postings (Capt. & Mrs R. P. Peter)

Room Outside†⊕ Goodwood Gardens, Waterbeach, 3 m. NE of Chichester ; take A27 from Chichester Motel ; after ¾ m. fork left on to A285 Petworth Rd ; after ½ m. turn left to Waterbeach, arriving after ½ m. at Richmond Arms Hotel. Part of old walled garden (½ acre) of Goodwood House transformed since 1973 into small but unique type of Garden Centre with modern showroom ; garden was designed by John Brookes on 3 levels, to show differing garden situations, e.g. orchard, patio, ponds, & inspire visitors with ideas for their own gardens. Wide variety of garden furniture, ornaments, & terracotta pots on display. Shop open. Tea Richmond Arms Hotel. *Collecting box. Sat. May 17 & Sat. June 14 (10–4)*

Rymans⊕ (The Hon. Claud & Mrs Phillimore) Apuldram, 1½ m. SW of Chichester. Witterings Rd out of Chichester at 1½ m. SW turn right signposted Apuldram ; garden down rd on left-hand side. Walled & other gardens surrounding lovely C15 stone house (not open) ; bulbs, flowering shrubs & roses. Teashops in Chichester. *Adm. 30p, Chd. 10p. Suns. April 6, May 4, June 22, July 20 & Aug. 24 (2–6.30)*

St Roche's Arboretum★†⅋ (E. F. W. James Esq) Singleton Hill, West Dean, 5 m. N of Chichester. Turn S off A286 Chichester–Midhurst, just W of Singleton, then 1 m. on to Goodwood. Bus: 258 & 260 to Singleton. The Trundle (ancient earthwork) & Weald & Downland Open-Air Museum (on Singleton Hill) open May–October on certain days each week. Rare trees & shrubs. NO DOGS. *Adm. 30p, Chd. 15p. Mon. May 5 daily to May 11; Mon. June 2 daily to June 8; Sun. Oct. 26 (12–5)*

South Corner House (Maj. & Mrs Shane Blewitt) Duncton, 3½ m. S of Petworth. On A285, 200 yds N of Duncton Hill. 1 acre ; mixed garden on different levels ; alkaline soil ; shrubs, herbaceous, roses (inc. shrub roses). NO DOGS. TEA & biscuits. *Adm. 25p, Chd. 10p. Sun. & Mon. Aug. 24 & 25 (2.30–6.30)*

South Lodge★⊕ (Miss E. Godman) Lower Beeding, SE of Horsham. Bus : 117 Horsham–Brighton, alight Crabtree, Lower Beeding. Flowering trees, shrubs, rhododendrons, azaleas, davidia. Tea St Peter's Café, Cowfold, 2 m. *Adm. 30p, Cars 5p. Suns. April 27, May 4, 25, June 1; Wed. May 14; Sat. May 24 (2–5)*

Standen (The National Trust—see p. ix) 1½ m. S of E Grinstead, signposted from Turner's Hill Rd, B2110. 10½ acres ; hillside garden with views across Medway Valley to Ashdown Forest ; setting for a late Victorian house by Philip Webb. *Adm. 25p, Chd. 10p. Sun. May 11 (2–6) & Sun. Oct. 5 (2–5)*

Stile House★⊕ (Mr & Mrs A. Archer-Wills) Gay St, 2 m. SE of Pulborough ; take A283 signposted to Storrington ; turn left to West Chiltington & Nutbourne ; then take 1st left to Nutbourne, then right down Stream Lane. 1¾-acre garden still in process of construction in some parts, although some of it is mature ; water plants, streams & a waterfall. NO DOGS. Cream TEAS. *Adm. 20p, Chd. 10p. Sat. & Sun. May 17 & 18 (2–5.30)*

Strawberry House (Mr & Mrs J. Dobbin) Square Drive, Kingsley Green. 1½ m. S of Haslemere on A286 Midhurst–Haslemere. Square Drive is 500 yds after the Kingsley Green sign on left. 4 acres on side of Blackdown ; 2 acres under cultivation ; flowering trees, shrubs, ornamental pool, waterfall & rockery, roses & herbaceous border. Sales table. NO DOGS. TEAS (& strawberries if available). *Adm. 30p, Chd. 10p. Sun. June 29 (2–6)*

Telegraph House★⅋⊕ (Mr & Mrs David Gault) North Marden, 9 m. NW of Chichester.

Entrance on B2141. From Petersfield to South Harting & on 2 m. From Chichester via A286 for 4 m. & N of Lavant turn W on to B2141. 1-acre enclosed chalk garden; nearly 700 ft above sea level; lilac blooms, shrubs, shrub roses, grey foliage, ground cover; 1 m. avenue of copper beeches; woodland walks through yew wood of 150 acres (for the intrepid); lovely views. House (not shown) in small park, built on site of semaphore keeper's cottage. TEAS. *Adm. 40p, Chd. 20p. Sat. & Sun. May 24 & 25; Sat. & Sun. July 5 & 6 (2–6); also by appt. June & July (2–5) (Tel. Harting 206)*

Treyford Manor⊕ (Mr & Mrs Bertram Aykroyd) Treyford, 6 m. SW of Midhurst; about 1 m. SE of rd leading from Harting via Elsted to A272, 2 m. W of Midhurst. Alternatively 4 m. W along rd from A286 at Cocking. Small garden with mixed shrub & herbaceous borders. Manor House (not open) with William & Mary facade in beautiful Downland setting. C15 dovecot etc. TEAS. *Adm. 20p, Chd. (if accompanied) 10p. Sat. & Sun. June 21 & 22 (2–6)*

Trotton Old Rectory† (Mr & Mrs L. H. P. Conner) Trotton, 3 m. W of Midhurst. A272 turning left over Trotton Bridge (from Midhurst); turning right opp. Trotton Church (from Petersfield). Medium-sized garden; azaleas, choice flowering shrubs & trees, herbaceous borders, hardy lilies, lake & water garden, fruit, vegetable garden. View of Trotton Bridge & R. Rother. TEAS. *Adm. 30p, Chd. 10p. Sun. May 18 & Sun. June 22 (2–6)*

Udimore Gardens, 3 m. W of Rye. Entrance on B2089. Bus: 30 Rye–Hastings; bus stops at gates (⅖-m. drive). The following 3 gardens will be open. (*Share to St Mary's Church, Udimore*). Home-made TEAS at White Fox Lodge. *Combined charge 60p, Chd. 10p. Sun. July 6 (2–6)*

Wick Farm (Robert Mair Esq) Medium-sized terraced garden; large herbaceous border, roses, picturesque setting with oast houses; views of Tillingham Valley. Exhibition of horse shoes. Swimming in heated pool 20p extra

Hammonds (Mr & Mrs D. Seward) Medium-sized mixed garden; roses, herbaceous borders, lawns, walled garden & goldfish pond. Fine views

¶**White Fox Lodge** (Mr & Mrs Sidney Horniblow) 2 acre shrub & rose garden developed from meadow since 1967 by owners. Extensive views. Plant stall

Uppark †⊕ (The National Trust—see p. ix) 5 m. SE of Petersfield; via B2141/B2146 Petersfield–Chichester rd. Medium-sized garden, mostly lawns, shrubs, large yews, beech & cedar trees; some flower beds. House built in 1690; re-decorated & embellished interior in 1754; little change since then; Chippendale furniture, original carpets

& curtains; collection of porcelain; domestic quarters also shown. Magnificent views of Solent & Isle of Wight. NO DOGS. Tea Dolphin & Anchor Hotel, Chichester; Concorde Hotel, Petersfield. Collection in grounds for N.G.S. *Adm. house & garden £1, Chd. 50p.* △*Sun. June 8 & Sun. Aug. 10 (2–6)*

Upper House (Mr & Mrs I. D. Greenwell) West Burton, 5 m. SW of Pulborough, ½ m. from Roman Villa, Bignor. Medium-sized garden; summer flowers & shrubs. TEA & biscuits. *Adm. 25p, Chd. 5p. Sun. & Mon. June 1 & 2 (2–7)*

The Upper Lodge (J. W. Harrington Esq) Stopham, 1 m. W of Pulborough; via A283 towards Petworth; Lodge is on left by telephone kiosk at Stopham. Small garden, mainly rhododendrons & azaleas with wide selection of shrubs for acid soil. NO DOGS. *Adm. 25p, Chd. 10p. Sun. May 25 (2–6)*

Warningcamp House⊕ (Maj.-Gen. & Mrs H. M. Liardet) Arundel. Almost opp. Arundel Station, turning to Burpham, off A27, & along 1 m. No Sun. buses. Medium-sized garden; spring flowers, daffodils, spring rockery. Car park free. *Adm. 30p, Chd. 5p. Sun. April 20 (2–5)*

Westbourne Gardens,⊕ 1 m. N of Emsworth. From A27 Chichester–Havant turn N for Westbourne; in village on B2145 at junction with rd to Southbourn. The following 2 gardens will be open with roses, shrubs & border plants. Plants for sale. *Combined charge for both gardens 25p, Chd. 5p. Sun. June 29 (2–7)*

Westbourne Court (Mrs M. J. Barrett)
Mile End House (Mr & Mrs Frank Stoddart)

West Burton House⅃⊕ (Mr & Mrs A. C. Benedict Eyre) 5 m. SW of Pulborough. 1 m. from Bignor Roman Villa. Turn off A29 at White Horse, Bury, ¾ m. Old walled garden under Downs; daffodils; summer flowers, shrubs & trees. *Adm. 20p, Chd. 5p. Sun. & Mon. April 20 & 21 Sun. & Mon. June 22 & 23 (2–6)*

●**West Dean Gardens***†⅃⊕ (Edward James Foundation) On A286, 6 m. N of Chichester (signposted West Dean College), nr Weald & Downland Open Air Museum. Bus routes 258 & 260 pass grounds. Large semiformal gardens famed for fine specimen trees, inc. large cedars, horse chestnuts, ginkgos, tulip trees & many rare & unusual species (labelled); pergola; gazebo; bamboo garden; borders; wild garden. Picnic & play area. Flint mansion (not open) now West Dean College of Arts & Crafts. NO DOGS. TEAS on Suns.; weekdays Singleton village (2 m. N). *Adm. 45p, OAPs 35p, Chd. 20p. Parties at reduced rates. April 1 to Sept. 30 daily except Sats. (Mon.–Fri. 1–6; Suns. & Bank Hols. 1–7, last adm. 1 hr before closing)*

West Sussex College of Agriculture,
Brinsbury House, North Heath, 3 m. N of
Pulborough on A29. Glasshouses will be open
showing various propagating techniques,
heating & plant illuminating. Commercial
glasshouses will show carnations, tomato,
cucumber, green pepper & variety of mixed
pot plants; also open new mushroom unit,
ornamental gardens & farm. Members of staff
will be on duty to answer questions. NO
DOGS. *Adm. 20p. Sat. May 10 (2—4.30)*

Whitehouse Cottage (Barry Gray Esq)
Staplefield Lane, 5 m. NW of Haywards Heath.
Garden is ½ m. E of A23; turn off the main rd
at Warninglid flyover; take the lane to
Staplefield (*not* the B2115 to Haywards
Heath & Cuckfield). Medium-sized garden;
mixed shrubs, old roses, with wood & ponds.
TEAS. *Adm. 20p, Chd. 5p. Sat. & Sun. June
28 & 29 (2—7)*

Winchelsea Gardens. The following 3
picturesque gardens in this historic 700-year-
old town will be open. TEAS at May Morning.
*Combined charge 60p, Chd. 10p. Sun. July 13
(2—6)*

¶**Cleveland House** (Mr & Mrs J. Jempson)
From Strand Gate take first turning left,
follow lane round to the right, house &
garden just on left. 1½ acres semi-formal
old garden with lawns, roses & ornamental
trees, in process of being restocked; large
vegetable garden

¶**Little Manor**† (The Misses B. & N. Lyle)
Mill Rd, opp. Castle Inn, Castle St. Small
cottage garden; two levels; one sunken
garden reputed site of bear pit used for bear
baiting. 300-year-old house (not open).
NO DOGS

¶**May Morning**† (Mr & Mrs I. Ferguson)
Mill Lane, nr restored Windmill in Winchelsea, just off A259 from Rye to Hastings. ⅓—
acre garden on 3 levels; one formed part of
original town ditch; roses, herbaceous
borders, rockery & vegetable garden. Stone
wall behind terrace dates from 1415. NO
DOGS. TEAS

WARWICKSHIRE
& part of WEST
MIDLANDS

Hon. County Organiser:
DENNIS L. FLOWER ESQ, Ilmington Manor
 Shipston-on-Stour, CV36 4LA

Assistant Hon. County Organiser:
MISS HELEN SYME, Puddocks, Frog Lane,
 Ilmington, Shipston-on-Stour
DATES OF OPENING

APRIL Friday 18 & Saturday 19
 ADMINGTON HALL, nr Stratford-on-Avon
APRIL Sunday 20
 ADMINGTON HALL, nr Stratford-on-Avon

ILMINGTON MANOR,
 nr Shipston-on-Stour
PUDDOCKS, Ilmington
APRIL Monday 21
 ADMINGTON HALL, nr Stratford-on-Avon
MAY Saturday 10
 SHERBOURNE PARK, nr Warwick
MAY Sunday 11
 HAYTOR, Stratford-on-Avon
 SHERBOURNE PARK, nr Warwick
MAY Sunday 18
 ILMINGTON GARDENS,
 nr Shipston-on-Stour
MAY Sunday 25
 ASHORNE HOUSE, nr Warwick
 DORSINGTON GARDENS,
 nr Stratford-on-Avon
JUNE Sunday 1
 HERMITAGE, Priors Marston,
 nr Southam
 MEADOWS, Draycote, nr Rugby
 SHUCKBURGH, nr Daventry
 THE SPRING, Kenilworth
 WROXALL ABBEY SCHOOL, Wroxall,
 nr Warwick
JUNE Sunday 8
 BARTON HOUSE, Barton-on-the-Heath
 LOXLEY HALL, nr Stratford-on-Avon
 THE OLD RECTORY, Ilmington
 PACKWOOD HOUSE, nr Hockley Heath
JUNE Sunday 15
 ALSCOT PARK, nr Stratford-on-Avon
 TYSOE MANOR, nr Stratford-on-Avon
 WROXALL ABBEY SCHOOL, Wroxall,
 nr Warwick
JUNE Sunday 22
 FOXCOTE, nr. Shipston-on-Stour
 MAXSTOKE CASTLE, nr Coleshill
 SAVAGES HOUSE, Bishops Tachbrook,
 nr Leamington Spa
 SHERBOURNE PARK, nr Warwick
JUNE Saturday 28
 BADGERS COTTAGE, Idlicote,
 nr Shipston-on-Stour
 THE OLD RECTORY, Oxhill,
 nr Shipston-on-Stour
JUNE Sunday 29
 BADGERS COTTAGE, Idlicote,
 nr Shipston-on-Stour
 THE OLD RECTORY, Oxhill,
 nr Shipston-on-Stour
JULY Sunday 6
 ALSCOT PARK, nr Stratford-on-Avon
 BRAILES HOUSE, Lower Brailes,
 nr Shipston-on-Stour
 FROG ORCHARD, Ilmington
 ILMINGTON MANOR,
 nr Shipston-on-Stour
 PUDDOCKS, Ilmington
 THE SPRING, Kenilworth
 UPPER BILLESLEY,
 nr Stratford-on-Avon
 WHICHFORD GARDENS,
 nr Shipston-on-Stour
JULY Sunday 13
 ASTROP HOUSE, Frankton, nr Rugby

CLAVERDON GARDENS, nr Warwick
THE DAVIDS, Northfield, Birmingham
JULY Sunday 20
LOXLEY HALL, nr Stratford-on-Avon
AUGUST Sunday 10
ARMSCOTE MANOR,
nr Shipston-on-Stour
SEPTEMBER Sunday 14
SHERBOURNE PARK, nr Warwick

DESCRIPTIONS OF GARDENS

Admington Hall&⊕ (Mr & Mrs J. P. Wilkerson) 6½ m. S of Stratford-on-Avon. Between A34 & A46, nr Quinton. Large garden; interesting water garden; mixed borders; extensive kitchen garden with greenhouses. (*Share to Gardeners' Sunday*) TEA & biscuits. *Adm. 30p, Chd. free. Fri., Sat., Sun. & Mon. April 18, 19, 20 & 21 (2–6)*

Alscot Park&⊕ (Capt. & Mrs James West) 2½ m. S of Stratford-on-Avon, via A34, on right (W) side of rd. Bus: Stratford–Shipston-on-Stour, alight at end of drive. Large garden & mid-C18 Gothic house; extensive lawns, borders, specie & shrub roses, fine trees; river & 2 lakes. Deer park. TEAS. *Adm. 30p, Chd. 15p. Sun. June 15 & Sun. July 6 (2–7)*

¶**Armscote Manor** (Mr & Mrs J. F. Docker) 4 m. N of Shipston-on-Stour. From A34 Stratford–Shipston rd, turn off W for Armscote; drive at beginning of village. 2–3 acres; walled gardens; wide variety of roses. House (not open) originally built 1590; currently in process of renovation. Tea Shipston-on-Stour. *Adm. 25p, Chd. 10p. Sun. Aug. 10 (2–6)*

Ashorne House⊕ (Mr & Mrs A. J. Sidwell) Ashorne, 5 m. S of Warwick. 1½ m. W of junction of A41 Warwick–Banbury; from junction follow signs to Ashorne. Entrance & car park in adjacent cricket pitch. 8 acres; typical English country garden combining a natural garden with a formal one. TEAS. *Adm. 30p, Chd. 15p. Sun. May 25 (2–7)*

Astrop House&⊕ (Mr & Mrs A. Harvey) Frankton, 6 m. SW of Rugby. Approx. midway between Rugby & Leamington & 9 m. SE of Coventry, from A423 turn off E at Princethorpe; or from A45 turn off W at Blue Boar flyover. 1-acre garden of C16 cottage; old-fashioned shrub roses & selection of trees & shrubs; charming grass areas. TEA & biscuits. *Adm. 30p, Chd. 10p. Sun. July 13 (2–6)*

Badgers Cottage (Dr & Mrs G. P. Williams) Idlicote, 3½ m. NE of Shipston-on-Stour. Adjoins village pond. From A34 turn off E at signpost 1 m. N of Shipston; or at signpost in Halford on Fosse Way (A429). Garden of ⅓ acre recently reconstructed, containing mixed borders, vegetable garden & an area devoted to alpines. C17 thatched cottage (not open). NO DOGS. Farmhouse teas, Upper Farm, Whatcote, 1 m. *Adm. 20p, Chd. 5p. Sat. & Sun. June 28 & 29 (2–7)*

Barton House★†&⊕ (Dr & Mrs I. A. Bewley Cathie) Barton-on-the-Heath, 3 m. E of Moreton-in-Marsh. 2 m. W of A34 at Long Compton; 1 m. N from A44 at Kitebrook. 5 acres; lawns, trees, flowering shrubs, particularly rhododendrons. Plant stall. TEA & biscuits. *Adm. 40p, Chd. 20p. Sun. June 8 (2–6.30)*

¶**Brailes House**⊕ (Maj. & Mrs R. F. Birch-Reynardson) Lower Brailes, 4 m. E of Shipston-onStour, via B4035 Shipston–Banbury rd, into Lower Brailes; gates opp. George Hotel. 3-acre garden in process of reconstruction started in 1976; new orchard, shrubs, spring garden, old-fashioned roses; ancient yew trees. TEAS. *Adm. 30p, Chd. 15p. Sun. July 6 (2–6)*

Claverdon Gardens. 5 m. W of Warwick; 3 m. E of Henley, off B4095 Warwick-Henley rd. Following 4 gardens will be open. NO DOGS. TEAS at The Grange. *Adm. 20p each garden, Chd. 10p. Sun. July 13 (2–7)*

¶**Barnmoor Farm** (Mr & Mrs S. R. Boddington) In Kington Lane. ½-acre cottage-type garden; herbaceous border

¶**The Grange** (Mr & Mrs B. R. Booth) 2-acre garden with lawns, shrubs & flower beds

¶**The Rockery**⊕ (Mr & Mrs G. A. Axtmann) In Langley Rd. Small (¼-acre) country garden

¶**Woodlands** (Mrs D. Button) In Langley Rd. ¾-acre garden with lawn, flower & rose beds

The Davids⊕ (Mr & Mrs L. J. Cadbury) Hole Lane, Northfield, Birmingham. A38 Bristol Rd, between Selly Oak & Northfield; on Birmingham side of the Royal Orthopaedic Hospital. Large town garden with roses, herbaceous borders, small pool & lawns. Collection of old cannons. *Adm. 30p, Chd. accompanied by adult 10p; unaccompanied 20p. Sun. July 13 (2–6.30)*

Dorsington Gardens,⊕ 7 m. SW of Stratford-upon-Avon. 6 lovely gardens welcome visitors. Teas in village. *Combined charge for all gardens 50p, Chd. 15p. Sun. May 25 (2–6)*

The Old Manor (Mr & Mrs J. Mills)
The Moat House (Mrs J. Saville)
The Old Rectory (Mrs M. Wilson)
Knowle Thatch (Mr & Mrs John Turner)
Windrush (Mr & Mrs I. Munro)
White Gates (Mr & Mrs I. Turner)

Foxcote† (Mr & the Hon. Mrs Holman) 4½ m. W of Shipston-on-Stour. From A429 Fosse Way, approx. 4 m. N of Moreton-in-Marsh, turn off N, following signs for Ilmington. Medium-sized terraced garden. NO DOGS. TEAS. *Adm. 30p, Chd. 10p. Sun. June 22 (2–6)*

Frog Orchard⊕ (Mrs B. R. Jewsbury) Ilmington, 4 m. NW of Shipston-on-Stour. Small new garden. Modern house; exhibition of paintings by local residents. TEAS. *Adm. 20p, Chd. 10p. Sun. July 6 (2–7)*

Haytor* (Mr & Mrs Douglas Hockerston-Tagg) top of Avenue Rd, Stratford-on-Avon. From the Warwick Rd at St Gregory's Church, up Welcombe Rd, an avenue of limes, & Haytor is at the top. 2-acre garden. Comprehensive herb garden. Plant stall. NO DOGS. *Adm. 35p, Chd. 15p. Sun. May 11 (2–6.30)*

Hermitage⊕ (Mrs M. Watson) Priors Marston, 5 m. E of Southam. 5-acre natural garden; 2 pools, herbaceous border, yew & beech hedges; interesting shrubs & ground cover. NO DOGS. TEAS. *Adm. 25p, Chd. 10p. Sun. June 1 (2–6)*

Ilmington Gardens, 8 m. S of Stratford-on-Avon, 4 m. NW of Shipston-on-Stour. 6 or more gardens open (inc. **The Manor**). Ilmington Morris dancers. Teas at Village Hall. *Rover's ticket (with map at all gardens) 70p, Chd. 30p. Sun. May 18 (2–6.30)*

Ilmington Manor*†⅋⊕ (Dennis L. Flower Esq) 4 m. NW of Shipston-on-Stour, 8 m. S of Stratford-on-Avon. Daffodils; herbaceous, shrubs, roses, clipped yews. House (not open) built 1600. Plants for sale. TEAS. *Adm. 40p, Chd. 20p. Sun. April 20 (2–6) & Sun. July 6 (2–7)*

Loxley Hall⅋⊕ (Col & Mrs Gregory-Hood) 4 m. SE of Stratford-on-Avon. Turn N off A422 or W off A429, 1½ m. SW of Wellesbourne. Modern sculpture, iris, shrubs, roses, herbaceous, trees. Old church adjacent can be visited. TEAS. *Adm. 30p, Chd. 10p. Sun. June 8 & Sun. July 20 (2–7)*

Maxstoke Castle †⊕ (Capt. & Mrs C. B. Fetherston-Dilke) nr Coleshill, E of Birmingham, 2½ m. E of Coleshill on A47 take right turn down Castle Lane; Castle drive is 1.2 m. on right. 4–5 acres of garden & pleasure grounds with flowers, shrubs & trees in the immediate surroundings of the Castle & inside courtyard; water-filled moat surrounding Castle. NO DOGS. *Adm. 40p, Chd. 20p. Sun. June 22 (2–7)*

Meadows⊕ (Mr & Mrs R. Law) Draycote, 5 m. SW of Rugby. 1 m. S off 'Straight Mile' on B4453 Leamington–Rugby. 1½ acres; a natural garden in heart of country with stream running through it; great emphasis on plants for foliage, waterside planting & ground cover & conifers; 2 heather beds with about 550 plants; waterfowl enclosure with 25 different species; trout. NO DOGS. TEA & biscuits. *Adm. 25p, Chd. 15p. Sun. June 1 (2–7)*

The Old Rectory, Ilmington*⅋⊕ (Mr & Mrs David Marland), 4½ m. NW of Shipston-on-Stour. 4½ acres; old-established garden with interesting trees, climbing roses & walled kitchen garden. *Adm. 40p, Chd. 20p. Sun. June 8 (2–6)*

¶**The Old Rectory, Oxhill**⊕ (Mr & Mrs D. Whaley) 11 m. SE of Stratford-on-Avon; 1 m. S of A422 Stratford–Banbury rd. From Stratford turn 1st X-rds E of Pillerton Priors. From Banbury 2nd X-rds after foot of Sun Rising Hill. Entering Oxhill from A422, take 1st left (signed village centre) & house is far end of village on left. 1½-acre garden, mainly shrubs, inc. shrub roses, designed for reduced work; few good trees. House (not open) C18. Nearby church has interesting architectural & historical features. Cream teas available at Upper Farm, Whatcote, 1 m. *Adm. 30p, Chd. 20p; under 3, free. Sat. & Sun. June 28 & 29 (2–7)*

Packwood House †⅋ (The National Trust—see p. ix) 11 m. SE of Birmingham. 1½ m. E of Hockley Heath (which is on A34 Birmingham–Stratford). Carolean formal garden & yew garden planted *c.* 1650, representing the Sermon on the Mount. Timber-framed Tudor house with collection of tapestry, needlework & furniture. NO DOGS. Tea Hockley Heath, Solihull or Knowle. *Adm. garden only 50p, Chd. 25p; house & garden 85p, Chd. 40p. △Sun. June 8 (2–7)*

Puddocks (Miss Helen Syme) Frog Lane, Ilmington, 4 m. NW of Shipston-on-Stour. Small owner-designed garden with village stream; rockeries & shrubs. Tea Ilmington Manor. *Adm. 20p, Chd. 10p. Sun. April 20 (2–6) & Sun. July 6 (2–7)*

Savages House †⅋⊕ (Mrs S. Hickson) Bishops Tachbrook, 2½ m. S of Leamington Spa. In village, on A452. Medium-sized garden; roses, old-fashioned roses, rhododendrons. Donkeys in paddock. House 1558 (not shown) was home of Walter Savage Landor, poet & dilettante. NO DOGS. TEAS. *Adm. 20p, Chd. 10p. Sun. June 22 (2–7)*

Sherbourne Park⊕ (The Hon. Mrs C. Smith-Ryland) 3 m. S of Warwick off A49; ½ m. N of Barford. Bus: MR 590 Coventry–Warwick–Stratford, alight Sherbourne corner; MR 518 Leamington–Warwick–Barford–Stratford, alight Sherbourne, ½ m. Medium-sized garden; lawns, shrubs, borders, roses, lilies; new lake. Church by Gilbert Scott adjacent to house (early Georgian, 1740). *(Share to Mid-Warwicks National Trust Centre)* Plants & shrubs for sale. TEAS (not May 10). *Adm. 30p, Chd. 5p. Sat. & Sun. May 10 & 11 (10.30–1 & 2–6.30); Sun. June 22 & Sun. Sept. 14 (2–6.30)*

Shuckburgh*†⅋ (Sir Charles Shuckburgh, Bt) W of Daventry. Nr Lower Shuckburgh on A425. Daventry–Leamington Rd. Large garden; trees, flowering shrubs, rhododendrons, azaleas; ornamental pheasants. C13 foundation church. NO DOGS. TEAS. *Adm. 30p, Chd. 10p. Sun. June 1 (2–6.30)*

The Spring⊕ (Miss H. Martin) Upper Spring Lane, Kenilworth. Off A46 Coventry–Warwick; or A452 Stonebridge–Leamington. Bus: 518 Leamington–Coventry, alight Water Tower, Kenilworth, 1 m. Medium-sized garden; azaleas & rhododendrons; herbaceous border & rose garden; walled kitchen garden & large lawns. Tea Kenilworth. *Adm. 20p, Chd. 10p. Sun. June 1 & Sun. July 6 (2–7)*

Tysoe Manor †⊕ (Maj. & Mrs Geoffrey Sewell) Tysoe, 12 m. SE of Stratford-on-Avon. Off A422; nr Compton Wynyates & Upton House. Large garden in peaceful setting; Irish yews, lawns, old shrub roses, lavender, etc. Attractive old manor house (not open). TEAS. *Adm. 30p, Chd. 10p. Sun. June 15 (2–6)*

Upper Billesley (Mrs Robert Ansell) 3½ m. W of Stratford-on-Avon. From Stratford via A422; turn N (right) at Western Farm Implements; 1 m. to 'T' junction then left; ¼ m. to gates on left. From Alcester via A422; after Stag Inn turn left; then 1st right up hill & gates on right. Medium-sized garden; rose & herbaceous gardens & swimming pool. NO DOGS. TEAS. *Adm. 25p, Chd. 10p. Sun. July 6 (2.30–7)*

Whichford Gardens, 6 m. SE of Shipston-on-Stour. Turn E off A34 at Long Compton for Whichford. Tea Shipston-on-Stour or Chipping Norton. *Combined charge for following 2 gardens 30p, Chd. 15p. Sun. July 6 (2–7)*

   Whichford House*†⊕ (George Rainbird Esq) Medium-sized garden; herbaceous & shrub rose borders set round classical Cotswold stone Queen Anne House; small alpine & wild gardens

   The Old Rectory†⊕ (Mrs Scott-Cockburn) Garden, designed for minimum upkeep; ponds, waterfall, water garden & paved rose garden. House (ground floor shown) was converted from a derelict farmhouse which had earlier been a rectory.

Wroxall Abbey School*†&⊕ (Miss K. M. Carter, Principal) Wroxall, 6 m. NW of Warwick. Nr Fiveways junction on A41. Bus: MR 157 Knowle–Leamington, passes gate. 27 acres; shrubs, rhododendrons & small enclosed flower garden. 'Nature trail' inc. comments on plants, flowers, etc. Evensong on June 15 in Chapel 5.30 p.m. NO DOGS. TEA & biscuits. *Adm. 25p, Chd. 10p. Sun. June 1 & Sun. June 15 (2–6)*

WILTSHIRE

Hon County Organiser:
MAJ. ANTHONY R. CARR, Blagden House, Keevil, Trowbridge, BA14 6LU
DATES OF OPENING
By appointment
   HUNGERDOWN HOUSE, Seagry

APRIL Easter Sunday 6
   WEDHAMPTON MANOR, nr Devizes
APRIL Easter Monday 7
   THE PYGMY PINETUM, Devizes
APRIL Sunday 13
   BROADLEAS, nr Devizes
APRIL Sunday 20
   SEVENHAMPTON PLACE,
      nr Swindon
APRIL Sunday 27
   EASTON GREY HOUSE, nr Malmesbury
MAY Sunday 4
   BAYNTON HOUSE, Coulston,
      nr Westbury
   OARE HOUSE, nr Pewsey
MAY Monday 5 (May Day Hol.)
   THE PYGMY PINETUM, Devizes
MAY Sunday 11
   BROADLEAS, nr Devizes
   SUTTON VENY HOUSE, nr Warminster
MAY Sunday 18
   IFORD MANOR, Bradford-on-Avon
   LUCKINGTON COURT, nr Chippenham
   SHELDON MANOR, nr Chippenham
MAY Sunday 25
   CONOCK MANOR, nr Devizes
JUNE Sunday 8
   BROADLEAS, nr Devizes
   KELLAWAYS, nr Chippenham
JUNE Sunday 15
   HEALE HOUSE, Woodford, nr Salisbury
JUNE Sunday 22
   FARLEIGH HUNGERFORD GARDENS,
      nr Trowbridge
   THE GRANGE, Edington, nr Westbury
   MONASTERY GARDEN, Edington,
      nr Westbury
   RAMSBURY GARDENS, nr Marlborough
JUNE Sunday 29
   LUSHILL, Hannington, nr Swindon
JULY Sunday 6
   ASHTON KEYNES GARDENS,
      nr Cirencester
   BUSHTON MANOR, nr Wootton Bassett
   CHALKE PIT HOUSE, Broadchalke
   THE MANOR HOUSE, Great Cheverell
   SEVENHAMPTON PLACE, nr Swindon
   STOURHEAD GARDENS, nr Mere
JULY Sunday 13
   BROADLEAS, nr Devizes
   FONTHILL HOUSE, nr Tisbury
   THE HALL, Bradford-on-Avon
   KEEVIL GARDENS, nr Trowbridge
   LACKHAM COLLEGE OF AGRICULTURE,
      Lacock, nr Chippenham
   STANTON HOUSE, Stanton Fitzwarren,
      nr Swindon
   STOURHEAD GARDENS, nr Mere
JULY Saturday 19
   MIDDLEHILL HOUSE, Box
JULY Sunday 20
   BIDDESTONE MANOR, nr Corsham
   LUCKINGTON MANOR, nr Chippenham
   MIDDLEHILL HOUSE, Box
JULY Sunday 27
   CORSHAM COURT, nr Chippenham

JOB'S MILL, Crockerton, nr Warminster
LAKE HOUSE, Lake, nr Salisbury
OARE HOUSE, nr Pewsey
SEALES COURT FARM, Upper Seagry,
nr Chippenham
WEDHAMPTON MANOR, nr Devizes
AUGUST Sunday 10
BROADLEAS, nr Devizes
NUNTON HOUSE, nr Salisbury
SEPTEMBER Sunday 14
BROADLEAS, nr Devizes
SEPTEMBER Sunday 21
HILLBARN HOUSE, Great Bedwyn,
nr Hungerford
OCTOBER Sunday 12
BROADLEAS, nr Devizes

DESCRIPTIONS OF GARDENS

Ashton Keynes Gardens. 5½ m. S of
Cirencester. From Cirencester take A419
towards Swindon for 3 m.; at Spine Rd
junction turn off W, following signs for
Ashton Keynes. From Cricklade via B4040 for
1½ m. to X-rds & turn off at sign to Ashton
Keynes 2 m. Following 4 gardens will be open.
TEAS at River House. *Combined charge for 4
gardens 50p, Chd. free. Sun. July 6 (2–6)*

¶**Ashton House**⊕ (Mr & Mrs John
Wilson) 2¾ acres with trees, shrubs, lawns
& ornamental lake. NO DOGS

¶**Virginia**⊕ (Mr & Mrs H. L. Greer) ½-acre
garden with shrubs, flower border & small
pond. NO DOGS

¶**2 Cove House**⊕ (Maj. & Mrs Hartland)
Approx. 1 acre with trees, shrubs & mixed
beds

¶**1 Cove House**⊕ (Mr & Mrs R. C. Threlfall)
Medium-sized, mature garden; herbaceous
border, rose bed & magnificent copper
beech; rear patio garden reached via garden
room with profusion of potted plants &
hanging baskets

Baynton House (Mr & Mrs A. J. Macdonald-
Buchanan) Coulston, 4 m. E of Westbury. On
B3098 between Edington & Erlestoke. 16-acre
gardens with spring bulbs, rock garden, wild,
woodland & water garden. TEAS. *Adm. 20p.
Sun. May 4 (2.30–6)*

Biddestone Manor†⊕ (Princess R. Loewen-
stein) Biddestone, nr Corsham, 5 m. W of
Chippenham. 3 m. N of Corsham. On A4
between Chippenham & Corsham turn off N;
or from A420, 5 m. W of Chippenham, turn
off S. Large garden with extensive lawns, small
lake, topiary & many unusual shrubs. Fine C17
manor house (not open) with interesting older
outbuildings. NO DOGS. *Adm. 25p, Chd. 10p.
Sun. July 20 (2–7)*

Broadleas*⅃ (Lady Anne Cowdray) S of
Devizes. Bus: Devizes–Salisbury, alight Pot-
terne Rd. Medium-sized garden; attractive
dell planted with unusual trees & shrubs,
azaleas & rhododendrons. Many rare plants in

rock garden & winter garden. Plants for sale.
(In addition to dates shown below in aid of
NGS, garden open April 2 to Oct. 29 every
Wed. *Adm. 25p*). *Suns. April 13, May 11,
June 8, July 13, Aug. 10, Sept. 14, Oct. 12.
Adm. 35p (2–6)*

¶**Bushton Manor**⊕ (Mrs George Loveday)
Bushton, 3 m. S of Wootton Bassett; via
A420 towards Chippenham & then turn off
left (S); or via B4041 to Broad Town & in ½ m.
turn off right (W). 1-acre garden with lawns,
yews & roses. House (not open) 1747 red
brick & stone-tiled roof. *Adm. 25p,
Chd. 15p. Sun. July 6 (2.30–6.30)*

¶**Chalke Pit House**⊕ (Lt-Col & Mrs J. G.
Jeans) Broadchalke, 8 m. W of Salisbury.
From Salisbury take A354 towards Blandford;
after 3 m., in Coombe Bissett, turn off right
(W) taking valley rd for 5 m. to Broadchalke.
3-acre garden; extensive lawns, herbaceous
border, roses, good trees; kitchen garden.
Swimming in heated pool (extra charge).
Plants for sale if available. Home-made
TEAS. *Adm. 25p, Chd. 5p. Sun. July 6 (2–6)*

Conock Manor⅃⊕ (Mr & Mrs Bonar Sykes)
5 m. SE of Devizes off A342. Lawns, borders,
flowering shrubs. C18 house in Bath stone.
(*Share to Gardeners' Sunday*) TEAS (home-
made cakes). *Adm. 25p, Chd. 10p. Sun. May
25 (2–7)*

Corsham Court*†⅃⊕ (The Lord Methuen)
4 m. W of Chippenham. S of A4. Bus: B 231/2
Bath–Chippenham, alight Corsham Town Hall.
Park & gardens laid out by Capability Brown
& Repton. Trees, flowering shrubs; some rare
specimens of flowering trees. Elizabethan
mansion; famous Old Masters in C18 state
rooms & C18 furniture by Adam etc. shown.
(*Share to R.N.L.I.*) Tea Methuen Arms,
Corsham, by arrangement. *Adm. gardens only
25p; house & garden 80p, Chd. 40p (parties
50p each).* △*Sun. July 27 (11–12.30 & 2–6)*

Easton Grey House†⅃⊕ (Mr & Mrs Peter
Saunders) 3½ m. W of Malmesbury on B4040
Bus: Bristol–Swindon, alight Easton Grey at
entrance. Intensively cultivated 9-acre garden
of beautiful C18 house also contains interesting Norman tower, font etc. of Easton Grey
Church. Superb situation overlooking sweep
of R. Avon & surrounding countryside; lime-
tolerant shrubs; tremendous display of spring
bulbs; many roses & clematis. Home-made
TEAS in garden or house; produce & cake
stall (in aid of Easton Grey Parish Church).
*Adm. Cars (inc. occupants) £1, Adults on
foot 25p, Chd. 10p. Sun. April 27 (2–6)*

Farleigh Hungerford Gardens, 3½ m. W of
Trowbridge on A366. TEAS at Castle House.
*Combined charge for both gardens 40p, Chd.
10p. Sun. June 22 (2–7)*

Castle House⊕ (Mr & Mrs Denis Purchas)
Immediately below Farleigh Castle. Parking
limited. Small cottage garden on site of old

woollen mill, made from wild by owners since 1966. Mill stream with water plants

Rowley Grange (Mr & Mrs Arthur King) Parking available. 5 acres; terraced garden leading to lawns; herbaceous borders; R. Frome forms boundary line & Farleigh Castle can be seen across it. The house was formerly 'Wiltshire Park Farm'; this side of river was the Wiltshire Park of the Hungerford family.

Fonthill House⊕ (The Lord & Lady Margadale) 3 m. N of Tisbury. W of Salisbury via B3089. Large garden; formal shrubs & wild garden. TEAS. *Adm. 25p, Chd. 10p. Sun. July 13 (2–6)*

The Grange (Col & Mrs J. S. Douglas) Edington, 4 m. E of Westbury. At Edington turn off B3098, Westbury–Lavington, for Edington Church; take 1st turning left (before reaching church) then 1st right (cul-de-sac); house is 3rd on left. ¾-acre garden with collection of varied shrubs, mostly planted since 1972. C18 house (not open). NO DOGS. TEAS. *Adm. 20p, Chd. 10p. Sun. June 22 (2–6)*

The Hall †⅃ (A. E. Moulton Esq) Bradford-on-Avon; nr centre of town, on B3107. Large garden beside R. Avon with lawns, fine trees, herbaceous & rose borders; interesting acoustic baffle fence. Fine example of Jacobean house set on high terrace; part house shown 10p extra, Chd. 5p. Boat trips on R. Avon. TEAS. *Adm. 25p, Chd. 5p. Sun. July 13 (2–6)*

Heale House †⅃ (Maj. & Mrs David Rasch) Woodford, 3½ m. NW of Salisbury. From A345 turn at High Post Filling Station, signposted Woodford. Bus: Salisbury–Amesbury, alight at gates. Medium-sized garden; herbaceous & mixed borders with hybrid, musk & other roses; exceptionally charming authentic Japanese water garden & house. House built 1585 & much associated with Charles II. (In addition to date shown below in aid of NGS, garden open Good Friday to Oct. daily). *Adm. 40p. Sun. June 15 (10–5)*

Hillbarn House (Mr & Mrs A. J. Buchanan) Great Bedwyn, SW of Hungerford. S of A4 Hungerford–Marlborough. Medium-sized garden on chalk with hornbeam tunnel, pleached limes, herb garden; some planting by Lanning Roper; a series of gardens within a garden. Swimming pool may be used (20p extra). TEA & biscuits. *Adm. 25p, Chd. 10p. Sun. Sept. 21 (2–6)*

Hungerdown House*⊕ (Mr & Mrs Egbert Barnes) Seagry, NE of Chippenham. Turn N off A420 at Sutton Benger Church for Seagry. Picturesque 4-acre garden with many interesting features; flowering shrubs & herbaceous plants in mixed borders; clematis; climbing & shrub roses; trees for autumn colour. *Adm. 25p, Chd. 5p. Garden open by appt. only. (Tel. Seagry 720317)*

Iford Manor*†⅃ (Mrs Cartwright Hignett) 2½ m. SW of Bradford-on-Avon. Entrance only through gates at Iford Bridge by the lanes. Medium-sized terraced garden with shrubs, plants & bulbs of interest. Italian marbles & bronze. Cloisters; many examples of archaeological interest. House not shown. NO DOGS except on lead. Tea Bradford-on-Avon. *Adm. 20p. Sun. May 18 (2–6)*

Job's Mill (The Marquess & Marchioness of Bath) Crockerton, 1½ m. S of Warminster. Bus: Salisbury–Bath, alight Warminster. Medium-sized garden; small terraced garden, through which R. Wylye flows; swimming pool & kitchen garden. Jumble stall. TEAS. *Adm. 30p, Chd. 10p. Sun. July 27 (2–7)*

Keevil Gardens⊕ 4 m. E of Trowbridge. Turn S off A361 between Devizes & Trowbridge. TEAS at Blagden House. *Combined charge for following 2 gardens. 50p, Chd. 10p. Sun. July 13 (2–7)*

    Keevil Manor (Mrs Vernon) Medium–large garden; fine trees & other features of general interest. Late Tudor house (not shown)

    Blagden House (Maj. & Mrs Anthony Carr) Medium-sized garden & kitchen garden of general interest. Queen Anne house (not shown) & stable block. TEAS

Kellaways (Mrs D. Hoskins) N of Chippenham. 3 m. N of Chippenham, A420 from Chippenham, 1st right through Langley Burrell on E Tytherton Rd. From M4, exit 17 (Chippenham & Cirencester) follow signs to Sutton Benger & thence right to East Tytherton & Calne. Small garden, worked entirely by owner; early C17 Cotswold stone house, Walled garden with herbaceous borders; irises. roses, shrubs; rock garden; large collection of old roses & many unusual plants. TEAS. *Adm. 25p. Sun. June 8 (2–7): also open by appt. May–Sept. (Tel. Kellaways 203)*

Lackham College of Agriculture*†⅃⊕ (Wiltshire County Council) Lacock, 4 m. S of Chippenham. Signposted N of Notton on A350. Few mins S of junction 17 on M4. Station: Chippenham, 4 m. Bus: Chippenham–Trowbridge, alight drive entrance, 1 m. walk. Large gardens; walled garden with greenhouses, tomatoes, pot plants, warm greenhouse plants, propagating house, fuchsias, begonias; lawn paths separating plots well laid out & labelled with great variety of interesting shrubs, usual & unusual vegetables, herbaceous plants & fruit. Pleasure gardens, mixed borders, herbs, shrubs & lawns; woodland down to river; large bird viewing hide. Famed museum of old agricultural machinery open separately in aid of museum funds (25p, Chd. free). Plants, inc. uncommon pot plants, for sale all afternoon; raffle drawn 4.30 p.m. Demonstration on sowing a hardy annual border at 3.30 p.m. Particulars of Lackham full- and part-time courses available. Light refreshments. Teas for coach parties by arrangement in advance. *(Share to Cheshire Home, Kingston Langley). Adm. 60p, Chd. if accompanied, free. Sun. July 13 (2–7)*

Lake House (Capt. O. N. Bailey, R.N.) Lake, N of Salisbury. Between Salisbury & Amesbury on Woodford Valley Rd. Station: Salisbury, 7 m. Large, mainly informal grounds; rose, herbaceous & woodland gardens; water; old yew hedges; pleached lime alley; peacocks. Jacobean gabled and flint house (not shown). TEAS. *Adm. 25p, Chd. 10p. Sun. July 27 (2–7)*

Luckington Court (The Hon. Mrs Trevor Horn) Chippenham. In Luckington village, 6 m. W of Malmesbury; turn S off B4040 Malmesbury–Bristol. Station: Chippenham, 10 m. Bus: Bristol–Swindon, alight Luckington. Medium-sized garden, mainly formal, well-designed & planted, amid exquisite group of ancient buildings; fine collection of ornamental cherries; other flowering shrubs. House much altered and rebuilt in Queen Anne times but ancient origins still evident; Queen Anne hall and drawing-room shown. Tea Manor House Hotel, Castle Combe. *Collecting box. Sun. May 18 (2.30–6)*

Luckington Manor (W. Greville Collins Esq) NW of Chippenham. 7½ m. SW of Malmesbury on B4040 Malmesbury–Bristol. Approx. 4 acres; 3 walled-in flower gardens; shrubberies & plantation. *(Share to Cancer Research)* Tea Manor House Hotel, Castle Combe. *Adm. 20p, Chd. 10p. Sun. July 20 (2–6)*

Lushill (Capt. & Mrs F. Barker) Hannington, 6 m. N of Swindon. 5 m. NW of Highworth, on minor rd between Hannington & Castle Eaton. 5-acre garden; extensive lawns; fine trees inc. very old Judas tree & weeping silver lime; shrub & rare old-fashioned roses; heated plant house. NO DOGS. Teashops in Lechlade & Fairford. *Adm. 20p, Chd. 10p. Sun. June 29 (2–6)*

The Manor House (Brig. & Mrs Oliver Brooke) Great Cheverell, 5 m. S of Devizes. Turn W off A360, 4 m. S of Devizes; take lane beside Bell Inn. Medium-sized garden; herbaceous borders; roses; interesting very old yew & box hedges. *Adm. 25p, Chd. 5p. Sun. July 6 (2–7)*

Middlehill House (Miss K. Harper) nr Box. Turn W from A4 at Northey Arms, signposted 'Middlehill & Ditteridge'. Bus: B Bath–Chippenham–Salisbury, alight Northery Arms, 7 mins. An intensive garden of much interest, a round C18 house. Mixed borders; many roses & shrubs; rock garden; kitchen garden; pools with ornamental fish a special feature. TEAS. *Adm. 20p. Sat. & Sun. July 19 & 20 (2–7.30)*

¶Monastery Garden (The Hon. Mrs Douglas Vivian) Edington, 7 m. E of Westbury. Mid-way between Westbury & West Lavington on B3098, adjacent to Edington Priory on Edington–Steeple Ashton rd. Bus stop in village, 600 yds. 5½ acres; wild garden with orchard, small pond, rose garden, shrub roses. Medieval walls of national importance. TEAS. *Adm. 25p, Chd. 10p. Sun. June 22 (2–7)*

Nunton House (Mr & Mrs H. E. Colvin) S of Salisbury. 400 yds W of main gate of Longford Castle on A338. Station: Salisbury, 3 m. Bus: WD 38, 244, Salisbury via A338. Garden of moderate size with herbaceous border, rose garden, woodland walk; good trees, inc. zelkova carpinifolia. Garden re-designed in 1955 by Brenda Colvin, Past President, Inst. of Landscape Architects. TEA & biscuits. *Adm. 25p, Chd. 5p. Sun. Aug. 10 (2–6); also by appt. (for parties only)*

Oare House (Henry Keswick Esq) N of Pewsey. 2 m. N of Pewsey on Marlborough Rd. (A345). Fine house (not shown) in large garden with fine trees and hedges, spring flowers and woodlands; extensive lawns & kitchen garden. *Adm. 25p, Chd. 5p. Sun. May 4 & Sun. July 27 (2–6)*

The Pygmy Pinetum *(Mr & Mrs D. van Klaveren) Hillworth Rd, Devizes. At S end of Devizes, turn into Hillworth Rd; pinetum on left. Bus: Bath–Salisbury; bus stop; Market Place, Devizes, 1 m. Small specialist nursery & pinetum containing the largest collection of dwarf & slow-growing conifers in British Isles & other interesting plants. Young plants for sale. Cups of TEA & biscuits. *Adm. 25p, Chd. 10p. Mon. April 7 & Mon. May 5 (11–7)*

Ramsbury Gardens. 5 m. NW of Hungerford; 5 m. NE of Marlborough. TEAS at Parliament Piece. *Combined charge for both gardens, 50p, Chd. 25p. Sun. June 22 (2–6)*
  The Old Mill (A. H. Ball Esq) Small garden planned around river, therefore not all under cultivation; attractive & colourful
  Parliament Piece (J. H. Pinches Esq) Medium-sized old walled garden with fine old trees; yew hedges, herbaceous border & rose garden. Interesting William & Mary house (not shown). TEAS

¶Seales Court Farm (Mrs Joan Small) Upper Seagry, 5 m. N of Chippenham. From Chippenham via A420 to Sutton Benger; turn left (N) before church; after 1 m. turn left to Seagry & entrance is 1st drive on left. 5-acre informal garden with typical English herbaceous borders. NO DOGS. *Adm. 25p, Chd. 10p. Sun. July 27 (2–6)*

Sevenhampton Place (Mrs Ian Fleming) Sevenhampton, nr Swindon. 6 m. W of Swindon, close to Sevenhampton village. Turn E from A361, 4½ m. N of Swindon. Exceptionally lovely & peaceful lakeside garden; many spring bulbs; rose garden with other shrubs & plants; woodland walks nr water; waterfowl. *Adm. 25p, Chd. 5p. Sun. April 20 & Sun. July 6 (2–6)*

Sheldon Manor*† (Maj. M. A. Gibbs) 3m. W of Chippenham turn S off A420 at Allington X-rds. Formal garden around C13 house; roses of all kinds; very old yew trees; many rare & interesting trees & shrubs. (In addition to date shown below in aid of NGS, garden open April 8 to Sept. 30 every Thurs., Sun. & Bank Hol.; also Weds. in Aug.). TEAS. *Adm. house & garden 70p, Chd. (5–15) 35p. Sun. May 18 (2–6)*

Stanton House (Sir Anthony & Lady Tritton) Stanton Fitzwarren. 3 m. due N of Swindon; from A361 Swindon–Highworth rd turn off N for Stanton Fitzwarren. 5-acre garden with lake, extensive lawns, herbaceous borders; walled kitchen garden & greenhouses. Plants for sale if available. NO DOGS. TEAS. *Adm. 25p, OAPs & Chd. 10p. Sun. July 13 (2–7)*

Stourhead Gardens*†⅃⊕ (The National Trust—see p. ix) Stourton, 3 m. NW of Mere on B3092. Bus: 25 from Salisbury (not Suns.); 480 from Shaftesbury; alight Zeals House, N Gate, 1¼ m. Great landscape garden dating from C18, one of the finest in Europe. 20-acre lake, temples & rare trees. Open every day of the year. NO DOGS. Lunch & tea Spread Eagle Inn, nr entrance. *Adm. 80p, Chd. 40p. Parties of 15 & over 60p each. △Suns. July 6 & 13 (8–7)*

¶Sutton Veny House⅃ (Maj. & Mrs J. C. Walker) 2 m. SE of Warminster. 1 m. S of A36 Warminster–Salisbury rd, nr Sutton Veny village; entrance by either N or S lodges (which will be marked by posters). 5½ acres; formal spring garden with rose garden, lily pool, lawns, orchard; main feature: blossom. TEAS. *Adm. 20p, Chd. 5p. Sun. May 11 (2–6)*

Wedhampton Manor (Mrs E. L. Harris) 5 m. SE of Devizes. Off N side of A342 (nr junction with B3098) Moderate-sized 'homely' garden; general mixed interest & a remarkable & rare specimen cut-leaved lime. Fine Queen Anne house (not open). TEA & biscuits. *Adm. 20p, Chd. 5p. Sun. April 6 & Sun. July 27 (2–7)*

WORCESTERSHIRE

See Hereford & Worcester

YORKSHIRE

Hon. County Organisers:
(N Yorks —Districts of Hambleton, Richmond, Ryedale & Scarborough)
MRS JOHN CHURCH, Osmotherley House, Osmotherley, nr Northallerton

(West & South Yorks & North Yorks Districts of Craven, Harrogate, Selby & York)
LADY VEALE, West House, Wetherby, LS22 4NH

DATES OF OPENING

APRIL daily
  CONSTABLE BURTON HALL, nr Leyburn
APRIL Sunday 20
  HARSLEY HALL, nr Northallerton
MAY daily
  CONSTABLE BURTON HALL, nr Leyburn
MAY Sunday 11
  OSMOTHERLEY HOUSE,
    nr Northallerton
MAY Sunday 25
  NAWTON TOWER, nr Helmsley
MAY Saturday 31
  PENNYHOLME, Fadmoor,
    nr Kirby Moorside
  YORK GATE, Adel, nr Leeds
JUNE daily
  CONSTABLE BURTON HALL, nr Leyburn
JUNE Sunday 1
  PENNYHOLME, Fadmoor,
    nr Kirby Moorside
  YORK GATE, Adel, nr Leeds
JUNE Saturday 7
  PENNYHOLME, Fadmoor,
    nr Kirby Moorside
JUNE Sunday 8
  THE HUTTS, Grewelthorpe, nr Ripon
  KEPWICK HALL, nr Thirsk
  PENNYHOLME, Fadmoor,
    nr Kirby Moorside
  SILVER BIRCHES, Scarcroft, nr Leeds
JUNE Saturday 14
  YORK HOUSE, Claxton, nr York
JUNE Sunday 15
  ELVINGTON HALL, nr York
  YORK HOUSE, Claxton, nr York
JUNE Monday 16
  ELVINGTON HALL, nr York
JUNE Sunday 29
  LING BEECHES, Scarcroft, nr Leeds
  ST NICHOLAS, Richmond
JULY daily
  CONSTABLE BURTON HALL, nr Leyburn
  GILLING CASTLE, Gilling East
JULY Sunday 6
  ARTHINGTON HALL, nr Otley
  THE HEATH, Adel, nr Leeds
  HOOTON PAGNELL HALL, nr Doncaster
JULY Sunday 6 & daily to Saturday 12 inc.
  SLEIGHTHOLME DALE LODGE,
    Fadmoor, nr Kirby Moorside
JULY Saturday 12
  OWSTON HALL GARDENS, Askern,
    nr Doncaster
JULY Sunday 13
  THE HEATH, Adel, nr Leeds
  HOVINGHAM HALL, nr Malton
  STOCKELD PARK, nr Wetherby

YORKSHIRE—continued

JULY Sunday 20
  OTTERINGTON HALL, nr Northallerton
  ST NICHOLAS, Richmond
JULY Sunday 27
  BRAWITH HALL, nr Thirsk
AUGUST daily
  GILLING CASTLE, Gilling East
AUGUST Friday 1
  CONSTABLE BURTON HALL, nr Leyburn
SEPTEMBER Sunday 21
  DUNCOMBE PARK, nr Helmsley

DESCRIPTIONS OF GARDENS

Arthington Hall&⊕ (C. E. W. Sheepshanks Esq) 5 m. E of Otley. A659, half-way between Harrogate & Otley. Buses: Leeds–Harrogate (stop Harewood Bar, 2 m.); Bradford–Harrogate or Skipton–Harrogate via Otley (stop Pool-in-Wharfedale, 2 m.) Large garden; 2 walled gardens; fruit & vegetables; roses, sweet peas & herbaceous borders; heather garden; interesting trees; attractive woodland walks. Fine view of Wharfedale. (*Share to Northern Horticultural Society*) NO DOGS. TEA & biscuits. *Adm. 35p, Chd. 10p. Sun. July 6 (2–7)*

Brawith Hall&⊕ (J. Consett Esq) 4 m. N of Thirsk. Between Knayton on A19 & Thornton-le-Street on A168. Station: Thirsk or North-allerton, 5 m. Bus: United X 99 Leeds–Thirsk–Northallerton–Middlesbrough (limited stop), alight Brawith Lane Ends, ½ m. Medium-sized garden. Roses & some fine hardwood trees; house (not open) has fine C17 S front. *Adm. 25p, Chd. 10p. Sun. July 27 (2–6)*

● Constable Burton Hall Gardens✻†&⊕ (Charles Wyvill Esq) 3 m. E of Leyburn. On A684 Bedale–Leyburn, 6 m. W of A1. Bus: United No. 72 from Northallerton, alight at gate. Large garden & woodland walks; something of interest all spring & summer; splendid display of daffodils; rockery with fine selection of alpines (some rare); extensive shrubs & roses. Beautiful John Carr house (not open) in C18 park; small lake with wildfowl. Beautiful countryside at entrance to Wensleydale. DOGS on leads only. *Adm. 30p, Chd. under 10, free; reduction for large parties. April 1 to Aug. 1 daily (9–6)*

Duncombe Park† (The Lord Feversham & the lessees, Queen Mary's School, Woodard Corporation) ½ m. W of Helmsley. Park gates just off A170 on Stokesley Rd from Helmsley. Large garden; C18 terraces with woodland rides & views of Rye Valley; C18 temples. Tea Helmsley. *Adm. 20p, Chd. 10p. △Sun. Sept. 21 (1.30–5.30)*

Elvington Hall&⊕ (Mrs Pontefract) 8 m. SE of York. From A1079 York–Hull, immediately after leaving York's outer ring rd, turn S on to B1228 for Elvington; entrance at far end of village. 3–4 acre garden in process of being re-made; terrace overlooking lawn sloping down to Ings (used for growing grass, some of it for the Wimbledon courts); fine trees, rockery, swimming pool & sanctuary with fishpond. Lawrence Sterne lived here at one time with his aunt. (*Share to Northern Horticultural Society*). TEAS. *Adm. 25p, Chd. 5p. Sun. & Mon. June 15 & 16 (2–7)*

Gilling Castle† (The Rt. Rev. the Abbot of Ampleforth) Gilling East. 18 m. N of York. Medium-sized garden. NO DOGS. *Adm. 20p, Chd. free. July & Aug. daily (11–5)*

Harsley Hall&⊕ (Mr & Mrs J. B. Barnard) 7 m. NE of Northallerton. 1½ m. W of A19; take turning approx. ½ m. N of Tontine Inn. 5 acres; terraced lawn; ground falls away to series of lakes & tree-lined walks with beautiful display of daffodils; C18 Italian temple. Traditional-style church on Saxon foundation adjacent to garden. *Adm. 25p, Chd. 10p. Sun. April 20 (2–6)*

The Heath✻&⊕ (Richard Wainwright Esq) Long Causeway, Adel, Leeds, 16. From A660 Leeds–Otley, turn right at Ring Rd roundabout; after short distance turn left. Bus: Leeds Cpn 28 Long Causeway; 30 Adel–Briggate opp. Debenhams every 20 mins, alight Duns Tarn Lane, few yds from gate. Herbaceous & rose borders; over 100 varieties of exhibition delphiniums; lawns; trees; fine views. (*Share to Friends of Old People's Welfare (Leeds)*) Picnicking in grounds. NO DOGS. *Adm. 30p, Chd. 10p. Suns. July 6 & 13 (2–7)*

¶Hooton Pagnell Hall& (Mr & Mrs W. G. A. Warde-Norbury) 7 m. NW of Doncaster. From Doncaster via A638; after 3 m. turn W on to B6422 & follow sign to Hooton Pagnell. 7 m. S of Pontefract. Bus: Doncaster–South Elmsall, bus stop at gates. Medium-sized garden on limestone; roses, lawns, small water gardens. Old tithe barn & garden house bounded by C14 house & Norman church. Cornish TEAS. *Adm. 35p, Chd. 15p. Sun. July 6 (2–6)*

Hovingham Hall†⊕ (Sir Marcus & Lady Worsley) 8 m. W of Malton. House in Hovingham village, 20 m. N of York; on B1257 midway between Malton & Helmsley. Medium-sized garden; yew hedges, shrubs & herbaceous borders. C18 dovecote, Riding School, Cricket ground. (*Share to Save the Children Fund*) Tea Worsley Arms Hotel, Hovingham. *Adm. 25p, Chd. 10p. Sun. July 13 (2–6)*

The Hutts (Maj.-Gen. Sir Charles Dalton) Grewelthorpe, Ripon. Ripon–Grewelthorpe Rd; turn left in village; thence 1 m. (signposted). Wild shrub garden; rhododendrons & azaleas; woodland walks in quiet & beautiful valley with 2 lakes; 800 ft above sea-level; magnificent views. Picnics allowed in woods. TEA, soft drinks & biscuits. *Adm. 30p, Chd. 15p. Sun. June 8 (2–6)*

Kepwick Hall (Mrs A. M. Guthe) 7 m. N of Thirsk. Turn E off A19. Large garden; woodland walks; fine trees. TEA & biscuits. *Adm. 25p, Chd. 10p. Sun. June 8 (2–6)*

Ling Beeches*⊕ (Mrs Arnold Rakusen) Ling Lane, Scarcroft 7 m. NE of Leeds. A58 mid-way between Leeds & Wetherby; at Scarcroft turn off W into Ling Lane, at signpost to Wike on brow of a hill; garden is ⅓ m. up lane on right. 2-acre woodland garden designed by owner with emphasis on labour-saving planting; unusual trees & shrubs; many ericaceous plants, but some species roses, conifers & interesting climbers. Plants for sale. NO DOGS please. TEAS. *Adm. 35p, Chd. 10p. Sun. June 29 (2–6)*

Nawton Tower*⊕ (D. Ward, Esq) Nawton, 5 m. NE of Helmsley. From A170, between Helmsley & Nawton village, at Beadlam turn N & on 2½ m. to Nawton Tower. Large garden; heaths, rhododendrons, azaleas & shrubs. Tea Helmsley. *Adm. 20p, Chd. 5p. Sun. May 25 (2–6)*

Osmotherley House (Mr & Mrs John Church) Osmotherley. On Yarm–Thirsk Rd A19, turn E at Clack Lane Ends up hill to village; turn right. Medium-sized garden; magnificent open view. Within national park. *Adm. 20p, Chd. 10p. Sun. May 11 (2–6)*

Otterington Hall⊕ (Miss M. Furness) 4 m. S of Northallerton. On A167, just N of South Otterington village. Medium-sized garden; roses, yew hedges, flowering shrubs. (*Share to St. John Ambulance Brigade*) TEA & biscuits. *Adm. 20p, Chd. 10p. Sun. July 20 (2–6)*

Owston Hall*†⊕ (Mrs K. M. Davies-Cooke) Askern, 6 m. N of Doncaster. A19 Doncaster–Selby Rd; from Doncaster entrance on left just before Rockley House, Dario's Restaurant. Bus stop at entrance. 7 acres; roses, herbaceous, shrubs, rock & paved garden; woodland walks; over 100 named specimen trees. Also (by kind permission of P Edwards Esq) unique hamlet under conservation order Owston Hall (let as flats), stone-built farm & cottages, bell tower, barns & stables, Saxon church all scheduled historical buildings. Garden & village 18 acres. (*Share to All Saints' Church Fabric Fund, Owston*). Morning coffee & TEA & biscuits available. *Adm. 30p, Chd. 10p. Sat. July 12 (10–7)*

Pennyholme* (The Countess of Feversham) Fadmoor, 5 m. NW of Kirbymoorside. From A170, between Kirbymoorside & Nawton, turn off N; ½ m. before Fadmoor turn left (at signpost 'Sleightholmedale only') and continue northwards up the dale, across 3 cattle-grids, to Pennyholme. No buses. Large, wild garden on edge of moor with rhododendrons, azaleas, primulas & shrubs. Tea Kirbymoorside. *Adm. 25p, Chd. 10p. Sat. & Sun. May 31 & June 1; Sat. & Sun. June 7 & 8 (11–6.30)*

St Nicholas*† (The Lady Serena James) Richmond. Bus: Darlington–Richmond, alight The Avenue, 500 yds. Medium-large garden of horticultural interest, shrubs, rock garden, topiary work. NO DOGS. Tea Terrace House Hotel, Richmond. *Adm. 20p, Chd. 10p. Sun. June 29 & Sun. July 20 (10–7)*

Silver Birches*& (Mr & Mrs S. C. Thomson) Ling Lane, Scarcroft, 7 m. NE of Leeds. A58 mid-way between Leeds & Wetherby; at Scarcroft turn off W into Ling Lane, at signpost to Wike; garden ½ m. up lane on S side. Bus: Leeds–Wetherby, alight Ling Lane, ½ m. 2½-acre woodland garden; foliage trees & shrubs; many conifers, rhododendrons & azaleas; good collection of heaths & heathers; pond; roses. NO DOGS. TEAS. *Adm. 35p, Chd. 15p. Sun. June 8 (2–7)*

Sleightholme Dale Lodge (Mrs Gordon Foster) Fadmoor, 3 m. N of Kirbymoorside. 1 m. from Fadmoor. No buses. Hillside garden; walled rose garden, rock garden, shrubs. Garden *not* suitable for wheelchairs). (*Share to N.S.P.C.C.*) TEAS (July 6 only). *Adm. 25p, Chd. 10p (under school age, free). Sun. July 6 & daily to Sat. July 12 inc. (2–6.30); also by appt. for parties*

Stockeld Park †&⊕ (Mrs Gough) 2 m. NW of Wetherby. On A661 Wetherby–Harrogate Rd; from Wetherby after 2 m. entrance is 2nd lodge on left. Bus: Wetherby–Harrogate, alight Stockeld lodge gates (¼ m. drive). 4-acre garden with lawns, grove & flowers, fine trees & roses. House built 1758 for Col Middleton by James Paine. C18 pigeon cote; chapel 1890. Tea Boat House Café, Wetherby. *Adm. to garden 40p; house 60p extra. Sun. July 13 (2.30–6)*

York Gate* (Mrs Sybil B. Spencer) Back Church Lane, Adel, Leeds 16. Situated behind Adel Church on the Otley Rd out of Leeds (A660). Bus: WY 34 Leeds–Ilkley; alight Lawnswood Arms, ½ m. An owner-made & maintained garden of particular interest to the plantsman, containing orchard with pool, an arbour, miniature pinetum, dell with stream, a Folly, nut walk, paeony bed, iris borders, fern border, herb garden, summerhouse, alley, white & silver garden, 2 vegetable gardens, pavement maze, all within 1 acre. NO DOGS. TEA & biscuits (June 1 only). *Adm. 50p, Chd. 10p. Sat. & Sun. May 31 & June 1 (2–7)*

York House⊕ (Mr & Mrs W. H. Pridmore) Claxton, 8 m. E of York, off A64. Bus: York–Scarborough, alight Claxton Hall (¾ m.). 1-acre plantsman's garden, planned & maintained by elderly owners; of interest as already 'well furnished' though practically nothing planted before 1975; old roses, herbaceous, shrubs, fruit. (*Share to Northern Horticultural Society*) Small paddock for picnics. *Adm. 25p, Chd. 10p. Sat. & Sun. June 14 & 15 (2–6)*

Please mention the National Gardens Scheme when replying to the advertisers

THE HOME OF GOOD PLANTS AND TRULY A GARDEN FOR ALL SEASONS.

The **Savill Garden**

IN WINDSOR GREAT PARK

Clearly signposted from Ascot, Egham and Windsor

The Garden is open from March 1st to December 24th daily from 10 a.m. to 6 or 7 p.m. or sunset if earlier.

Ample Free Car/Coach parking adjoining the garden in Wick Lane, Englefield Green.

Admission: Adults 75p. Children 45p. Senior Citizens 65p. Parties of 20 and over 65p.

A Licensed Self Service Restaurant is open from March 1st to October 31st. Also our well stocked Plant-Gift-Book Shop is open throughout the season.

GARDENERS DELIGHT

A selection of Garden Weekends
**Hosted by Professor Alan Gemmell
with guest speakers including**
Geoffrey Smith, Clay Jones and Fred Leads
APRIL—**Three Great Gardens**
Kew, Savill, Wisley
MAY—**Wales and the Wirral**
Bodnant Ness, Tatton Park
JUNE—**Pennines and Peaks**
Hardwick Hall, Haddon Hall, Chatsworth
SEPTEMBER—**Great Houses and Gardens**
Stourhead, Wilton, Pusey House, Blenheim Palace
OCTOBER—**Golden Autumn**
Westonbirt, Westbury, Hidcote, Batsford Arboretum
Brochure now available from
**HANSON TRAVEL
2 Jones Street, Berkley Square,
London W1   Tel.: 01-493 8771**

Please mention the National Gardens Scheme when replying to the advertisers

Two very special holidays arranged for the RHS in 1980

Once again Rankin Kuhn and P&O Cruises have combined their expertise to offer RHS Members two unique holidays.

Holiday No. 1 4-30 November (25 days - or longer)

The Caribbean - Venezuela - Colombia - Mexico

This exciting holiday combines the delights of the Caribbean with an interesting tour of Venezuela and Colombia and finishing with a relaxing stay aboard the luxurious "Sun Princess" as the cruise makes its way from Acapulco to Los Angeles.

Accompanying this tour will be Frances Perry, A Vice President of the RHS and Gardening Correspondent of 'The Observer'.

"I am looking forward to re-visiting Venezuela and Colombia; these fascinating countries are rich in little-known and mysterious flora. In Barbados we will visit two of the most beautiful sub-tropical gardens I have ever seen anywhere".

Frances Perry

Travelling with Frances will be her husband Roy Hay, Gardening Correspondent of 'The Times'.

Tuesday 4th November 1980 - The RHS party flies from London to Barbados for a relaxing stay in an idyllic island setting before continuing South to the exciting city of Caracas and a five-day stay in Venezuela to see the breathtaking scenery, and wild flowers of this exotic latin American country. Before leaving South America the tour heads South-west to Colombia to see the cultivated and wild flowers as well as a chance to view the splendid "Pre-colombian Gold Exhibition" - The Gold of El Dorado in Bogota. Then on by air via Mexico City to Acapulco to join the luxurious "Sun Princess" for a seven-day cruise along the Mexican coastline. Ports of call will include Ixtapa, Puerto Vallarta and Mazatlan before arriving in Los Angeles to join your London bound British Airways flight - arriving London 30th November. (An optional stopover in the United States of America can be arranged.)

Cost per person from £1798.00

P&O Cruises

Please mention the National Gardens Scheme when replying to the advertisers

Holiday No. 2   5th October - 4th November 1980 (30 days)

See the Wild Flowers of Australia and Cruise the Pacific

Following the success of a similar holiday in 1979 Rankin Kuhn and P&O are offering RHS the chance of seeing the wild flowers of Western Australia together with Sydney and a cruise of the Pacific Islands in the Autumn of 1980.

Last year's tour was led by Frances Perry.
"Last year many people were disappointed as they were unable to join our limited small group to the South Pacific and Australia where we saw so many unique wild flowers in their natural surroundings. The next tour will be led by an Australian friend of mine who is a leading authority on Australian flora and his local knowledge will ensure that the party will have an informative and unforgettable holiday."

5th October - The RHS Party flies from Heathrow to Perth for a week in Western Australia, touring the wild flower areas in the South-western corner of the State and relaxing or sightseeing in Perth. This is followed by a short stay in Sydney before joining P&O's luxurious "Sea Princess". P&O will pamper you for two weeks aboard their magnificent 27,000 ton ship as you cruise to the enchanting Pacific Islands. The cruise will include two calls in Tonga, beautiful Vavau and Nuku'alofa home of the much-loved Queen Salote, also two calls at the Fijian ports of Suva and Lautoka and Noumea in French Polynesia. The cruise returns to Sydney for a three-day stop before returning to London.

Arrangements can be made to extend the stay in Australia or for a return via New Zealand.

Cost per person from £1685.00

We are currently planning a tour to South China in the spring of 1981. Please tick the appropriate box if you would be interested in receiving information when this is available.

Please mention the National Gardens Scheme when replying to the advertisers

152

Please mention the National Gardens Scheme when replying to the advertisers

Useful gardening items

Shear Sharpener

Country Garden Price
£2.75

Keep your shears and lawn edgers in perfect condition. This simple to use sharpener will maintain or cut a keen edge on your tools with just a few gentle strokes – no need to dismantle them. Use it for scissors too.

Knee Pads

Country Garden Price
£2.95

Treat yourself to comfortable weeding. These cushioned knee pads are ideal for kneeling jobs in the garden: they are very light, but strong and damp-proof.

Long Arm Fruit Picker

Country Garden Price
£10.95

Now the tantalising top-of-the-tree fruit easily within your grasp with this lightweight Fruit Picker. Telescopic tubular aluminium sections adjustable up to 13' length and total 18' reach. The unique transparent collection bag helps you pick large and small fruit without bruising or damage.

The Donkey

Country Garden Price
£3.95

The famous garden carry-all. Spread it on the ground, throw your weeds, leaves, clippings, etc. on to it, and when it is full, pick it up by the four strong corner handles and it forms a giant bag for you to take and empty on to the compost heap. Made of strong woven polypropylene with strengthened carrying handles. Approximately 5' square.

Rose Sucker Cutter

Country Garden Price   £4.50

A specifically designed tool to remove rose suckers at the root and stop them growing again. You can do it the right way without even getting your hands dirty.
Quality steel, cadmium plated with a plastic handle grip. Ideal gift for the rose enthusiast.

Please mention the National Gardens Scheme when replying to the advertisers

from The Country Garden.

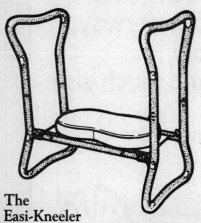

These are just a few of the items which The Country Garden offers to the enthusiastic gardener. If you place an order from this selection, we shall be pleased to send you our beautiful catalogue, with over 180 different tools, implements and gadgets.
Customer Queries –
tel: 053672 3710

The Easi-Kneeler Stool
Country Garden Price
£17.95

An invaluable aid in garden and home. Safe, robust, extremely practical. So many uses. Reverses to make comfortable bench seat. Supplied packed flat in carton. Top quality rubber kneeling pad included. Stool: 24" high x 20" wide x 12" deep.

Seed Dispenser
Country Garden Price
£2.95

An ingenious little gadget for precision seed sowing. Accuracy in drills and even sowing in boxes. Useful for dispensing fertiliser around plants and in pots.

Small Sprayer
Country Garden Price
£1.75

A versatile small sprayer specially made for The Country Garden. Non-corrodable polythene. Adjustable nozzle. Trigger Spray. Holds 600cc, over 1 pint.

Please mention the National Gardens Scheme when replying to the advertisers

Please mention the National Gardens Scheme when replying to the advertisers

157

158

ALL-CEDAR GREENHOUSES

C. H. Whitehouse Ltd. have made quality greenhouses for over fifty years and have established a reputation for reliability. Each All-Cedar Greenhouse is individually built by one of a team of skilled craftsmen. Western Red Cedar from Canada is used throughout, chosen for its resistance to rot, attractive appearance and long-lasting qualities with the minimum of maintenance.

Brick-Base Greenhouses are made for new or existing bases and purpose-built greenhouses can provide for the different needs of orchids, alpines, carnations etc. Advice gladly given on the choice of heating, watering and ventilating equipment to provide the conditions desired.

C. H. WHITEHOUSE LTD.

Buckhurst Works, FRANT, (nr. Tunbridge Wells) Sussex.   Phone: Frant 247

'Ferndowne' garden furniture

ELEGANCE, COMFORT & DURABILITY. Are brought to you by Ferndowne "Britain's most beautiful garden furniture", made in aluminium and finished in lustrous weather resisting epoxy enamel.

Manufactured by:
A. E. (METALS) LTD., Wood Lane, Erdington, Birmingham B24 9QR. Tel: 021-373 2207.
THE ASSOCIATED ENGINEERING GROUP

Please mention the National Gardens Scheme when replying to the advertisers

SCOTTS NURSERIES
and
GARDEN CENTRE
MERRIOTT SOMERSET

Telephone: CREWKERNE 72306

Two miles north of Crewkerne—
between the A30 and the A303

OUR STOCK IS THE MOST VARIED IN THE
WEST COUNTRY AND WE HAVE OVER
SEVENTY ACRES OF GROWING PLANTS

Open every weekday 8 a.m. - 5 p.m.
and on Sundays, 2 p.m. - 5 p.m.

Plenty of space for parking and picnics

Our 224-page Catalogue is 50p Post Free

MEADOW HERBS

**47 Moreton Street, S.W.1
London 01-821 0094**

The simple secret of flourishing gardens!

Sudbury kits tell not only a soil's lime needs,
and how deficient or rich it currently is in
nitrogen, phosphorus and potash nutrients –
but exactly what to do to change it for the
better.

Home Gardeners (*pictured*) **£5.24** inc. VAT
De luxe **£7.97** inc. VAT

SUDBURY SOIL TEST KITS

From garden shops or send appropriate cheque
to Sudbury, Corwen, Clwyd.

DESIGNERS
AND MAKERS OF
NATURAL
AROMATIC HERB
PRODUCTS

SPECIALIST
SUPPLIERS OF
AROMATIC OILS
AND POT-POURRI
INGREDIENTS

Send S.A.E. for price list

Please mention the National Gardens Scheme when replying to the advertisers

160

PAY YOUR HOME A COMPLEMENT

Your home says a lot about you. It reflects your style, your personality, - your way of life.

For over a Century, Richardsons of Darlington have brought a touch of gracious living to the homes of the discerning.

The conservatory. Elegant. Luxurious. The peace and tranquility of a garden with the warmth and comfort of the home.

Once part of Richardsons, Amdega continue the tradition. The finest conservatories, built by our craftsmen using the highest quality cedar. Using the versatile modular system you can choose the perfect complement for your home. Or if you prefer, express your individuality with a conservatory designed exclusively for you.

Does your home deserve a complement?

For further details, write to Dept NGG/380 at the address below:

Amdega Ltd., Faverdale Industrial Estate, Darlington, Co. Durham DL3 0PW. Telephone: (0325) 68522

GARDEN TOURS

Coombe Cross Hotel. The Misses Hebditch arrange a programme each year of Special Interest weeks and weekends. Their 'Holidays for Garden-Lovers' this year have been arranged for March 27–April 3; May 8–15; June 5–12; June 26–July 3; July 17–24; Oct. 9–16. Write to The Misses Hebditch, Coombe Cross Hotel, Bovey Tracey, Devon (Tel. Bovey Tracey 832476).

Country Homes & Castles, R & I Tours Ltd arrange for visitors from overseas to stay as guests of British families in their own homes on a highly personal basis. These homes vary from thatched cottages to large mansions. Further information from R & I Tours Ltd, 138a Piccadilly, London W1V 9FH (Tel. 01-491 4272).

Premier-Albanian Coaches include in their programme day-trips to Beaulieu, Berkeley Castle, Blenheim Palace, Bowood, Bressingham, Broadlands, Chartwell, Cliveden, Compton Acres, Compton Wynyates, Frogmore, Hampton Court, Hatfield House, Hever Castle, Kew, Leonardslee, Nymans, Penshurst Place, Rochford House Plant Nurseries, Savill, Springfields, Syon Park, Waddesdon Manor, Wisley. Departures from Watford, St. Albans and Hemel Hempstead areas. Write to Premier-Albanian, 105-107 Queens Avenue, Watford, Herts WD1 7NU (Tel. Watford 23590).

Scotland's Gardens Scheme arranges tours of gardens in Scotland. In 1980 there will be a 6-day tour in Dumfries and Galloway (May 27–June 1) and a 6-day tour in Fife and Cental Scotland (June 26–July 1). There will also be day tours during the Edinburgh Festival. For partiuclars write to Scotland's Gardens Scheme, 26 Castle Terrace, Edinburgh EH1 2EL (Tel. 031-229 1870)

The English Tourist Board's publication 'Visit an English Garden' includes two pages of Garden Tours and Excursions. (see page iii at the beginning of this book).

16 mm FILMS ABOUT GARDENS in colour

In Search of an English Garden: 20 mins; hire charge £4.50 + VAT. Made for The National Gardens Scheme by Fisons Ltd, this film shows a representative selection of gardens opened in aid of the charity, and has been described as an exceptionally beautiful film. On hire from Guild Sound & Vision, Woodston House, Oundle Rd, Peterborough, PE2 9PZ.

Open To-day: 30 mins. Made for Scotland's Gardens Scheme, the film gives a short history of the Scheme together with pictures of a wide variety of gardens open to the public during the season. On hire to societies and clubs from The National Trust for Scotland, 5 Charlotte Square, Edinburgh, EH2 4DU.

A Garden for all Seasons: 23 mins; hire charge £5.15 + VAT. Made for The Royal Horticultural Society by Fisons Ltd, this is devoted to the Society's garden at Wisley and reveals the varied beauties of the 150-acre garden including splendid panoramic shots taken from a helicopter. On hire from Guild Sound & Vision, Woodston House, Oundle Rd, Peterborough, PE2 9PZ.

Chelsea Flower Show 1973: 22 mins, hire charge £5.15 + VAT. Made by the B.B.C., with a commentary by John Braham and Ann Scott-James, describes scenes, events and exhibits at the Show. This film is in the nature of a private view since it was made before the Show was open to the public. On hire from Guild Sound & Vision, Woodston House, Oundle Road, Peterborough, PE2 9PZ.

A Garden Grows: 25 mins; free. Made for The Royal Horticultural Society by ICI, the film covers the first year of construction and planting of a small garden within the RHS garden at Wisley. On hire from ICI Film Library, Thames House North, Millbank, London, SW1.

Capability Brown: 20 mins; free (except for postage). The life and work of Capability Brown, showing the great influence he had on the development of landscape design during the 18th cent. Over 200 estates were laid out by him and the film includes examples of some of these 'stately homes'. Apply to The Film Library, Ransomes Sims & Jefferies Ltd, Nacton Works, Ipswich, IP3 9QG.

A compost for all gardeners: 24 mins. Free. Fisons Ltd. Spectacular time-lapse photography used to illustrate plant growth in a film showing development work on peat-type composts, with a step by step guide on seed-growing and a wide variety of methods and situations in which the composts can be used. Obtainable from Guild Sound & Vision, Woodston House, Oundle Road, Peterborough, PE2 9PZ.

Capital Garden: 37 mins; free. Made for the Royal Botanic Garden, Edinburgh, includes a brief history of the garden since 1670, sequences on work being done in the herbarium, laboratories, glasshouses and library, and 9 mins showing the garden throughout the seasons. Available from Guild Sound & Vision, Woodston House, Oundle Rd, Peterborough PE2 9PZ (Scottish applicants : Scottish Central Film Library, 16/17 Woodside Terrace, Glasgow, G3 7XN).

163

THE ROYAL HORTICULTURAL SOCIETY

CHELSEA FLOWER SHOW 1980

to be held in the Royal Hospital Grounds, Chelsea

Wednesday May 21, 8.00 am to 8.30 pm. (Adm. £5.00: after 4 pm £4.00)

Thursday May 22, 8.00 am to 8.30 pm. (Adm. £4.00: after 4 pm £3.00)

Friday May 23, 8.00 am to 5.00 pm. (Adm. £3.00)

(Private View, Tuesday May 20: admission only to holders of Private View tickets)

SHOWS HELD IN THE SOCIETY'S HALLS

in Vincent Square and/or Greycoat Street, Westminster

February 19 (11-6) and 20 (10-5)	Flower Show
March 11 (11.30-6) and 12 (10-5)	Early Spring Show
March 25 (11-8) and 26 (10-5)	Flower and Garden Equipment Show
April 15 (11.30-6) and 16 (10-5)	Spring Flower Show
April 29 (11-6) and 30 (10-5)	Flower Show
June 17 (11-6) and 18 (10-5)	Early Summer Show
July 8 (11.30-6) and 9 (10-5)	Flower Show
August 5 (11-8) and 6 (10-5)	Summer Flower Show
September 23 (11-8) and 24 (10-8) and 25 (10-5)	Great Autumn Show
October 7 (11-6) and 8 (10-5)	Flower Show and Fruit and Vegetable Show
October 28 (11-6) and 29 (10-5)	Late Autumn Show
November 18 (11-6) and 19 (10-5)	Flower Show

Entrance to Westminster Shows, first day 60p, second day 40p.

The following Shows will also be held, August 27 National Dahlia Society's Show; September 3 and 4 The Royal National Rose Society's Autumn Show; September 16 and 17 National Chrysanthemum Society's Show; October 31 and November 1 National Chrysanthemum Show.

THE SOCIETY'S GARDEN AT WISLEY, NR. RIPLEY, SURREY

The Garden is open throughout the year, except on Christmas Day. Adm. 90p; children 5 years and under, no charge; from 6 to 14 years, 45p. Dogs not admitted. Party rates. Admission charges for parties of 20 or more booking and paying in advance, 80p (children 40p).

Jan., Nov. and Dec. 10 am to 4.30 pm (Sundays from 2 pm).
Feb. to Oct. 10 am to 7 pm or sunset, whichever is the earlier (Sundays from 2 pm)
On Sunday mornings (10 am to 2 pm) admission is by member's ticket only.
The Garden is 20 miles from London, between Cobham and Ripley in Surrey, on west side of the main London-Portsmouth Road (A3).
From London. *By rail:* Waterloo to Esher, then to Wisley by Green Line Coach No. 715. Waterloo to West Byfleet and then by hired car.
By Green Line Coach No. 715: Oxford Circus coach stop. Upper Regent Street (opposite the Polytechnic) to Wisley. *via* Hammersmith and Esher (1 hr 20 mins).
From Guildford. By Green Line Coach No. 715: Commercial Road Bus Station to Wisley (20 mins).

There is a **free car park** at the Garden. Restaurant or Cafeteria open mid-February to mid-November. Information centre and shop and plant sales centre open at all times when the Garden is open. A brochure in colour may be obtained from the Secretary, The Royal Horticultural Society, Vincent Square, London, SW1P 2PE.

Ideas grow into gardens at The Inchbald School

Designing and planting a garden is an exciting challenge, whether it be several acres incorporating natural water and woodland or a 'garden room' in the heart of town.

You can meet that challenge with confidence using the knowledge and experience gained from the Ten Week Garden Design Course at The Inchbald School. This highly intensive course, now in it's fifth year, teaches the basic principles of landscape design and their application to all types and sizes of site. Lectures and studio tutorials, held at Eaton Gate by well known practising designers and horticulturists, are combined with a weekly visit to the Chelsea Physic Garden and to other significant gardens and designer's offices.

The syllabus includes a series of lectures on the History of Garden Design – General Landscape & Horticultural Technique – Plants and their use in Design – and Basic Constructional Methods.

In the studio students learn how to relate perspective levels, to analyse a brief and to demonstrate their solutions with plans and specifications. Even those with no previous draughting experience can develop an acceptable level of proficiency.

So whether you are an aspiring amateur or plan a career as a professional landscape designer – turn your ideas into reality at The Inchbald School.

The Inchbald School of Design **isd**

For further information contact: The Secretary, Room 4,
7 Eaton Gate, London SW1W 9BA. Tel: 01-730 5508.

Thirty-six of the most glorious gardens in Great Britain
described by the women who created them

THE ENGLISHWOMAN'S GARDEN

Edited by Alvilde Lees-Milne and Rosemary Verey
Foreword by Dr Roy Strong
Illustrated throughout with over 200 full colour photographs

• From the Countess of Haddington's commanding estates in East Lothian to Moira Reid's cottage garden at Liskeard in Cornwall, this beautiful book takes us into the gardens created by some of the most famous and talented of English women gardeners. The gardens themselves are as distinctive as the women who made them.

• First serial rights sold to **Harpers & Queen**

• Second serial rights sold to **Homes & Gardens**

• Feature in **House & Garden**

160 pages   £9.95

CHATTO & WINDUS

Please mention the National Gardens Scheme when replying to the advertisers

166

GARDENS
OPEN TO THE PUBLIC
1981

PUBLISHED MARCH —
PRICE 75p including UK postage

(Europe 85p; U.S.A. $3.50; Canada $4)

To: The National Gardens Scheme
57 Lower Belgrave Street, London, SW1W 0LR   01-730 0359

Please send to the address below...copy/copies of
Gardens Open to the Public, for which I enclose Postal Order/Cheque

value..(Postal Orders and Cheques should be made
payable to The National Gardens Scheme and crossed. If sending money
from abroad please use International Stamps or International Money
Order.)

Name (Mr/Mrs/Miss)...
(BLOCK LETTERS)

Address ....
(BLOCK LETTERS)

....

Date ....

Note: The book/s will be posted on publication. If meantime you wish to
receive an acknowledgement of your order, please enclose an s.a.e.

Please mention the National Gardens Scheme when replying to the advertisers